# World Yearbook of Education 2018

This latest volume in the *World Yearbook of Education* Series considers changing space-times of education by asking how they become unevenly textured as our worlds globalise, horizons shift and familiar points of reference melt and are remade. Acknowledging the reach of economic and cultural change, digital communication, geopolitics and persistent inequalities, the chapters trace processes that are re-making education and societies. Examining the depth of their impact on practices, methods and concepts reveals the significance of knowledge-building and socially embedded forms of reasoning in emerging patterns of educational governance, pedagogic and policy reforms as well as in lived understandings of self and social worlds.

The organisation of the collection into three sections – Making Spaces, Troubling Temporalities, and Mobility and Contexts – begins to map out an ambitious project. It calls on education researchers and professionals to write the present as history by grasping the socio-spatial, historical and political dimensions and effects that frame, form and filter the educational present. This research calls for a revitalised historical sociology and novel forms of comparative education that can provide productive insights, inform creative problem solving and suggest practical directions for education. This agenda recognises:

- the unevenness of educational space-times
- the making of education as a social institution
- the persistence and effects of social embeddedness, eventful space, situated knowledge and geosocial thinking
- the present as history and multiple temporalities in education
- different registers of transformation that become visible through lenses such as identity, work, citizenship and mobility.

The *World Yearbook of Education 2018* continues the project of compiling worldwide research on globalising education. These volumes offer a powerful commentary on how and why space-times of education are changing and emphasise the importance of forms of knowledge that materialise categories of professionals, policies and practices. This volume will be of interest to academics, professionals and policymakers in education and social policy, and also to scholars who engage in historical studies of education and debates about the socio-material formations that contribute to educational inequalities and dynamics of difference.

**Julie McLeod** is Professor of Curriculum, Equity and Social Change in the Melbourne Graduate School of Education, University of Melbourne, Australia.

**Noah W. Sobe** is Professor of Cultural and Educational Studies at Loyola University Chicago, USA, where he also directs the Center for Comparative Education.

**Terri Seddon** is Professor of Education, La Trobe University, Australia.

## World Yearbook of Education Series

Series editors:
**Julie Allen**, University of Birmingham, UK
**Gita Steiner Khamsi**, Teachers College Columbia, USA
**Terri Seddon**, La Trobe University, Australia

For a full list of titles in this series please visit www.routledge.com/World-Yearbook-of-Education/book-series/WYBE

**World Yearbook of Education 2017: Assessment Inequalities**
*Edited by Julie Allan and Alfredo J. Artiles*

**World Yearbook of Education 2016: The Global Education Industry**
*Edited by Antoni Verger, Christopher Lubienski and Gita Steiner-Khamsi*

**World Yearbook of Education 2015: Educational Elites, Privilege and Excellence**
*Edited by Stephen Ball, Agnes van Zantén and Brigitte Darchy-Koechlin*

**World Yearbook of Education 2014: Governing Knowledge**
*Edited by Tara Fenwick, Eric Mangez and Jenny Ozga*

**World Yearbook of Education 2013: Educators, Professionalism and Politics**
*Edited by Terri Seddon and John Levin*

**World Yearbook of Education 2012: Policy Borrowing and Lending in Education**
*Edited by Gita Steiner-Khamsi and Florian Waldow*

**World Yearbook of Education 2011: Curriculum in Today's World**
*Edited by Lyn Yates and Madeleine Grumet*

**World Yearbook of Education 2010: Education and the Arab 'World'**
*Edited by Andre Elias Mazawi and Ronald Sultana*

**World Yearbook of Education 2009: Childhood Studies and the Impact of Globalization**
*Edited by Marilyn Fleer, Mariane Hedegaard and Jonathan Tudge*

**World Yearbook of Education 2008: Geographies of Knowledge**
*Edited by Debbie Epstein, Rebecca Boden, Rosemary Deem, Fazal Rizvi and Susan Wright*

**World Yearbook of Education 2007: Educating the Global Workforce**
*Edited by Lesley Farrell and Tara Fenwick*

**World Yearbook of Education 2006: Education, Research and Policy**
*Edited by Jenny Ozga, Terri Seddon and Thomas S. Popkewitz*

**World Yearbook of Education 2005: Globalization and Nationalism in Education**
*Edited by David Coulby and Evie Zambeta*

# World Yearbook of Education 2018

Uneven Space-Times of Education:
Historical Sociologies of Concepts,
Methods and Practices

**Edited by Julie McLeod, Noah W. Sobe
and Terri Seddon**

Routledge
Taylor & Francis Group

LONDON AND NEW YORK

First published 2018
by Routledge
2 Park Square, Milton Park, Abingdon, Oxon OX14 4RN

and by Routledge
711 Third Avenue, New York, NY 10017

*Routledge is an imprint of the Taylor & Francis Group, an informa business*

© 2018 selection and editorial matter, Julie McLeod, Noah W. Sobe and
Terri Seddon; individual chapters, the contributors

*British Library Cataloguing-in-Publication Data*
A catalogue record for this book is available from the British Library

*Library of Congress Cataloging-in-Publication Data*
A catalog record has been requested for this book

ISBN: 978-1-138-23048-4 (hbk)
ISBN: 978-1-315-36381-3 (ebk)

Typeset in Minion Pro
by Swales & Willis Ltd, Exeter, Devon, UK

# Contents

# Contributors

**Robert Cowen** is Emeritus Professor of Education in the UCL Institute of Education and a former President of the Comparative Education Society in Europe. Currently he is Chair of the Editorial Board of *Comparative Education*. As a specialist in comparative education, he has been privileged to reside or to work frequently in Australia, Argentina and Brazil, China and Japan, the USA and Canada, and a pleasing number of countries within continental Europe. His current interests include the impact on academic comparative education of new forms of 'applied comparative education' – funded research, PISA, the World Bank and so on; and the shift in the theoretical assumptions of the field of study away from the simplicities of juxtaposition of two descriptive narratives about education and society and a subsequent search for the causes of similarities and differences.

**Inés Dussel** is Researcher and Professor at the Department of Educational Research, CINVESTAV, Mexico. PhD, University of Wisconsin-Madison. Director of the Education Area, FLACSO/Argentina, from 2001 to 2008. She has researched extensively on the history and theory of education, and on the material and visual culture of schools. Her research interests focus on the relationships between digital media and schooling.

**Eleftherios Klerides** is Assistant Professor of Comparative Education at the University of Cyprus and the Secretary-Treasurer of the Comparative Education Society in Europe (CESE). He has worked in various capacities in a variety of academic and (educational) political contexts including the UCL Institute of Education, the American University of Beirut, the Georg Eckert Institute for International Textbook Research, the Collège de France, the World Bank, UNESCO (Beirut) and the Greek Ministry of Education, Research and Religious Affairs. He has published numerous articles and book chapters in the fields of cross-border mobility, transnational governance, identity formation and textbook theory. His current scholarly concern is how to revitalise comparative educational thinking with the help of concepts from international political theory.

**Jamie Kowalczyk** is an Assistant Professor and Principal Program Leader for Curriculum & Instruction in the Department of Teaching, Learning & Diversity at Concordia University, Chicago. Her scholarship and research interests focus on migration and education, multicultural/intercultural education, and school reform policy discourses.

**Paolo Landri** is a Senior Researcher of the Institute of Research on Population and Social Policies at National Research Council in Italy (CNR-IRPPS). His main research interests concern educational organisations, professional learning and educational policies. He edited with Tara Fenwick a Special Issue on 'Materialities, Textures and Pedagogies: Socio-Material Assemblages in Education' in *Pedagogy, Culture and Society* 20(1) March 2012, and published recently 'The Sociomateriality of Education Policy' in *Discourse* 36(4) November 2014.

**Marianne A. Larsen** is an Associate Professor at Western's Faculty of Education. Her research is situated within the field of comparative and international education. She has studied the complex ways that international service learning (ISL) experiences shape university students as global citizens. Out of this research, she produced an edited book (2015), *International Service Learning: Engaging Host* Communities, which investigates the impact of ISL on Global South host communities. Her 2016 book, *Internationalization of Higher Education: An Analysis through Spatial, Network and Mobilities Theories* brings together her interest in post-foundational theories and global processes of higher education internationalisation. Dr Larsen is interested in pushing the boundaries about how we think about the effects of globalising processes within educational contexts, and challenging taken-for-granted assumptions about how we (should) conduct our research and play out our roles as academics within internationalised and corporatised universities.

**Martin Lawn** is an Honorary Professor, University of Edinburgh. He is a well-known scholar in the domain of comparative education, educational policy and educational history. He is the Founding Editor of the *European Educational Research Journal*, the academic journal of the European Educational Research Association. He is also a Fellow of the UK Academy of Social Sciences. His main research interests are the European policy space in education – its conceptualisation, development and practices – and the sociology and history of the education sciences. Recent books include *Governing Europe's Spaces: European Union Re-Imagined* (with Caitriona Carter) (Manchester University Press, 2013); *Rise of Data in Education Systems – Collection, Visualisation and Use* (Symposium Books. Comparative Histories of Education Series, 2014), and *Europeanizing Education – Governing a New Policy Space* (with Sotiria Grek) (Symposium Books, Oxford, 2012).

**Nancy Lesko**, PhD, is Maxine Greene Professor at Teachers College, Columbia University and teaches in the areas of curriculum, social theory, gender studies, and youth studies. She is the co-editor with Susan Talburt of *Keywords in Youth Studies: Tracing Affects, Movements, Knowledges* (Routledge, 2012).

**Chin-Ju Mao** is Professor at the Department of Education and Graduate Institute of Curriculum and Instruction, National Taiwan Normal University. She received her PhD in Educational Policy Studies from University of Wisconsin-Madison, USA. Her research interests revolve around educational/curricular reform as identity politics and its effect of/on social change, locally and globally. She has conducted many research projects supported by the National Science Council of Taiwan, such as 'The Global and the Local: The problematic of cultural identity in Taiwan's discourses of curriculum reform, 1987–2003'; 'The Travel and Movement of Reform Ideas in the Global and the Discursive Practice of Curriculum Reform Policy in the Local'. Mao also joined an international collaborative project, 'Educating the Global Citizen: Globalization, educational reform and the politics of equity and inclusion in 12 countries', led by Professor Carlos Alberto Torres at the University of California – Los Angles, and another collaborative project, 'Fashioning National Identity Through Curricular Reform: A comparative analysis of Australian and Taiwanese national curricula as responses to global times', with Professor Catherine Ann Doherty at the University of Glasgow.

**Julie McLeod** is Professor of Curriculum, Equity and Social Change in the Melbourne Graduate School of Education and Pro Vice-Chancellor (Research Capability) at the University of Melbourne. Julie researches in the history and sociology of education, with a focus on youth, gender, and social change. She was an editor of the journal *Gender and Education* (2011–16), held an Australian Research Council Future Fellowship (2012–16) and is a Fellow of the Academy of Social Sciences Australia. Books include *Rethinking Youth Wellbeing: Critical perspectives* (2015), *The Promise of the New and Genealogies of Educational Reform* (2015), *Researching Social Change: Qualitative approaches* (2009), and *Making Modern Lives: Subjectivity, schooling and social change* (2006).

**Beatrix Niemeyer** holds the chair for Adult and Further Education at the University of Flensburg, Germany. She holds a diploma in Social Work and one in Education Sciences and has worked in international contexts both in and outside university. She has been nominated as an expert member of PEYR – the pool of European youth researchers in 2011 and engaged in transnational activities both in and outside university. Her research interest is on the boundaries between work and learning and the related reconfigurations of professional education, with a special focus on school-to-work transition. As head of the MA-program 'Education in Europe' she is teaching and researching on the construction of Europe as an education space and transnational practices of knowledge building.

**Alyssa D. Niccolini**, PhD, received her doctorate from Columbia University's Teachers College. Her research focuses on affect and its intersections with secondary education and has been published in journals such as *Gender and Education*, *Girlhood Studies*, *Journal of Gender Studies*, *Sex Education*, and *International Journal of Qualitative Studies in Education*.

**Arwen Raddon** has worked as an academic and researcher at a number of different institutions in the UK and Singapore, including universities and government bodies. Having recently returned to the UK after six years working as a researcher in Singapore, she is both an independent researcher and is branching out into a healing career, being a qualified yoga and meditation teacher and Reiki healer. She holds adjunct positions with the University of Liverpool and the University of Leicester. Her interest in time, space, and the sociology of education began in the early 2000s, when she was researching issues around gender and distance learning for her PhD. She continues to be fascinated by how quantum mechanics is still only scratching the surface of how time operates, and how insightful ancient spiritual ideas on time and space can be when appreciating our concept of the social world.

**Terri Seddon** is Professor of Education at La Trobe University, Melbourne. She examines education in global transitions through historical sociologies of learning and educational work. Her research focuses particularly on workplace learning and governance in tertiary, adult, and post-compulsory learning spaces. This research program, anchored by concepts of 'space', 'place' and 'boundary politics', asks questions about knowledge, authority, worker-citizen-professional formations, and the conditions for practical politics that are making and re-making societies, schooling and an emerging global order. She is a Fellow of the Academy of Social Sciences Australia and is editorial board member for the European Educational Research Journal. She has been series editor of the *Routledge World Yearbook of Education* since 2006 and edited the 2006 volume on *Education Research and Policy* (with Jenny Ozga and Tom Popkewitz) and the 2013 volume, *Educators, Professionalism and Politics* (with John Levin).

**Noah W. Sobe** is Professor and Program Chair of Cultural and Educational Policy Studies in the School of Education at Loyola University Chicago where he also directs the Center for Comparative Education. He is a historian of education and comparative education researcher whose research examines the global circulation of educational policies and practices, with a particular focus on the ways that schools function as contested sites of cultural production for the making up of people, peoples, societies and worlds. He is President of the Comparative and International Education Society (CIES) (2017–18). He is co-editor of the journal *European Education*, affiliated with the Comparative Education Society of Europe (CESE) and also serves on the Executive Committee of the International Standing Conference on the History of Education (ISCHE).

**Hannah M. Tavares** is Associate Professor in the Department of Educational Foundations at the University of Hawai'i at Mānoa. She received her PhD in educational policy studies and curriculum and instruction from the University of Wisconsin-Madison. Her research interests include cultural histories, curriculum histories, philosophy of education, and the use of visual archives in studies of education. She has completed a monograph, *Pedagogies of the Image: Photoarchives, cultural histories, and post-foundational inquiry* (Springer, 2016) and a book chapter, 'Postcolonial Studies and Education', in B. R. Warnick and L. Stone (Eds.), *Philosophy: Education* (Macmillan Interdisciplinary Handbooks: Philosophy series, 2017).

**Lorraine White-Hancock** completed her PhD in 2017 with the Faculty of Education at Monash University in Melbourne, Australia. Lorraine's background is as a practicing artist and object designer. After initially studying art and design (specialising in gold and silversmithing) at RMIT University (Melbourne, Australia), she completed a BA (Fine Art/Film) from the University of Melbourne and a Master of Education at Monash University. Lorraine was granted an Australian Postgraduate Award (Australian Government) and the Centre for Work and Learning Studies Award (Faculty of Education, Monash University) to support her PhD studies. Until 2013, Lorraine was the Course Co-ordinator of the Adv. Dip. Engineering Technology (Jewellery Design and Metalsmithing) in the Centre for Creative Industries at Box Hill Institute in Melbourne.

**Michalinos Zembylas** is Professor of Educational Theory and Curriculum Studies at the Open University of Cyprus. He is Visiting Professor and Research Fellow at the Institute for Reconciliation and Social Justice, University of the Free State, South Africa and at the Centre for Critical Studies in Higher Education Transformation at Nelson Mandela Metropolitan University. He has written extensively on emotion and affect in relation to social justice pedagogies, intercultural and peace education, human rights education and citizenship education. His upcoming books are *Psychologized Language in Education: Denaturalizing a regime of truth* (with Z. Bekerman), and *Socially Just Pedagogies in Higher Education* (co-edited with V. Bozalek, R. Braidotti, and T. Shefer). In 2016, he received the Distinguished Researcher Award in 'Social Sciences and Humanities' from the Cyprus Research Promotion Foundation.

# 1 Reclaiming comparative historical sociologies of education

*Terri Seddon, Julie McLeod and Noah W. Sobe*

The 'blue marble' photograph published in 1972 offered an iconic image of the earth. Taken from the Apollo 17 spacecraft at a distance of 45,000 kilometres, it shows a small blue and white planet in the vast darkness of space. That image prompted romantic and sometimes apocalyptic self-understandings of humanity relative to the immensity of the universe. It extended people's horizons and imaginaries from the relational intimacies of families, clans and communities, beyond the bordering and ordering of nation-states, towards the idea of earth as an imaginable social whole – a system that had to be self-sustaining. Such narratives helped to make everyday life knowable and actionable, reminding people of their responsibilities and stewardship of the planet. They prompted scientific debates about extending the geological time-scale beyond the Holocene, the warm period since the end of the last ice age, to recognize the Anthropocene, when human activities leave geological traces on the earth (Chakrabarty, 2009; Monastersky, 2015). These narratives also stimulated political will, driving developments that helped to reconfigure practices of governing and encouraged people to re-imagine their role in the world and how they were implicated in place, planet and permanence (Seghezzo, 2009). Such shifting boundaries of space and time, human self-understanding and practices of governing also opened the door to education reform and ways of working with difference.

Yet the reforms that have re-oriented education over the last thirty years are premised on particular patterns of knowledge building and methodological choices. For example, New Zealand educational researcher John Hattie explains the reasoning behind his research into *Visible Learning* by telling the story of Elliot and his treatment for leukaemia. His narrative reveals how he reviewed certain research reports as evidence for developing the idea of 'visible learning'. As a researcher, Hattie acknowledged how his insights came from somewhere; in his case, a concern with children and the challenges of learning. His research orientation was mediated by a particular form of reasoning that linked educational ways of looking to bio-medical logics, which used particular forms of evidence to identify a 'best way' forward. Recognising these methodological choices, Hattie also acknowledged the limits of his own knowledge building, declaring at the outset what his book was *not* about:

> It is not a book about classroom life, and does not speak about the nuances of what does and doesn't happen in classrooms . . . It is not a book about influences that cannot be addressed in classrooms – thus critical discussions about class, poverty, resources in families, health in families and nutrition are not included – but NOT because they are unimportant . . . It is not a book that includes qualitative studies.
>
> (Hattie, 2009: iix–ix)

But these nuances of research slipped past many education policy-makers and professional educators.

The idea of 'visible learning' went viral through education policy and professional networks because it offered an evidence-based educational improvement. It was knowledge from somewhere that was transferred to other places and its capacity to travel and realise reform success rested on particular methodological choices. Hattie's research topic, children's learning, and his key resource, educational reasoning inflected by bio-medical logics, used certain kinds of abstracted evidence to build knowledge about successful education. That evidence did not include direct engagement with learners or those who enabled their learning, and it did not interrogate the particularities of persons or places – the why or where learning occurred. Instead, the idea of 'visible learning' became a de-narrativised thing that was disconnected from the terms and conditions of its own formation. In this abstracted form, the meaning of visible learning could travel as endorsed policy scripts and remake local places by governing through knowledge. *Visible Learning* became an attractive product because it was 'commercialisable' in a hungry, competitive and hyper-accelerated global education market. But what is overlooked with the normalisation of this 'what works' gaze in education? And how does knowledge building affect the making and remaking of education and societies?

This volume of the *Routledge World Yearbook of Education* considers transformations in contemporary education that have accompanied global imaginaries. Our interest in globalising education is centred by the problem of knowledge building and what we are calling its 'embeddedness' (to use a broad descriptor). The blue marble photograph can be understood, we suggest, as a shift in horizons that ruptures familiar space-time boundaries that frame, form and filter everyday life. This rupture has unfolded with the globalising and regionalising dimensions of economic and cultural change, digital communication, geopolitics and policy instruments that encourage global horizons such as the Programme for International Student Assessment (PISA). Novelty is experienced through encounters with unfamiliar social worlds and unpredictable rhythms of time, which affect people's ways of knowing and doing everyday life *in situ*, irrespective of whether they move or not. These experiences of novelty, positive or negative, have a role in disrupting established ways of knowing and doing education by disturbing familiar frames of reference and space-time boundaries that mark out what is known and how it should be done.

Given these global shifts, this volume attempts to grasp, situate and historicise the specificity of these re-spatialising phenomena. We approach this task by interrogating how social worlds become knowable and actionable through the ways in which they are framed in the present. The question that informs this volume is: how space-times of education and forms of educational knowledge and practice are being, and have been, disturbed by these globalising phenomena and with what effects on reconfiguring education.

## Researching education space-times

This research agenda focuses attention on forms of education that unfold as particular historical formations of educational practices, concepts and research methods. The overarching problem that we tackle is how reconfiguring space-time boundaries affects education as a social institution. The chapters offer various ways of understanding these contexts of education and how they become differentiated. Our object of inquiry is 'changing contexts' – where change can be read as both an adjective and a verb. Like Hattie, we have made certain methodological choices in setting up the research discussed in this volume. Tracing how the research context located our point of departure and how the dialogue between the volume editor's respective vantage points oriented the project, we foreground two key propositions: first, that a robust engagement with changing contexts to re-examine ways of seeing, knowing and educating confronts the concept and effects of 'social embeddedness'; and second, that a research imaginary informed by historical sensibilities offers a valuable entry point for understanding the re-spatialisation of education that we see as currently underway.

### *The research context of this edited volume*

We take up the problem of social embeddedness as a way of contributing to a larger story about globalising education. Our entry point is partly defined by the current state of educational knowledge and research. But it also builds on a systematic inquiry into the re-spatialisation of education that has been organised through thematic volumes of the *World Yearbook of Education* between 2006 and 2017. The editors of the 2018 volume have different perspectives on this conscious knowledge-building project. Terri Seddon has been series and occasional volume editor since 2006. Noah Sobe has contributed chapters to the 2011 and 2013 volumes. Julie McLeod knows the *World Yearbook of Education* series as reader rather than writer. These different perspectives mean that this volume combines insider and outsider knowledge in order to understand how the re-spatialisation of education has become knowable and actionable, in part, through the *World Yearbook* project.

The specific *World Yearbook* focus on the re-spatialisation of education departed from the 2005 volume, which examined how the relation between globalisation and nationalism affected education around the world (Coulby & Zambetta, 2005). Coordinated and organised through the series editorship of the *Yearbook*, each subsequent volume addressed a particular dimension of globalising education by examining the relation between 'travelling ideas and local places' to understand how spatially distributed formations of knowledge build-ing and practices of 'governing through knowledge' reconfigured education. Over twelve years, the book series used the opportunity afforded by a *world* yearbook to map how governing knowledge emerged and was renegotiated through shifting space-times of education. This *World Yearbook* project offered 'proof of concept' understandings of globalising education. It also troubled established education concepts and research methods that defined fields of education research.

This dialogue within and between fields of education research came into sharper focus with the publication of *WYB* 2012. That volume speaks back to the tradition of comparative education by troubling the established concepts of policy lending and borrowing (Steiner-Khamsi & Waldow, 2012). As a thematic focus within the larger *World Yearbook* project, it was conceived as a contribu-tion to an emerging field of 'comparative policy studies'. The introductory essay indicated that aim of the volume was to look beyond normative judgements that saw travelling ideas as either good or bad and, instead, better 'describe, ana-lyse and understand policy borrowing and learning in an era of globalisation' (Steiner-Khamsi, 2012: 3). This research agenda was located at the intersection between comparative education and policy studies, and mapped the research history that now informs understandings of policy borrowing and lending. Its core argument underlines the importance of researching local policy contexts where simple notions of policy implementation are disrupted by unpredictable policy effects.

The essay identified three generations of researchers who contributed to this emerging field of comparative policy studies. The first generation reached out from separate histories in comparative education and education policy studies: establishing foundational concepts, such as 'selective policy borrowing and lend-ing' 'externalisation' and 'cross-national policy attraction', and through policy studies, focusing on the mechanisms that make globalising education knowable and actionable. The second generation named and captured the significance of travelling ideas and their effects through local policy contexts. They also extended the geographic range of policy and local contexts by tracing the effects of glo-balising education through developing countries. And, as Steiner-Khamsi noted, that middle generation also supported third-generation scholars through targeted institutional support, for example, that organised by her own university, Teachers College Columbia (2012: 9). With that support, an emerging network of compara-tive policy researchers has become visible, and lines of inquiry are exploding in many directions. The design of the 2012 *World Yearbook of Education* captured the conceptual contributions of this body of work by surfacing four lines of inquiry: the shift from bilateral to international frames of reference; understandings of logics or forms of reasoning that order systems and cases; the methodological repercussions of a 'globalisation optique' and how 'policyscapes' trouble nation-state case study research, and the analysis of cross-national policy attractions through 'projections', where the portrayal of one school system is ordered, dis-torted, simplified and smoothed with reference to address the priorities and social logics of another place.

The move towards codification of the academic field in the 2012 volume served as a provocation in its claiming and naming the primary object of inquiry as 'policy'. This focus on policy had been centre-stage within the field of education since the 1990s (Dale, 1992). But sociology of education, and the larger World Yearbook project, had a longer history that was tensioned between policy and practice. Yearbooks focusing on educational improvements have been published since the late 19th century. In the US, progressive education movements and universities established agencies, such as the US-based National Society for the Study of Education which, from 1901, produced the *Educational Yearbook* that remains associated with Teachers College Columbia. The *Yearbook of Education* was initially conceived through Kings College London in 1932, with Lord Eustace Percy as the editor-in-chief until 1935 (Holmes, 1974: 387). The war stopped publication from 1940 to 1946, and it relocated to the London Institute of Education in 1953. This institutional support incubated a British tradition of comparative education that referenced the needs of England and Wales, set in an international context and addressed using 'common British traditions' (Holmes, 1974: 390). There were associations with Teachers College Columbia from 1938, when Isaac Kandel joined the editorial board. The prefix *World* was added in negotiation with comparative education scholars from Teachers College Columbia, particularly George Bereday (joint editor from 1957 to 1967), which filled the gap created by the suspension of Teachers College's *Educational Yearbook* (Keller, 1949). But as Holmes suggests, this *World Yearbook of Education* retained an British orientation. By the 1960s, British and US interests in comparative education were diverging as US scholars extended their research into the developing 'Third World', with British scholars remaining focused on Britain and its Commonwealth.

It was the process of europeanisation that cut across this Anglophone world and its visible networks and research orientations. The effects of the novel europeanising narrative unfolded at three levels, all of which had an impact upon ways of knowing and doing education. First, the process of making Europe unfolded through the establishment of a supra-national European state. The post-war union of European nation-states for economic purposes became a novel space of governing, where the supra-national state mobilised forms of soft governing to coordinate networks of actors: not only governments but also communities, professionals and researchers. Second, this networking revealed the deep social embedding of education and how logics of education were anchored by certain forms of reasoning that sedimented particular educational practices, concepts and research methods, often in taken-for-granted ways. These ways of looking and seeing were materialised through policy and professional ways of knowing and doing education that re-made policy processes, and prompted the concept of 'governing through knowledge and numbers' (Ozga, 2008). Finally, this novel supra-national space of 'Europe' and its practices of governing became an object of inquiry, which was identified initially as *Fabricating Europe* through a 2002 collaboration between Portuguese comparativist António Nóvoa and British historical sociologist Martin Lawn (Nóvoa & Lawn, 2002).

The concept of 'europeanisation' framed research on the making of a European educational space. It was a research agenda that centred formation of the *European Education Research Journal.* It also informed the *World Yearbook* project, which was re-conceiving its own objects of enquiry in more globalised, one-world ways, in line with the shift from a British to a more European/international editorial board.

The idea of europeanisation as the making of a supra-national European space bumped up against the 2012 idea of comparative policy studies within the *World Yearbook* project. Where comparative policy studies prioritised policy research through studies of 'local policy contexts', the study of europeanisation focused on the re-spatialisation of national education systems through the emergence of a supra-national European educational space and its effects on 'local places' (Alexiadou & Jones, 2001). In practice, the main trajectory of europeanisation research prioritised 'Europe', the supra-national space of governing, and highlighted the way knowledge-based regulatory technologies, such as policies, audit and data practices, resourced and oriented the emerging European educational space. These methodological choices co-existed with research that also examined how the space of experiencing Europe was affected by the process of europeanisation (Niemeyer & Seddon, forthcoming). And for researchers that were not 'from Europe', there was scope to explore how the long shadow of europeanisation was framed by larger processes of globalising education, as well as by the historic effects of colonisation that had made a eurocentric world (and made its historical specificity invisible) through eurocentric knowledge building (Connell, 2007; Chen, 2010; Caruso & Sobe 2012; Seddon 2015; Takayama et al. 2017).

However, defining this emerging field of europeanisation research as comparative policy research seemed to lose some of the complexities of globalising education. The process of chunking up fields of inquiry is a necessary methodological step, and makes it possible to discipline research through the use of specific concepts, methods and practices of knowledge building. Yet a focus on 'policy' and investigations of 'local policy contexts' foregrounds social worlds that are bordered and ordered with reference to policy. Whereas studies of europeanisation foreground the relation between forms of state and civil society: an object of inquiry that sprawls across forms, scales and disciplinary formations, and also builds on often unacknowledged geographies of knowledge. In contrast to policy studies, research on europeanisation was tracing emergent spaces that unfolded through the spatialisation of knowledge networks of state and non-state actors, and also the coordinating effects of their antagonistic and collaborative forms of reasoning. This work prompted a place-based, rather than a policy orientation. It incubated a sociology of locality that could be policy focused but could also plunge into the borderland spaces between policy and practice, governing and experience, 'representations (mental space)' and 'real space', that is 'the space of people who deal with material things' (Lefebvre, 1991: 4). This line of inquiry had its own intellectual history at the intersection, not between comparative education and policy studies, but between social history and sociology of education.

### Historical and sociological vantage points

The codification of comparative policy studies raised questions about the unit of reference that frames, forms and filters knowledge building about globalising education. It also served as a reminder that the naming of a field of inquiry pinpoints the methodological choices that inform its way of looking and seeing, which, in turn, orients its associated educational practices. However, bumping into that name – comparative policy studies – brought particular methodological choices into relief along with an awareness of the mostly taken-for-granted assumptions and premises that inform knowledge building within a particular field. In part, it was the juxtaposition of a field defined by comparative research of policy and policy effects with the largely unarticulated framing of sociology of education that prompted this 2018 *World Yearbook of Education*. Its aim has been to examine space-times of education and account for their unevenness by interrogating the changing contexts that make educational practices, concepts and research methods as seen from three vantage points: sociology of education, history of education and comparative education.

Research into globalising education through these three fields of education research brings conceptualisations of space, time and mobility into sharp focus. However, it is the intersecting effects of these concepts – used as either research topic or conceptual resource – that can give historical sociology its somewhat sprawling and elusive character. The core project of historical sociology is to understand

> . . . what people do in the present as a struggle to create a future out of the past, of seeing that the past is not just the womb of the present but the only raw material out of which the present can be constructed.
>
> (Abrams, 1982: 8; original emphasis)

It is a line of inquiry that has unfolded through generations of researchers: from Marx, Durkheim and Weber, through second-wave scholars like E.P. Thompson, Barrington Moore and Theda Skocpol, to a proliferating third wave, where feminist and post-colonial contributors have also struggled to understand and act within and through emerging forms of modernity (Delanty & Isin, 2003). As C. Wright Mills noted, 'all sociology worthy of the name is "historical sociology" . . . an attempt to "write the present as history"' (1967: 146). It is a research orientation that aims to grasp an emerging present by triangulating knowledge building based on detailed analyses of history, social structures and biography (Kumar, 2015).

The aim of writing the present as history underpins the methodological standpoint of the 2018 *World Yearbook of Education*. As noted above, our interest in globalising education is captured in two key propositions. The first substantive proposition is that a robust engagement with changing contexts confronts the concept and effects of 'social embeddedness' which, we argue, is crucial for any re-examining of ways of seeing, knowing and doing education. This is because who sees what, from where and for what purposes invites a reconsideration of the ethical and political dimensions of knowledge building and its material effects. This substantive dimension raises questions about the unevenness of education and how the texturing of space-times contributes to inequality. For example, naming and addressing the 'uneven space-times of education' recognises that the compression and stretching of space and time are not only policy effects but are also experienced differently by people, how they know their place and act out their sense of permanence. The apparent 'smoothing' of global configurations through dominant policy scripts and standardising social technologies are also implicated in the fabrication of principles and practices that are lived and often taken for granted as unevenness, distance and shifting forms of inequality. Acknowledgement of these contradictions and of how dilemmas are experienced marks this volume of the *WYB* as a contribution to the long tradition of educational inquiry that looks past the uncertainties of any particular present to better understand the points of leverage that steer educational change and continuity in ways that make futures.

The second methodological proposition is that a research imaginary informed by historical sensibilities offers a valuable entry point for understanding the re-spatialisation of education. As Edward Sojo has long argued, there is a 'growing awareness of the simultaneity and interwoven complexity of the social, the historical and the spatial, their inseparability and interdependence' (Sojo, 1996: 3). For example, a field named 'comparative policy studies' is provocative because it makes the methodological choice to focus on one context, centred by policy and policy effects, rather than engaging the messy multiplicities of space, place and context that, in practice, spatialise entities-identities, relationships and cultures (Massey, 2005). Foregrounding time and temporalities makes it possible to think about encounters with the spectres of a past and a future, where historical memory and future-oriented imagination colour story-telling in the present. Temporalities also suggest the 'over-writing' of identities where traces and smudges persist, haunting and unsettling the present and unevenly moving into the future (McLeod, 2014). Temporalities also play through institutional spaces and processes of knowledge building by congealing particular recontextualisations that can disturb, transform and sometimes produce things anew. Categories and concepts are used to objectify a 'here and now', but they are also entangled with contextual narratives and habits of mind, which carry traces of 'there and then'. Narrating a context inter-crosses – criss-crosses and weaves between – temporal spaces in ways that are also interrupted by things that move, travel and live through particular patterns of mobility and fixity (Sobe & Kowalczyk, 2012).

One challenge of historical sociology lies in how to write the present as history, where each present is both an input to and outcome of social forms and formations. The delineation of what is dead and past, and what is live and emergent provides a well-known methodological circuit breaker in this kind of intellectual iteration, and marks a distinction between history and historiography (Spiegel, 2014). Comparison is a parallel methodological strategy and, in the form of longitudinal, epochal and cross-border comparison, is central to historical sociology

(Kumar, 2015). Those research traditions that traced *longue durée* as social forma-tions and sedimented knowledge cultures have become *histoire croisée* – analyses that investigate concepts as inter-related and often associated with transnational history (Werner & Zimmermann, 2006).

These different forms of comparison open up analysis in ways that are dif-ferent to the distinction of past from present. First, lateral comparison offers a way of juxtaposing particular presents for purposes of analysis, for example, the present narrated as 'policy studies' and the present narrated as 'europeani-sation', or the present experienced in diverse geo-social settings. Second, depth comparison reveals how a particular event or artefact, such as education or supra-national 'Europe', is fabricated through particular formations of knowl-edge, knowledge building and social learning that make and remake identity, relationships, cultures and their effects. Finally, criss-crossing (*croisée*) com-parison makes it possible to look both at and behind the landscape of tangible things to surface patterns and processes of knowing and doing that configure globalising education. This move, which examines space-time contexts and their histories and effects together, reveals the significance of knowledge build-ing, methodological choices, and also more or less habitual ways of looking and learning. We see the concept of 'space-times of education' as offering a way of investigating spaces of governing and experiencing where, for example, dilemma-driven policyscapes, learning spaces and workplaces sediment mean-ings through material practices, with reference to certain contexts, concepts and congealed social interests.

### Entangled histories

This trajectory of comparative historical sociology leads, we believe, towards an understanding of the present as arising from 'entangled histories'. The idea of 'entanglement' focuses attention on events, such as travelling ideas, people and goods that interrupt a particular present, and the effects of those interrup-tions that distort, diffract and disturb established forms of education and society. 'Entanglement' also acknowledges how each of these elements also has their own history and how narratives fix these histories as if they just unfolded through path-dependent knowledge building and social organisation. Entangled history addresses issues of convergence, contingency, diverse and unexpected collisions of forces and effects, which are all features of such entanglement. This orienta-tion that acknowledges interlocking flows and forces has gained traction across the social sciences and humanities. However, we should not rest on the assertion of 'entanglement' as a sufficient concept to account for the complexity of the present or the past. Neither should we be satisfied with the 'finding' of 'entangle-ment' as the sufficient outcome of scholarly research. Rather, the imperative is to trace out the specificity of relations and the forms that unfold with particular entanglements.

In the case of historical sociologies of education, we can see how comparison of events with reference to particular (and messy) space-times of education helps to account for globalising education. It offers concepts and methodologies for tracing how and with what effects education, and the educational logics of learning, working and governing, become entangled with socio-cultural and geo-social transformations, such as globalisation. As Burson explains:

> The notion of historical entanglement is the manner in which an "object" of historical study (for example, a concept, discourse, or identity) is constituted at the meeting point or intercrossing among various historical contexts as opposed to its being considered in only one isolated discursive context. Entanglement may be considered to operate on at least three levels: multicultural entanglement (the intercrossing of synchronous cultures); transdiscursive entanglements (the intercrossing of theological, scientific or ethico-political debates, for example); and diachronic entanglement (the arguably inevitable way in which scholarly analysis interjects itself into, and alters, the past by the very process of attending to the first and second entanglements).
>
> (Burson, 2013: 3)

In this volume of the *World Yearbook of Education* we draw on concepts and methods associated with entangled history to write about globalising education as an historical phenomena. Initially, this rationale was hard to pinpoint and we struggled to identify the core line of argument. The relative invisibility of historical sociology in the field of educational research was part of the problem. It complicated the selection of chapter authors because there was no visible bookshelf or college of easily identifiable scholars grappling with entangled histories in the sphere of sociology of education and policy studies. Pragmatically, therefore, we organised the volume in three sections, with chapter authors selected with reference to each editor's particular interest in time and identity, space and work, and context and mobility. Yet the movement of changing socio-political contexts has also affected the volume. Working on the 2018 volume of the *World Yearbook of Education* since 2016 means that it has come to fruition alongside the disturbing effects of war in the Middle East/North Africa (MENA) region, the disconcerting farce of Brexit and the Donald Trump US presidency, and the dislocating geopolitical ripple effects, which now intensify political violence in Europe and increase sabre-rattling in East Asia. This lived history contextualised the volume but has also confirmed the importance of recognising knowledge and developing methodologies that can interrogate and understand such entangled histories.

As the volume came to completion, the contributions helped us to grasp the significance of space-times in globalising education. In particular, it helped us to understand why an earlier framing of the *World Yearbook* project as one of 'comparative policy studies' had served as such a potent methodological provocation. Such entanglements suggested how space-times of education were implicated in globalising education, but they also highlighted the salience of 'social embeddedness' as a key concept in writing the present as history.

## Entangled space-times

The expansive essay by Bob Cowen, which immediately follows this opening chapter, introduces many of the concerns that initially prompted this volume of the *World Yearbook of Education* by highlighting the way space and time are troubled by globalisation. Speaking through academic comparative education, Cowen suggests that 'what works' research, such as the study of visible learning, has built on 'fix-it' forms of comparative education that have operated with simplified understandings of space and time, where

> . . . [s]pace is places in which some version of research by 'field-work' (i.e. the collection from educational sites of systematically organised data) shows that successful or non-successful action on education occurs. Space is locales of educational success and failure. Good space is where success is clearly visible (e.g. once upon a time, Japan; Finland; or last year, Shanghai). Bad space is where failure is occurring (say, Pisa-shocked Germany or Spain). Exciting space is a scientific version of the promised land: the happy, evidence-sensitive, places where data-informed reform will occur.
>
> (Cowen, this vol p. XX)

This pragmatic, action-oriented form of comparative education reasoning has unfolded through policy and activities focused by particular understandings of modernisation. Its underlying logic was to produce 'successful' education through 'successful' reforms, when seen from the vantage point of international politics. Fix-it comparative education, as Cowen argues, looks across geographic areas to identify successful education landscapes and reforms. It draws on histories of policy borrowing and lending that are seen as having proven capacity to extend and generalise the success of 'successful countries' to those deemed unsuccessful.

But what counts as success? Whose success is in view in fix-it comparative education? And whose success is at stake in visible learning? For comparative historical sociologists one challenge is to understand how such simple views of time and space shape or indeed impede our ways of knowing the space-time of education, arguably distorting the frame of reference that orients and motivates how we act and know in any particular present.

We argue here that such questions are not answered directly by established practices derived from either fix-it or academic comparative education. As Cowen notes, while comparative education is consciously renewing concepts, methods and practices, its epistemological debates have congealed in ways that continue to surface narratives about educational change and continuity which are premised on analysis of the education landscape without explicitly acknowledging imperium. By 'imperium', Cowen means the social organisation of power whereby the governing effects of knowledge that materialise as habits of mind as well as the exercise of authority, play through everyday practical politics of education and societies. For example, world culture theory offers a counter-narrative to fix-it comparative education by highlighting the significance of global scripts that now rewrite educational activities (Silova & Brehm, 2015). However, in researching education landscapes through lateral comparison rather than depth or criss-crossing comparisons that reveal the play of knowledge-authority regimes, world culture and fix-it narratives do not fully render the complexities of transfer, translation and transformation. As Cowen notes, the new as well as the old directions in comparative education are limited by the way that field has conceptualised 'context'. Reducing space and time to linear trajectories looks past the effects of social embedding and its implications for policy borrowing and lending. It encourages knowledge building that writes linear, progressivist histories of past, present and future; it doesn't write the present as history.

Yet despite these limitations, the gaze that realises 'what works' agendas through comparative education continues to dominate education policy and practice. It is a gaze that has particular significance because of its orientation, persistence and effects in globalising education. The ascent of fix-it comparative education as the *modus operandi* of globalising education over the last thirty years has steered the remaking of education, while its ontological and epistemological habits, even in academic comparative education, mostly look beyond or ignore reflexive anxieties. Our dis-ease thus rests on warranted concerns about the usefulness and adequacy of concepts, methods and practices associated with comparative education and its logics of policy borrowing and lending. The problem, as Cowen observes, is that these simple fix-it understandings of time and space rest on particular ways of understanding education as an instrument of governing that can steer social change and achieve the success of a promised land.

This problem of 'context', we suggest, is fundamental to 'what works' research and 'fix it' comparative education. The reduction of context to a simple backdrop or container for knowing and doing education fails to grasp the entangling effects of space and time, and of knowledge and narrative. Similarly, not looking at context, as if contextualisation had no effects, makes it possible to look away from the social embeddedness of learning, knowledge networks and education systems. We critique both logics because they make it possible to sustain a future-oriented gaze but in ways that imperfectly acknowledge how effects of work and learning can change education and society.

Looking towards a future without also acknowledging its present and past as history overlooks the entanglements that cohere educational practices, concepts and methods of knowledge building into forms of education. Downplaying the persistent effects of imperium, not only through landscapes of the present but also through the deep reach into the hearts and souls of a social body, risks making the narrative formation of contexts invisible. Neglecting histories and sociologies of knowledge and authority makes it hard to see the unpredictable consequences of educational practices, concepts and methods, and how they shape the space-times of education.

This line of reasoning has motivated our analysis of the space-times of education. As an intellectual project, it is a critique of 'what works' research and 'fix it' comparative education. But problematising space-times of education and social embeddedness also re-opens debates about what is not seen through a 'quick fix' policy-research lens and the implications of those partial narratives and invisible effects for globalising education. The chapters that follow Cowen's essay take this agenda forward by laying out more explicit conceptualisations of space-times of education and their effects. Each chapter draws on detailed knowledge-building work to engage with concepts of 'space', 'time' and 'mobility', employing diverse research approaches that deepen understanding of the multiple dimensions of globalising education.

### Eventful space

The assumption that space is eventful, an active force in the making and remaking of education and societies is central to the concept of space-times of education. This premise acknowledges that concepts, methods and practices are events that occupy, orient and form particular 'places'. These events are embedded and given meaning, significance and social force because of the way they unfold through a certain space of social relationships, habits of mind and practices of governing. The situating of these events makes places, where learning, working and governing have effects; this knowledge building and the exercise of authority fix circuits of labour and circulations of knowledge that also steer and sustain everyday life. As Gieryn (2000: 465) notes, 'place' is a distinct spot, which is distinguished by geographic location, material form, and invested meanings. It is doubly constructed, being 'built or in some way physically carved out' [and] also 'interpreted narrated, perceived, felt, understood, and imagined'. These processes entail knowledge building that makes meaning through referencing a particular space-time and how it is narrated as context: fixing a space-time as a unit of reference (as in the very concepts of 'national education' or 'international education') is a way of governing through knowledge.

Space, therefore, is not just a container or a simple event in a flat world. It is rather an ontological unfolding that is not only influenced by a single context. The production of space rests on entanglements between multiple contexts where the concepts, methods and practices that make space are also mediated by ways of seeing and experiencing space and place. Doreen Massey (1993) identifies eventful 'space' with reference to the 'stories-so-far' that are framed by particular geometries of power, which make space and also configure and orient place. Space making, she suggests, is, first, a 'product of interrelations' and is constituted through interactions, 'from the immensity of the global to the intimately tiny'. Second, seeing space requires us to recognise the relational processes that play through forms of interaction, multiple voices, logics and directions. Spaces therefore locate 'multiplicity in the sense of contemporaneous plurality', 'co-existing heterogeneity' and 'distinct trajectories'. Finally, these features mean space is always under construction: 'Without space, no multiplicity; without multiplicity, no space . . . Multiplicity and space as co-constitutive' (Massey, 2005: 9). But the sum of the-stories-so-far is never just one space; those stories emerge through spatialities that rest on different ways of seeing space and understanding spatial organisation (Lefebvre, 1991). Space is produced as those spatialities perceived as 'spatial practices' prompt conceptions or 'representations of space', and are felt as an experienced 'space of representation' that is lived affectively.

There are echoes here with Donna Haraway's (1988) concept of 'situated knowledge' and her now-famous call for researchers to acknowledge the contexts in which knowledge is produced and made possible – the relationship between epistemology and perspective. This has been an influential concept in the humanities and social sciences, and especially among feminist and qualitative researchers. Its citational popularity has coincided with an autobiographical turn and critical attention to the reflexivity and power of research encounters. However, in many respects this has resulted in rather thin applications of the concept of situated knowledges, such that it risks becoming a simple phrase to describe the personal and political positioning of the researcher, thereby diminishing some of its analytic power and reach. In explaining their associated concept of the 'geosocial', Mitchell and Kallio (2017) have made a convincing case for not confining the argument of 'situated knowledges' to 'the personal subjectivity of the knower alone'. Rather, they urge making 'situated knowledge locatable in "actually existing spaces"' (2017: 14). To do so, they look to the messy intersection of macro, geopolitical, geo-economic, globalising forces and local, everyday micro practices and social relations: 'Tracing the connections between these human practices and social, environmental, and political-economic worlds, and constantly thinking and rethinking the meaning of the 'ground' and 'politics' in the twenty-first century, is the aim of geosocial thinking' (Mitchell and Kallio 2017: 14).

The chapters in the 'Space' section of this book elaborate the idea of 'eventful space' by considering the work that makes space and how forms of labour fix time as a particular present and a platform that both locates and orients subsequent space making. The first two chapters address the making of education as a social institution. Beatrix Niemeyer reflects a Germanic reading of education back to Anglophone researchers. She introduces the concept of 'space of orientation' to trace how the German tradition of letter writing made a normative public space, a context that framed, formed and filtered what it meant to be an educated person. She suggests that this space making served as both an input to the formation of education as a public space and also embedded particular kinds of knowledge and narrative as certain social movements steered the institutionalisation of public schooling. Through these processes, women learned their own subordination, as men learned their privileged access to public space.

The remaining chapters offer more detailed analyses of specific space-times of education. Martin Lawn targets the space of governing made through europeanisation by tracing particular circuits of labour and ideas that remade European education at the nexus between policy and research. He shows how the knowledge-building habits of comparative education networks and their particular methodologies and pragmatic work practices made a distinctive European educational space. He gives the idea of 'governing through knowledge' meaning and also shows how researchers are implicated in this governing work that steers education through cultural resources that make education knowable and actionable. Chin-Ju Mao analyses the unevenness of educational space-times by comparing two high schools in wealthy and poor parts of Taipei. She shows how the context of school choice reconstitutes the status order through the normative bordering and ordering of relationships, rules and resources at each school.

The two final chapters in this section surface interventions intended to change space-times of education. Arwen Raddon uses the concept of 'time-space' to analyse Technical and Vocational Education (TVET) in Singapore. Combining insights from Barbara Adam and Doreen Massey, she considers how the low status of TVET is both embedded within geometries of power and also constantly renewed through habits anchored by Anglophone colonial histories and popular culture. Tracing interventions in TVET, Raddon documents the difficulties in dislodging socially embedded associations between working-class education and low status learning. Finally, Lorraine White-Hancock asks, how can space-making enable innovation? Using the concept of 'learning through working', she traces how scientists and artists create borderlands within STEM that realise innovation through unlearning and relearning embedded concepts, methods and practices. This expansive learning depends on space-times that combine appropriate work organisation and a culture order that is open to transgression. She argues that innovative work and learning mobilises educational logics to orient and authorise workplaces as learning spaces.

### Troubling temporalities

These various constructs – social embeddedness, eventful space, situated knowledge and geosocial thinking – all offer ways of understanding and analysing the tricky terrain of space and its inherited, contested, volatile and sedimented meanings and social effects. We can add and subtract emphases and elements, but the ethical and methodological challenge remains that of trying to understand the shifting grounds on which educational research, practice and policy takes place. Crucial to this, as we have argued, is the dynamic between space and time, which is by no means self-evident. Of course, all research takes place in and over time and research methods and ways of knowing and theorising emerge and take hold of imaginations in particular times and places and in ways that can be fateful, nonreversible, in their effects. Our own endeavours in this volume arise in the context of a 'temporal turn' across the social sciences, which is associated with a range of approaches that privilege time as an object of analysis, allow for understanding of the social in greater time perspective and interrogate the presumed linearity of temporal processes (Savage, 2010; Thomson and McLeod, 2015). In our discussions, temporality is engaged 'not as a fancier word for time, but as signifying the messy, moving relations between past, present and future' (McLeod, 2017; see also Harootunian, 2007; Lorenz and Bevernage, 2013).

The shifting horizons of globalisation, as noted above, accelerating ecological changes and the messing with time, speed and presence made possible by digital communication, among other phenomena, are bringing time and temporalities into sharp relief, from big historical and epochal time to everyday micro experiences of time. The philosopher of history, Helge Jordheim writes of these 'multiple temporalities' not as discrete layers – such as in geological formations – with the rhythms of daily life on top, and the slow change of the environment on the bottom. Rather he suggests that 'it might be more useful to imagine different temporalities existing in a plane, as parallel lines, paths, tracks, or courses, zigzagging, sometimes touching or even crossing one another, but all equally visible, tangible, and with direct consequences for our lives' (Jordheim 2014: 508). Jordheim employs the term 'temporal regimes' to characterize 'the plurality of times inherent in the plurality of social phenomena' (2014: 509).

The chapters comprising the second section of this volume, 'Identity and shifting temporalities' take up the challenge of exploring different registers of transformations in educational space-times through the lenses of identity, citizenship and pedagogy. In each chapter, the focus and topic is historicised and this historicity is brought into the foreground. Jordheim's concepts of multiple temporalities resonates here, as the chapters variously trace the criss-crossing of policy change, national affiliation, colonising and decolonising agendas, and the remaking of teacher and student identities via pedagogies and rhetorics that engender complex affective responses. As each chapter illustrates, subjective and everyday experiences bear the marks of longer historical processes and also point to some of the ways in which educational aspirations and policy regimes take root and gain meaning. The traces and memories of earlier temporal regimes continue to haunt the educational present yet, at the same time, this present is forcibly interrupted by, among other phenomena, the promise of digital communication and pedagogies or policy-reform discourses directed to more standardised governing of teachers and learning. While it is not easy to disentangle the layers that constitute the temporal regimes of the educational present, these chapters offer ways of doing so that give analytic priority to the subjects visibly populating the space-times of education – teachers, students, citizens – those who are also typically cast as the beneficiaries, mediators, or objects of educational policy reform.

Inés Dussel considers the ways and extent to which digital media in schools are 'reconfiguring the space-times of education'. She questions the standard debates of these pedagogical changes (accelerating or compressing time, inaugurating different rhythms of teaching and learning), and calls for new ways of approaching the concepts of space and time that step away from seeing them as still 'linear and homogenous'. In particular, she draws out new types of archival work, attached to digital media in schools, addressing the function and politics of images, 'their relationship to truth claims, memory, and the representability of the real'. Memory figures powerfully in Michalinos Zembylas's analysis of education policy in Cyprus, taking as a focus the affective charge and orthodoxies of the 'I don't forget and I struggle' policy. A key aim of this policy was to encourage Greek-Cypriot children not to forget national struggles and to preserve a particular conception of 'history, memory and identity'. Here history and memory operate at several levels: in historicising the production of the curriculum and policy texts, in historicising national and collective memory – the 'emotional archive of the nation state' (Kenway & Fahey in Zembylas) – and the politics and affect of memory mediated in the space-times of education and pedagogies. Here policy reform meets affect studies, and this encounter dramatizes the ways in which the educational present inherits and is constituted by complex memories and emotional legacies – hope, nostalgia, bitterness, sentimentality, loss.

The importance of attending to affective responses in order to grasp the reach and character of globalising education is also a central theme in Nancy Lesko and Alyssa Niccolini's chapter on school reform and public feelings teachers. They work with the notion of 'viscosity', understood as a 'spatial and temporal event' that aggregates people/bodies over time, to analyse how antipathetic and nega- tive feelings accrue to teachers, who are grouped and pitted as 'at odds' with the public. Their lively analysis shows how 'the brisk and sharp affects that mobi- lize . . . reform strategies at the macro level of politics have congealed with the slow and unglamorous work of teaching at a more micro level'. Traversing the micro and macro effects of policy-reform agendas is a focus as well of Hannah Tavares's chapter, which explores the 'temporal legacies of colonial situations' in relation to questions of identity, citizenship and the broader space-times in which education – as government, as colonising, as otherwise – takes place. Focusing on Hawai'i, Tavares's discussion places colonialism as vital in theorising temporality and in understanding constructions of normative and desirable educable citizen subjects. This chapter is also a necessary and timely reminder of what attention to globalisation, europeanisation, or other forms of regionalisation can exclude from view and the concomitant imperative to embrace a robust account of the historicity and geo-social politics of knowledge, where knowledge that matters is named as central, not peripheral or 'merely' local.

## *Problematising mobility*

Coming to terms with mobility, circulation and flow is essential to grappling with the uneven space-times of education. Scholarly interest in people and objects in movement or in 'flux' has exploded in step with the study of globalisation. As discussed above, a recent *World Yearbook* project sought to deepen our field's understanding of 'policy borrowing and lending' (Steiner-Khamsi &Waldow, 2012) by directing attention at the global movement of educational policies and practices. But by harkening back to earlier scholarship, in some cases the diffu- sionist paradigms of early anthropology as well as political science engagements with concepts such as Westernisation and modernisation, a wealth of insightful scholarship on the cultural exchanges, flows and circulations of educational prac- tices, policies, objects and individuals has emerged in recent years (for example, Caruso & Roldán Vera, 2005; Popkewitz, 2005, 2016; Cowen, 2009). In addition to considering the transnational as one of the criss-crossing layers of educational time-spaces, this work often also directs careful attention to travelling, movement and mobility as key aspects of 'changing contexts' (again used here in the double sense of adjective and verb). The third section of this *WYB* volume consists of four chapters that surface the linking of mobility with the time-spaces of schooling.

Flow and movement are seen as positive, necessary component elements of one-worldist globalisation. James Clifford (1997) pointed out some time ago that the customary academic paradigm has been to attribute movement and the advantages that accrue from the ability to occupy multiple positions to cultural elites, academic researchers among them. Settlement, stability and all that remains *in situ* is then easily coded as a 'backwards' provincial remainder needing to be reformed/transformed by 'forces' seen as moving in from the outside. Connected to this is the analytic and cultural paradigm that views 'authentic' forms of mobility as inhering exclusively in the free (and freeing) movements of subjects for whom journeys/departures are a matter of choice, in contrast, for example, to forced mobility of refugees. Sobe and Fischer (2009) have argued that this dichotomy is clearly evident in the completely opposing ways that 'student mobility' is discussed in European and American contexts. This final section of the volume problematises mobility in an effort to help us move further beyond limited temporalised and spatialised notions of context. Anna Tsing (2000) evocatively recommended that we pay attention to the ways that global flows make and remake channels, and in this section contributors use what we would characterise as criss-crossing comparison approaches to develop new understandings of the texturing of the time-spaces of education.

In the first chapter of this section, Noah W. Sobe and Jamie Kowalczyk propose that examination of 'big C' Context – meaning the categories and concepts used to define social embeddedness – is an essential part of developing criss-crossing comparisons. In proposing a reconceptualisation of context as a weaving and an assemblage, they draw on Bruno Latour's (2004) distinction between 'matters of fact' and 'matters of concern' to argue for the importance of researcher reflexivity and for conceptualising of objects of analysis in the first place.

The mobility of academic researchers is carefully examined by Marianne Larsen in a chapter that questions contemporary vogues for academic movement and considers the (im)mobilities that are mutually embedded with mobilities and help to generate the unevenness of the space-times of higher education teaching and research labour. Drawing on network and assemblage metaphors, Larsen presents a historical sociology of the role mobility plays in constituting a global academic assemblage. She uses Bærendoldt's (2013) notion of 'governmobility' to illustrate the ways in which mobilities become self-governing principles, and she draws the important conclusion that mobilities don't just happen on top of existing institutions or societies, but constitute them.

In the subsequent chapter, Elefterios Klerides comes at mobility and the uneven space-times of education through a historical sociology of interculturalism in history teaching that is informed by a careful analysis of changing theories and practices in the field of international relations. Contrasting the production of *homo nationalis* with a *homo interculturalis*, Klerides offers a window into changing contexts of schooling through fine-grained discussion of textbook revision politics and initiatives. The chapter accomplishes a significant rethinking of the contexts of history teaching by convincingly showing that realist, liberalist and constructionist approaches to international relations are useful in helping us to identify the political principles and social structures that make different modalities of imagining the relationship between history and identity possible.

The final chapter of the volume presents a call for the sociology of education to 'move beyond itself' towards a 'mobile' sociology of education. Paolo Landri argues that this entails opening up the ways in which researchers engage with the space-times of education, examining the co-implication of the human and non-human in social ties, and moving from accounts of policy to more complex analyses of practices. He proposes that a sociomaterial gaze helps us to escape from the pitfall of methodological nationalism. Shifting the lens from policy to practice similarly brings visibility to the materialities of education. Not losing sight of the importance of liveable time-spaces of education, Landri's mobile sociology invokes nomadic thinking and practice to underscore the openness of everyday life.

## Globalising space-times and contextualising embeddedness

Despite these extensive debates about space and time in cognate fields that are revealed through the chapters, the history of educational policy and practice tends to flatten out education. The failure to look at the ontological depth and epistemological complexities of educational space-times means the term 'context' is widely used by policy makers and professional educators. But that concept rests on evacuated notions of time and space and, at best, offers a thinned-down gesture towards the complexities of space-times of education that look past the effects of embeddedness. One irony is that this understanding of context, which frames future-focused advocacy of fix-it comparative education and simple here-and-now versions of visible learning, informs official policies of globalising education, just as we enter a new game of globalising space and time. So, what does this new game mean for knowing and doing education?

As Cowen notes, globalising education is a new game of space and time; it troubles the warp and weft that once anchored educational concepts, methods and practices, which fixed forms of education. But the main trajectory of education research has largely focused on the making of education space-times within the parameters defined by schoolwork and its particular learning identities. These preoccupations with the professional practice of education focused attention on 'education *in* society', while studies of 'education *and* society' were left to academic educational studies that rested on relations with cognate fields. The effects of globalising education, however, have now troubled that tidy division in educational research between professionalised and academic studies. They have done so in part by drawing professionalised research as well as professional work and learning into the thin practices of visible learning that are endorsed by fix-it comparative education (Ball, 2008). The normalisation of this way of knowing and doing education is an effect of globalising space-times, where advocates work the transnational borderlands between governments, professions and edu-business, and roll out knowledge-based regulatory tools, which are making a global space-time of educational governance.

Yet the challenge for education research is to understand how education now 'morphs as it moves'. It requires research into the re-spatialising effects of globalising education and how they unfold through inter-crossings between globalising space-times and contextualised embeddedness. We began this introductory essay by troubling the trajectory of globalising education. Focusing on knowledge building, we asked two questions: what is overlooked with the normalisation of this 'what works' gaze in education? And how does knowledge building affect the making and remaking of education and societies? The chapters collected in this *2018 World Yearbook of Education* offer insights into the first question by evidencing many effects of space-times of education that are often rendered invisible by the normalised gaze of a 'what works' knowledge formation. In concluding this essay, we address the second question by building on Cowen's commentary that invites us to codify the perspective, project and research voice that informs this study of space-times of education and what it adds to this present and the new game of globalising education. Organising our concluding comments on this basis clarifies our contribution to knowledge through this thirteenth volume of the *World Yearbook* project and suggests an agenda for further research on globalising education.

### Perspective

In this essay, we have sought to canvas some of the challenges and conceptual puzzles that arise in research on globalising education. Sociologies and histories of education have long examined forms of education by documenting the nature and effects of concepts, methods and practices as they take form through space-times of education. But our individual formations embedded in sociology of education, history of education and comparative education have created an interdisciplinary context, where we have surfaced the processes of knowledge building that intrigued us, individually and as an editorial team. Our collaboration has revealed how the concepts of space, time, mobility, and the methodological choices around comparison complicate research centred by globalising education. The earlier *World Yearbook* provocation of naming 'comparative policy studies' highlighted for us how contextualisation is an effect of knowledge formations. Being alert to space and time, and also scale, subjectivity and steering effects, reveals how knowledge and narratives make forms of education and contribute to imperium, all of which unfold through policy scripts, embedded habits of mind and differentiated capacities for mobility and immobility. But as Cowen notes, continuing to disagree about labelling a field of research also indicates a live knowledge politics and invites us to clarify and codify the rules of engagement that define particular practices of knowledge building and the problematics, the field of concepts and methodological choices, which distinguish fields of research. Our perspective recognises that interdisciplinary inquiry requires re-disciplining rather than de-disciplining research (Bonnell & Hunt, 1999).

On this basis, we name the *2018 World Yearbook of Education* as a contribution to knowledge in comparative historical sociology of education. We take Cowen's point that studies of space and time can overcomplicate research in education, but suggest the broad concept of 'space-times of education' is a useful objectification.

It permits investigations into the nature and effects of education that employ methodological choices selectively to avoid the encaging consequences of common-sense assumptions: for example, about education as schooling, about local, national or global scale of analysis, about particularities (e.g., age, gender, ability) of learning identities, about the purpose of education. We also show, through the chapters of this book, that comparative historical sociology, as a knowledge formation, has developed a range of concepts and methods, particularly different methods of comparison, for understanding education. The challenge is to turn those conceptual resources towards globalising education which, as Cowen suggests, means recognising how education and imperium inter-cross through the social organisation of knowledge and authority that mobilises education as a ' "text" for transfer, translation and transformation' (this volume, p. 36).

### Project

The historical sociology of globalising education is a project that requires us to write the present as history. We investigate space-times of education to better understand the inter-crossings between forms of education and formations of concepts, methods and practices that fix mobile and immobile boundaries of space and time. We target 'context', 'education' and 'narrative' as effects of imperium. The problem of 'context' is writ large when 'education in societies' no longer references national education systems, and 'education and societies' reference globalising 'one-world' narratives rather than the embedded histories and narratives, which distinguish national and regional knowledge cultures. The significance of 'education' becomes apparent as 'long-term social learning processes' are mediated by the politics of individual and educated identity. Such education is not reducible to 'schooling' but, rather, references how space-times are bordered and ordered by imperium. Education as an effect is realised through lived cultures and their processes of socialisation, and through period cultures, which steer learners through teachings. But it is through the borderland tensioned between these long-term social learning processes that 'education as text' unfolds as a specialist space-time, which is purposefully designed, resourced and rule-governed as 'schooling' (Hamilton, 1989). In the *Long Revolution*, for example, Raymond Williams (1976) focuses explicitly on this institutionalisation of culture and how education, like journalism, theatre and books, fixes cultures of selective tradition. Williams was writing a history of the present – 1960s Britain – by tracking the institutional forms and formations of concepts, methods and practices that produced the political revolution of democracy, the economic revolution of industrialised societies and which was unfolding during the 1960s as a social revolution through the effects of mass literacy.

In this present, these effects of generalising literacy across peoples and places on a wide scale are now chicken and egg with globalising education and societies. We investigate globalising education by tracing narratives that reveal how the re-spatialisation of education and societies disturbs knowledge building. This intellectual move shows how patterns of reasoning and geographies of knowledge have material effects that govern everyday life (Bonnell & Hunt, 1999; Popkewitz, 2015). Marking out text and context shows space to be communicative and eventful, while temporalities can seem fateful when narratives disturb the familiar experience of time, space, affect structures and social learning processes. Tracing narratives also pinpoints inter-crossings between education and imperium by revealing novel entanglements between knowledge and networks, where practices of governing rub up against the socially embedded concepts, methods and practices that distinguish particular space-times of education and societies. These effects of knowledge building arise because narratives are not simply representations but social epistemologies. They take tangible form as processes of narrativity construct 'constellations of relationships (connected parts) embedded in time and space, constituted by causal emplotment' (Somers, 1994: 616). This distinctive form of cultural-political boundary work is central to education and imperium because it constructs meaning by contextualising everyday life with reference to particular boundaries of space and time. For as

> . . . we come to know, understand, and make sense of the social world . . . it is through narratives and narrativity that we constitute our social identities . . . whether [or not] we are social scientists or subjects of historical research, but that all of us come to *be* who we *are* (however ephemeral, multiple, and changing) by being located or locating ourselves (usually unconsciously) in social narratives *rarely of our own making*.
>
> (Somers, 1994: 606; original emphasis)

### *Voice*

In naming this project a comparative historical sociology, we also claim a vantage point for looking with a certain critical distance at globalising education. As Cowen suggests, this claim to understand space-times of education is associated with a certain kind of voice; it offers academic interpretation to inform 'views on what is a good society, what is good knowledge, and by extension what is a good education' (p. 37). Rather than accepting the space-time assumptions of 'what works' research, we look past its 'happy land' promised through pragmatic, action-oriented forms of visible learning and comparative education. We see its future-oriented gaze and, by looking through historical contexts, also see how the social organisation of education and imperium has become entangled with certain economic logics and free-trade imperatives. We question this trajectory for education and societies because, despite the narratives of 'quick fix' reform, there is persistent evidence of social embeddedness (e.g., Brexit). This means long memories and our responsibilities to a long future are matters of fact for which education and imperium have long been and will continue to be accountable.

Through this project we glimpse our questions and concerns about globalising education as a collective project, not simply idiosyncratic interests. Our jolting realisation is that by working together, our insights both reflect and are shaped by broader political, historical and theoretical currents, and in this way, also represent the *zeitgeist*. But with this glimpse of our present as history, we also recognise our complicity. We acknowledge the embeddedness and historicity of our research approaches, and how the ideas and ways of seeing that are appealing to us also have urgency now. And we name our project and claim its methodological choices because warrantable assertions are necessary if the academic voice as Cassandra is to speak truth to power.

# References

Abrams, P. (1982). *Historical Sociology*. Shepton Mallet, Somerset: Open Books.

Alexiadou, N., & Jones, K. (2001). Travelling policy/local spaces. Paper presented at the Congres Marx International 111, Paris.

Ball, Stephen J. (2008). Some sociologies of education: A history of problems and places, and segments and gazes. *Sociological Review*, 56(4), 650–669.

Bærendoldt, J. O. (2013). Governmobility: The powers of mobility. *Mobilities*, 8(1), 20–34.

Bonnell, V. E., & Hunt, L. (Eds.). (1999). *Beyond the Cultural Turn: New directions in the study of society and culture*. Berkley: University of California Press.

Burson, J. D. (2013). Entangled history and the scholarly concept of enlightenment. *Contributions to the History of Concepts*, 8(2), 1–24.

Caruso, M., & Roldán Vera, E. (2005). Pluralizing meanings: The monitorial system of education in Latin America in the early nineteenth century. *Paedagogica Historica*, 41(6), 645–654.

Caruso, M., & Sobe, N.W. (2012). Editorial introduction: European Education Outside Europe Historical Perspectives on Perceptions and Practices. *European Education*, 44(4), 3–7.

Chakrabarty, D. (2009). Climate of history, *Critical Inquiry*, 35(2), 197–222.

Chen, K.-H. (2010). *Asia as Method: Toward deimperialization*. Durham, NC: Duke University Press.

Clifford, J. (1997). *Routes: Travel and translation in the late twentieth century*, Cambridge, MA: Harvard University Press.

Connell, R. (2007). *Southern Theory: The global dynamics of knowledge in social science*. Sydney: Allen and Unwin.

Coulby, D., & Zambetta, E. (2005). Globalization and nationalism in education, *2005 World Yearbook of Education*. Abingdon, Oxon: Routledge.

Cowen, R. (2009). The transfer, translation and transformation of educational processes: and their shape-shifting?, *Comparative Education*, 45(3), 315–327.

Dale, R. (1992). Recovering from a pyrrhic victory? Quality, relevance and impact in the sociology of education. In M. Arnot & L. Barton (Eds.), *Voicing Concerns: Sociological perspectives on contemporary education reforms*. Oxford: Triangle.

Delanty, G., & Isin, E. F. (2003). Reorienting historical sociology. In G. Delanty & E. F. Isin (Eds.), *The Handbook of Historical Sociology* (pp. 1–8). London: Sage.

Gieryn, T. F. (2000). A space for place in sociology. *Annual Review of Sociology*, 26, 463–496.

Hamilton, D. (1989). *Towards a Theory of Schooling*. Brighton, Falmer Press.

Haraway, D. (1988). Situated knowledges: The science question in feminism and the privilege of partial perspective. *Feminist Studies*, 14(3), 575–599.

Harootunian, H. (2007). Remembering the historical present. *Critical Inquiry*, 33, 471–94.

Hattie, J. (2009). *Visible Learning: A synthesis of over 800 meta-analyses relating to achievement*. Abingdon: Routledge.

Holmes, B. (1974). The World Yearbook of Education: A postscript, in Philip Foster, James R. Sheffield (Eds.). *World Yearbook of Education 1974: Education and Rural Development*. London: Evans Brothers.

Jordheim, H. (2014). Introduction: Multiple times and the work of synchronization. *History and Theory*, 53(4), 498–518.

Keller, George F. (1949) A meritorious achievement. Review of the Yearbook of Education 1949, *Journal of Higher Education*, 21(6), 334–335.

Kumar, K. (2015). The past in the present: Mills, Tocqueville and the necessity of history. *Journal of Historical Sociology*, 28(3), 265–289.

Latour, B. (2004). Why has critique run out of steam? From matters of fact to matters of concern. *Critical Inquiry*, 30(2), 225–248.

Lefebvre, H. (1991). *The Production of Space* (D. Nicholson-Smith, Trans.). Oxford: Blackwell.

Lorenz, C., & Beverage, B. (2013) *Breaking Up Time: Negotiating the borders between present, past and future*. Göttingden, Germany & Bristol, CT: Vandenhoeck & Ruprecht,

Massey, D. (1993). Power geometry and a progressive sense of place. In J. Bird, B. Curtis, T. Putnam, G. Robertson, & L. Tickner (Eds.), *Mapping the Futures: Local cultures, global change* (pp. 59–69). London: Routledge.

Massey, D. (2005). *For Space*. London: Sage.

McLeod, J. (2014). Temporality and identity in youth research. In A. Reid, P. Hart and M. Peters (Eds.), *A Companion to Research in Education* (pp. 311–313). Dordrecht: Springer.

McLeod, J. (2017). Marking time, making methods: Temporality and untimely dilemmas in the sociology of youth and educational change. *British Journal of Sociology of Education*, 38(1), 13–25.

Mills, C. Wright (1967/2000). *The Sociological Imagination*. Oxford: Oxford University Press.

Mitchell, K., & Kallio, K.P. (2017). Spaces of the geosocial: Exploring transnational topologies. *Geopolitics*, 22(1), 1–14.

Monastersky, R. (2015). Momentum is building to establish a new geological epoch that recognizes humanity's impact on the planet. But there is fierce debate behind the scenes, *Nature*, 519(7542), 1.

Niemeyer, B., & Seddon, T. (forthcoming). Special issue: Experiencing Europe. *European Educational Research Journal*.

Nóvoa, A., & Lawn, M. (Eds.). (2002). *Fabricating Europe: The formation of an education space*. Dordrecht: Kluewer.

Ozga, J. (2008). Governing knowledge: Research steering and research quality. *European Educational Research Journal*, 7(3), 261–272.

Popkewitz, T. S. (2005). Inventing the modern self and John Dewey: Modernities and the traveling of pragmatism in education—An introduction. In his *Inventing the Modern Self and John Dewey* (pp. 3 36). New York: Palgrave Macmillan US.

Popkewitz, T. S. (2015). *The "Reason" of Schooling: Historicizing curriculum studies, pedagogy, and teacher education*. New York: Routledge.

Popkewitz, T. (ed.) (2016). *Rethinking the History of Education: Transnational perspectives on its questions, methods, and knowledge*. Springer.

Savage, M. (2010). *Identities and Social Change in Britain since 1940*. Oxford: Oxford University Press.

Seddon, T. (2015). Academic identity formation: Reframing the long shadow of Europe, in J.Nixon and L. Evans (Eds.), *Academic Identities in Higher Education: The changing European landscape*. London; Bloomsbury.

Seghezzo, L. (2009). The five dimensions of sustainability. *Environmental Politics*, 18(4), 539–556.

Silova, I., & Brehm, W. C. (2015). From myths to models: The (re)production of world culture in comparative education. *Globalisation, Societies and Education*, 13(1), 8–33.

Sobe, N. W and Fischer. M.vG. (2009). Mobility, migration and minorities in education. In R. Cowen and A. M Kazamias (Eds.), *International Handbook of Comparative Education* (pp. 359–371). Dordrecht: Springer.

Sobe, N. W., & Kowalczyk, J. (2012). The problem of context in comparative education research. *Journal for Educational, Cultural and Psychological Studies (Rome)*, 6, 55–74.

Sojo, E. W. (1996). T*hirdspace: Journeys to Los Angeles and other real-and-imagined places*. Malden, MA: Blackwell.

Somers, M. R. (1994). The narrative constitution of identity: A relational and network approach, *Theory and Society*, 23, 605–649.

Spiegel, G. M. (2014). The future of the past: History, memory and the ethical imperatives of writing history. *Journal of the Philosophy of History*, 8, 149–179.

Steiner-Khamsi, G. (2012). Understanding policy borrowing and lending: Building comparative policy studies. In G. Stein-Khamsi & F. Waldow (Eds.), *Policy Borrrowing and Lending in Education: World Yearbook of Education, 2012* (pp. 3–17). London: Routledge.

Steiner-Khamsi, G. & Waldow, F. (Eds.) (2012). *Policy Borrowing and Lending in Education: World Yearbook of Education, 2012*. London: Routledge.

Takayama, K., Sriprakash, A. and Connell, R. (2017). Toward a postcolonial comparative and international education. *Comparative Education Review*, 61(1; Supplement), S1–S24.

Thomson, R. and McLeod. J. (2015). New frontiers in qualitative longitudinal research: An agenda for research. *International Journal of Social Research Methodology*, 18(3).

Tsing, A. (2000). The global situation, *Cultural Anthropology*, 15(3), 327–360.

Werner, M., & Zimmermann, B. (2006). Beyond Comparison: Histoire croisée and the challenge of reflexivity, *History and Theory*, 45(1), 30–50.

Williams, R. (1976). *The Long Revolution*. Harmondsworth: Penguin.

# 2 The warp and weft of comparative education

## Time and space

*Robert Cowen*

## Introduction

A long, long time ago, space and time in comparative education were non-problematic. Comparison meant searching for examples of educational success and failure in spaces where the provision of educational institutions and practices was increasingly systematic, and therefore could be categorized by observers. Most histories of the field of study have Marc-Antoine Jullien as an icon who, in the process of creating his peculiar positivist version of comparative education and calling it a science, described and compared (among other things) educational provision in some of the cantons of Switzerland (Fraser 1964). "Time" was also non-problematic. Jullien was concerned with nineteenth-century educational policies and practices: their similarities and differences, their relative success and failure, and their potential transfer. Thus comparative-time in our early history was both "modern" and chronologically ordered.

However, "comparative time" gradually became less simple. It mutated into "successful policy time": a core theoretical and practical aspiration of comparative education. This is "time" of peculiar duration, measurable by the practical success of a specific policy in one place and (after transfer) the time in which it works well in its new social context. The point is not merely an intellectual abstraction: "successful policy time" was a core policy question for educational reforms in both Japan and (West) Germany in 1945, a crucial theme in Soviet educational actions in Eastern Europe soon after 1945, and within a variety of rubrics (e.g., "world-class universities") the theme remains very much with us.

Pragmatic, action-oriented, forms of comparative education aiming at successful practical intervention in the world require neither a long memory nor (necessarily) a long future. "Action-framed comparative education" includes both Jullien and PISA (Programme for International Student Assessment): in ideology and political assumptions they are both aspirational "fix-it" forms of comparative education, with similar assertions about their own scientific status. Past and future time become short (i.e., assess-and-measure time; then the period needed for approval for action and inter-national transfer; and, post hoc, another period of assess-and-measure time). Jullien and the public stance of PISA occupy the same theoretical ground: data-as-a-science for the improvement of educational systems by the inter-national transfer of educational practices. Both Jullien and PISA would offer the same prayer ("From 'the whims' of educational administrators may good science protect us"); though as far as I know, only Jullien has done so explicitly (Fraser, 1964). Jullien and PISA make very similar assumptions about time and space. Space is places in which some version of research by "fieldwork" (i.e., the collection from educational sites of systematically organized data) shows that successful or non-successful action on education occurs. Space is locales of educational success and failure. Good space is where success is clearly visible (e.g., once upon a time, Japan, Finland, or, last year, Shanghai). Bad space is where failure is occurring (say, PISA-shocked Germany or Spain). Exciting space is a scientific version of the promised land: the happy, evidence-sensitive, places where data-informed reform will occur.

Thus, within this quadrille of conceptions of time and space and policy and action, danced to the tune of Becoming Modern, comparative education is remarkably coherent. From 1817 to 2017, its strategic agenda of attention was identifying similarities and differences in societies and distinguishing between successful and failing systems of education; its agenda of action was the transfer of the successful and the useful; and its aspirations for impact or power (as a metaphor: dalliance with the Minister of Education) remained basically undisturbed.

## Time: warping the warp?

However, almost in the middle of this 200-year period, one author disturbed the rhythms of the dance. Almost all histories of the field of study invoke the name of Michael Sadler (1900) who, while asking himself about the transfer of the useful, insisted on the significance of battles long ago and of course the problem with "battles long ago" is that they are serious double discords: Thermopylae, Kosovo, Lepanto, Waterloo, Stalingrad are violent and historical markers of empires lost and identities gained, and they are also dramatic interrupters of simple linearities in time and space. They hint that comparative education may have to deal with futures that stretch into the past.

It is the fascinating ambiguities of this essay by Sadler that have made him iconic. He can be made to fit all ontologies (at least the relatively trivial ones imagined in comparative education). He illustrates the classic action anxiety: how far may we learn anything practical by doing comparative education? And he illustrates the classic academic anxiety of comparative education: how to understand the social embeddedness of educational systems. Thus, Sadler may be used, and has been used, in our normal historical accounts of ourselves, to make a claim about the significance of future time – the time of action, transfer and practicality – *and* to make a claim on the vital importance of past time: history as a form of understanding and, by extension of the theme of "battles long ago", the recurrent claim that "history" is the necessary and proper way to do comparative education.

Among the comparative educationists who were widely read in the 1960s and 1970s, Nicholas Hans and Andreas Kazamias emphasized the importance of time-past. They both embraced the significance of history as a way of understanding what is often called "context" in comparative education, though their approaches to history varied. Hans (1958) emphasized the continuing importance of a range of "factors" – such as language, race, religions and selected political belief systems – on which he offered narratives normally labelled "historical". Kazamias tends to stress the idiographic rather than the nomothetic implications of history for comparative education and even, in his recent conversations, to stress what he calls the "singularities" of history.

However, as Kazamias himself (2009) has pointed out, historical ways of treating "time" within mainstream comparative education weakened. The rejection of time-past (and of the much-quoted aphorism of Kandel that "comparative education may be considered a continuation of the study of the history of education into the present" [quoted by Kazamias, 2009: 46]) began in the 1960s. Brian Holmes emphasized that comparative education should deal with time-future. Over the years his methodology became increasingly cumbersome, but it retained a simple radical core: a rejection of the usefulness of concepts of cause. Instead, he argued that explanation, scientific explanation, is defined by successful prediction. Necessarily therefore, he was explicit about the importance of time-future and about his reluctance to let comparative education continue to be "historical" (Holmes 1965, 1986). Noah and Eckstein (1969), albeit within a different model of science, aspired to a comparative education in which variables could be intellectually organized in a quasi-mathematical form that would be academically rigorous (cf. econometrics) and, like Holmes, they wished for a comparative education that was policy-useful and future-oriented.

This vision of comparative education has not disappeared: a version of comparative education as a science of policy transfer is reconstrued within each generation as a vivid new ambition (Steiner-Khamsi 2012: 3–18). This is a perfectly proper ambition, provided we remind ourselves that comparative education is a bit more complicated than rocket science. Crashing and burning space satellites is expensive, but somewhat less serious than crashing and burning social systems.

One illustration of this complexity is that the older visions of a successful science of policy transfer tended not to see the problem of space: Holmes, and Noah and Eckstein, were not unusual in failing to offer theoretically self-conscious definitions of space and they were not unusual in gliding by the politics of space (despite Harold Noah's interest in the financing of Soviet education).

In the 1960s in comparative education, specialists tended to investigate spaces within what George Bereday (1964) in Teachers College, Columbia, termed "the northern crescent" – the arc of countries stretching from the USA and Canada, to Scandinavia and Europe, and the USSR and China and Japan. For example, in West Germany, comparative educationists looked eastwards to Czechoslovakia, Poland, the USSR and of course East Germany. Comparative educationists within the USSR investigated the other socialist countries (as well as the USA).

For example, in the Department of Comparative Education in the Institute of Education in London, attention was given to Japan and China, the USSR and Eastern Europe, Scandinavia and the rest of Europe, the USA and Canada, with the occasional invocation of Australia and New Zealand.

This early notion of "the northern crescent" carried both an epistemic and a political definition of space which made it different from "the south". The "south" was not labelled, as such. It was lumbered with multiple names; all of which were politically sensitive as terms for space. This was especially – indeed institutionally – the case in London. In the period before 1990 in the UK, "the south" was largely left to specialists in former colonial areas; in pre-war and immediate post-1945 days, often to those who had administered education in Africa. This British "south" was the residual south of empire. (It was only in later parlance and within a different discourse, that "The South" became a new political label.) This lack of self-consciousness and political alertness about space led to various discords.[1]

More generally, the comparative education of this time period was not overtly self-conscious about its own international political positioning in time and space. There is little sustained analytical acknowledgement in the literature (with the notable exception of Steiner-Khamsi 2009) that, for much of the 1945 post-war period, comparative education functioned in political spaces called socialist and capitalist. Similarly, until recently, there has been little explicit acknowledgement that comparative education in northern Europe and northern America was peculiarly framed in time: it was "modernist" (Cowen 2014), trapped within "policy time" in industrialized countries – the kind of time in which short-term social engineering and meliorist and gradualist change is to be attempted. These assumptions about time and mission express implicitly a political position which was in silent opposition to revolution and Marx and to planned change in state-socialist political spaces. The epistemic consequences of this lack of intellectual alertness about the politics of space were considerable and include the failure to make explicit – and then to debate – the proposition that the increased significance of the politics of development-and-education was precisely because of the Cold War. That was part of the broader failure to debate Empire(s).

The consequences included a loss of intellectual grip on concepts of both space *and* time.

Concepts of space became part of a seriously muddled discourse. "Space" became epistemically fractured: its naming marked a division of labour, as in the distinction between the *International Journal of Educational Development* and *Comparative Education*. The specialist comparative education people were talking about "northern crescent countries" and were naming *political* spaces: Denmark, Japan, Italy and so on; while the "development education" specialists – at the same time as they were also talking about countries such as Ghana or India – were giving priority to an *economic* labelling of space. There was also the sustained use of binary economic space-categories – for example, "developed" and "developing" countries; a vocabulary which became rapidly mixed with other names of spaces that stressed economic formations: industrialized and non-industrialized and newly industrializing. The words "colonialism" (Altbach and Kelly 1978) and "cultural imperialism" (Carnoy 1974) were indeed made very visible in the 1970s but were (in the work of Altbach and Kelly on "colonialism") poorly defined conceptually or (in the case of Carnoy's book on "cultural imperialism") were illustrated with historical sketches of uneven quality. Unfortunately, as hinted earlier, the word "Empire", which as a thematic might have powerfully shown the need to rethink concepts and relations of space-and-time, was not given a sustained analysis in the 1980s either by the "comparative" specialists or by the "international" specialists (Cowen 2014).

Concepts of time did not become part of a seriously muddled discourse, but they did become part of a separation of discourses: "time" became a principle of exclusion. Books might be published on the shaping of educational systems over time (Archer 1979; Green 1990; Muller, Ringer and Simon 1987; Skocpol 1979); but comparative articles which chose an historical perspective became rarer in the specialist journals whose editorial rubrics were increasingly stressing "policy". There was a further strand of separation: those who wrote "history" – such as Archer and Skocpol – were creating sociological histories with a political edge. "Comparative history" was beginning to migrate out of comparative education to become a slightly separated field of study, with a widening range of scholars who did not (always) self-identify with comparative education but whose work and forms of understanding are crucial to it (Charle, Schriewer and Wagner 2004; Lawn 2009, 2013; Popkewitz 2013; Troehler 2011).

These centrifuging views of space and time, and the different languages to label space and time (e.g., as in W.W. Rostow's "stages of development", whose phrase obviously labels both) come as sharp counterpoint to the optimism of the 1960s, notably Bereday's (1964: 25–28) excitement about "total analysis", at that time allegedly just out of reach. It stayed out of reach. History and historical notions of time had begun to leach out from both "comparative" and "the international" writing. Major work on the international agencies (treated not as saviours but as problems in the comparative universe), the re-theorization of European space, and work on Empires was still to come. There was no new furore over "method". "Normal puzzle" comparative education – the juxtaposition of social spaces and educational descriptions, the identification of similarities and differences, and the search for causes – continued without much disturbance, except for increasingly lengthy statements about the rigour of new methods of approach.

Thus, as late as the 1990s the future of comparative education was certainly not going to be written by those practising history as a discipline, but it was far from clear how the maze of theoretical culs-de-sac that marked the field might become coherent. Nor was it clear what we should do with our quaint treasure trove of contradictory concepts of space and time that had developed since the 1960s.

## Space: warping the weft?

Happily, fortune sometimes favours the timid. Comparative education's muddled and partial theories of space-and-time were overwhelmed when the world was labelled a *globalized* world. Literature from outside of the field of education, such as the brilliant *oeuvre* of Castells, Frederick Cooper, and Wallerstein and the new systematizations and questions of Held et al. (1999) and Robertson (1992), raised new questions about space and time. Comparative education could calmly "lose" history: if the world was new and globalized, there was little point in looking at an old world. Comparative education could become even more of a social science: more and more rigorously researching and more and more organizing knowledge as a means to action.

The literature exploded and all of the conventional topics of comparative education – which (given our ideological aspiration to be "useful") tend to be a naming of the parts of educational systems – reappeared. Secondary education, teacher education, vocational-technical education, curriculum, higher education, universities, the administration of education (aka "leadership"), "adult education" (aka "lifelong learning") had books written about them or were the themes of large edited volumes: in other words, this was fairly "normal comparative education", stirred – by the addition of the word "globalization" – but not shaken.

Of course, some of the work within this new burst of literature in comparative education had an edge – questions about world systems and the dialectic of the global and the local (Arnove 2009; Arnove and Torres 1999) or themes such as "the space of flows" offered new thinking. And there are excellent analyses (notably on the themes of the growth of international testing, knowledge-based technologies of governance, and the creation of "European space") which have added powerfully to the literature. However, the great virtues of these new analyses in the early part of this century is that they were serious and relatively precise "readings of the global" (Cowen 2000) around the time that the concept of "globalization" itself was starting to lose its analytical edge because of over-casual use by academics and its absorption as a catch-all concept by the mass media. Certainly, the best article in this period written on comparative education as a field of study (Nóvoa and Yariv-Mashal 2003) – a succinct strategic reconceptualization of the history of the field – uses the word "globalization" hardly at all (i.e., only within a quotation, or to refer to a category of theory which has limitations). In addition, many of the most original books in the period – books of major theoretical significance for comparative education by Alexander (2001), Bernstein (2000), Nóvoa and Lawn (2002), and Popkewitz (2005) – did not take globalization as their starting point and thus managed to create an intellectual agenda that comfortably crosses the decades.

Nevertheless, what can (at the risk of inventing a new cliché) be called "globalization shock" was important for comparative education. It offered a sharp reminder that the conventional problematics of comparative education needed to be rethought.

The old practical problem had been how a successful educational space might help another failing educational space, though there was the irritating phenomenon of "battles long ago": in other words, the puzzle of social context. Since Jullien, the practical problem of comparative education has been the transfer of educational policy-and-practice. However, it has proven difficult to create a practical geometry of insertion – or even to sketch a *theory* of a geometry of insertion. (The British Empire for example, much more than the French or the Soviet, refused such an approach.) Despite all of the experience of the post-1945 world, including the occupation of countries by conquering armies, we are only now beginning to understand some of the complexities of the shape-shifting puzzle: "transfer, translation and transformation" (Cowen 2009a, 1281). The books that investigate this theme, deeply, are few, though some of them are brilliant (Meyer 2017; Troehler 2011). It is, in practice, easier to avoid the problem. Forms of "solution-comparative-education" (and these are far more widespread than just PISA research) tend to deal with the problem by giving it to the locals, or by blaming them for failures. Perhaps this will become less and less acceptable as a social and political practice.

In counterpoint with space, the traditional epistemic problem was that history might explain the problem of context, or permit a form of understanding of context sufficient for transfer to occur. The pessimistic version of this theory was the Hans factors; "pessimistic" because they are too powerful to be easily manipulated by educational policy makers. The optimistic version of this theory came from Holmes: the task of history is merely to identify those "specific initial conditions" that (like variations in air pressure) might affect, in an unusual way, predictions of the outcomes of an experiment – here, a transferred policy or practice. Revisionist versions of context theory have been part of the work of Michael Crossley (2009). His unremitting attention to the problem of context has been courageous, which is not the same as suggesting that we have solved the problem (Sobe and Kowalczyk 2012; Sobe and Kowalczyk this volume). What we probably now need is some revisionist thinking about the significance of history for a comparative education that aspires to be more than merely pragmatic. Of course that thinking has already begun, even within the field of comparative education (Phillips 2014) and there are several chapters within Thomas Popkewitz's *Rethinking the history of education* (2013) which are directly relevant to rethinking comparative education.

We also retain the classic problem of the very different politics of space, time, and alliances which characterize comparative education and "international education"; though the rapid growth of new forms of "international education" probably means that the situation has become so complex that attention can now be given to a serious discussion of analytical concepts, political assumptions and what counts as good theorization within the seductive kaleidoscopic glittering ball that is currently called, in some English-speaking places, comparative and international education.

However, disturbance to the old assumptions about the practical purpose of comparative education, new contradictions in concepts of time and space, and the contemporary political attractiveness of comparative education (to almost everyone from politicians and consulting agencies to students and a wide range of academics) came not only with the assertion of "globalization" as the theoretical *Gestalt* for comparative education or from tensions within the literature of comparative education itself. As usual, there was a flow of ideas from outside of comparative education and there was also a rapid shifting of the institutional base that was creating forms of "comparative education".

## The new game of time and space

The ideas from "outside" were multiple. Clearly, many French theoreticians (illustratively, Bourdieu, Derrida, Foucault, Lefebvre) offer refreshing and difficult ways to think about time and space. Particular fields of study (e.g., sociology) have been declared (by sociologists) to be in difficulty because they have indulged, sinfully, in methodological nationalism. There has clearly been "a geographic moment" or "spatial turn" within the social sciences generally – sufficient for the theoretical stakes to become "temporality" and "spatiality". Post-colonialism and post-socialism (as spaces and times within historical processes) raise major questions for comparative education, as do contemporary analyses in academic social science that address, in a sustained way, themes of identity, such as gender, race, and religion (and, of course, combinations of gender, race and religion). Manifestly, a range of post-theorizations (e.g., of post-structuralism or of post-modernity) have rewritten past and future space and time. Historians are placing a new emphasis on comparative and transnational history. Specialist texts on time and on space continue to be published. Allegedly, we live at a special moment of time-space compression – and so on. Overall, the potential bibliography is enormous.

Thus, clearly, comparative education, as it so often has done, can revitalize and simultaneously damage itself by simplistically importing "saviour theoreticians" from other fields of study. Very fortunately, there is already considerable theorization about space and time coming from within the field of comparative education. "We" are already beginning to generate new interpretations of space-and-time (Larsen and Beech 2014; Rappleye and Komatsu 2016; Sobe 2013).

However, before we become too self-congratulatory, three caveats seem appropriate.

First, what counts as "comparative education" has changed. What used to be a university subject has developed new versions of itself in new institutional sites; and thus a new politics of itself. The new institutional sites for comparative education include both international or regional agencies, such as the World Bank, or OECD or the EU. As agencies, they have made excursions into the world of education through conceptualizations of world-class universities, or PISA tests, or notions of a triple helix of government, business and universities. These forms of "advocacy-comparative-education" (a specific form of "solution-comparative-education") carry their own concepts of space and their own definitions of time. For example, UNESCO, given its concern for Education for All, necessarily must create definitions of social time and social space within which such huge international projects will occur and can be measured. Thus (perfectly properly, as a matter of logic), there emerge concepts of project-space and project-time which, in this UNESCO illustration, could be called mind-the-gap time, measure-the-gap-time, and mend-the-gap time in places selected because they are gap-places.

*Mutatis mutandis*, this applies to what is probably the fastest growing sector of "comparative education" which is funded contract research, in which the funder (e.g., the EU, etc.) specifies the purposes, the research agenda, and offers some general expectation about the strategic shape of research results. The expectations of both the EU (and probably the contract researcher) cluster round "social impact" and policy change. Again, this is perfectly proper – these are open contracts arrived at within democratic societies in which the new economic and political roles and social responsibilities of carefully supervised neo-liberal universities have been made more and more explicit in a variety of "evaluative States" (Neave 2012). Even given such constraints, there has been a huge growth in consultancy work which addresses the reform of "education elsewhere".

Thus, we are seeing the growth of an "applied science", comparative education which is not institutionally located within the university sector (as were former departments or professorships concerned with "Education in Developing Countries"). Contemporary versions of applied comparative education are located in political space (e.g., the World Bank) or in economic space (e.g., McKinsey and Company); even if university-based academics may be taken into that work force as contracted, paid, short-term labour. The caveat is that these forms of comparative education as an applied science contain explicit and operationally sensible definitions of space and time which (for the moment at least) do not much help with rethinking notions of space and time in academic comparative education; though they very much confirm the continuing significance of the rather cumbersome concept I sketched earlier: "successful policy time".

The second caveat is that comparative education as a specialist university subject and as a field of study linked to the education of teachers is under considerable adverse pressure, at the very least in the USA and in the UK (Kubow and Blosser 2016). Perhaps in those places, some traditional forms of "university comparative education" may well begin to disappear.[2] Perhaps the optimistic corollary is that we will – in departments which are more and more interdisciplinary – have to think hard about how to revitalize our MA and doctoral forms of pedagogy, as well as rethinking our notions of time and space as we extend our analyses into multicultural education and "peace" education, notions of fragile and failed States (and so on).

The third caveat is simple: old academic versions of time and space will continue – and will continue to be contradicted. For example, the tradition of textbooks of the kind pioneered by E.J. King in his series, *Society, schools and progress in . . .* [specific countries] has received contemporary reaffirmation, on very tight, occasionally legalistic, definitions of space, in a series of nearly twenty textbooks (*Education around the world*) masterminded by Colin Brock whose own interests in space and especially geography (Brock 2016; Symaco and Brock 2013) were unremitting throughout a long career within comparative education. This tradition will coexist within efforts to rethink the subject and indeed will coexist within efforts to rename the subject. One example is *CIDE*: comparative and international and development education, emphasized in this instance within the interesting theme of "beyond the comparative" (Weidman and Jacob 2011).

Thus, we are in the presence of new games of time and space, new versions of the permanent warp and weft of comparative education; "permanent" because it is very difficult to see how these two "unit ideas" of comparative education

(Cowen 2009b) can ever disappear from any form of comparative education that aims to be more than *Auslandspädagogik* contract research. And so, what do we do next?

First, I think it is important that we continue to disagree on how we label ourselves (CIDE? "comparative education"? and so on); that we disagree on specific major theorizations, e.g. world culture theory (Carney, Rappleye and Silova 2012; Schriewer 2012); and that we worry about what I take to be the most interesting theoretical challenge to comparative education that we have had for a long time: the question of its "Westernness" (Rappleye and Komatsu 2016; Takayama 2016).

Second, it is probable that we have new "readings of the global" to create. This is probable because the economic framing of the world economy slowly created and refined since 1945 gave us increasingly confident assumptions about the permanence of economic free trade – and thus by extension a sense that (economic) globalization was a "deductive rationality" (Cowen 2005) on the basis of which we could interpret comparatively patterns of education in the present and the future. I have little doubt that forms of "global" educational governance (in tension with conceptions of personal and historical and educated identity) will need decipherment and interpretation for several decades. I am less confident that what we are currently calling (economic) globalization can continue to be our core "deductive rationality" from which can deduce (never mind "should deduce"!!) good educational systems.

Third, I think it important that we control the Pandora's box of "time and space". It is relatively simple to make both very complex. For example, the concept of time can be made puzzling, quite rapidly, by putting a qualifier before the word "time", thus: chronological-time and school-time and life-time; or western time, Jewish time, Chinese time; or biological time and cultural time. In turn, a larger category can be used to construct contradictions: thus, notions of "school-time" frame the potential contradictions which come from thinking about curriculum-time and exam-time, personal-biological and "age-grade" time. There is also "disciplinary" time-framing: time that can be labelled economic, sociological, historical, anthropological: not quite ad infinitum but the list can clearly be extended as indeed it is, whenever we discuss and refine in any abstract way notions of "comparative education time".

So, paradoxically, a final overture seems to be appropriate.

What do we want out of the Pandora box of "time and space" – if we assume that the core question is not what is happening in applied comparative education but in academic comparative education? That of course depends on what you think academic comparative education is and what it should become in the next couple of decades. Therefore, we will finish up with multiple versions of what is "good space and time" for comparative education; but maybe with a higher level of sensitivity about why our forms of understanding – offered under the generic label "comparative education" – are different. One hopes: productively different.

In the interim, I think we merely want forms of academic comparative education which are self-conscious about why they work with specific times and places. An obvious first step towards that is to theorize broadly time and space. But sooner to later, time and space have to come home to roost, as it were.

My own version of academic comparative education is that it is: a field of study based in universities which works to understand theoretically and intellectually the shape-shifting of "education" as it moves transnationally amid the interplay of international political, cultural and economic hierarchies with domestic politics and forms of social power (Cowen, 2012: 20). Within this emphasis on international relations, especially international political relations, it studies "imperium" (let us say, the power of command as this flows from social framings such as political or religious ideologies, or official disciplinary measures of the performativity of academics by administrators in universities).

The trick of course is to tie it all together, analytically, but *en passant* note that such a comparative education can be explored in the time and space called classical Greece, Roman Britain, Machiavelli's Italy, and Togugawa Japan (as well as the world after Jullien and Auguste Comte). This kind of comparative education begins in the politics of the international (or, if the word grates, the politics of the ancient world, the Middle Ages, the time of European expansionist empires, etc.) and, via imperium, finishes in the politics of individual and educated identity.

And, within such a broad framing, the detailed concern is with the "text" of transfer, translation and transformation as an educational practice or an institution (e.g., the education of princes, the German university, the "English" version of school curriculum knowledge, Soviet socialist education) moves to another "place"; is translated (by whom – the Soviets or the Chinese?) and is transformed within the new social context (e.g., the 6–3–3 American system of school structures in post-1945 Japan).

As it moves, it morphs. Fine, examples can be relatively easily narrated for lots of places and times. But what is the morphology? What are the rules of these educational mobilities and metamorphoses? What is the point of fussing on with descriptions of education in different places and different times and narrations and illustrations of my aphorism "as it moves it morphs"?

The academic answer is that we would then be closer to understanding "imperium"; for example, the remarkably corrosive effects of internationally mobile systems of the university management of performativities, as these are demanded by "the State", whether that be in its Australian or English or Danish or Flemish forms.

And the academic answer is another aphorism: the Cassandra voice. Understanding, academically and intellectually, the morphologies of educational principles and practices in different times and spaces (i.e., comparatively) permits the voice of "the University" a modest independence, of the kind for which it was, in its modern form in a certain time and place, invented: to speak truth to power; Or, more modestly, an independence which permits it to offer the kind of "warranted assertions" which follow from scholarship, university research, and a great deal of thinking and discussion inside the university. It is this independence, coming from an institutional base different from the international and regional agencies and commercial consultancy agencies which construct "applied comparative education", that begins to permit a worthwhile and sustainable "Cassandra voice", albeit not one conferred by a god.

Clearly, the Cassandra voice (hers of course, but potentially ours) is a tragic voice if universities are urgently rewritten as institutions which exist only to have economic impact. In principle, we exist also to offer independent views on what is a good society, what is good knowledge, and by extension what is a good education. However, it is not easy within the angry politics of the early part of this century and the quotidian rush to institutional efficiency and measured social impact to insist that the university – per se – as an academic institution has to comment critically on a future that stretches, ethically and morally, historically and sociologically, politically and culturally, into the past. But we should, not least because "comparative education" itself, with its concerns for the education of human beings in different times and spaces, does that too.

## Notes

1 One example is the tension over nomenclature which occurred in London. There was a Department of Comparative Education – but only from 1947 onwards. The names used for a separate and parallel department – which predated "comparative" work and which predated the Second World War – had labels such as "Education in the Colonies" and "Education in Tropical Areas" (Little 2000). These became politically awkward. They mutated into the label "Education in Developing Countries". This in turn has changed into the current naming: "Education and International Development". Shifting nomenclatures and discords about the political significance of space-naming also attended struggles over the titles of departments in the USA and some of the academic Societies of "comparative education". The struggles whirled around the apparently anodyne word "international". The Americans and the British moved to CIES and BAICE; the Spanish and the Japanese and the Comparative Education Society in Europe stayed with "comparative" (Epstein 2016).
2 That would be both sad and bad: pedagogically for example, using different spaces and times and exotic educational patterns to shock students in initial teacher education courses out of their traditional assumptions about good education has always offered the possibility of exciting cathartic teaching and learning; a sort of academic version of the child-drawn picture of "Lucy in the Sky with Diamonds" which so startled John Lennon.

## References

Alexander, R. J. (2001). *Culture and pedagogy: International comparisons in primary education*. London: Wiley-Blackwell.

Altbach, P. G. and Kelly, P. G. (Eds.). (1978). *Education and colonialism*. London: Longmans.

Archer, S. (1979). *Social origins of educational systems*. London and Beverly Hills, CA: Sage Publications.

Arnove, R. F. (2009). World-systems analysis and comparative education in the age of globalisation. In R. Cowen and A. M. Kazamias (Eds.), *International handbook of comparative education* (pp. 101–119). Dordrecht: Springer.

Arnove, R. F. and Torres, C. A. (Eds.) (1999). *Comparative education: The dialectic of the global and the local*. Oxford: Rowman & Littlefield.

Bauman, Z. (1987). *Legislators and interpreters: On modernity, post-modernity and intellectuals*. Cambridge: Polity Press.

Bereday, G. Z. F. (1964). *Comparative method in education*. New York: Holt Rinehart & Winston.

Bernstein, B. (2000) *Pedagogy, symbolic control and identity* (revised edition). Lanham, MD: Rowman & Littlefield.

Brock, C. (2016) *Geography of education: Scale, space, location in the study of education.* London: Bloomsbury.

Carney, S., Rappleye, J. and Silova I. (2012). Between faith and science: World culture theory and comparative education. *Comparative Education Review*, 56(3), 366–393.

Carnoy, M. (1974) Education as Cultural Imperialism. New York. Longman

Charle, C. Schriewer, J. and Wagner, P. (Eds.). (2004). *Transnational intellectual networks: Forms of academic knowledge and the search for cultural identities.* Chicago, IL: Chicago University Press.

Cowen, R. (2000). Comparing futures or comparing pasts? *Comparative Education*, 36(3), 333–342.

Cowen, R. (2005). Extreme political systems, deductive rationalities, and comparative education: Education as politics. In D. Halpin & P. Walsh (Eds.), *Educational commonplaces: Essays to honour Denis Lawton* (pp. 177–194). London: Institute of Education, University of London.

Cowen, R. (2009a). The transfer, translation and transformation of educational processes: And their shape-shifting? *Comparative Education*, 45(3), 315–327.

Cowen, R. (2009b). Then and now: Unit ideas and comparative education. In R. Cowen, & A. M. Kazamias (Eds.), *International handbook of comparative education* (pp. 1277–1294). Dordrecht: Springer.

Cowen, R. (2012). Robustly researching the relevant: A note on creation myths in comparative education. In L. Wikander, C. Gustaffson, and U. Riis. (Eds.), *Enlightenment, Creativity and Education: Polities, politics, performances* (pp. 3–26). Rotterdam: Sense Publishers & CESE.

Cowen, R. (2014) Comparative education: Stones, silences, and siren songs, *Comparative Education*, 50(1), 3–14.

Crossley, M. (2009). Rethinking context in comparative education. In R. Cowen and A. M. Kazamias (Eds.), *International handbook of comparative education* (pp. 1173–1187). Dordrecht: Springer.

Epstein, E. H. (2016). Why comparative and international education? Reflections on the conflation of names. In Patricia K. Kubow and Allison H. Blosser (Eds.), *Teaching comparative education: Trends and issues informing practice* (pp. 57–73). Oxford: Symposium Books.

Fraser, S. E. (1964). *Jullien's plan for comparative education 1816–1817.* New York: Teachers College, Columbia University.

Green, A. (1990). *Education and state formation: The rise of education systems in England, France and the USA.* London: Macmillan.

Hans, N. (1958). *Comparative education: A study of educational factors and traditions.* London: Routledge & Kegan Paul.

Held, D., McGrew, A., Goldblatt, D. and Perraton, J. (1999). *Global transformations: Politics, economics and culture.* London: Polity Press.

Holmes, B. (1965). *Problems in education: A comparative approach.* London: Routledge & Kegan Paul.

Holmes, B. (1986). Paradigm shifts in comparative education. In P. G. Altbach and G. P. Kelly (Eds.), *New approaches to comparative education* (pp. 179–199). Chicago, IL: University of Chicago Press.

Kandel, I. L. (1933). *Comparative education.* Boston, MA: Houghton Mifflin.

Kazamias, A. (2009). Forgotten men, forgotten themes: The historical-philosophical-cultural and liberal humanist motif in comparative education. In R. Cowen and A. M. Kazamias (Eds.). *International handbook of comparative education* (pp. 37–58). Dordrecht: Springer.

Kubow, P. K. and Blosser, A. H. (Eds.). (2016). *Teaching comparative education :Trends and issues informing practice.* Oxford: Symposium Books.

Larsen, M. and Beech, J. (2014). Spatial theorizing in comparative and international research, *Comparative Education Review, 58*(2), 191–215.

Lawn, M. (Ed.). (2009). *Modelling the future: Exhibitions and the materiality of education.* Oxford: Symposium Books.

Lawn, M. (Ed.). (2013). *The rise of data in education systems: Collection, visualization and use.* Oxford: Symposium Books.

Little, A. (2000). Development studies and comparative education: Context, content, comparison and contributors. *Comparative Education, 36*(3), 279–296.

Meyer, H.-D. (2017) *The design of the university: German, American, and "world class".* New York and London: Routledge.

Muller, D. K., Ringer, F. and Simon, B. (Eds.). (1987). *The rise of the modern educational system: Structural change and social reproduction 1870–1920.* Cambridge: Cambridge University Press.

Neave, G. (2012). *The evaluative state, institutional autonomy and re-engineering higher education in Western Europe: The prince and his pleasure.* London: Palgrave Macmillan.

Noah, H. J. and Eckstein, M. A. (1969). *Toward a science of comparative education.* New York: Macmillan.

Nóvoa, A. and Yariv-Mashal, T. (2003). Comparative research in education: A mode of governance or a historical journey? *Comparative Education, 39*(4), 423–438.

Nóvoa, A. and Lawn, M. (Eds.). (2002). *Fabricating Europe: The formation of an education space.* Dordrecht: Kluwer.

Phillips, D. (2014). Comparatography, history and policy quotation: Some reflections, *Comparative Education, 50*(1), 73–83.

Popkewitz, T. (Ed.). (2005). *Inventing the modern self and John Dewey: Modernities and the traveling of pragmatism in education.* New York: Palgrave Macmillan.

Popkewitz, T. (Ed.). (2013). *Rethinking the history of education: Transnational perspectives on its questions, methods, and knowledge.* New York: Palgrave Macmillan.

Rappleye, J. and Komatsu, H. (2016). Living on borrowed time: Rethinking temporality, self, nihilism, and schooling, *Comparative Education, 52*(2), 177–201.

Robertson, R. (1992). *Globalization: Social theory and global culture.* London: Sage Publications.

Sadler, M. (1900). How far can we learn anything of practical value from the study of foreign systems of education? In: J. H. Higginson (Ed.). (1979), *Selections from Michael Sadler* (pp. 48–51). Liverpool: Dejall & Meyorre.

Schriewer, J. (Ed.). (2012). Special issue (45): Re-conceptualising the global/local nexus: Meaning constellations in the world society, *Comparative Education, 48*(4).

Skocpol, T. (1979). *States and social revolutions: A comparative analysis of France, Russia and China.* Cambridge: Cambridge University Press.

Sobe, N. (2013). Entanglement and transnationalism on the history of American education. In T. Popkewitz (Ed.), *Rethinking the history of education: Transnational perspectives on its questions, methods, and knowledge* (pp. 93–107). New York: Palgrave Macmillan.

Sobe, N. W. and Kowalczyk, J. (2012). The problem of context in comparative education research. *Journal for Educational, Cultural and Psychological Studies, 6*, 55–74.

Steiner-Khamsi, G. (2009). Comparison: Quo vadis? In R. Cowen and A. M. Kazamias (Eds.), *International handbook of comparative education* (pp. 1143–1158). Dordrecht: Springer.

Steiner-Khamsi, G. (2012). Understanding policy borrowing and lending: Building comparative policy studies. In G. Steiner-Khamsi and F. Waldow (Eds.), *World yearbook of education 2012: Policy borrowing and lending in education* (pp. 3–17). London & New York: Routledge.

Symaco, L. P. and Brock C. (Eds.). (2013). Special Issue (47): The significance of space, place and scale in the study of education. *Comparative Education, 49*(3).

Takayama, K. (2016.). Deploying the post-colonial predicaments of researching on/with 'Asia' in education: a standpoint from a rich peripheral country. *Discourse: Studies in the Cultural Politics of Education, 37*(1), 70–88.

Tröhler, D. (2011). *Languages of education: Protestant legacies, national identities and global aspirations.* London: Routledge.

Ulich, R. (Ed.). (1964). *Education and the idea of mankind.* Chicago, IL: University of Chicago Press.

Weidman, John C. and Jacob, W. J. (Eds.). (2011). *Beyond the comparative: advancing theory and its application to practice.* Rotterdam: Sense Publisher.

# Section I
# Making spaces

## 3 Training female ways of knowing or educating (in) a common sense

## A historical analysis of space-times of (adult) education

*Beatrix Niemeyer*

### Times of education – introduction

With the paradoxical challenge to care for both social continuity and change, education is caught from both ends by past and by future. As a normative project, education is inevitably linked to a collective imagination of time as a constant flow from past to future. Building on past experiences, memory, formerly accumulated explicit and implicit knowledge, and confined to the situatedness of presence, educational activities are prompted by and directed towards imaginations of a coming future. Whether training for a career or learning for a language test, whether designing a curriculum or being introduced to a community of practice, any kind of learning and teaching – whether formal or informal, individual or collective, private or public and no matter if paid or offered for free – is built on the idea that there is a present need for change. Simultaneously it is tied to the belief that efforts undertaken will pay off in the future.

Without this imagination of time as a constant flow towards a future, which needs to be secured and improved, any educational endeavour would be senseless (Schmidt-Lauff 2012). Being aware of the importance of the dimension of time underpins the historical approach to the following reflections on space-times of education. Re-reading history through the lens of the present in order to build on past experiences and prepare for future challenges is a typical pattern of learning. This historical learning is, however, not meant as accumulation of codified knowledge or a collecting of facts and findings. This chapter rather intends to re-construct a historical case of making space-times of education in view of the present need to better understand when and how education as a social practice of "doing knowing" takes place.

The retrospection that informs this chapter is situated in a specific space-time and shaped by a specific perspective on education. This way of knowing education is anchored by the cultural context of Germany; it builds the historical point of departure for the journey to the past, with the imprinted thoughts and ideas of critical thinkers including Humboldt, Marx, Weber, Adorno, and Negt, and less famous but more critical female scholars, from Dorothea Leporin to Karin Hausen. Their history is wrapping the following reflections in a specific cultural context, providing collective memories, terms and concepts for a common understanding and the making of a common sense on education in a specific way. The concept of *Bildung*, which is itself a historically transforming concept, reflects the constant endeavour to understand how a subject and his or her surroundings, the self and the world are interrelated in a way which allows for continuity and change, duration and development of both individual and society.

Education is often considered as a purposeful, constructed process taking place in a carefully designed exclusive space for learning – most commonly thought of as a school. But I argue that space-times of education are not limited to certain places. Instead, they open up in the course of history whenever the relation of individual and society, self and world, enters in a process of transformation. Talking about "informal learning" would not completely capture this phenomenon, because learning – at least to German ears – refers to the gathering and acquiring of codified and therefore pre-processed and pre-selected knowledge. The concept of *Bildung*, however, shifts the focus to the individual transforming as an autonomous subject, building a personal biography (Ahlheit and Dausien 2009; Koller 2012; Marotzki 1991) *and* conceptualises the individual as a political being (Negt 2010; Faulstich 2011; Zeuner 2001). It is with reference to this tradition of critical adult education theory in Germany that the political dimension of *Bildung* is underlined. In that tradition, *Bildung* entails the capacity of making a difference (Negt 2010). In this context, the individual is understood as a political being and *Bildung* inevitably includes knowing about the relation between one-self and the world, believing that this relation is socially constructed, and therefore knowing how to engage in these constructions to alter them. According to this understanding, space-times of education open up in moments or periods in history, when change is made. They capture the moments or periods in history (or in a biography), when the relation of self and surrounding, subject and world is ultimately transforming.

There are quite a lot of indicators suggesting that we find ourselves at such a transforming point at present. In this present, the visible limits of growth are disturbing the imaginations of the world to come; probably for the first time in history, the collective future seems to be at a man-made risk. How is education, as an individual and as a social project, institutionalised or informal, affected by these insights? How are the concepts of knowledge and knowledge building transforming? How and where are the space-times of education emerging to process new uncertainties and old inequalities?

In order to identify the social practices of bordering and ordering that fix space-times of education, I suggest a historical comparison. I centre my arguments on a case study of the collective learning practices of a social group, situated in a period of major social change when the collective imaginations of a future were reconfigured, and when knowledge-building practices incorporated new technical developments, improved and accelerated means of transport and ideas of a social order were generally subject to challenge. Towards this aim, I draw back on my earlier work (Niemeyer 1996a, 1996b, 1997), which dealt with the establishing of a bourgeois gender order in the German-speaking states of the eighteenth century.[1] Collections of private letters from this time speak about the desire of women for education and provide an insight in the formation of a gender ideology based on "natural" differences as a foundational part of the upcoming bourgeois society. In hindsight these processes of letter writing appear as specific space-times of education; transforming familiar, and establishing new, social practices of spreading knowledge and "doing knowing".

## Making space-times of education – a historical case study

When the development of transportation allowed for fairly regular correspond-ence and printing techniques permitted the wider distribution and copying of texts, knowledge was circulated by letters and the exchange of journals. From the perspective of adult education, a process of generalisation and popularisation of images and stories about the world and the abilities of humans to dominate nature and profit from it, started. At a certain moment in history, knowledge building no longer appears as an elitist project; producing, gathering, sharing and distributing the new ideas and imaginations of the world became a popular practice, before the changing power structures and (re)established social hierarchies regulated, once again, who could access the domes of knowledge and who was allowed to engage in the exciting business of increasing and distributing ideas and inventions. The relating socio-historical transformations included a renegotiation of gender rela-tions, by exchanging and circulating, publishing and pushing narratives of how to be male or female in an appropriate (bourgeois) way. Women were neither silent nor passive in this process, but developed and put into practice female strategies of learning about broadening horizons and expanding worlds, discoveries and inven-tions. Handbag-sized microscopes for diverting tea-times are one image illustrating the female desire to join the exciting rise of natural sciences; anonymised cover-pages of books written by female authors are the other side of the coin signifying the perpetuation of social inequality that silenced women writers.

Already in the seventeenth century, so-called "scholarly letters" (*Gelehrtenbriefe*) were published and distributed in a larger scale. Letters were an important means of communication for the early academic community in pre-national times; exchanging letters with a scholar counted as evidence of belonging to the aca-demic community. More and more academic texts and literature took the form of letters, thus imitating the feature of oral communication. However, those early correspondences of the *res publica litteraria* – the republic of scholars – were com-posed according to strict formal regulations. (*Salutatio, captatio benevolentiae, narration, petition* and *conclusion* were the formal features according to which writers structured their texts.)

Letters were constitutive for building what today would be called a network and keeping up distant communication; they treated topics of friendship and phil-osophical disputes, or discussed and distributed pieces of literature. Exchanging letters was considered to be useful, because they were thought to be testimonies of the writer's personality. Using Latin as the common language further allowed the exchange of research methods and results, thus contributing to the growing community of scholars and a growing body of common knowledge, connecting scholars throughout Europe long before the establishment of nation states. Even if the letters probably were written by a single author, they were usually read by a wider audience and could be printed and published. Libraries of that time had special departments for the collection of letters. Members of this early European republic of scholars were listed in lexica, the social construction of belonging built on knowledge and the ability to read and write in Latin. Interesting enough gen-der was no explicit criteria for in- or exclusion (Niemeyer 1996b), a considerable number of women's names are to be found in these lists. With technical progress, the exchanging of letters became more and more popular and transcended the limited boundaries of the community of learned scholars.

A major precondition then was the general availability of this medium. When the postal system was developed so that letters could be delivered within a calculable time to almost any place, the writing of letters needed nothing but the ability to read and write, and the money to afford paper and ink. A common lexicon from 1733 underlined that letters could be written by anybody about anything; it would not be necessary to express the social position of the writer (*Zedlers Universallexikon* 1732). What seems to be self-understood from today's perspective must be read in contrast to feudal society, in which nobles held the privilege of long-distance communication within their networks over Europe. At the same time, German as a written language gained momentum in contrast to French, which was the language of the nobility on the one hand and to Latin, the language of learned scholars, on the other.

The assertion of German as written language, of scientific texts, literature and letters, contributed to the growing popularity of letter writing. Likewise it contributed to the general distribution of knowledge, about the latest literature, findings of natural science, journeys alongside with descriptions of everyday life. It is in this context that we can trace the ideological formation of a bourgeois society. Collections of letters of those times give evidence of a process of spelling out and testing of new habits and ideas of social orders – with the negotiation of gender relations, the spelling of modes of femininity being one of the most prominent topics.

The vivid exchange of letters within the educated German community then was a shared social practice of knowledge building and a common means of self-education. It marks a present, a particular period of history that, in the German context, is considered as the dawn of the bourgeois society. Letters written by women between the sixteenth and nineteenth centuries, as well as style-guides covering the period allow for an insight into this collective project. Communication via the exchange of written, seemingly private, individual letters was of major importance for the formation of a bourgeois self-understanding. An increasing exchange of letters considerably contributed to the self-image of the educated community, so that finally the eighteenth century is referred to as the century of letters (Niemeyer 1996a; 1997).

Gender then was an important topic for discussion; the "right" way of being female was expressed by men and women in letters and literature. Scholarly women became subject of caricatures, and Latin letters lost attention, while a more general, popular exchange of thoughts and information took place in journals, with letters maintaining their prominent social importance. Especially for women, who were excluded from the initial institutions of formal education, corresponding with teachers, writers and philosophers became an accepted way of participating in the intellectual community of the early bourgeois times. Collection of letters and style-guides from the eighteenth century give evidence to the ideological struggle going along with the social reconfigurations, in the years before general schooling was introduced, general education became formalised and electricity speeded up the means of transport and communication.

The complex balancing of continuity and change within a transforming order of societies included the paradoxical task of living and holding on
to the democratic paradigms of *liberté, egalité* and *fraternité*, while obviously
excluding the female half of the population from the access to these newly con-
quered human rights. A gendered society, with distinct places and spaces for
men and women, was the model. It centred on the so-called bourgeois ideal
of femininity, declaring children, kitchen and church as "natural" spaces for
women, with housekeeping and raising of children as their "natural" profession (Hausen 1976). The division between public and private sphere emerged
together with the establishing of a complementary gender order. (German) letters and literature between 1720 and 1820 can be read as a large-scale education
project, likewise engaging men and women in developing the blueprint of bourgeois femininity (and masculinity) and a gendered society, valid and working
throughout the coming 250 years.

### Spelling out femininity

Exactly because letters were exercising private attitudes without being private,
they could serve as a vehicle of normative ideas of femininity:

> The origins of the private bourgeois letter turns it into a public affair at the
> same time. In turn, the conventions of a bourgeois privacy are only produced
> by the public forum, in which – mostly fictive – letters are reproduced. By
> reading weekly papers, the writing of letters is learned; when writing letters,
> they are potentially addressing the public (of these newspapers) . . . and it is
> not unusual that the letter itself is topical and subject to moral and theoretical
> considerations in them.
>
> (Nörtemann 1990: 219, translation BN)

The staging of privacy needed an audience. Authors had to be aware of the fact
that their writing, their ideas, their self-representation would be handed on,
distributed and discussed and potentially criticised within a wider circle of an
interested supposedly like-minded audience. This interplay of producing and
reproducing these gendering norms was nothing but a male-dominated project.
But by cultivating their correspondence, women actively engaged in it.

Against this background, the letters of women can be seen as a practice of
negotiating the social gender order. When analysing correspondences of women
through the course of the eighteenth century, the sharing of knowledge, exchanging
of news and innovations seems to fall back against elaborated descriptions of multiple aspects of idealised femininity. Hence, it was not least by writing letters that
gender differences were ascribed and women learned how to behave as a female
in a socially appropriate way, for example, women's letters should be written in a
delicate handwriting in a nice and readable way. These recommendations for the
letters' formal appearance soon were transferred to the contents: nice thoughts
should be expressed in a noble (*sic!*) language in a most natural way. In the second

half of 1700, learning by letters was considered especially appropriate for the female mind. Letters had turned into the teaching material of becoming female within a reconfiguration of social orders; they promoted the equality of the *citoyen*, while society still was built and continuously depended on the inequality of women.

Interestingly enough, the German fashion of female writing was drawing on French models. Madame Sevigné (1627–1696) was praised in France as "*modèle inimitable dans le genre épistolaire*" (*Biographie Universelle*, Paris 1821). Her letters were admired examples of expressing emotions in an "honest" way. Nature generally was the main argument for connecting femininity and the writing of letters. Letters were a "natural" way for women to express their thinking and feeling; the "natural" model of a letter would be a conversation. The structure of a letter should no longer follow the rigid forms that were valid for scholars' writings but flow in a "natural" way. A multitude of "nice" and "natural" letters were now published and circulated. Nature served as a model for the connection of writing style and femininity.

Modern readers are puzzled by the repeated apologies that seemed to be a regular element of letters from women. Usually taking a standpoint, elaborating an argument, or uttering an opinion was preceded by a longer paragraph, in which the authoress excused herself for daring to express her thoughts, highlighting her modesty and thereby relativising her point of view. Thus, by writing letters, women trained female ways of behaving and presenting themselves. The writing of letters – like caring and maintaining for the private sphere – was declared as female activity and served as a representation of femininity. While letters were teaching female behaviour, women were spelling out gender differences in their letter writing. Correspondences of engaged couples especially can be read as a common training of gender relations and female subordination.

By the beginning of 1800, women increasingly refrained from having their letters printed and published. Topics had changed from exchanging news and knowledge to describing female ways of living. Representations of the everyday life of housewives became topical and the little ideal conditions of writing were shining through the lines. Space and time for writing became scarce within the daily routine of a housewife-mother. Often enough, there was, literally, no place for a bourgeois housewife to write. Letters were often interrupted, writing disturbed by children, visitors and distractions of all kinds. In the end, the writing of a letter appears as part of housework.

Still, there is a tension shining through the writings, marking a gap between the normative expectation, the social norms of being female, and women's aspiration for education and engagement in the joy of sophisticated discussions. Putting this tension into words reflects a process of *Bildung*. While the desire for education is disappearing as a letter-writing topic, the representation and staging of gender differences gains momentum in correspondences of the late eighteenth century. The main features of bourgeois femininity – such as female virtue, usefulness, housekeeping knowledge and childcare – are central topics of letters of this time. It appears that the exchanging of letters no longer was intended to share information and knowledge, and shape opinions, but served to train female behaviour instead. This historical process culminated in the – probably ironic – intention to completely refrain from "holding the hard pen in their soft hands" (Meta Moller 1728–1758, in Tiemann 1956: 390).

## Reading space-times of education historically

Education as an organised process of generalising and distributing knowledge on the one side and enabling individuals to acquire and share it through reading, writing and communicating on the other was a general project of enlightenment. Emancipatory adult education still refers to these bourgeois roots with the actual concepts of empowerment, civic engagement and lifelong learning. However, the construction elements, the concepts and conditions of the space-times of education have changed considerably. So, is there still a message sent from this period in history? Are there historical parallels?

Today, the reading of letters collected 300 years ago seems strange, the constant arguing in favour of what today appears as unbearable gender inequality is hard to bear. The big "why" dominates questions about the how and what of a historical process. Asking why women consent to a self-image of becoming an uneducated housewife and mother "by nature", is one question that prompted research on the history of women's education (Schmid 1986). The other question, on the present agenda, is what does this story tell about space-times of education? What can be drawn from the historical comparison of settings, how does memorizing the collective educational project of so-called gender characters help us to understand and theorise the re-making of space-times of education of today?

The transition from feudal to bourgeois society made and legitimised a gender order to secure social continuity under changed conditions. This historical process was lubricated by the broadly developing natural sciences, the gradual replacement of monarchies, the rise of industry with a resulting societal labour division, a growing body of general knowledge about nature in combination with rationalities that called for renewed arguments. Reading and writing in a common, popular language facilitated this process. The emerging broad literature on how to make (or not make) use of newly acquired knowledge about the world and the establishing of female ways of knowing appeared as an educational project; it gave reason to the (re)construction of gender differences and enabled men and women to consent to it.

I argue that the writing of letters in the eighteenth century can be understood as a practice of making space-times of education. The historical comparison is evidence of the transforming practices of communities/societies managing the basic contradictions of continuity and change, balancing differences and inequalities and mediating the relations between individuals and societies. What was at stake was a new model for European societies, based on the civil rights of rational individuals, in need of renewing the arguments for social inequalities.

Reconsidering the past thus allows a specific view on education as a collective practice enabling change and innovation; those collective practices provide space for orientation to develop and test new or alternative modes of relating to the world and oneself within it. The analytical revision of women's correspondence in the eighteenth century allows us to reconstruct one aspect of this social b/ordering within a particular space-time of education. Within their writing practices, women then built spaces of orientation, as they spread news and information and distributed knowledge, first in an unregulated, popular, informal way.

Only in a second step did these travelling ideas or knowledge flows congeal as "educational movements", and only after that would they be governed by law and governmentality.

The analytical perspective calls for further reflection on questions of access to learning and knowledge and, in turn, the evident but less visible practices of making education an exclusive project. It calls into question the commonality of a 'common sense' and the generality of 'general education' as, quite obviously, the era of enlightenment was a mainly male project.

## Messages from history

Space-times of education emerge in historical situations when there is need for orientation. When established patterns of social borders are called in question, "education movements" emerge as self-organised activities: creating spaces for orientation in times of social reconfigurations, allowing for the testing of alternative practices, providing further knowledge and negotiating contradicting interests. Hence, space-times of education extend according to social needs – and in ways that socially make sense. They are built through socially situated practices of interacting individuals and collectives. In this way, they are directed at mediating social inequalities, providing and producing collective narratives to explain and legitimise social differences and to enable individuals to consent.

These space-times of education promote and generate social orders and borders. They do not have defined borders or places, but may also be considered as locations for doing boundary work (cf. Newman, Niemeyer, Seddon and Devos 2014). The gathering, sharing, distributing and acquiring of knowledge is embedded in and framed by social norms; governing the modes of knowing and ways of learning by developing a common understanding of what is considered as knowledge or as being knowledgeable, as well as the access to sources of knowledge and communities of knowers. The writing and exchanging of letters therefore can be interpreted as a social practice of "doing knowledge" by engaging in the informal activities of organising, providing and processing the know-how and know-what needed to allow for change of not less than the ideal of a society.

Then, as well as now, the reconfigurations which promote informal education and provide individual and orientating norms address central dimensions of social orders. When social, technical and economic developments call for a revision of the social organisation of working and living, and traditional arguments to legitimise social orders become outdated, ways of learning re-produce categories of social differences and establish modes and models for social relations. Education as a normative project then engenders modes and models of knowing in socially appropriate ways. It is not only directed at a societal general orientation but likewise addresses individual members of society as subjects, delivering models of making a living and building individual biographies. After all, the bourgeois pattern of femininity with its stunning inequalities offered a meaning to men and women at that time. Presenting the idealised and admired counterpart to the rough world of labour, supporting the hard struggle against the evil of a competitive society, in which personal achievement had replaced the right of birth as reason for social positioning might have been attractive to women who were supposed to balance the more and more restricted features of masculinity.

As the example shows, time is always changing and there will always be need for social reconfigurations. It is not exclusively us who live in a liquid modernity (Baumann, 2000) and experience times of uncertainty (Luhmann 1984). Certainly, the historical example of female writing does not serve as a best-practice example. It cannot be directly transferred to present education spaces. Today's email correspondence is no direct equivalent for their letters; the worldwide web no replacement for former dictionaries. As airplanes differ from carriages in speed, capacity and range of transportation, the means and media of communication allow for more, faster and wider exchange of facts and stories. However, the retrospective may help to explore some of the constitutive elements of space-times of education.

Space-times of education are made in times of historical change. When means of communication, and social and technical development had led to major social reconfigurations, the respective space for education opened up in an informal and self-organised way. Material conditions such as technological development impact on social relations and, vice versa, the means and modes of communication pre-shape the building and maintaining of (educating) human relationships. Furthermore, education involves training modes of applying knowledge in a socially accepted way. This includes the negotiation and legitimisation of social differences.

Seen from this angle, education is always political; making space-times of education is active engagement in knowledge policies. This certainly includes the regulation of formal learning, the design of curricula, the agreement on accreditation as constitutive social practices of relating individuals and society, defining what should be learned, when and by whom. However, it is worthwhile to similarly look for spaces of self-organised education outside the domes of knowledge building today and to identify those informal, not yet governable, spaces of education in the present. The exercise of making a difference and alternative practices of living, working and learning may emerge in unexpected spaces, outside of the reach of educational institutions. To value informal, self-organised activities of sharing knowledge, to look out for emerging space-times of education in places where social relations are to be reconfigured, is a current topic for critical (adult) education research. The categories identified here may help to continue the study of hidden dynamics of knowledge sharing, the topics at stake, the interests engaged, the differences made – in short, to question what is common in the common sense.

## Note

1  At that time Germany consisted of multiple petty states; travelling from Hamburg to Munich involved the crossing of as many as eleven borders.

# References

Alheit, P. and Dausien, B. (2009): "Biographie" in den Sozialwissenschaften. Anmerkungen zu historischen und aktuellen Problemen einer Forschungsperspektive. In B. Fetz (Ed.). *Die Biographie – Zur Grundlegung ihrer Theorie* (pp. 285–315). Berlin and New York: De Gruyter.

Bauman, Z. (2000). *Liquid modernity*. 'Cambridge: Polity Press.

Faulstich, P. (2011). Aufklärung, Wissenschaft und lebensentfaltende Bildung. Geschichte und Gegenwart einer großen Hoffnung der Moderne. Bielefeld: Transcript.

Hausen, K. (1976). Die Polarisierung der "Geschlechtscharaktere"– Eine Spiegelung der Dissoziation von Erwerbs- und Familienleben. In W. Conze (Ed.). *Sozialgeschichte der Familie in der Neutzeit Europas* (pp. 367–393). Stuttgart: Ernst Klett.

Koller, C. (2012). *Bildung anders denken. Einführung in die Theorie transformatorischer Bildungsprozesse*. Stuttgart: Kohlhammer.

Luhmann, N. (1984). *Soziale Systeme*. Frankfurt am Main: Suhrkamp.

Marotzki, W. (1991). Bildung, Identität und Individualität. In D. Benner and D. Lenzen (Eds.). *Erziehung, Bildung, Normativität* (pp. 79–94). Weinheim: Juventa.

Negt, O. (2010). *Der politische Mensch. Demokratie als Lebensform*. Göttingen: Steidl.

Newman, S., Niemeyer, B., Seddon, T., and Devos, A. (Eds.) (2014). Understanding educational work: Exploring the analytic borderlands around the labour that enables learning, *Globalisation, Societies and Education*, 12(3), 321–35.

Niemeyer, B. (1996a). Der Brief als weibliches Bildungsmedium im 18. Jahrhundert. In E. Kleinau and Opitz, C. (Eds.). *Geschichte der Mädchen- und Frauenbildung* (Vol. I, Vom Mittelalter bis zur Aufklärung) (pp. 440–452). Frankfurt am Main: Campus.

Niemeyer, B. (1996b). Ausschluß oder Ausgrenzung? Frauen im Umkreis der Universitäten im 18. Jahrhundert. E. Kleinau and Opitz, C. (Eds.). *Geschichte der Mädchen- und Frauenbildung* (Vol. I, Vom Mittelalter bis zur Aufklärung) (pp. 275–294), Frankfurt am Main: Campus.

Niemeyer, B. (1997). "Angenehme Sittenlehrer". Briefe und Weiblichkeit im 18. Jahrhundert. Kritische Anmerkungen zu Norbert Elias. In G. Klein and K. Liebsch (Eds.). *Zivilisierung des weiblichen Ich* (pp. 185–205). Frankfurt am Main: Suhrkamp.

Nörtemann, R. (1990). Brieftheoretische Konzepte im 18. Jahrhundert und ihre Genese. In A. Ebrecht, R. Nörtemann and H. Schwarz (Eds.). *Brieftheorie des 18. Jahrhunderts* (pp. 211–224). Stuttgart: Metzlersche Verlagsbuchhandlung.

Schmid, P. (1986). Das Allgemeine, die Bildung und das Weib. Zur verborgenen Konzipierung von Allgemeinbildung als allgemeiner Bildung für Männer. In T. Heinz-Elmar (Ed.). *Allgemeine Bildung. Analysen zu ihrer Wirklichkeit, Versuche über ihre Zukunft* (pp. 202–214). Weinheim & München: Juventa Verlag.

Schmidt-Lauff, S. (2012). Grundüberlegungen zu Zeit und Bildung. In: S. Schmidt-Lauff (Ed.). *Zeit und Bildung. Annäherungen an eine zeittheoretische Grundlegung* (pp. 11–62). Münster: Waxmann.

Tiemann, Hermann (ed.) (1956), *Klopstock, Martha, gen. Meta, geb. Moller, Briefwechsel mit Klopstock, ihren Verwandten und Freunden*. Vol. I, p. 390.

*Zedlers Universallexikon* (1732). *Grosses vollständiges Universallexicon aller Wissenschafften und Künste, welche bishero durch menschlichen Verstand und Witz erfunden und verbessert worden*. Halle and Leipzig: Johann Heinrich Zedler. Retrieved May 1, 2017 www.zedler-lexikon.de/index.html?c=blaettern&seitenzahl=4&bandnummer=01&view=100&l=de.

Zeuner, C. and Faulstich, P. (2001). *Erwachsenenbildung und soziales Engagement – historisch-biographische Zugänge*. Bielefeld: Bertelsmann.

# 4 Europeanizing through expertise

## From scientific laboratory to the governing of education

*Martin Lawn*

The European educational space is a portmanteau term, able to contain sets of knowledge-building movements and institutional relations, and allowing continuities, disruptures and post-comparative analyses to be made over time and space in Europe and beyond. While cross-border influences and transnational relations are the core of this spatial idea, it is driven by capital and governing acts as well. This chapter is focused on the emergence of cross-border meetings by senior educational researchers which took place in a reconstructing Germany and under the auspices of the American (and later) British Zone commanders. Post-war development in European expert collaborations in educational research began with the post-war occupation of Germany and continued into the post-Sputnik world of Western Europe (Lawn and Grek 2011). These meetings may be viewed as limited historical cases but they are treated here as the forerunners of the later European Union strength in research data and the creation of a common European educational research space.

## Europe and Europeanization

Europe is a project (political, social, economic and educational), an idea, a form of governance and a forward projection: it is not a fixed space of stable policy and territorial legitimacy. If Europe is viewed in this way, then it appears in focus as meaning making, a governing laboratory, a series of collaborations and forms of constructed commonality. The field of education, in our immediate post-Second World War example, can no longer be regarded as locked into national territories and politics but fluid, accessible and unstable. In the post-war world, the European fields of education have become promiscuous, sharing ideas, knowledge, visits and techniques across their sites and borders. The idea of national systems of education as warehouses of traditions and cultures, impregnable to foreign influences, is long gone. It is not sustainable, faced with a constant interplay of its specialist actors and their tools and texts, which has grown significantly since the 1920s.

These actors, drawn from specialist research centres, state services, government offices and the extended field of education, may be regarded as independent performers, providing professional services and exchanges. Their networks aimed to construct common languages in education or opportunities to innovate or create rational comparison, and to do this, they had to produce common and comparable data about European education. The methods and the categories of educational research were shared, and these common tools and practices had to be tested in use. This was a constant process of creation, integration and standardization.

Over time, these sets of collaborations provided the infrastructure upon which growing political and economic cooperation in Europe depended. These attempts to create order and meaning by researchers were of increasing value to the governing of education in Europe. As an innovative and fluid concept, Europe, shaping itself as it moves, needed a governing discourse by which its legitimacy and purpose could be determined. It needed information and reliable data. By the year 2000, the European Union had established statistical systems which were collecting data on trade, industry and social issues, including education. In effect, education experts created the foundations for the "calculative rationality" needed to create this Europeanization process in education.

The European Union has itself been characterized as a "network of networks". To create and manage European policy without its own major departments of government, the European Union works with networks of experts, in private and public units. A large range of partners has to be negotiated with; they exist within complex networks, which span intergovernmental, producer, professional and expert forms (Bellier and Wilson 2000; Shore 2000). Today, they may represent highly organized industry or voluntary sector groups, or loose, but important, specialist academic associations. Increasingly, it appears that these networks, woven into sets of linked relations, represent a form of governance unique in Europe in which state borders are crossed, research units are linked and professionals with different traditions of work and administration are linked up. The informality of their organization, the complexity of their knowledge relations and exchanges, the hybridity of their institutional associations, combine with their overall interdependence to produce a distinctive form of governance in Europe. This form of governance in education cannot be understood as simply instrumental in transmitting policy or in mediating it. Policy is made in this process of governing through knowledge. The sum of this space of flows in education can be portrayed, as a space comprised of organizing networks, where territorial proximity has been replaced by network virtual proximity, and its actors exchange information and expertise within trust relations (Hannerz 1996; Lawn 2008).

The networks are working on their own trajectories – following their own preferred goals, often to do with cooperation and some sense of usefulness, usually derived from national responsibilities. At the same time, the networked policy-research space is providing necessary and vital services in European governance: it is linking countries and expertise, developing common standards, and creating possible policy solutions. From the 1950s onward, this form of network governance in research connects up, integrates and works on a wider and specialized front with research networks. This process works with funding programs for network formation and steers science and policy tasks. Over time, research networks have worked more closely with the aims of the EU policy centres, which is a source of stability at times. Governing pressures shape the networks and their work is steered; at the same time, they have independence, and are not forced into awkward relations or uncomfortable directions. European governance is constantly created and reformed as it moves along.

The following case takes this view of European governance, but applies it to the pre-history of the European Union, when post-war institutions were in an embryonic stage. From the late 1940s, European and American networking in education was focused around Hamburg, and the American and British Zones of Occupation in Germany. The foundation of the UNESCO Institute aided the formation of networks of national, European education experts who were drawn from their recently established national centres and institutes. In its early period – from the late 1940s to the early 1960s – it was home for research projects, devised by research experts, who, in retrospect, can be seen as providing the basis for what was to become a much more closely woven European research space in the following decades.

The approach taken here is about knowledge construction and its post-war actors, their sites and associations, and uses methods and concepts derived from transnational histories. Processes of Europeanization occur at particular sites or hubs, with particular actors that are mobilized by governing desires as well as their own scholarly interests. A consequence of the post-war period was an uneven but prevailing association between national institutes and the flourishing postwar statistical and survey expertise: this led to a gradual involvement in national governmental tasks by education experts and the standardization of educational research and commissions.

A confluence of problems and opportunities across the war-damaged landscape of Europe, combined with favoured governing interventions, created a series of comparable acts which grew together with strong outcomes in the governing of education, in Europe and then more globally. The scientific question about what is needed or what works became interwoven with the governing question about what has to be done and whose expertise is needed. From the insistent necessity of managing an Occupied Germany, to the support of national institutes and actors into a European association, the emergence of research agreements and common standards happens over a relatively short time in the late 1940s and the 1950s.

What is established in this period is a major consolidation of pre-war work in quantitative research but tied into a significant European governing effect. Educational research is one of the ways in which Europe becomes more governable. It does so because of the growing relation between national scholars and institutes, emerging Cold War and European governing trends, and the creation of common knowledge and standards in educational research. Early scholars' meetings, and their subsequent research together, created standardized subjects and research methods, and put in place a community of experts working across diverse statist jurisdictions, network organization, and politics. The importance of this work in the 1950s and early 1960s is not directly connected to acts of European governing, but the relation between the growing professional solidarities of senior researchers and the formation of common standards and knowledge would eventually allow the development of "governing at a distance" in Europe.

This chapter is in several parts: first, the post-war context and the American Occupation in West Germany; the creation of the UNESCO Institute in Hamburg; the formation of the International Project for the Evaluation of Educational Achievement (IEA); the problems of research cooperation in Europe, and, finally, the formation of a community, data and standards.

## Europe post-war

Professors of education in Western Europe were few in number but often they had knowledge of each other, due to common language use and book and journal publishing. It was the related fields of intelligence testing and factorial studies, which was a dominating influence in the relatively small field of educational research: "The group of researchers that coalesced in the early history of IEA, who possessed a solid background in psychometric methods and an interest in evaluation, set about to develop the instruments required" (Husén 1979 p.381).

In the field of education, the growth of national research centres, of various kinds, their collaborations and their involvement in European projects have been and continue to be crucial in the process of a transnational European policy space. National centres began to develop in the early 1930s and then again in the 1950s. National actors in their centres of education research moved to a new level of regional and international organization in the early post-war years.

The formation of research capacities at the European level, in transitory or heterogeneous networks, as well as in more settled hubs, was to become important in the gradual formation of a connected European space for educational research. W.D. Wall, in 1951 Head of the Unit for Education and Child Development at UNESCO in Paris, and a leading expert on the relation between psychology and education (and by 1956, the Director of the National Foundation for Educational Research in England), said:

> prior to the 1939–45 war research in education and related sciences was artisanal in character. Most of the empirical work was done by university teachers in time left aside from their lecturing and tutorial duties, and by students, the majority of them working part time for higher degrees. Outside the United States, with a few conspicuous exceptions . . . little support was given from public or private funds. Hence prior to 1945 in Europe, we find research addressing itself principally to the rather limited issues which can be handled by one person over a brief period of time.
>
> (Wall 1970: 484–485).

With one major exception, which Wall notes, this is true: the exception was Godfrey Thomson in Edinburgh who was heavily involved in the national survey of school children, the International Examinations Inquiry and the recipient of a 1930s Carnegie research grant. However, senior post-war scholars, like Husén, often had a common history in their research expertise and understandings: they had experience in quantitative surveys, statistical data and factorial analysis in their own pre-war work. This enabled them to work together quite quickly even if they had not met previously. Wall's point still stands though; generally, their research was managed through their own time as professors or with small organizational grants, and it was specific: "Its influence was mainly upon teaching method; until the 1950s, little of it touched directly upon major issues of educational organization, administration" (Wall 1970: 487). Wall then argued that objective tests of verbal ability and basic attainment together with the appraisals of experienced teachers would predict subsequent academic success. The Second World War gave a powerful impetus to changes which had been under way before – particularly to ideas concerning the responsibility of the state towards its less fortunate citizens, and reflected the citizens' demands upon the state. So, by the late 1940s, European states saw the necessity for social reform, and educational policy was a key element in this reform:

> Most European governments had to intervene more actively in the lives of their citizens in the period of reconstruction . . . In the forties and fifties, a number of countries (UK, Denmark, Norway, Sweden, Belgium, Finland, German Federal Republic) had set up commissions and organizations of varying degrees of independence concerned with the conduct and fostering of educational research directly concerned with policy making.
>
> (Wall 1970: 488)

The idea of a common Europe, or at least, a common Western Europe, as a political idea, partly followed cooperation in research areas, including education research. Even though political borders were transcended by actors who sometimes appeared to know each other through scientific communications and congresses, cooperation was not easy and needed catalytic agencies, like the new UNESCO, or the American Occupation Government in Germany, to bring them together at a Western European level.

There was urgency about the actions of these agencies, and the actors they supported, focused on the creation of modern, democratic education systems in Europe. The role of the new Hamburg UNESCO Institute, founded in 1951, appears to have been central in support of the groups of comparativists, psychologists and curriculum designers who worked together on projects and reports. An early catalyst for effective action was the need to govern an Occupied Germany. In 1942, the Allies began discussing post-war cooperation and laying the groundwork for new international, intergovernmental organizations. During the late war years, from 1943 to 1945, a continuing collaboration between the key players in the Allies seemed assured.

It is not surprising that in reconstructing German education, at least within the American Occupation Zone, the Americans would invite experts who reflected their national norms in educational research. In August 1952, a six-week workshop on the role of educational research was organised jointly by the American High Commissioner's office and the recently formed German Institute for International Educational Research (DiPF) in Frankfurt on the use that educational research could have on current problems in German school education. As it was made clear in statements about the Summer School workshop and DiPF, German educational issues included selection for types and stages of schooling, the exclusion of lower-income children from higher schools, and individual differences and teaching. The workshop members included six educational psychologists from the United States, 13 from Austria, Denmark, England, Holland, Italy, Norway, Sweden and Switzerland and 38 German professors.

The aim was to secure from each European country the presence of one out-standing professor of educational psychology and a younger professor who was the most promising person in this field. It was not only a reconstruction of educational research through the application of educational psychology in Germany but its internationalization, and in effect, its European formation as a community. The aims of the High Commission at the time were the internal reconstruction of Germany, but also externally in the creation of a European union (US High Commissioner Office 1949–51).

*In effect, educational psychology, associated with testing and selection, became the foundation of post-war educational research in Europe, and its actors the core of a professional community.* International projects and organizations began working in education, and their international actors were psychometricians, often coming together for the first time in proximity. These actors used the tools of testing, and its foundational ideas on factorial analysis and intelligence. The results of their work – sets of national education data – were soon to lose their singular scholarly purpose as European countries became part of blocs and blocs were increasingly in competition; this was especially the case when the success of the Soviet Sputnik in the late 1950s provided a powerful impetus to competition and change:

> In the decade after the Second World War, a definite willingness of governments to support and utilise research in education appeared in the belief that the studies would be useful to the formulation and conduct of educational policy. Government agencies turned to research workers for "answers" to what was considered to be basically the "scientific" problems involved in planning educational reforms. Policy-orientated research increased rapidly. [The 1967 "Plowden Committee" in Great Britain, the German Education Commission 1966–75, and the "School Commission" in Sweden established in 1946, are cases in point].
>
> (de Landsheere, 1997: 8)

Psychology began to be the mainstay of policy, and in the particular form it took – intelligence studies and factorial studies – it constituted a new international, and certainly European, language.

## Hamburg, UNESCO and the IEA: constructing Europe through research

In the mid-1950s, while the focus of educational research stayed the same as in Germany, researchers from European countries met regularly, particularly at the newly formed UNESCO Institute for Education in Hamburg, to examine common policy problems, for example, about school structures and organization, selection processes, examinations and school failure, and to devise ways of investigating education systems comparatively empirically, mainly through small expert meetings.

In 1956, UNESCO and the AERA (American Educational Research Association) held a joint meeting in the US, the First International Conference on Educational Research; amongst other things:

> The Conference recommended that UNESCO convene an international commission at an early date to study the possibility of developing common methods and techniques, international scales and measuring instruments, and essential terminology in educational research. Such a commission would probably require considerable time and financial support for its work since the nature of the task is one requiring inter-national cooperation and agreement in the highest degree. The dictionary referred to above could well be one of the responsibilities of such a commission.
>
> (Noll 1958: 85)

Soon after, Dr W. D. Wall (representing the NFER and UNESCO) chaired a 1958 meeting of European researchers in Hamburg and also meetings in Eltham Palace, England.[1] At those meetings, it was decided to carry out a pilot study to discover if an international research project would be administratively possible and meaningful (Postlethwaite 1966: 358). As Wall reflected later:

> The very fact that international scientific co-operation in educational research can be effectively organized implies the existence of powerful and highly developed research institutions in the member countries and a much more widespread technical and scientific competence than might have been expected ten years ago.
>
> (Wall 1970: 497).

These meetings became the basis for one of the most influential of the new European associations, working across policy and research: the International Project for the Evaluation of Educational Achievement (IEA). Soon after the 1958 meeting,

> The UNESCO Institute for Education accepted the proposal that an "international study of intellectual functioning" be undertaken and invited several directors of educational research organizations to meet in Hamburg in June,

1959, to consider the proposal further, and to decide whether they wished to participate in such a study. As it happened, the second meeting of represent-atives of European Centres of Educational Research was scheduled to take place near London a week later, and the proposal was described there also, with the result that some centres not represented at the Hamburg meeting also joined in the project.

Each of the participants was to bear the costs of test administration within his own country. The UNESCO Institute paid the cost of travel and mainte-nance for the European participants at the three meetings finally held, and furnished extensive coordinative services.

(Foshay 1962: 8)

By 1962, and with a significant US grant, other countries joined. It was coordi-nated from the UNESCO Institute in Hamburg. Beginning with a study of school mathematics, through tests and questionnaires, and across the range of parental, organizational and method, it provided the template for later studies on Science, French and English as foreign languages, Reading Comprehension, Literature and Civic Education:

The representatives of the Research Centres from these twelve Countries formed themselves into a Council whose main task was to agree on the overall policies of the research work. On average, they met once a year. They elected a Standing Committee of five of their members and their task was, if necessary, to take major decisions between Council meetings on behalf of the Council. Furthermore, a Chairman/Technical Director (Professor Husén of Sweden[2]) was elected, whose task was to attend to the day running of the project. He was assisted by a Project Co-ordinator, who was appointed in 1962 and placed in the UNESCO Institute for Education, Hamburg.

In its turn, each National Centre, although using most of its own staff

. . . on the national work involved in the project, sometimes used sampling consultants. At the content analysis stage at the beginning of the project, each National Centre had to organise national committees of mathematics educa-tors and at the coding and punching stage, they often had to employ extra coders (mostly university students).

(Postlethwaite 1966: 359)

Husén had attended the crucial Summer School workshop in Frankfurt in 1952 and was becoming well known to UNESCO, and the main educational psy-chologists who were grouping together within it. His new position reflected his linguistic capabilities (in German and English), his experience in factorial stud-ies and testing, and Sweden's position as a fair mediator in post-war Europe. The effect of this steered collaboration was to enhance and stabilize research institutions in education across Europe and to develop advanced technical and scientific competence as a cross-European resource. It had the further effect of making systems more transparent to national policy makers and across Europe. Ways of measuring complex variables in education systems also had the effect of aiding their shape and direction:

> There is no doubt that IEA had a very substantial influence on the development of educational research activities in all the countries that it has involved in any way, particularly in those countries where, previously, education research efforts had been of small extent and sophistication. Overall, this influence has been highly beneficial, resulting in the professionalization of educational personnel in the area of educational achievement measurement, statistical analysis of data, and the management of large scale educational projects. Again, it can be said that these developments would have had minimal likelihood of occurring without the existence of IEA. This was partly because IEA had to develop, in different countries, cadres of educational researchers that could help carry out IEA's investments.
>
> (J. B. Carroll 1994, quoted in de Landsheere 1997: 10)

Like the IEI in the 1930s (Lawn 2008), this movement of European researchers reflected American policy, was supported by American funding and involved American expertise and services. Again like the IEI, it had strong links with Teachers College, Columbia, but also, in this case, with Benjamin Bloom in Chicago: "A research grant from the United States Office of Education was received in the summer of 1962, and this covered the international costs and the United States national costs only" (Postlethwaite 1966: 359).

The data were filed on magnetic tape at the University of Chicago Computation Centre:

> Needless to say, with approximately fifty million pieces of information, this study could never have been completed without the use of a computer. That the whole project (mathematics phase) was completed within four years, even with the help of a computer, was, in itself, an enormous achievement – the work on content analysis was begun at the beginning of 1962 and the final manuscripts were completed at the end of 1965; this success was due to the dedication, enthusiasm and ability of all the educational researchers concerned.
>
> (Postlethwaite 1966: 360)

### Overcoming difficulties

The ambitions of the early scholars, based upon their common interests, was strained by the growing scale of their work, by funding problems and especially by differential speeds and contexts of new national partners. In describing an early study, it is clear that this new organization took some time to create a stable and scientific way of working:

> This is an exploratory study. The participants in this study were working with no extra funds, no extra allotment of time, and without the benefit of a previously developed set of procedures.
>
> It will therefore be apparent that both the tests and the sampling procedures do not meet the standards that might otherwise be required. For these shortcomings we are not apologetic; it was necessary to accept them, and hence to restrict the statements based on the data gathered, if the study was indeed to be undertaken.
>
> (Foshay 1962: 9)

Given the research and linguistic complexities of the early years, the difficulties are not surprising: "The tests were originally prepared in either English, French, or German. They had to be translated into eight languages: English, Finnish, French, German, Hebrew, Polish, Serbo-Croatian and Swedish. The problem of translation was, of course, of great concern" (Foshay 1962: 19).

The scale of the (first mathematics) study was huge: "133,000 pupils from 5,400 schools were tested, and that questionnaires were filled in by 13,500 teachers and 5,450 head teachers, it can be appreciated that the time to record these data in the various national research institutes was enormous" (Postlethwaite 1966: 363).

Creating an international project is a delicate business – who will be legitimate partners, who is listened to, how will the research be paid for, how will the research be undertaken in the time scale and in comparable ways, and how is trust established:

> The administrative centre for the project was the UNESCO Institute in Hamburg. The participants met there three times, each time for one week: in June, 1959, to plan the project and construct trial forms for the tests; in October, 1960, to take a final look at the project before testing, and in June, 1961, to examine the data and to plan for interpretation and publication.
>
> (Foshay 1962: 11)

Analysing the conditions for the success of an international research project, which were nearly unknown in education in the 1950s, Pidgeon (from the English NFER) isolated several points drawn from his experience of the IEA. Unlike Wall, he didn't make reference to the powerful institutes involved, but the lack of an empirical tradition and so, an expertise in it, and the care needed in selecting competent researchers. Pidgeon continued with reference to the IEA coordinating centre and the problem of international representation within it: "few of the countries likely to participate in research of this kind can spare their 'competence' and hence either the central organisation will necessarily be run by competent workers from two or three countries only" (Pidgeon 1969: 248).

Another issue was the status of the institute, is it independent or part of a government department?

> ... if a co-operative research project is to be successful, it must be a joining together of competent research institutions in the various countries ... They are more likely to achieve this if they come together on a voluntary basis than if some of their number are "officially" appointed, and, moreover, until such time as trained and experienced researchers are generously available in all participating countries, there is less danger of some relatively incompetent workers coming into the team if they were allowed, as it were, to choose themselves.
>
> (Pidgeon 1969: 249)

Without question, the group of researchers meeting in Frankfurt and the founding group of the Hamburg UNESCO meetings, overcame their national, linguistic, financial and methodological difficulties and made a solid foundation for an early European education space. In the 1950s, Hamburg became a nodal point in the distributed laboratory model of scientific testing and its community of workers. Indeed, they not only cooperated but, as Husén said, they began with pupil cognitive development in different countries and by the late 1950s, had begun to realize how little empirical evidence was available to substantiate the sweeping judgements that were commonplace about the relative merits and failings of various national systems of education (Husén 1979). Now the world was to be conceived as more than a meeting place: it was to be an educational laboratory where different practices in terms of school organization, curriculum content and methods of instruction were experimented with. The laboratory soon had multiple coordinated national sites and complex procedures and finance:

> A feasibility study was launched with the purpose of finding out whether, methodologically and administratively, instruments could be developed that were cross-nationally valid and could be administered uniformly over a range of countries with different school systems. We also wanted to find out whether data could be made accessible in order to make the processing of data and statistical analyses possible at one central place.
>
> (Husén 1979: 374)

The scientific possibilities – producing cross-national generalisations about input and output factors – began to shift toward the idea of comparative results and system improvements. In turn, the strength of a particular way of seeing comparative education grew – what Husén called the empirical-positivist "paradigm", comparing through quantitative methods. Previously, there had been no instruments by means of which one could assess cross-nationally the level of student competence in various systems.

Funding was always a problem for this research work, and to the consistent support from the US Office of Education, other sources were added: the UK's Leverhulme Trust, the German Volkswagen Foundation, and the Swedish Tercentenary Bank. Increased funding came when the Sputnik crisis grew, and competition with the Soviet bloc increased. A focus on the efficiency of national systems and types materialized naturally from its earlier work (Husén 1979).

## Standardization

A major aspect of this 1960s work was not only the knowledge which was accrued, through its Pilot study and Curriculum projects, but the methods by which the subject was investigated. It was producing proof not only about the effectiveness of transnational European research projects but also about their methods. Even more important than a community of European educational researchers, was the creation of standardized means of investigating education and validating it. They had normalized the use of sampling by random probability sampling techniques and specially constructed specific testing instruments. The first carefully designed study in one subject area (mathematics) had developed over the years into a series of studies. Husén, who had participated from the early days, chaired and coordinated the Office, and would write several accounts about what had become IEA, revealing the scale of the work and the ambition of its aims: "One could, indeed, ask about the rationale for embarking on a venture which has included 250,000 students in 9,700 schools in 19 countries with all its far-reaching administrative implications and formidable technical complexities" (Husén 1975b: 1).

Partly through the far sightedness of Husén, but also emerging from the enthusiasm of experts drawn together in common tasks, the scope of the research developed from scholarly interest in the possibility of comparative data, and into differential outcomes and their causes. Now,

> ... the world could be conceived of as one big educational laboratory where different practices were experimented with in terms of school organization, curriculum content and methods of instruction. But before trying to analyze cross-nationally the "effects" of various input factors on educational outcomes, it was necessary to devise internationally valid evaluation instruments ... Therefore the prime concern during the first years of IEA research was the construction of appropriate measuring techniques that could result in the establishment of adequate international yardsticks.
>
> (Husén 1975b: 7–8)

The IEA researchers, or at least, the coordinators, had to face the difficult problems of the relationship between input factors in the social, economic and instructional domains and output as measured by international tests covering both cognitive (student performance) and affective behaviours (student attitudes and motivation), and comparability between the student tests. Additionally, they had problems associated with the assessment of "productivity" of a national system of school education. So, as Husén said, "this research community [in the IEA] brought about the accumulation of strategies and techniques, which could begin to be utilized routinely in analysing national curricula and their goals, across cultures" (Husén 1975a: 23) and "Routines for data collection in the schools have been tried out in a wide variety of contexts. Finally, experiences have been gained in data processing that lend themselves to nation-wide evaluation surveys" (Husén 1975b: 20).

In these statements, Husén reveals how a small, informal meeting of educational researchers in a sponsored post-war meeting could develop and be encouraged to develop an international organization capable of producing joint data which could make comparisons between systems and about progress and achievement.

## Conclusion

The idea of Europeanization draws attention to the emerging and transforming condition of Europe, and away from notions of stasis and stability. This is a useful device in the studies of European governance which have tended to rely on intra-governmental relations and regulations. While Europe, and the European Union, transforms through multidimensional and heterogeneous channels which draw attention to significant acts and events, there is also a congruent process of accumulation and bureaucratization. This produces standards, programmes, codes and organizations. Involved in the transformation and in the standardization are mutable communities of researchers and their agreed technologies.

Our understandings of European governance are about acts of funding (research and innovation), persuasive power (Lawn 2006), and governing by experts (Ozga, Dahler-Larsen, Segerholm and Simola 2011). What may appear as loosely connected or even coincidental events or relations accumulate and are made serviceable in the act of governing at distance; a practical necessity in the European Union. It is governing at a distance and through instrumentalization, turning ideas and actions into instruments of governing, which has resulted in new forms of non-state power (Miller and Rose 2008: 205). It has the advantage of appearing to exclude politics and yet produce workable solutions to governing problems.

The use of experts in this way is an interesting phenomenon in relation to Europeanization acts of governance. The experts are bound within their world of technical problems, professional community obligations, urgent tasks and agreements, funding and the overcoming of weaknesses. They accumulate knowledge about systems and agreements about the nature and conceptualization of nations, systems and schooling. They agree common and unfolding standards about how the problem can be defined, studied and what should be excluded. They produce abstract and commensurable units, enabling exchange across borders and places, and producing a newly transparent domain. At the same time, through their effectiveness in negotiating about funding or close proximity to national policy colleagues, their work has political value. Its usage, as data and standards, become a vital governing tool in the formation of a common governable and operational Europe.

Studies of European associations, research projects, and networks can be crucial in the development of significant tendencies, dominant interpretations and governing technologies, in this case in European education. The UNESCO Institute and its related researcher network, the IEA, became one of the emerging groups of researchers, in their own right, or linked to the emergence of the OECD or the Council of Europe in the decades following the late 1940s. These studies can be significant in understanding how powerful and emerging institutes of education research and research centres worked together, and were strengthened by evolving common ideas, a community of practice, and shared and agreed standards of inquiry and analysis. Often describing their work through the solving of "theoretical or technical problems", they eventually achieved the means to "assess how school systems are performing, how, why, and under what conditions education makes a difference" (de Landsheere 1997: 7). In contemporary Europe, this crucial understanding is now absorbed into policy and political discourse. It is no longer scholarly but technical.

The formulation of educational knowledge – what is important to know and what should or should not be reflected in the study and practice of education – has historically been a consequence of social and political as well as academic developments. More than an epistemological or methodological discussion, these developments entail a process that is historically contingent, vulnerable and reflective of the political mood and intellectual space that they express (Nóvoa and Yariv-Mashal 2003: 423). The problem of modernizing and democratizing postwar Germany, in the American Zone of Occupation, was the first step in the 1940s to bring into being a commonality of purpose and explanation between disparate groups of academics, many working in war-torn societies. This commonality was produced through a process of selection and recommendation, with an emphasis on the new and meritocratic techniques of testing and selection.

This increasingly dominant trend in educational psychology, especially in the US and the UK, was used to shape and unite European researchers, and in so doing, knowingly build a united Europe (or at least, its Western edge). The Military Government, and then the High Commissioner in the American Sector, funded this heavily through its support for the Frankfurt DiPF and the Summer Schools. Their support for UNESCO and the Hamburg Institute, and later in the face of the Sputnik advance in scientific progress, meant that this embryo research community was favoured (even though it had to constantly search for funding). Researchers like Husén, Wall, Walker, Hotyat, de Landsheere, Takkala and their US colleagues, like Bloom and Thorndike, began to speak the international languages of research in education, moving along from differentiation and testing into the evaluation and reconstruction of the school. Husén's ideas about school differences emerge out of this group work (Husén 1979, 1993) and their joint work in the UNESCO journal, the *International Review of Education*.

IEA was founded during this historical turning point in the history of educational research. In the decade after the Second World War, a definite willingness of governments to support and utilize research in education appeared in the belief that the studies would be useful to the formulation and conduct of educational policy. Government agencies turned to research workers for "answers" to what was considered to be basically the "scientific" problems involved in planning educational reforms. Policy-orientated research increased rapidly. The emerging concentration within this community on variations between systems became crucial in the European context. As was said, reflecting on the 1960s and the IEA:

it seems that what had been learned by the students in different subjects in different systems could well vary considerably. There were certain differences between school systems in terms of age of entry to school, the structure of the system, the curriculum content, teaching methods, teacher training and the like. Would it be possible, they asked themselves, to conduct international (or inter-system) studies on a comparative basis which would yield results from which each system could learn about improving itself?

(Postlethwaite 1993: 689)

This was a defining moment in the Europeanization in education. Now the community, the standards, the capacity and the expertise were ready when governing at a distance across European education, post-Maastricht, and through PISA, was materializing:

Europe is diversified but it is now in a period of integration of its trade and labour markets. At the same time, as an institution, the role of the school is rapidly changing: more and more European youth are in schools and not in work. In relation to work, and to European identity and consciousness, the school has a crucial role.

(Husén 1993: 501).

Europeanization is a fast-moving process and the relations between researchers, policy and context have changed their purpose and their value to the governing of Europe as well.

## Acknowledgement

Research funded by the Swedish Research Council *From Paris to Pisa. Governing Education by Comparison 1867–2015* (2015–17).

## Notes

1 Those attending the meeting were: Benjamin S. Bloom of the University of Chicago; Arnold Anderson; Robert L. Thorndike of Teachers College, Columbia University; Douglas Pidgeon, NFER; David Walker, Scottish Council for Research in Education (SCRE); Martti Takala, Finland; Fernand Hotyat, Belgium; Gaston Mialaret, France; Walter Schukze, Germany; Moshe Smilansky, Israel; Torsten Husén, Sweden; Wells Foshay; Harry Passow and Donald Super from Teachers College.
2 An exemplar of this kind of new European networking at this time was Torsten Husén, a major educational researcher in Sweden and its first professor of applied education research in Stockholm in the 1950s. By the late 1950s, he had already become part of the Hamburg group, which emerged as the IEA, an expert in changes in post-war German education, as a consultant to the US administration, and had visited the US several times. With close colleagues, he worked with a major Swedish Commission of comprehensive education on its content, methods and ways of comparing pupil achievement. So, at the same time that there was growing governmental recognition of the value of strong links between educational research and educational reform policies, and a consequent increase in funding, experts like Husén became useful and found opportunities for work

elsewhere in Europe. Husén became a major expert and ubiquitous figure in the seminars and consultancies of UNESCO and the OECD, as well as crucial to the IEA. He was both a technical expert and a policy advisor.

## References

Bellier, I. and Wilson, T.W. (2000). *An Anthropology of the European Union: Building, Imagining and Experiencing the New Europe*. Oxford: Berg.

de Landsheere, G. (1997). IEA and UNESCO: a history of working cooperation. Retrieved 20 January 2014 from: www.unesco.org/education/pdf/LANDSHEE.pdf (pp. 1–22).

Foshay, A. W. (1962). The background and the procedures of the twelve-country study in educational achievements of thirteen-year-olds in twelve countries. Results of an international research project, 1959–61 (pp. 7–19). Hamburg: UNESCO Institute for Education.

Hannerz, U. (1996). Transnational Connections: Culture, People, Places. London: Routledge.

Husén, T. (1975a). *International evaluation of educational systems and its role of building research competence in less-developed countries*. HEP Seminar on "The evaluation of the qualitative aspects of education," 30 September 30–4 October 1974. Paris: UNESCO, International Institute for Educational Planning.

Husén, T. (1975b). *Multi-national evaluation of school systems*. IIEP (International Institute for Educational Planning) Occasional Papers. Paris, UNESCO: International Institute for Educational Planning, Paris.

Husén, T. (1979). An international research venture in retrospect: The IEA surveys, *Comparative Education Review*, *23*(3), 371–385.

Husén, T. (1993). Schooling in modern Europe: Exploring major issues and their ramifications. *International Review of Education/Internationale Zeitschrift für Erziehungswissenschaft/Revue Internationale de Pedagogie*, *39*(6), 499–509.

Lawn, M. (2006). Soft governance and the learning spaces of Europe. *Comparative European Politics*, *4*(2), 272–288.

Lawn, M. (Ed.). (2008). *An Atlantic crossing? The work of the IEI, its researchers, methods and influence*. Oxford: Symposium Books (Comparative Histories of Education Series).

Lawn, M. (2011). Standardizing the European education policy space. *European Educational Research Journal*, *10*(2), 259–272.

Lawn, M. and Grek, S. (2011). *Europeanizing education: Governing a new policy space*. Oxford: Symposium Books.

Miller, P. and Rose, N. (2008). *Governing the present: Administering economic, social and personal life*. Oxford: Polity Press.

Noll, V (1958). International cooperation in educational research. *International Review of Education/Internationale Zeitschrift fuer Erziehungswissenschaft/Revue Internationale de Pedagogie*, *4*(1), 77–87.

Nóvoa, A. and Yariv-Mashal, T. (2003). Comparative research in education: A mode of governance or a historical journey? *Comparative Education, 39*(4), 423–438.

Ozga, J., Dahler-Larsen, P., Segerholm, C. and Simola, H. (Eds.). (2011). *Fabricating quality in education: Data and governance in Europe*. London: Routledge.

Pidgeon, D. (1969). Technical problems of international co-operative research projects. *International Review of Education*, *15*(2), , 247–253.

Postlethwaite, N. (1966). International Project for the Evaluation of Educational Achievement (IEA) *International Review of Education*, *12*(3), Celebration of the 20th Anniversary of UNESCO, 356–369.

Postlethwaite, T. N. (1993). Prospects, *International Bureau of Education*, *23*(3/4), 677–686.

Shore, Cris (2000). *Building Europe: The cultural politics of European integration*. London: Routledge.

US High Commissioner Office Information Bulletins 1949–1951 *Germany under Reconstruction*. Retrieved 6 October 2016 from Digital Library, University of Wisconsin http://digicoll.library.wisc.edu/cgi-bin/History/History-idx?type=header&id=History. omg1951Aug.

Wall, W. D. (1970). Research and educational action. *International Review of Education*, *16*(4): 484–501.

# 5 A global-local mixture of educational reform policy in Taiwan

## Taking school choice policy as an example of unevenness of educational opportunity[1]

*Chin-Ju Mao*

## Introduction

Neo-liberal policy initiatives are reshaping educational systems in complex and varied ways globally and locally (Popkewitz 2000, 2003; Rizvi 2004). As such, Taiwan's borrowing of neo-liberal educational reform ideas produces different meanings locally. Although its neo-liberal ideas of education reform derive from the United States and other Anglophone countries, local entities have reformulated these policies and re-inserted them into local schooling contexts to meet particular local interests and personal needs. Efforts in education reform must deal not only with global concerns, such as global competitiveness and efficiency, but also with local educational problems, such as educational democratization and education fanaticism in Taiwan.

There are always multiple logics behind the local adoption and adaptation of global discourses of educational reform and restructuring. Moreover, an uneven assembling of global ideas and local practice can be observed. This study uses school choice as an example of how the state and reformers integrated a neo-liberal sense of educational reform policies into a public school system and how the local participants (especially parents) transformed the choice policy into a hybrid model that combined civil rights' participation and market competition as "school choice". Behind this hybrid model, there is a social space in which particular social relations are not only stretched out, but also contribute to a new unevenness of educational opportunity.

Combining the global and local levels of policy borrowing and hybridization, I take two junior high schools in Taiwan as examples of what happens as these neo-liberal reform policies travel down to the local level and are refracted through a local system that has already developed its own local practice of school choice. In the following, theoretical perspectives about global policy travel, and reformulation and local adoption are first discussed. Secondly, I introduce Taiwanese school culture and school choice practices, and how, since the 1990s, they have been reshaped by the neo-liberal education policies formulated in response to Taiwan's education reform movement. Thirdly, I discuss how a hybrid model of choice came about and analyzed its impact on Taiwanese educational system and social effect. Finally, I reflect on the implications of the school choice case for the theoretical perspectives of global-local mixture and the remade space of educational politics in terms of educational opportunity.

## A global and local mixture as a theoretical frame

Post-colonial theorists suggest that the flow of cultural globalization is complex and fragmented, and is more often characterized by cultural hybridity than by cultural domination (Young 1995; Spivak 1992; Bhabha 1994). There are considerable forces of fragmentation and hybridization that makes globalization not a homogeneous process (Barker 2000). While researching the process of globalization, in addition to the phenomena of cultural synchronization, we also need to understand that the flow of cultural discourse is not always unidirectional. As many theorists point out, there is a global convergence of educational restructuring in which global ideas of reform are usually internalized within a national debate. When a society adopts the international language of reform (such as market, choice, and deregulation), it serves not only as a functional strategy of reform, but also as a local discourse that projects particular national interests and political ideologies (Ozga and Lingard 2007; Ozga, Seddon and Popkewitz 2006; Popkewitz 2000, 2003).

Applying the concept of hybridity to the interactive process of globalization and localization, Popkewitz (2000) asserts that when applied at the national level many educational reforms interact and overlap with one another, such that it becomes rather difficult to categorize them according to traditional concepts such as liberal and conservative. For example, when educational reform measures are implemented in Latin America or Africa in cooperation with an international organization based in Europe or North America, due to the influence of national interests and the domestic political environment, they aren't necessarily an exact replication of a pre-existing reform model, but rather a hybrid.

There are two levels of hybridization. One is the level of hybridization between the international and the national. This is where scholars of comparative education tend to use terms such as policy "lending" and "borrowing". Steiner-Khamsi (2004) examines the politics, the processes, and the "agents of transfer" underlying instances of educational borrowing and lending, and pays particular attention to historical and contextual dimensions. Popkewitz (2000) created the new term "indigenous foreigner" to explore how any discourse of educational reform was a hybridity that appropriated global discourses into national concerns. To pursue the idea of indigenous foreigner, he pointed out that when a nation deploys a global discourse of reform to reformulate its national educational system, reform ideas tend to be adopted without a history of time and place. They travel across national boundaries in the form of universal principles, but also are reformulated into transmogrified forms that meet particularly national and local interests.

However, there is another level of hybridization: from the national to the local and the individual. According to Anderson-Levitt (2003), world culture theory proposes that education around the world would, over time, undergo reforms reflective of a similar model, but that school systems would tend to reflect national culture and that local people would institute school-system changes reflective of local realities.

This emphasis on the process of mediation and innovation carried out by individuals and social groupings, suggests the hybrid cultural discourse of post-colonialism has superseded the globalization discourse based on the process of cultural conflict or homogenization. The strength of such an anthropological perspective is that it helps to show how a policy travels down to the local, what effects it generates, and how it is refracted in a local system within a nation that is often regarded as a mere borrower of a global language of reform policy. Moreover, in its analysis of the process of globalization, post-colonialism gives due importance to non-linear logic, deviation-generating potentials, and contingent outcomes in the local. With respect to policy formulation, problem solving, and institutional forms, each country has its own way of interpreting and adapting reform models.

As discussed, a study on the globalization and localization of educational reform necessarily has dual focal points. One of these concerns the development of supra-national convergence and the bricolage and hybridization of the concept of reform on the international level; the other focal point concerns local divergence and fragmentation at the intra-national level. Therefore, in addition to supra-national convergence and the adaptation of reform concepts, such research needs to investigate how globalized reform concepts are adapted and applied at the local level, in terms of re-assembling, bricolage, fragmentation, and hybridization, as well as what impact they have on schools, how educators respond and how parents react. Globalization becomes a social space of people who deals with real issues of education, such as educational opportunity and quality, mobility and choice, resources and tensions, etc.

Therefore, how is it that such neo-liberal ideas as privatization, marketization, standardization, decentralization, and deregulation (Arnove 2003; Burbules and Torres 2000; Morrow and Torres 2003) become the conceptual framework of the educational reforms being adopted in numerous countries? Why have these countries accepted or adapted these alien concepts and used them to formulate their reform policies? How have local schools and communities been affected by these reform policies, and how have they responded to and act upon them? These issues deserve to be explored.

In this research, I examine the highly complex and interactive process of globalization and localization in Taiwan, describing Taiwanese reform policy as superimposed, complex, and chaotic, which nevertheless clusters around main nodal points, such as choice and deregulation. In regarding the adoption and implementation of educational policy as a type of cultural practice, my focus is to shift through multiple layers of adaptation and the logic of transformation, to show how a complicated global-local mixture of reform policy in local community schools is recognized and realized, or distorted and recreated, a dynamic and changing process. This implies a lived educational world, in which there is a simultaneous multiplicity of educational spaces, made up of social networks and actions. Therefore, it is important to pay particular attention to how local actors adopt, appropriate, or subvert global-borrowing policy. On the one hand, it resides in macro-level of global flows and national politics, and on the other, it is embedded in their daily practices, implying a multiple micro-social space constituting multiform maneuvering of individuals.

This chapter uses two junior high schools as examples with which to explore both what happens at the school level and how neo-liberal senses of reform policy, as they travel down to the local, are employed by local actors and results in unexpected outcomes. The following section introduces local Taiwanese senses of school culture and school choice practice, and how, since the 1990s, they were reshaped by neo-liberal education policies that constituted the governmental response to Taiwan's education reform movement.

## Local sense of school choice in the catchment area system

In the Taiwanese education system, elementary school education and lower-level secondary education are compulsory and free for children from the age of 6 to 15. Recent statistics show that 98 per cent of elementary and junior high schools are public, with only a very small number of private schools (2 per cent) (Ministry of Education, 2017a). Allocating students into public elementary and junior high schools rests on an administratively operated system of catchment areas. The system conducts geographic distributions of public schools to manage school enrollment and, more specifically, to ensure that students can attend nearby schools, according to rules laid out in the Constitution.[2] This school system aspires to a model in which equal opportunities are created through equal funding for all schools and regulated enrolment. Such a public education system reflects the assumption that each public school provides the same quality of education as others.

However, parents are concerned that their children pass the future competitive entrance examination for prestigious high schools. There is a gap between providing equal quality of public education and the personal desire for upward social mobility. As many Western studies point out, where you live can significantly affect the quality of your children's educational experience (Elmore 1986; Wells and Crain 1992). However, for some parents in Taiwan, this quality is more an issue of which schools your child attends than an issue of where you live. Therefore, local parents believe that only "superstar schools"[3] can achieve better academic performance to compete for entrance to prestigious high schools. Thus, some local parents either choose or transfer to "superstar schools," which are often outside their catchment areas.

There are many choice strategies appropriated by such parents. They can simply change their family's registered residence without actually moving into the area. Parents devote much energy to deciding which school to enroll their children in, where to live, and how to maneuver their choice strategy, all of which cause problems for popular schools because applications far exceed available places. Such situations are much worse in highly populated areas and in metropolitan areas, than in less densely populated regions (Lin 2000; Chang 2000).

## The Taiwanese Educational Reform Movement since the late 1980s

While local parents continuously update and share their local knowledge of school choice strategies in the catchment system of public schools, Taiwanese society and the Taiwanese education system have also been undergoing rapid changes. Beginning in 1987,[4] Taiwan underwent a drastic process of social and state reformation (Hsiao 1991). On April 10, 1994, tens of thousands of protesters marched in the streets demanding education reform, an event later called the landmark 410 Educational Reform Movement (Xue 1996). The heady aroma of democracy created a strong sense of civil rights, which echoed middle-class parents' vocal demands for educational rights (Mao 2001, 2008; Ho 2009). There were two camps of supporters within the movement: one for liberalism and the free market, the other for social justice. The call for deregulation in the education system was first proposed by some university professors, including those who self-identified as liberal believer of economists.

At the moment of transforming from an authoritarian state to a democratic one, the government's new policies, in a way, are to build a new imagination of democratic society and its own political legitimacy. The government and some economists who were later in charge of a scheme for managing and redistributing resources for reform programs chose to align with the market model, which was considered a low-cost reform policy (Ho 2009). Thus, the educational authority employed the ideas and framework of neo-liberalism to devolve its power to local government and communities, and to deregulate a rigid system of schooling in response to the domestic trend leading toward democratization (Mao 1997, 2001).

Education reform ran parallel to the democratization of society. It was argued that by deregulation, the power of making educational decisions can be transferred to the public and decrease state's central control. Therefore, the educational system needs to be decentralized. The ideas of deregulation and decentralization as a scaffolding enables a discursive field for developing more reform projects in education. The emergence of such a discursive field was more connected with the political zest of democracy than economic concerns of efficiency in early 1990s. During the 1990s, discourses of deregulation and decentralization were strongly intertwined with the national idea of democracy and state re-formation. Parent participation, educational decentralization to local government and deregulation, and rights-based reform issues constituted the discursive field of educational reform (Mao 2001, 2008; Mao and Chang 2005; Ho 2009).

Therefore, the democratic movement argued for deregulation by transferring educational decision-making powers from the state's central control to public control. In this way, parents' right to exercise choice over their children's education embodied the democratic ideal and individual civil rights. Promoting parental choice and parental involvement also justified the push to make schooling more diverse and more responsive to the needs of parents. It was claimed that parental choice and involvement could serve not only to correct an overly authoritarian style of schooling, but also to improve educational quality at the same time (Yang and

Lin 1994; 410 Education Restructuring League 1996). Therefore, since the 1990s, discourses of deregulation and choice have been strongly intertwined with the ideas of democracy and civil society. The call for education reform in the 1990s echoed the social trend of democratization and efficiency that involved a range of initiatives to increase local autonomy and the transfer of state control to local management.

## Education rights and the Fundamental Education Act of 1999

In the aforementioned social and political context, the discourses of parental choice, parental involvement, and education rights finally became a part of the Fundamental Education Act, approved by legislators in the national assembly and announced in 1999. Promulgation of the Act was essentially a politically symbolic move. The status of this Act is equal to the status of an educational constitution that sets out the basic principles of educational development. The Act states in the beginning that it is "enacted to protect people's rights to learning and educa-tion" (Ministry of Education, 2017b). A right to education is part of one's civil rights, making it clear that educational affairs should be decentralized to the local level. The Act clearly states that the government should provide the opportunity of choice for parents, promote private-sector involvement in establishing schools, and allow the "publically funded"-"privately run" model of a school in the public school system. It provides a legal basis by which parents are eligible to partici-pate in the decision-making processes underlying the formation and execution of all school policies and have the right of educational choice in terms of select-ing schools, educational content, and instruction methods. Because of this Act, a Parent Association (PA), as a formal organization within the school structure, is expected to work in partnership with the school principal and staff.

## Stories about School A and School B[5]

While the Fundamental Education Act legally ensures parents' right to choose their children's education and choosing a school outside the catchment area is not uncommon in the past decades, how does this global idea of neo-liberalism in terms of choice become appropriated, and generate possibly deviation or unex-pected outcomes? Here are two schools, A and B, junior high schools located in the greater metropolitan Taipei area. They are taken as examples to demonstrate how their parents as local actors recognize and maneuver their choice strategies at a micro-level of multiform practices and reconfigure social space of education, contributing to the unevenness of educational opportunity.

School A is located in a prosperous area of Taipei City. The socio-economic status of the students' parents is, on average, higher than that for School B. Many of School A's parents work at big corporations and a hospital nearby. Because a consistently high percentage of its students attend top-end high schools, School A is among the few public schools in Taipei to attract parents who aspire to enroll their children in the institution. School A is widely recognized as one of the trendiest superstar schools in Taipei. A teacher at School A pointed out a salient phenomenon:

... people have usually said that our school has the quality of a private school but the price of a public school's tuition, but our efficiency [i.e., the school's capacity to churn out graduates eligible for attendance at top-end high schools] is more like a cram school's.

(Mao, 2015a: 3)

**School B** is located in one of Taipei's satellite cities and stands not far from an intersection of two major highways and quite close to a soon-to-be-established line of the MRT (Metropolitan Rapid Transit). Because of its convenient location and flexible transportation options, new housing projects started growing in this region twenty years ago, attracting many new families and young couples who could not afford the prohibitively expensive real estate in Taipei City. School B serves both old and new communities, and features a racially and ethnically diverse student body. It usually accepts graduates of three elementary schools in its catchment area. The three elementary schools respectively represent three different kinds of communities in the region: traditional, aboriginal, and new. The traditional community comprises people who have lived there for many generations working in occupations related to agriculture. This area also attracts many aboriginals from the east coast of Taiwan looking for work. They form the second community, labeled "aboriginal." The third community comprises residents who have arrived in the area in the last decade, whose ethnic and racial background tends to be Han Chinese, and who tends to hold professional, white-collar jobs.

The following table compares the two schools in terms of their campus size, the average space for each student, the number of students, teachers, and classes, the ratio of students to teachers, and the percentage of graduates attending one of Taipei's top three high schools and the percentage of graduates attending public high schools.

As the table indicates, a huge difference does not exist between the two schools in terms of student-to-teacher ratios owing to the equal distribution of educational resources under national educational provisions. However, there is a significant difference regarding four matters: the number of students, the average space for

*Table 5.1* Basic information about School A and School B

| Statistics 2016 | School A | School B |
| --- | --- | --- |
| Space | 27,421 m$^2$ | 34,248 m$^2$ |
| Average space for each student | 10.07 m$^2$ | 28.05 m$^2$ |
| Number of classes | 72 | 39 |
| Number of students | 2725 | 1213 |
| Number of teachers | 171 | 84 |
| Ratio of students to teachers (national average is 15.1) | 15.93 | 14.54 |
| Total number of graduates | 926 | 506 |
| Number and percentage of graduates who attend public HS | 648 (70%) | 89 (18%) |
| Number and percentage of graduates who attend one of Taipei's top three HSs | 226 (24%) | 11 (2%) |

each student, the percentage of graduates who attend one of Taipei's top three high schools, and the percentage of graduates who attend a public high school.

The Fundamental Education Act enshrines parents' right to participate in school affairs. Article 8 of the Act outlines two dimensions of parental rights to educational participation. One is parents' rights in the selection of schools, educational content, and methods of instruction. The second is their right to participate in decision making in all school policies and development. The Act requires reserving at least one-fifth of school-board positions for PA members.

On the other hand, traditionally, Taiwan society highly valued the status of teachers. Parents respect the position of teachers and appreciate what schools do for their children. However, such an unconditional respect and appreciation for teachers was somewhat residualized with the call for parents' rights in education. Rather than preferring to work in equal partnership with parents of students, both school administrators and teachers have preferred parents to respond to teachers' requests for assistance, such as support at special events and class supervision. Mixing the feeling of traditional respect for educators with awareness of the right to participate school affairs, means the function of PA, in general, turns out to be one of financial contribution and resource supplements, with very limited involvement and participation of parents otherwise. However, for School A, benefiting from its PA's donations as well as parents' devotion of substantial amounts of time and intelligence to school-related matters, there also builds up an increasing ambivalence on the part of teachers toward parents' involvement in school-related matters. Some of School A's parents participate not only in classroom management and teaching, but also in the school's decision-making process, including the review and selection of principals, curriculum development, and the allocation of homeroom teachers and subject teachers. Some teachers resent this parental monitoring of teachers, resulting in a contradictory blend of parents' polite support of school-initiated matters and parents' sometimes forceful efforts to guide certain affairs, especially regarding children's "best" interests in achieving outstanding academic performance.

Some powerful, resource-blessed parents at School A were able to exercise significant influence over the school not only by identifying and exercising loopholes in admission procedures, but also by forming an information-sharing network. They are able to "find" relevant and up-to-date information regarding matters ranging from the state of school enrollment to teachers' classroom performance. These parents dominated the school board and steered school policy toward their personal interests. In this way, parents and the school were not working in partnership. Teachers felt that the PA had them under observation, which created unhealthy competition amongst teachers for winning over parents' support and praise. Therefore, parents' choice of and involvement in School A have made it highly competitive with other schools because School A operates under the formidable pressure of parents' constant monitoring and comparing.

In contrast, School B's diverse student body (reflecting three different demographic groups) had left School B's PA less united and less competent than School A's. There were factions within School B's PA, and opinions about future development of the school were divided. Some parents supported the school's policy of keeping a special program on aboriginal culture in the curriculum as a way of gaining extra funding from the government, while some parents were strongly against it, claiming that it tainted the school's reputation, resulting in lower enrollments over time. An overarching consequence of these differences, in short, was that School B's PA had difficulty achieving consensus in their group. There was a growing distrust between the school administrative team and parents, as well as among parents. The different orientations among School B's three communities helped weaken, or even sever, connections among parents, who divided into factions, causing further distrust between and among school staff and parents and essentially paralyzing the function of the PA.

Most parents of School B seem relatively passive as market-based consumer-choosers. However, some of School B's parents from the middle-class-new community are quite active in responding to their sense of community improvement. They see School B as a part of the community and expect that their involvement in the school can perhaps improve not only the school but the community as well. Nevertheless, divisions exist within School B, its PA, and the wider community. School B's vulnerability is specific to its diverse social space. Faith or pride in the school is not easy to come by. The school suffers from multiple deprivations, yet struggles to improve itself.

## School choice as historical legacy and systems of social relationships

According to Taiwan's Constitution, educational authorities must provide Taiwanese children with equal access to good-quality schools. Regardless of social status or location, students are entitled to a good education. Parental choice of education in the Fundamental Education Act first rested upon the notion of citizenship rights, as stated earlier. When the Ministry of Education integrates parental choice into public schools, it assumes that parents can act on their best interests, and the policy can thus strengthen parental democratic participation in public schools. This policy is viewed not only as providing avenues for exercising citizenship rights, but also as a strategy to improve the schools. However, the implementation of such a policy needs to be situated in a historically embedded choice practice and culturally bounded social network.

In a democratic society, education plays a key role in developing democratic capacities that enable people to become involved in a democratically political process. This was the aim of enacting the Fundamental Education Act in the context of political democratization and educational liberalization of Taiwan during the 1990s. The Act states that educational rights are part of one's civil rights. It protects individuals from unwarranted action by government and ensures people's ability to participate in school affairs without discrimination. Promoting parental involvement gives the impression that granting opportunities for participating in a decision-making process will create a sense of collective choice for bettering schools within communities. However, as the two cases showed, the translation from school-choice strategies to forms of parental participation meant there was a huge difference between two schools' PA operation and human interactions. A long-standing habit of middle-class parents choosing superstar schools also poses a challenge to the Act and its assuming collectivism of the community.

Levin (2007) mentioned that local management is different from parental involvement. He asserted that local management and parental involvement are only sensible if the policy assumes a genuine interest in the community. However, there are two senses of community: a social group in a specific locality, and a group sharing common characteristics and interests. Levin defined "community" in the former sense. In this regard, the current school system, in terms of superstar schools and community schools, shows that the school staff of School A was very proud of their most able and talented students but had a less pronounced sense of being a community school. As School A's Head of Academic Affairs noted, "We are not a community school . . . [But] our school attracts students from at least fifty-four different elementary schools" (Mao, 2015a: 4).

As study showed, involved parents in School A had their own sense of community (sharing the same interests and characteristics) because many of their children had attended the same primary school together. These parents exercised collective strategies for participating in school life, and shared similar economic, cultural, and social capital, giving rise to a network in which parents looked to other parents for help in deciding how to get involved in their school. The objective of this involvement was to strengthen their children's future prospects. Parents with economic, cultural, and social resources could compensate for perceived deficiencies in the school budget, teaching resources, and teaching practice. By congregating together in a PA, these parents could wield even more power over school practices. Whether acting individually or in coordination with one another, parents at School A participated in decision making in the name of the school's development, but by doing so, favored the welfare of their children.

This situation also applied to School B. Parents in School B who were involved as volunteers also created strong links with each other and maintained close contact with the principal and classroom teachers. They drew on resources to protect their children's interests. As the head of the PA pointed out bluntly, parents sought elected membership in the PA in order to strengthen opposition to the school's establishment of the aboriginal program. Furthermore, members of the PA persuaded the principal to apply for a "talented and gifted students" program in the hopes of both attracting better students to the school and producing graduates who would end up attending a top-end high school.

The Act and related new policies have helped formally redraw the boundaries between parents and schools, effectively creating new incentives for parental involvement in school affairs; one aspect of these redrawn boundaries is an interaction between the policies of parental involvement (including choice) and parents' historically fanatical preoccupation with their children's exams. Unlike the educational systems of Western countries, where a neo-liberal sense of parental choice rests on perceptions of school differentiation, the Taiwanese educational system has created a hierarchy of junior high schools, ranked according to graduates' performances on exams. The test-driven admission system favors superstar schools. The new act ensures PAs' roles and promotes general parental involvement in schools. In this regard, some parents have gained ground in mobilizing school resources to ensure that their own child's purportedly "best" educational interests are met.

The public school system promotes parental participation following Taiwanese society's awakening sense of citizenship rights. However, local parents, with their past superstar school complex and less trust in equal quality of public schools, have appropriated this feature of the system in order to insert themselves in school affairs and, thereby, to expand resources that can strengthen their children's performance on entrance exams. As a result, superstar schools do not have to fight for a greater share of the educational market or struggle to be distinctive in finding their market niches. All they have to do is to keep responding to parents' demands for students' high scores on exams. Such a cycle leaves little room for either innovation in school development or diversity in educational programs, both of which are critical if schools are to meet the diverse needs of students in schools in a democratic society.

## Conclusions

From 1987 through the 1990s, deregulation and liberalization as discourses of the educational reform movement strongly intertwined with the national idea of democratization (Mao 1997, 2001; Xue 1996). They resonated in accordance with Taiwan's social leanings toward democratization, which involved a range of initiatives to increase local autonomy and strengthen civil society relative to authoritarian state control. Thus, the reformulation of global ideas of neo-liberalism for educational reform in the Taiwanese context has not necessarily been the same as the corresponding formulations discursively constructed in the contexts of the United States or Britain (e.g., Apple 2000; Whitty 1997). It was a process of hybridization that was under way when the global idea of neo-liberalism for educational reform was adopted in Taiwan during the 1990s. The discourses of these reform efforts were not only tied to the ideas of national democratization and social justice, but also heavily relied on borrowing deregulation and choice strategies from neo-liberal ideas of educational restructuring.

The neo-liberalism of educational reforms in the late 1980s looked like a part of the international circulation of reform ideas but also partially projected particular national interests and political ideologies. The global concept of neo-liberal reform did not follow a direct route, but circulated and then was internalized as a national debate. It is interesting to note that when the crossed boundaries of global ideas were introduced into the local space, they were rearticulated and reformulated into indigenous discourses. Foreign qualities are masked by local qualities, and new elements are generated within this process of global and local framing of reform policy.

The problematic of a global-local mixture of policy enactment indicates a theoretical sensibility in which choice as the global idea of reform, rather than following a direct route, circulates and is then incorporated into existing local practices. The issues here include three dimensions. On the international level, Taiwan's educational reform is contingently moving in the same direction toward neo-liberalism. At the national level, the policy frames parental choice and involvement as civil rights with regard to the domestic context of political democratization. However, at the daily local level, parents who pursue the best interests of their children have already learned to adopt choice strategies, such as either transgressing the catchment area system by changing their home address or buying a piece of real estate in a catchment area attached to their desired school. The three levels are interwoven and interpenetrated. Instead of making a clear-cut distinction between levels of policy borrowing and reformulating, in reality, from the Taiwanese case, we can see a new educational space is created within a particular time frame and contributes to a new unevenness of educational opportunity.

This is what happens to fragmented local realities. Where choosing a school outside the catchment area is not uncommon and the Fundamental Education Act legally ensures parents' right to choose their children's education, the reforms produce a hybrid model of educational choice policy, blending civil rights' pursuit with a true market force (Mao 2008). A civil rights model entails decentralization and giving more authority to schools and parents. A market model sees parents as consumers who choose schools, in which parents act according to their own best interests when choosing a school. The compounding effects of such a new reform policy on local school's practice result in an increasing school disparity. Due to parental school choice and their different capacity and degree of school involvement, differences are created among schools in terms of teachers' morale, curriculum development, and school management.

Taiwan's school choice policy mixes a civil rights' model with a market model. Such a mix consists of two ironies. First, Taiwan's democratization-inspired political impulse to strengthen people's right to education derives largely from neo-liberal ideas of choice, but has been channeled into initiatives that have widened the gaps among public schools. Although the Fundamental Education Act provides moral and legal grounds on which parents can choose schools and participate in school affairs, the very limited selection of types of schools, programs, and school curriculum means that choice is a catchword referring chiefly to public schools whose graduates perform well on exams. The Taiwanese education policy's encouragement of parental participation in educational matters can create further disparity among public schools and facilitate stratification in the public-education system.

The second irony is that in the public-education system, the value of social diversity and equity contradict the value of market competition. Social diversity is a value embedded in the design of public school system of Taiwan. Yet the same system keeps schools such as School B divided while School A, as one of the superstar schools, is far more homogeneous. To what extent can a regular public school be diverse and competitive at the same time?

The Fundamental Education Act provides a legal basis for promoting school choice and parental participation. However, both the continuation of the influential competitive entrance examination and the absence of diverse schooling have resulted in little change to parental school-choice strategies since 1999. The only difference since 1999 is that the law's promotion of parental involvement has consolidated the reputation of superstar schools, helping them acquire significant advantages from the impressive resources of the schools' highly involved parents and from the enrollment of able students. In this sense, it is possible that school choice imbued with parental involvement and participation will lead to heightened social competition and segregation rather than community management and improvement. If there is no public alertness and interventions, "parental school choice and involvement" results in a spontaneous yet unregulated school market and culture, a class-related divided school system that contradicts the Constitution of the Article 159 which states, "People's educational opportunities shall be equal."

The stories of Schools A and B show that there are different spaces of educational politics, in which different social networks and their ways of knowing are in play. Things like class location and resource mobilizations of parental networks constitute uneven spaces of education contributing to differentiation in terms of educational opportunities and social justice. The dissonance between global idea of choice and local practice of parental involvement reveals that, as Seddon (1993) pointed out before, educational reform should be understood in its social ecology through which a matrix of socio-political milieu, habits of local culture, and institutional rules formed a particular context and culture of education.

## Notes

1 This chapter employed two cases data from Mao (2015a) "Between public good and private interest: exploring values of public education in the level of junior high schools as multiple cases study", a report funded under Ministry of Science and Technology and partly revised from an article by C.J. Mao (2015b).
2 According to Article 21 of the Constitution, "People have a right and obligation to national education." Article 159 states, "People's educational opportunities shall be equal."
3 Because junior high graduates must take a very competitive entrance examination to attend senior high schools, parents are anxious about—and pay attention to—which junior high schools have a higher percentage of graduates admitted to prestigious public senior high schools. This percentage becomes a dominant and major indicator of school performance, enabling parents to sort out junior high schools in a region (such as the Taipei metropolitan area). Such a ranking is not an official record, but popular information circulating among parents and the public. Schools having a high percentage of graduates going to prestigious public senior high schools become the most desirable junior high schools. Such highly popular junior high schools are typically termed "superstar" schools.
4 The year when the martial law was abolished. After 1987, it has been called the post-martial era.
5 School A and School B were two of the multiple cases that were studied through the research project "Between public good and private interest: exploring values of public education in the level of junior high schools as multiple cases study," funded by Ministry of Science and Technology in Taiwan.

# References

Anderson-Levitt, K. (Ed.). (2003). *Local meanings, global schooling: Anthropology and world culture*. New York: Palgrave Macmillan.

Apple, M. W. (2000). Between neoliberalism and neoconservatism: Education and conservatism in a global context. In N. C. Burbules and C. A. Torres (Eds.). *Globalization and education: Critical perspectives* (pp. 57–78). New York and London: Routledge.

Arnove, R. F. (2003). Introduction: Framing comparative education—the dialectic of the global and the local. In: R. F. Arnove and C. A. Torres (Eds.). *Comparative education: The dialectic of the global and the local* (2nd ed.) (pp. 1–23). New York: Rowman & Littlefield.

Barker, C. (2000). *Cultural studies: Theory and practice*. London, Thousand Oaks, CA and New Delhi: Sage.

Bhabha, H. (1994). *The location of culture*. New York & London: Routledge.

Burbules, N. C., & Torres, C. A. (2000). Globalization and education: An introduction. In N. C. Burbules and C. A. Torres (Eds.). *Globalization and education: Critical perspectives* (pp. 1–26). New York & London: Routledge.

Chang, B. H. (2000). The study of factors influencing the school choice of parents. In S. W. Yang (Ed.). *School choice of parents* (pp. 95–250). Taipei: Shining Culture Publishing (in Chinese).

Elmore, R. F. (1986). *Choice in public education*. Santa Monica, CA: Rand Corporation.

Ho, M. S. (2009). From Humanism to neo-liberalism: Policy response to the Taiwanese educational reform movement. Paper presented at the Conference for "The Era of Social Movement." Kaohsiung, Taiwan. June 12–13.

Hsiao, H. M. (1991). The changing state-society relation in the ROC. In R. H. Myers (Ed.). *Two societies in opposition* (pp. 127–140). San Francisco, CA: Stanford University Press.

Levin, B. (2007). The lessons of international education reform. In S. Ball, I. Goodson and M. Maguire (Eds.). *Education, globalization and new times* (pp. 47–63). London and New York: Routledge.

Lin, M. H. (2000). The public school choices of parents (Unpublished thesis), National Taiwan University, Taipei (in Chinese).

Mao, C. J. (1997). Constructing a new social identity: Taiwan's curricular reforms of the nineties. *International Journal of Educational Reform, 6*(4), 400–406.

Mao, C. J. (2001). An analysis of curriculum reforms in Taiwan from the perspective of political sociology. *Taiwan Journal of Sociology of Education, 1*(1), 79–102 (in Chinese).

Mao, C. J. (2008). Fashioning curriculum reform as identity politics—Taiwan's curriculum in the new millennium. *International Journal of Educational Development, 28*(5), 585–595.

Mao, C. J. (2015a). Between public good and private interest: Exploring values of public education in the level of junior high schools as multiple cases study. A report funded under the Ministry of Science and Technology in Taiwan.

Mao, C. J. (2015b). Choice as a global language in local practice: A mixed model of school choice in Taiwan. *International Education Journal: Comparative Perspectives, 14*(2), 101–112.

Mao, C. J. and Chang, C. C. (2005). Between the local and the global: Shifting discourses of curriculum reform after the post-martial law era of Taiwan. *Taiwan Journal of Sociology of Education, 5*(1), 39–76 (in Chinese).

Ministry of Education (2017a). *A general review of schools in each level*. Retrieved on June 18, 2017 at http://depart.moe.edu.tw/ED4500/cp.aspx?n=1B58E0B736635285&s=D04 C74553DB60CAD.

Ministry of Education (2017b). *The Fundmental Education Act*. Retrieved on June 18 2017 at http://edu.law.moe.gov.tw/LawContentDetails.aspx?id=FL008468&KeyWordHL=.

Morrow, R. A. and Torres, C. A. (2003). The State, globalization, and educational policy. In N. C. Burbules and C. A. Torres (Eds.). *Globalization and education: Critical perspectives* (pp. 27–56). New York and London: Routledge.

Ozga, J. and Jones, R. (2006). Travelling and embedded policy: The case of knowledge transfer. *Journal of Education Policy*, *21*(1), 1–17.

Ozga, J., Seddon, T. and Popkewitz, T. (Eds.). (2006). *Education research and policy: Steering the knowledge-based economy (World Yearbook of Education 2006)*. New York and London: Routledge.

Ozga, J. and Lingard, R. (2007). Globalisation, education policy and politics. In J. Ozga and R. Lingard (Eds.), *The Routledge Falmer reader in education policy and politics* (pp. 65–82). London: Routledge.

Popkewitz, T. (Ed.) (2000). *Educational knowledge: Changing relationships between the state, civil society, and the educational community*. Albany: State University of New York Press.

Popkewitz, T. (2003). National imaginaries, the indigenous foreigner, and power: Comparative educational research. In J. Schriewer (Ed.). *Discourse formation in comparative education* (pp. 261–294). Frankfurt am Main: Peter Lang.

Rizvi, F. (2004). Theorizing the global convergence of educational restructuring. In S. Lindblad and T. Popkewitz (Eds.). *Educational restructuring: International perspectives on traveling policies* (pp. 21–41). Greenwich, CT: IAP.

Seddon, T. (1993). *Context and beyond: Reframing the theory and practice of education*. London: Falmer.

Spivak, G. (1992). The politics of translation. In M. Barrett and A. Phillip (Eds.). *Destablizing theory: Contemporary feminist debates* (pp. 177–200). Stanford, CA: Stanford University Press.

Steiner-Khamsi, G. (2004). Introduction: Globalization in education—real or imagined? In G. Steiner-Khamsi (Ed.). *The global politics of educational borrowing and lending* (pp. 1–11). New York and London: Teachers College Press.

Wells, A. S. and Crain, R. L. (1992). Do parents choose school quality or school status? A sociological theory of free market education. In P. W. Cookson Jr. (Ed.). *The choice controversy*. Newbury Park, CA: Corwin Press.

Whitty, G. (1997). Creating quasi-markets in education. In M. W. Apple (Ed.). *Review of Research in Education* (Vol. 22) (pp. 3–47). Washington, DC: American Educational Research Association.

Yang, I. J., and Lin C. (1994). *The education reform of Taiwan*. Taipei: Vanguard Publishing (in Chinese).

Young, R. (1995). *Colonial desire: Hybridity in theory, culture and race*. London and New York: Routledge.

Xue, H. H. (1996). *The education reform of Taiwan: The analysis of state and society*. Taipei: Vanguard Publishing (in Chinese).

410 Education Restructuring League (1996). *The Blueprint of civil society: Towards a structural change of social justice*. Taipei: China Times Publishing (in Chinese).

# 6 Producing the institutional timescape

## The case of technical and vocational education in Singapore

*Arwen Raddon*

## Introduction

Technical and Vocational Education (TVE) has an image problem. In Singapore, the national Institute of Technical Education (ITE) is an institutional space that has been central to the transition from colonial rule through independence and on to being an important hub in today's globalised world.[1] Yet, despite decades of effort and investment, institutionally and nationally, to improve the image of TVE, there is a persistent stigma related to TVE and the institution. When local Singaporeans asked where I worked, almost without fail they would follow up with "Hey, do you know what ITE stands for?" Surprisingly to them, given that I'm an *Ang Mo* (the local term for a Westerner), I would respond, "Yes, I know . . . *It's the end.*" This infamous line from a popular local movie refers to the idea that TVE is a dead end.

Although not local, I'm very familiar with the Singaporean context, having conducted extensive research on the national workforce development system, among other things (e.g., World Bank 2012), and worked in different areas of education and training as a long-term resident. So I would extend these exchanges by explaining why I felt that view of ITE is no longer valid. Generally, they would agree that it does *look* externally very different to the past. Taxi drivers often came out with this phrase and some were keen to share their own stories of studying at the institution's predecessor. Usually they talked of early failure, some unruly behaviour and later redemption. But their characterisation of ITE as a dead end feels like an injustice with real consequences for how students and the institution are viewed in society.

So why, after millions of dollars of investment, many changes, and very public success stories in business and industry, does ITE still have an image problem? When ITE students do well and are celebrated for progressing to higher learning, why are parents today still scolding their children at primary and secondary level that they will "go to ITE" if they don't do well? What is it about the time-space of ITE as an educational institution that keeps school pupils debating on public forums whether ITE is really "as bad" as *the end* would suggest (Reddit 2016)?

## Time, space and the making of educational institutions

Time and space are often taken for granted in our lives. They may be perceived as a mechanistic "clock" function in the case of time, with space as a static background (a room, a building, a country). These pre-conscious mindsets have also inflected the sociology of education (Lingard and Thompson 2017; McLeod 2017). When treated as givens, these features make time-space analyses both a challenging and deeply important area to explore further in education.

Although our common understanding of time in the modern world is of mechanical, industrial clock time – that *tick tock* which marks our lives – this wasn't always the case and isn't necessarily the primary experience of time across cultures (Adam 1998; Davies 1990; Lewis 2006). Early human social timings were closely tied to natural and biological cycles, be it the seasons, the sun, or the moon and tides, accepted as a more rhythmic, less precise aspect of human life. Later, sundials were invented and bells were sounded to mark certain parts of the day as they showed on the sundial, based on diurnal patterns of sunrise, midday and sunset. The mechanical pendulum clock was invented in the mid-seventeenth century, but clocks weren't widely available and accessible in Europe until the 1900s, with the expansion of the railway (Landes 2000). The eventual spread of the clock allowed time to be rationalised, bringing about a major shift in some key human functions such as daily routines and habits, how work was regulated and measured for productivity, and how communications and transport functioned (Davies 1990; Landes 2000). Growing prevalence of the mechanical clock enabled local time to be replaced by standard time in the UK in the early 1880s, with the US and Canada following suit. In 1884, Greenwich Mean Time was instituted and, shortly thereafter, international standard time. Clock time, a relatively recent human "invention" within the scientific revolution, swiftly took precedence in society over the natural rhythms of the human body and nature. The ability to record time with great accuracy was central to industrialisation and modernity (Landes 2000). Today, astoundingly, atomic time is only one second out every 100 million years.

Though quite ordinary to us now, the concept of mechanical clock time has deeply shaped, and is shaped by, our social reality. Indeed, each different form of time is productive: these are not just abstract words to describe life, but are involved in producing the very social conditions in which we live. The growth of linear clock time facilitated and shaped emergence of early sociological research such as childhood and youth studies, which in this mindset can only move forward (Popkewitz 2013). The problem, however, is that this linearity remains so strong that there is, for example, "scant scholarly and policy recognition of how the past leaves a mark on the educational present" (McLeod 2017: 14). Indeed, diverse fields of understanding illustrate how time is multiple and deeply complex; for example:

- In clock time, some people are perceived to have more time than others, due to material wealth or alternatively because they are unemployed. In reality, they have quite distinct experiences of that "free" time. For example, this overlooks the "inner time" among those who are uncertain of their future, whether that's an unemployed miner whose industry has disappeared, or concentration camp prisoners whose lives and identities are stripped away: days go on endlessly (and hellishly), yet a week passes by almost without notice (Frankl, 1959/2006: 79).

- Many today feel that most, if not all, of their (clock) time is "owned" by employers, even, ironically, as "zero hours" contracts are on the increase (Inman 2016).
- Studies of communication, work organisation (e.g., deadlines, decision making) and leadership highlight how understandings of time and space differ far more across cultures than we appreciate, easily leading to cultural "collisions" (Lewis 2006).
- We often remain unaware of our natural, cyclical times and biological rhythms to the detriment of our health and mental well-being (Davies, 1990; Koukkari and Sothern 2006).
- Popular stress reduction techniques, such as mindfulness, draw on ancient knowledge and a very different concept of time. Interestingly, mindfulness alters our perception, and thus experience, of time: by meditating we focus on the present moment, rather than contemplating the past or future, both of which can cause anxiety (Kabat-Zinn 2015).
- Quantum physics continues to demonstrate that, as yet, we have neither the measurement tools nor the language to fully describe what time might actually be (e.g., perhaps multiple and parallel options running concurrently) (Musser 2016).

Regardless of our awareness, various forms of time are subtly and not so subtly shaping our lives. We can start to see here how time is produced in multiple ways, productive, and power-laden (Adam 1998), and why it's worth looking deeper at this experience of time in relation to the sociology of education. Our conception of space is often similarly problematic, as will be noted below.

## Applying a time-space lens

In the context of the sociology of education, there has been interest in spatial aspects but time has been rather overlooked as a nuanced object of analysis and a key factor shaping education. Time and space are often considered separately or hierarchically (Lingard and Thompson 2017). This chapter will apply a time-space lens to explore how time and space relations are inherently and often invisibly connected to power and social inequalities with real, material impacts within and on educational institutions. I draw on what I regard as the complementary notions of the "timescape" (Adam 1998) – a concept developed in sociology and environmental studies – and "power-geometry" (Massey 1993) – a concept developed in critical geography. They don't provide specific instructions on how to perform a spatial and temporal analysis, but act instead as a heuristic device and a form of "lens" through which to re-view the institution of education. Thus they serve to decentre our normal assumptions, helping us to understand and thereby potentially re-visualise how time-space shapes social life, power relations and structures in any given environment. Reflexive disruption of commonly held or even subtly embedded views, norms, assumptions, or habits involves an often discomforting but vital process of "interruption", potentially challenging hegemonic truths and facilitating social justice (Faulkner 2012: xiii). Are inequalities being re-produced (despite our best efforts), for example, due to factors that we've overlooked or normalised? Of particular interest in the following discussion is how the time-space of the educational institution both shapes and is shaped by changing socio-economic relations and the persistence of certain perceptions in society, even when the institution has radically altered its physical appearance.

## The timescape

Adam (1998) developed the concept of the "timescape" when exploring environmental concerns and temporal factors. It has since been applied to a number of social, political and cultural topics, such as analysis of: experiences of distance education (Raddon 2004, 2007), the meaning of time in everyday life (Holland 2011), the European Union (Goetz and Meyer-Sahling 2012), and technology and liberal democracy (Hassan 2009). Adam (1998) uses the term "timescape" to do a number of things that include:

- flagging the multiplicity and complexity of times shaping the social world;
- underlining how the social and geographical "scape" runs through and around these times, with time and matter being intertwined; and
- highlighting how time and space are power-laden.

The timescape uses the idea of the landscape as a means of delving deeper into social life. A landscape, whether natural or man-made, has both visible and hidden layers as well as hints about that which came before but is no longer visible (Adam, 1998). Thus, history is imprinted on the present in different ways: some of which are plain to see, some we know from historical records or memories, some we may only be able to guess at or imagine, whilst others are indeed hidden from us as part of wider power relations. Just as when we look at a landscape, how two individuals see any given social situation differs. The landscape can also give us an indication of potential futures that may be used to build scenarios and to walk through where current time-space relations might take us. Central to the timescape concept, then, is that we should be open to multiple and simultaneous possibilities, potentialities and forces shaping social life, which are akin to the outer and inner layers of a landscape.

When working with the timescape concept in the past (Raddon 2004, 2007), I felt time was being foregrounded rather heavily. At that time, Adam (1998, 2008) argued for placing time at centre-stage because writers were arguing for the ascendance of space over time in the modern world. Authors such as Castells (2000) declared we had entered a "timeless time" in the networked world. Two decades on, however, both time and space remain relevant to an analysis of the fundamental organising relations of social life. Indeed, it's impossible to exist beyond time, if we appreciate its multiplicity of meaning and experience (Raddon 2004) and its centrality in the fabric of the universe (Musser 2016). Thus, I also draw here on Massey's (1994) concept of *power-geometry*, which she developed through her critical social geographical research on space, gender and power.

## Power-geometry

I find Massey's "power-geometry" to be a useful complementary concept to further tease out some of the deeper layers of an educational institution's "timescape". In particular, it emphasises the geo-political aspects and productive nature of time-space as a source of differential power and inequality in the social setting.

Key to Massey's (1993, 1994) work is that space is not a blank canvas against which social life occurs, but a productive and evolving *process*. She uses the concept of "power-geometry" (1993) to illustrate the way in which individuals, communities, institutions and locations are differently positioned within networks of spatial relations, creating hierarchies of engagement and differential access, power and control. For example, some people are highly mobile, such as an individual jetting around the world to make business deals, while others are unable to move, such as someone trapped in poverty who barely, if ever, leaves their neighbourhood (Massey 1993). Furthermore, spatial relations are not fixed in one place, but can stretch across times and spaces, thereby extending social and power relations via "spatial reach", such as in the case of multinational corporations or indeed governments (Massey 1994: 158).

Essentially, Massey aims to demonstrate that when some groups exercise their greater control, it creates inequalities and lessens the control of others. A good example of this is globalisation, which is popularly claimed to have led to a compression of time-space and, ultimately, a convergence of access to and experience of the globalised, postmodern world (Harvey 1989). However, due to the power-geometry of time-space, not only are different groups and individuals positioned in different ways in relation "to these flows and inter-connections . . . [but] some people are more in charge of it than others" (Massey 1994: 149). Thus, the impact of globalisation is differential, such as the environmental impact in emerging economies of producing the resources to sustain consumption by industrialised countries.

Indeed, the effect of power-geometry also means that the reaction to spatial reach can be quite different, depending on the position of the affected group. The experience of time-space compression is often described (by Westerners) as creating a new and sad sense of loss, when the familiar town is now filled with an array of "imported" shops (Massey 1993: 59). As Massey notes, however, centuries back, this same sense of the unfamiliar was no doubt felt by locals in countries colonised by Europeans, with their way of life being radically altered by European values, technologies and practices. Moreover, it wasn't just the *appearance* of Europeans on the streets (like the popping up of "foreign" shops), but an often heavy-handed imposition of colonial laws, practices, cultures, social norms and beliefs (Chen 2010). These multiple perspectives on the framing of local-global relations reflect the power-geometry that exists within the "dialectical interaction" between colonisation and decolonisation, creating differentiated local histories and dynamics (Chen 2010: 66). Thus, Western powers regarded colonisation as legitimate, whereas globalisation causes uneasiness, reflecting the changing flow and spatial reach of power relations over time.

These relations are also relevant to understanding increasingly internationalised educational settings. I personally draw on this concept of "power-geometry" as a form of analytical "mapping", where we can visualise how individuals, institutions and nations are placed at different points across space-time. Massey (1994: 66) refers to "a particular constellation of relations, articulated together at a particular locus [or] articulated moments", which map across time-space connections, networks, social relations, flows of power and capital. When layered with the concept of the timescape, we can start to think about how the context under study (e.g., an institution) is shaped by the past/present, the visible/invisible, the local/global, and relations of power-geometry which shape how individuals access and experience that context. This analytic approach recognises the fact that time-space relations are differential and productive: they simultaneously create opportunities, resources *and* inequalities. At the same time, the flow is bi-directional: just as time-space produces social life, so our activities also shape concepts and experiences of time-space.

Turning a time-space lens to the development of Singapore's technical and vocational education system, offers ways of seeing and understanding the emergence of the national Institute of Technical Education and its persistent image problem. The motivation for focusing on this particular case comes from the repeated experience of derisory comments about ITE as 'the end' that arose repeatedly while I was working at ITE.

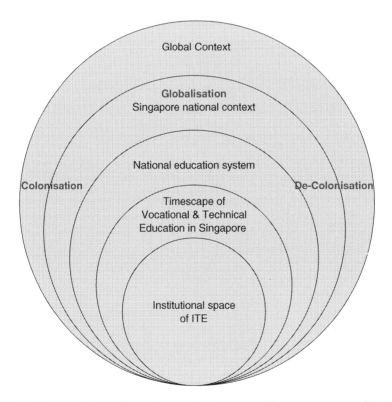

*Figure 6.1* Key layers of the institutional timescape and power-geometry of TVE in Singapore

The following diagram maps out the timescape and power-geometry of my chosen institutional space, and the different layers through which the analysis travels. I've focused primarily on institutional analysis for the purposes of this chapter, though an extended analysis could potentially overlay the constellations of power-geometry of individuals, be they students, teachers, policy makers, or those who are excluded from participation.

The concentric layers in Figure 6.1 illustrate that, in order to understand the layering of this institution's timescape and power-geometry, it's necessary to walk though some historical and political background before homing in on the educational institution itself. I start by taking a broad approach to the national timescape, before focusing in on the specific institution to ask what productive work time-space is doing in this particular context, and the implications for the institution and students.

## Locating Singapore

Singapore's socio-economic history and development is quite unique in a number of ways and the institution examined here is central to that story. So it's important to locate Singapore's timescape and power-geometry as a key layer underpinning the institutional setting.

### Geo-spatial and historical context of Singapore

The Republic of Singapore is a small, relatively "young", urban city-state, located off the tip of Malaysia. Affectionately referred to as the "Red Dot" (i.e., easily covered by a pin on the world map), the population is approximately 5.5 million, 30 per cent of whom are non-residents (i.e., foreign workers). Four official languages reflect the historical, political and spatial imprint of its specific trading and colonial heritage as a one-time entrepôt, comprising: Malay (the national language, as part of the Malay Archipelago), Mandarin, Tamil and English.

After being governed and taken over by various local and European rulers, the island became a British colony in 1819 until 1962, with the exception of the Japanese invasion of 1942–45. Following a period of self-government, Singapore broke away from Britain in 1962 and, after a short time as a state within the Federation of Malaysia, it, somewhat reluctantly, became an independent republic on 9 August 1965. Given its small size and history, establishing a self-sufficient, strong nation was an important task for the Singaporean government, which some commentators considered near impossible (Lee 2000). In reality, its geospatial location was advantageous, being a popular stopping and trading point; even today it has the fifth busiest airport in the world. There were major challenges in the 1960s, such as racial riots, high unemployment and poverty. However, following an economic development strategy in the late 1960s to early 1970s, going against advice from international agencies, Singapore soon experienced rapid economic and social development (Ngiam 2011; Sung 2006; World Bank 2012). Aiming for a quality of life similar to that of Switzerland, Singapore shifted from a developing to advanced economy in a matter of decades (Ngiam 2011; Sung 2006). It now ranks second in the Global Competitiveness Index (2015–16) (GCI 2016), experiencing remarkable GDP growth since the 1960s. Given its strategic location for production, shipping and trade, Singapore is heavily linked into the global economy and TVE was seen to be an important element in its development.

### Singapore's political landscape

The political landscape is another key layer within the broader time-space context of TVE in Singapore. This can probably be said for any system, since changing governments and national policies shape provision (e.g., funding, target groups). However, the longevity of the ruling political party makes this of particular interest.

The People's Action Party (PAP) has led the country since 1959. Singapore has a democratic parliamentary system, based initially on the British political system but with mandatory voting. The PAP has faced little challenge except during the "landmark" General Election of 2011, when the opposition Worker's Party made historical gains (BBC 2011; Tan and Lee 2011). Despite some critiques of the long-run leadership and minimal opposition, the government is widely perceived to offer security and a strong track record. Stability in office has enabled more long-term strategic policy planning than might be possible in nations where the ruling party changes every few years. Interestingly, Caplan asserts that, in electoral terms, Singapore needs to be regarded as a city rather than a country: "In the United States, big city politics is often about as lopsided as Singaporean politics. Democratic mayors have won without interruption since 1931 in Chicago and 1964 in San Francisco" (Caplan 2009).

Indeed, whilst this government stability seems remarkable from a Western perspective, if we take the relations of power-geometry into account, it's worth noting that stability is a core objective for Confucian thought and Asian society (Mauzy and Milne 2002). Moreover, what are labelled as "Asian values" in Singapore often mirror British colonial attitudes from the Victorian era, which were variously admired, absorbed and indeed already practiced by the establishment in Singapore (Mauzy and Milne, 2002: 57). As Chen (2010) notes, the influence of colonial thought isn't necessarily about external imposition by the "Other", but can also be about merging with and amplifying some long-standing local cultural beliefs. When this occurs, marginal local views can grow and allow seemingly external beliefs to take root fairly easily. Moreover, when the influence of such thought becomes habit, it does not simply decline and disappear with the end of colonial rule. This spatial reach through the interplay of colonialisation and decolonisation (Chen 2010) continues to influence TVE today.

It is also important to consider the role of citizens within what has been described as a "symbiotic" relationship between workers, union, government and employers (Sung 2006: 159). A discourse of being "*all in this together*" has built up through the passage of Singapore's prosperous economic and social development. Where the UK government used this same cynically received slogan in 2012 to garner support for government spending cuts (*Guardian* 2012), the Singaporean version represents "win-win". This relation is expressed materially in both rhetoric and realities of very low unemployment (around 2 per cent), and a stable economy with relatively rapid exit from economic downturns, such as the 2008–09 financial crisis. There are also government incentives such as national bonus payments when the economy does well, a spectrum of established government subsidies and union cooperatives to reduce the costs of living, and a strong social housing scheme under the Housing Development Board (HDB) (Sung 2006; World Bank 2012). Nevertheless, the high cost of living and widening gap between rich and poor is a growing concern (Low 2014).

### The role of education in national economic development

It's also important to understand how education is positioned in the national timescape. Prospects for a small nation like Singapore were fairly grave after it broke away from Britain in 1962 and from Malaysia in 1965. The lack of abundant natural resources weighed heavily on politician's minds as they considered how to build their nation. If you ask what helped Singapore move from developing to advanced economy in just three decades (the envy of many newly industrialising nations), a standard response is to point to its solid education and training system. The first leader of independent Singapore, Lee Kuan Yew, emphasised from the outset that citizens (human capital) were Singapore's only natural resource (Lee 2000). This commonly cited and powerful discourse can still be heard, from the current Prime Minister's National Day Rally speeches right down to the ordinary person on the street.

As a result, education and training have always been considered central to Singapore's "Developmental State" approach to nation building (Ashton, Green, James and Sung 1999; World Bank 2012). They remain fundamental in the government's "tactical" response to the requirements and risks of globalisation (Koh 2010: 21). This "developmental model" means the government has taken a strategic and interventionist approach through which the market and key stakeholders are "incentivised" to steer work towards government objectives and realise economic growth and development (Sung and Raddon, 2017). The system is capitalist, but delivered via a government-led approach, as opposed to the neoliberal, market-led approach advocated in Western economies (Johnson, 1999).

This government-led development means the national education system is closely managed. A ministerial-level National Manpower Council (established in 1979) oversees the types of programmes and places available in each stream and level of education (including TVE), based on both present and future national economic needs (World Bank 2012). Within this highly managed national education timescape, it is not just policy and institutions that are being strategically formed and managed, but also individual subjectivities, which are oriented towards the impacts of globalisation within the national timescape and power-geometry: "this social experiment with schooling is seen as a vehicle to incubate, train, transform and reproduce a populace of human capital capable of sustaining Singapore's economy in the years to come" (Koh 2010: 19).

## The timescape of technical and vocational education (TVE) in Singapore

To understand the timescape of TVE today means delving into the layers of time-space historically, politically and in terms of physical and geographical space. During Singapore's times as a British colony, a variety of general educational institutions were established, but TVE was one area that was long felt to be lacking. The timescape of TVE was very visibly marked by time-space relations, replete with "colonial attitudes and prejudices . . . legacy systems and mindsets that became ingrained and difficult to change later, especially regarding education that served the colonial service and not the state's growing needs nor the individual's economic mobility" (Varaprasad 2016: 1–2).

From 1900, various reports were produced on the topic of TVE but with few outcomes, beyond demonstrating the colonial government's lack of commitment to TVE in Singapore (Varaprasad 2016). The colonial government rejected continued calls from local groups for the establishment of TVE schools, claiming there was no evident need, that the "Asiatic parent" was not supportive, and "local boys had an aversion to manual crafts" (Varaprasad 2016: 3–4). By implication, the timescape meant TVE was not in the colonial interest (Varaprasad 2016). The meaning of TVE reveals the "spatial reach" and power-geometry of colonial politics and power at work (Massey 2004).

The first Government Trade School was finally introduced in 1929. Until this point, TVE was provided via night classes for adults and young people. However, there was still no support for including TVE in the general education system. A 1937 report recommended increasing trade schools and incorporating some vocational training within general education in British Malaya as a way to improve employment. Meanwhile, in Singapore the next TVE school, St Joseph's Trade School, was set up by monks from the Catholic Mission in 1938 (not by the government), to train poor and homeless boys. Around the same time, one additional Government Trade School was approved for construction. However, the advent of the Second World War and the Japanese invasion duly halted any expansion (Varaprasad, 2016).

There wasn't a great deal happening in the field of TVE at this time in history. The power-geometry around this timescape meant it was never regarded as a preferred or desirable career pathway, such as in the German context (Deissinger 2004). Instead, TVE was regarded as a low-level pathway for those who truly had no options: destitute young boys were positioned in this particular constellation of power, access and politics. British colonial influence helped shape this view: "The colonial government was cautious and deleterious in taking vocational education initiatives, reflecting perhaps the class attitudes of the home country" (Varaprasad 2016: 8).

Indeed, TVE was equally marginal in Britain. There was a high rate of child labour and little in the way of education for young people and the working classes in the nineteenth century, until the emphasis on basic adult education (no TVE of value) at night schools in the late nineteenth to early twentieth centuries (Deissinger 2004).

Nevertheless, this particular power-geometry meant that these views from the West were "one cultural resource among many others" (Chen 2010: 223). The prevailing view of TVE is likely a result of the *combined* European-Asian context of colonial Singapore. Manual trades have long had a particularly low status within traditional Chinese culture, which linked mental work to the ruling classes, and manual work to the working classes, whose implicit role was to follow behind (Schulte 2003). The colonial administration reported that Asian parents did not want to send their children for manual-work-related studies and the boys were not keen to attend. This negative foundational layer of the TVE timescape has a longevity well beyond the colonial period; it resurfaces continuously in my analysis of the ITE institutional timescape.

When the Japanese surrendered and Singapore was returned to colonial rule in 1945, both the local political scene and attitudes towards TVE were changing. Private education continued to lead the growth of TVE. New schools opened up, including providing craft and housekeeping skills for girls. However, a low perception of TVE persisted and students were performing poorly. For example, in 1951, over half of the small number of students from one school who qualified to sit UK City & Guilds exams failed (Varaprasad 2016). As Singapore's economy began to change, there was increasing pressure from industry for better TVE provision. The colonial government eventually published a number of "milestone" reports in the late 1950s (Varaprasad 2016). The result was the establishment in 1958 of Singapore Polytechnic, with a grand opening by HRH Prince Philip, painting quite a different image to that of TVE for destitute boys! However, whilst tertiary technical education proved popular, and the Polytechnic timescape was modern and attractive, ITE was an institution that emerged to cater to struggling primary and secondary students. It occupied a very different position in this constellation.

In 1959, Singapore became self-governing and the PAP government was voted into office. The TVE timescape changed rapidly, as the power-geometry shifted towards an education system designed to meet *local* rather than colonial needs. Where TVE had been of little interest to the colonial government, for the new nation it was positioned (and proved correctly) to be key in supporting the new government's strategy. The result was industrialisation, attention to high levels of unemployment, and a reduction in reliance on supplying goods and labour to British military bases (World Bank 2012). TVE swiftly became a steady source of skilled workers, enabling the newly independent nation to strategically attract multi national companies (World Bank 2012). At the same time, education generally was emerging as a means of creating "new subjectivities" among citizens (Koh 2010: 27). In TVE, that meant students were prepared to build the new nation through their manual and technical efforts (Koh 2010).

## The impact of institutional space on the technical education timescape: from "the end" to new beginnings

Out of this timescape for TVE, the national Institute for Technical Education would emerge as the key institutional space. Despite establishment of a number of TVE secondary schools, by the end of the 1960s, the majority of primary and secondary school leavers were still entering the academic stream. Since the government required higher numbers to be prepared for technical trades, measures were taken to raise the profile of TVE and reshape the mindset of students and parents, including requiring exposure to technical skills in general curriculum hours, and building high-profile industry partnerships to deliver training (Law 2015). Nevertheless, government reviews in 1976 and 1978 found many short-comings. The Vocational and Industrial Training Board (VITB) was formed in 1979, providing training and national, as opposed to UK, certification for TVE for primary and secondary leavers and adult learners. This is the first formation of what would later become the Institute of Technical Education (ITE).

The VITB was able to train sufficient numbers of students to fulfil industry needs, but the image of the institution remained poor in the public's eyes (Law 2015). Unlike those entering VITB after completing secondary level, students who entered direct from primary school (being ineligible to proceed to second-ary school based on their Primary School Leaving Examination [PSLE] results), had just a 40 per cent success rate, probably due to the low level of literacy and numeracy (Varaprasad 2016). At this time, teaching staff came with industry skills but were "lowly qualified professionally" and it would be some time before higher levels of training were required for TVE teachers (Law 2015: 67).

Overall, the general public perception was that VITB was a less than desirable option. At this time, progression from VITB to Polytechnic was far from the norm, with TVE preparing young people for blue-collar work and direct entry to industry (Varaprasad 2016). Of particular interest to a time-space analysis, com-pounding and likely sustaining TVE's image was the physical, spatial setting of the institution. Early VITB institutions were housed in ageing, repurposed buildings, such as former school, army and government buildings. The physical timescape was not built-for-purpose or attractive. Even today, older staff and past students recall the heat and dust they experienced in workshops, which had basic facilities and fans at best.

After another government review in 1992 recognised that the TVE system was sorely in need of upgrading, VITB was subject to sweeping reforms. The mile-stone change for the institution and for TVE was that it became a post-secondary institution, enabled by an important parallel change in the general education sys-tem whereby students would complete a minimum of ten years' general primary and secondary schooling before they could move on (i.e., secondary pathways were made available for those who failed the PSLE). This repositioned not just the education provided but the institution itself within the national education framework and, notably, the national psyche. Indeed, a key objective was to shift away from the poor perceptions of TVE and the institution as a last-choice for primary dropouts. Instead, the goal was to be a viable post-secondary pathway for students who were less academically inclined, but gifted in more practical skills (Law 2015). Importantly, to mark these changes, new buildings and upgrad-ing of older premises were planned, with ten small campuses to be located near high-density population areas. This substantially altered the physical landscape of the institution. Moreover, the institution's name was changed to the Institute of Technical Education (ITE), recognised internally as a highly tactical rebranding to shift away from being "the last place of resort for those who had failed in schools" (Law 2015: 122).

The major policy lesson is that, after decades, and numerous student cohorts, government recognised the problem of status: positioning TVE "at the bottom of the ladder . . . is highly demotivating for students as well as damaging for the employers who have to employ them" (Varaprasad 2016: 166). Education policy, and how TVE sat in the power-geometry of society, had a material impact on many students' lives. Despite numerous reforms, sixty years after the early TVE institutions were opened for those with few options in life, that foundational layer of the timescape and its unequal power-geometry meant inequality and lack of opportunity were still fundamentally visible in the modern-day institutional space-time and had pervasive effects on the individuals who inhabited TVE. That past and this present are not linear, but deeply connected and existing simultaneously (Adam 1998; Davies 1990; McLeod 2017).

The non-linear flow of time-space relations produces an institutional timescape where the effects of history have not disappeared today, but persist as both an experienced spatial reach and temporal layer. Thus despite changes, the image of the institutional space remained an ongoing niggling issue for ITE. The upgraded facilities of the 1990s still lacked something compared to the large, attractive and well-catered facilities of the growing number of Polytechnics, which were partly able to leverage on their industry partnerships to provide advanced facilities. Equally, the underlying historical layers persisted, including perceptions of manual labour as low-value and low-class, and technical studies being for what are locally referred to as CMIs or "cannot make it" types. These factors were both deeply buried and yet just beneath the surface of the institutional timescape, (re)producing negative social perceptions of ITE in the 1990s to 2000s, as well as reflecting real social inequalities and power-geometry. So ITE still caters to the lowest performing (in academic terms) 25 per cent of the secondary school cohort and many of its students come from lower socio-economic groups. A survey showed that 74 per cent of the 1998 cohort came from lower-income families (Law 2015).

## Remaking educational cultures

Despite all of the strategic and policy work, the image of ITE took a blow in 2002, when in the movie *I Not Stupid* was released. Respected local film-maker Jack Neo portrayed a young boy and his friends struggling with their studies and scolded for being placed in the lower stream. One character worries bitterly that if the boy can't do well in his exams, he will surely end up at ITE, standing for "*it's the end*". In other words, his future will be hopeless. There is humour in Singaporeans' love of abbreviations and acronyms, be that for national institutions, swear words, insults, or popular everyday phrases (Tan 2014). But in the timescape of both TVE and ITE as an institution, this damning tagline summed up the past and its material experience of deep disappointment amongst those students and parents who felt let down by the education system. It expressed the hidden power relations and inequalities that played out through the TVE timescape. In the movie, there is also the inference that TVE is for "Ah Bengs and Ah Sengs". This Singlish (Singaporean English) slang comes from Hokkien, meaning uncouth individuals, but having a deeper connotation of referring to the lower classes, again echoing earlier Chinese and colonial views on TVE and manual labour.

Neo deliberately set out to highlight the heavy social pressure on children and the very real social stigma experienced by those in lower educational, particularly technical, streams. Far from being a mere passing joke, this film is credited with sparking parliamentary debate about the education system and prompting subsequent reforms to provide more opportunities for less academically inclined students (Tan 2008). But the catchphrase seems to have become just as much a part of local culture as the institution itself.

Reforms to education streams (though they remain) and greater opportunities for progression to tertiary education from the technical pathway have substantially improved the image of ITE in the last decade. In addition to major efforts on institutional marketing campaigns, there has been heavy government investment and significant changes to teacher professionalisation through new work systems and quality measures (Law 2015). As well as work on the mental space of the institution, part of the mindset change is also linked to radical improvements in the physical space. In the last decade, ITE moved from the various dispersed colleges and separate HQ, to three large, purpose-built "mega campuses" located in the east, west and centre of Singapore. Space is not merely a backdrop to social life: physical space and architecture can be significant in shaping the human psyche, impacting how individuals feel and behave, and on the sense of community and level of pro-social behaviour. Buildings incorporating attractive outdoor spaces, recreation areas and natural settings, for example, can enhance well-being and social engagement (Heerwagen 2008). The mindset towards TVE and the radical improvement of the built environment of this institutional timescape is likely to have had a positive effect on student behaviour and self-esteem (Roberts and Russell 2002).

Many of the classrooms still look rather standard (whiteboard at the front, individual desks facing the board), but the "mega-campuses" each incorporate attractive designs and innovative use of space. Workshops are bright and well laid-out, with good ventilation and air conditioning (not always the case in the industries students enter), but it is the external areas that are notably very different to the past premises. Large, modern campuses have vertical gardens, running water features, attractive courtyards with outdoor seating and palm trees, open-air performance spaces, shopping and banking facilities, built-in sports and recreation venues such as an Olympic-size, open-air swimming pool, climbing wall, running tracks, large conference-style facilities, a small hotel and upmarket restaurants where hospitality students can hone their skills with real-life guests and real aircraft housed outside the aerospace department.

The facilities rested on an investment of S$800 million (GB£500 million or US$630 million) (Wee, 2013). But this funding also reflected the government's serious intent and the institutional commitment to upgrade TVE. Citizens and the press now often equate ITE and the Polytechnics, which represents a significant change in view. As more people visit the facilities, the national mindset is slowly shifting. TVE is being recognised as a legitimate and positive pathway for young people, instead of an early dead end. Past alumni often remark on the astonishing difference between the current facilities compared to their times in the 1970s to

1990s, when going to VITB and later ITE was considered shameful and they were written off as the "naughty kids" and dropouts.

A newspaper article marking ITE's twenty-first birthday and "coming of age" expressed similar sentiments. It noted that the "schools are a far cry from the hand-me-down premises that ITE used to occupy. Alumni are amazed at the transformation," seeing them more like universities and worth attending. Indeed, current students appear more inclined to feel a "sense of pride" (Varaprasad 2016). Moreover, around 20 per cent of ITE students go on to a Polytechnic today, with others studying with private and overseas institutions. That the institutional space now *looks* spatially a lot like a Polytechnic perhaps narrows the mental and social gap between the institutions. The gradual shift away from classed perceptions of ITE, as the school for "Ah Bengs and Ah Sengs", is doubtless helped along by the new institutional space.

The Prime Minister's televised National Day Rally speech has been hosted at ITE several times, with the impressive new facilities becoming a source of national pride. Delegations from newly industrialising nations often visit ITE to learn from the approach and marvel at the kind of facilities that now make up Singapore's TVE timescape, now held up as world class (Ganapathy 2016; Law 2015; Ng 2016; Spykerman 2015; Varaprasad 2016). A key lesson for overseas policy makers from this timescape is that a desirable space, along with good funding and quality curriculum and certification, is an important means of legitimising TVE as a viable option for young people (Law 2015; Varaprasad 2016).

Taking a simple linear approach to the history of the institution might lead us to conclude that times have changed, things have progressed as they do (time moves forward) and we're at a happy ending. However, our time-space lens tells us something different to the linear temporal story. If we peel back the layers of the timescape to consider the multiplicity of times and the power-geometry, we can instead conclude that today's layer doesn't supersede, but instead overlays those deep, foundational layers which *continue* – since the past exists in the present – to mark the timescape mentally and materially as "the end". People still ask, "do you know what that stands for?" because more recent layers of time-space cannot simply supplant ingrained cultural depth, particularly given material impacts and connections to social power and inequality. Instead, the additional layer to this timescape provides an opportunity to *decentre* the other layers, enabling the institutional space to produce and reproduce alternative outcomes and constellations for students and for TVE. These interventions provide a chance to re-imagine TVE as a positive educational opportunity.

## Conclusions

Historicising institutions as a timescape reveals education as an uneven time-space. It is produced by and produces a combination of temporal and spatial layers, and simultaneously shifting constellations of power. Mapping these timescapes helps to pinpoint some of the underlying and pervasive socio-economic relations that continue to produce educational institutions today, often in ways that are beyond our immediate level of awareness or concern. Clearly, the past history of an educational institution is not something which is easily replaced and progressed from. For the space is far more than a mere physical building that houses educational activities, even if we generally take the institutional environment for granted.

A time-space lens starts to map out how space and time are integral elements of everyday activities, which affect future outcomes for students. This approach is no less relevant to general and tertiary education, since similar issues are likely to arise between different types of tertiary institution (i.e., "new and old", red brick, etc.), and schools (e.g., failing schools, revamped schools, schools within poorer versus more prosperous communities). It can be challenging to move away from our commonplace understandings of time as mechanical clock time and space as a disinterested backdrop to the social, particularly as these time-space lenses are heuristic devices requiring a change of mindset and philosophical understanding, rather than providing functional steps of analysis. Historical studies and the past in education has not been a major concern in recent sociology of education (McLeod 2017). Nevertheless, decentring everyday understandings of time-space in our analyses of educational spaces can create an openness to nuances of time-space relations, and reveal productive rather than reactive forces. In practice, it means researchers seek to uncover how time-space operates around education and is involved in creating (constituting) the everyday experiences of those learning and working within any given educational institution. These constellations also have effects that shape future outcomes and social trajectories beyond their time in that institution.

Time-space analysis offers ways of thinking about educational change and how historic features of education might be de-linked. In the case of TVE in Singapore, even a radical change in the institutional space could not remove the past, but it could slowly start to reshape the national psyche. Spatial redesign began the move towards acceptance of TVE as a positive educational option rather than a negative dead-end destination. Yet at the same time, this is a two-way process: time-space shapes social relations, but social relations also shape concepts and experiences of time-space. This raises further questions about how the changing nature of education also re-shapes the multiple meanings of time-space – for example, how digital technologies are impacting on the lived experience and power-geometries of time-space in educational institutions. As changes occur in how we learn, teach or carry out administrative and management functions, so too do conceptions of and differential access to time-space.

## From the end to the beginning – a poem[2]

> *A drop out kid, a "cannot make it"*
> *So I'm a failure, me*
> *School time dragged, studying sucked*
> *My only chance was ITE.*
> *Scolded, teased: The End, they said*
> *But here it's not like school*
> *I'm learning about cinematography*
> *Now, I think it's pretty cool!*

# Notes

1 The author worked at ITE from 2014 to 2016, however, any reference to the institution in this chapter is based on publicly available information.
2 This poem is written based on various stories I heard from students and is not related to any specific person.

# References

Adam, B. (1998). *Timescapes of modernity: The environment and invisible hazards*. London: Routledge.

Adam, B. (2008) Of timescapes, futurescapes and timeprints, Lüneburg Talk Web, 17 June 2008, Lüneburg: Lüneburg University.

Ashton, D. N., Green, F. J., James, D. and Sung J. (1999). *Education and training for development in East Asia: The political economy of skill formation in newly industrialised economies*. London: Routledge.

BBC (2011). Singapore opposition make "landmark" election gains (May 9). *BBC Asia*. Retrieved from: www.bbc.co.uk/news/world-asia-pacific-13313695.

Caplan, B. (2009). Singaporean Political Economy: Two Paradoxes, *Ethos*, 6. Retrieved September 2010 from: www.cscollege.gov.sg/Knowledge/Ethos/Issue%206%20Jul%20 2009/Pages/Singapores-Political-Economy-Two-Paradoxes.aspx.

Castells, M. (2000). *The rise of the network society*. Oxford: Blackwell.

Chen, K.-H. (2010). *Asia as method: Towards deimperialization*. Durham, NC: Duke University Press.

Davies, K. (1990). *Women, time and the weaving of the strands of everyday life*. Aldershot: Avebury.

Deissinger, T. (2004). Apprenticeship systems in England and Germany: Decline and survival, pp. 28–45 in CEDEFOP (2004) *Towards a history of vocational education and training (VET) in Europe in a comparative perspective, Proceedings of the first international conference October 2002, Florence, Volume I The rise of national VET systems in a comparative perspective*, Cedefop Panorama series; 103 Luxembourg: Office for Official Publications of the European Communities.

Faulkner, J. (Ed.) (2012). *Disrupting pedagogies in the knowledge society: Countering conservative norms with creative approaches*. Hershey, PA: Information Science Reference.

Frankl, V. (1959/ 2006). *Man's search for meaning*. Boston, MA: Beacon Press.

Ganapathy, N. (2016, October 3). Training centre in Rajasthan: A collaboration with Singapore. *Straits Times*. Retrieved from: www.straitstimes.com/asia/south-asia/training-centre-in-rajasthan-a-collaboration-with-singapore.

GCI (2016). Global Competitiveness Index. Retrieved November 2016 from: http://reports. weforum.org/global-competitiveness-report-2015-2016/competitiveness-rankings/.

Goetz, K. H. and Meyer-Sahling, J.-H. (Eds.). (2012). *The EU timescape*, Journal of European Public Policy Series. Abingdon, Routledge.

Guardian (2012, March 24). Osborne's budget: All in it together? Or are we ever more divided as cuts bite. *The Guardian*, Retrieved from: www.guardian.co.uk/uk/2012/ mar/24/george-osborne-budget-divisive-inequality.

Harvey, D. (1989). *The condition of post-modernity: An enquiry into the origins of cultural change*. Oxford: Blackwell.

Hassan, R. (2009). Crisis time: Networks, acceleration and politics within late capitalism. Retrieved December 2016 from: www.ctheory.net/articles.aspx?id=618.

Heerwagen, J. (2008). Psychosocial value of space. Retrieved December 2016 from: www.wbdg.org/resources/psychspace_value.php.

Holland, J. (2011). Timescapes: Living a qualitative longitudinal study. *Forum Qualitative Sozialforschung / Forum: Qualitative Social Research, 12*(3). Retrieved December 2016 from: www.qualitative-research.net/index.php/fqs/article/view/1729.

Inman, P. (2016, September 8). More than 900,000 UK workers now on zero-hours contracts. *The Guardian*, Retrieved from: www.theguardian.com/uk-news/2016/sep/08/uk-workers-zero-hours-contracts-rise-tuc.

Johnson, C. (1999). The developmental state: Odyssey of a concept. In M. Woo-Cummings, (Ed.). *The developmental state* (pp 32–60). Ithaca, NY: Cornell University Press.

Kabat-Zinn, J. (2015). Meditation: It's not what you think, *Mindfulness*, 6, 395.

Koh, A. (2010). *Tactical globalization: Learning from the Singapore experiment*. Bern: Peter Lang.

Koukkari, W. L. and Sothern, R. B. (2006). *Introducing biological rhythms – A primer on the temporal organization of life, with implications for health, society, reproduction and the natural environment*. New York: Springer.

Landes, D. S. (2000). *Revolution in time: Clocks and the making of the modern world*. Cambridge, MA: Belknap Press of Harvard University Press.

Law, S. S. (2015). *A breakthrough in vocational and technical education: The Singapore story*. Singapore: World Scientific Publishing.

Lee, K. Y. (2000). *From third world to first. The Singapore story: 1965–2000, Memoirs of Lee Kuan Yew*. Singapore: The Straits Times Press.

Lewis, R. D. (2006). *When cultures collide: Leading across cultures* (2nd Ed.). Boston, MA and London: Nicholas Brealey International.

Lingard, B. and Thompson, G. (2017). Doing time in the sociology of education. *British Journal of Sociology of Education, 38*(1), 1–12.

Low, D. (2014). The four myths of inequality in Singapore. In D. Low and S. Vadaketh (Eds.). *Hard choices: Challenging the Singapore consensus* (pp. 17–30). Singapore: National University of Singapore Press.

Massey, D. (1993). Power-geometry and a progressive sense of place. In J. Bird, B. Curtis, T. Putnam, G. Robertson and L. Tickner (Eds.). *Mapping the futures: Local cultures, global change* (pp. 59–69). London and New York: Routledge.

Massey, D. (1994). *Space, place and gender*. Cambridge: Polity Press.

Massey, D. (2004). Geographies of responsibility, *Geografiska Annaler, Series B: Human Geography, 86*(1), 5–18.

Mauzy, D. K., and Milne, R. S. (2002). *Singapore politics under the People's Action Party*. London and New York: Routledge.

McLeod, J. (2017). Marking time, making methods: Temporality and untimely dilemmas in the sociology of youth and educational change. *British Journal of Sociology of Education*, 38(1), 13–25.

Musser, G. (2016, January 19). Quantum weirdness now a matter of time, *Quanta Magazine*, Retrieved from: www.quantamagazine.org/20160119-time-entanglement/.

Ng, K. (2016, October 24). 2,000 Indians vie for 400 places at skills centre opened with Singapore's help. *Today Online*. Retrieved from: www.todayonline.com/singapore/more-nations-taking-leaf-out-spores-vocational-training-books.

Ngiam, T. D. (2011). *Dynamics of the Singapore success story: Insights by Ngiam Tong Dow* (introduced and edited by Dr Zhang Zhibin). Singapore: Cengage Learning.

Popkewitz, T. (2013). The sociology of education as the history of the present: Fabrication, difference and abjection. *Discourse: Studies in the Cultural Politics of Education, 34*(3), 439–456.

Raddon, A. (2004). Feminist perspectives on times and spaces in distance learning (Unpublished PhD thesis). University of Warwick: Coventry.

Raddon, A. (2007). Timescapes of flexibility and insecurity: Exploring the context of distance learners. *Time & Society*, *16*(1), 61–82.

Reddit (2016, January 12). Is ITE as bad as everyone makes it out to be? [Online discussion thread]. Retrieved from: www.reddit.com/r/singapore/comments/40oy4o/is_ite_as_bad_as_everyone_makes_it_out_to_be/.

Roberts, C. and Russell, J. (2002). *Angles on environmental psychology*. Cheltenham: Nelson Thornes Ltd.

Schulte, B. (2003). Social hierarchy and group solidarity: The meanings of work and vocation/profession in the Chinese context and their implications for vocational education. In Bray, M. (Ed.) *Comparative education: Continuing traditions, new challenges, and new paradigms* (pp. 213–239). Dordrecht: Kluwer Academic Publishers.

Spykerman, K. (2015, November 24). Indian PM Modi tours ITE College Central during Singapore visit. Retrieved from: www.channelnewsasia.com/news/singapore/indian-pm-modi-tours-ite/2289422.html.

Sung, J. (2006). *Explaining the economic success of Singapore: The developmental worker as the missing link*. Cheltenham: Edward Elgar Publishing.

Sung, J. and Raddon, A. (2017). Skills demands in the Asian Developmental States. In J. Buchanan, D. Finegold, K. Mayhew and C. Warhurst (Eds.). *Oxford handbook of skills and training*. Oxford: Oxford University Press.

Tan, K. P. (2008). *Cinema and television in Singapore: Resistance in one dimension*. Leiden and Boston, MA: Brill.

Tan, K. Y. L. and Lee, T. (2011). *Voting in change: Politics of Singapore's 2011 general election*. Singapore: Ethos Books.

Tan, X. Q. (2014, November 14). 10 acronyms only S'poreans can come up with, *Mothership. sg*, Retrieved from: http://mothership.sg/2014/11/10-acronyms-only-sporeans-can-come-up-with/.

Varaprasad, N. (2016). *50 years of technical education in Singapore: How to build a world class system*. Singapore: World Scientific Publishing.

Wee, C. F. (2013, April 25). ITE comes of age as it celebrates its 21st anniversary. *Straits Times*. Retrieved from: www.straitstimes.com/singapore/ite-comes-of-age-as-it-celebrates-its-21st-anniversary.

World Bank. (2012). *SABER workforce development country report: Singapore 2012*. Washington DC: Author. Retrieved December 2016 from: http://documents.worldbank.org/curated/en/101071468299971244/SABER-workforce-development-country-report-Singapore-2012.

# 7 Space-times of innovation

## Collaborative, cross-disciplinary work and learning

*Lorraine White-Hancock*

Governments around the globe increasingly acknowledge innovation as essential to economic prosperity and well-being. Much government support for innovation in Australia has focused on collaboration within or between STEM fields (science, technology, engineering and mathematics) and business. Yet innovation and collaborative work and learning that produces innovation are not restricted to STEM fields, they are also evident in the arts. In recent times of rapid change, new spaces of innovation involving collaborative work between the arts and science are emerging. These developments raise questions about what supports collaborative cross-disciplinary work and learning to generate innovation in these "borderland" art-science spaces as traditional, temporally embedded disciplinary boundaries are disturbed.

I use the concept of "transgression" to understand the workplaces and people's ways of learning through working that produce innovation. I draw on Donna Haraway's discussion of transgression to understand innovation where transgressive practices disrupt established knowledges, moving ways of thinking and doing in new directions. This conceptual framework suggests innovation is a particular kind of transgressive learning through working that is contingent on the organisation and culture of workplaces and how authority relations permit or regulate transgressive practices.

This chapter reports on one case study of a *Synapse* artist-in-residence project that supported an artist to work in collaboration with scientists in their organisation as a means of encouraging innovation. Analysis of interview data shows how the effects of the cross-disciplinary collaboration disturbed the taken-for-granted understandings of scientists and created a "space for innovation", where the artist challenged workplace, disciplinary, and organisational orders in ways that materialised as innovations.

I argue that innovation materialises transgression which is embedded in cross-disciplinary borderland workplaces. Learning through working together across diverse disciplinary boundaries becomes transgressive when prevailing cultural and social conventions and boundaries are disturbed and set novel processes in train. In the moment of transgression, past understandings shift and possibilities for a new future are set in motion so space-time boundaries shift. Innovation only materialises in collaborative, cross-boundary spaces when workplace conditions combine with a culture-order that permits rule breaking. These materialisations are not visible in the moment of innovation, but become evident through the unfolding effects of transgression framed by the particular space-time of innovation.

## Arts practice and innovation

Artist Chris Henschke was awarded a *Synapse* Residency Program grant, supported by the Australian Network for Art and Technology (ANAT)[1] to work on a project with scientists, particularly Dr Mark Boland, Chief Scientist, at Australian Synchrotron (Melbourne, Victoria, Australia). This facility houses a third-generation large hadron collider (particle accelerator). This machine accelerates electrons (through space) at almost the speed of light (time). Light created as the electrons are deflected through magnetic fields is channelled down "beam lines" to be used for research at experimental workstations (Australian Synchrotron, 2013).[2] The following excerpt from an interview with Henschke reveals his approach to understanding the nature of synchrotron science and the particle accelerator:

> In terms of Einstein-Rosen bridges[3] and sort of pushing the Ricci tensor[4] and actually curving, bending the space/time dimension as they do in the machine, to get my head around that was, it still is really difficult . . . but I did lots of experiments trying to visualise that very thing . . . Talking about space and architecture, I'm trying to imagine it from the electron's perspective.
>
> (White-Hancock, 2017: 143)

In the interview, Henschke explained his exhilaration at eventually being allowed access inside the particle accelerator. He had to be fully gowned-up to protect himself from intense levels of radiation. He knew how dangerous this activity was, but Henschke happily took the risk. The artist pointed out that few people, let alone artists, ever got a chance to experience the inside of a synchrotron, and it was this experience that led and inspired his work as artist. In the spirit of the pioneer, Henschke went where few artists had gone before. It was the artist's direct experience of this space as a frontier zone which he believed was groundbreaking that prompted him to cross boundaries. His collaborative work meant being there, inside the machine, which enabled him to gain a new perspective on the space. This was a perspective that was different to that of the scientists. For Henschke, the space and the electrons were far more than sources of data for scientific experiments. Imagining the inside of the synchrotron from the electron's perspective seemed to capture the "life-force" of the machine. In 2010, this artist made a short film, *Lightcurve-fraction,*[5] giving visual form to the "body" of electrons that race through the space, making the invisible, visible.

*Lightbridge* was the name of Henschke and Boland's *Synapse* project. It suggests a phenomenon (light) that links different environments or bridges boundaries. As the Chief Executive Officer of ANAT explained in a phone conversation, one reason the project was seen to be innovative was because it was rare for an artist to work in this kind of physics environment. According to Boland, the concept of the *Lightbridge* project was both innovative and transgressive because it pushed the boundaries of what was permissible in the organization and the scientific community in terms of access to data. Boland explained "how closely guarded data is . . . that's just solid gold. So, you don't just give that [data] away. [That control of data is] a kind of a boundary that scientists wouldn't cross" (White-Hancock, 2017: 172). Data sharing beyond the field was a sensitive area for the collaborators in terms of dealing with Synchrotron management. The artist, Henschke, was initially forbidden access to the machine because a senior manager found the idea unacceptable; it transgressed accepted practices and protocols of who should gain entry.

As this commentary suggests, innovations are practices, material artefacts or ways of using artefacts that are considered novel relative to established empirical and normative practices and conventions in particular contexts. The intellectual-practical work of an artist uses techniques, skills, available knowledges and imagination to use and make artefacts.

This idea of "transgression" is more than the perception that something is different. Rather, the concept recognises the encounter with the artefact or new practice as a particular moment defined by space, time, knowledge practices and relationships (Haraway 2008). The encounter with the artefact and its ripple of new practice produces an experience and affective response to difference; the response rubs up against norms and conventions, which are anchored by patterns of social organisation and established habits of mind. In this way, the innovation has effects that disturb social and cultural boundaries that order knowledge and authority. I understand "innovation" in ways that reference the arts context and see innovativeness in terms of transgressive effects. From this perspective, I define innovation as an effect of work and learning through workplaces where the context permits the transgression of existing empirical and normative practices and boundaries.

## Boundaries, boundary crossing and transgression

The notion of "boundaries" has been the focus of much research as a way of understanding differences between social spaces. Well-established sociological traditions focus on boundaries that become fixed and maintain power structures. For example, Durkheim (1965) considered the division of labour and boundaries between the sacred and secular aspects of everyday life. Marx (1948) examined class and labour boundaries, while Weber (1978) considered ethnic and status group boundaries. Discursive boundaries are means of controlling "subjugated knowledges", by disengaging history or local knowledge from the knowledge hierarchy of science (Foucault 1973). The persistence of boundaries helps to account for: collective identities; inequalities of class, ethnicity, and gender; professional demarcations based on specialist knowledge and claims about science; and the social organisation of communities, national identities and spatial boundaries (Lamont and Molnár 2002: 168). In these contexts, boundary work makes space, territories and institutions, but also depends on continuous maintenance, and is disrupted by boundary-crossing and things that shift between spaces.

Boundary-crossing and "in-between" spaces where shifts occur have been the subject of much research interest since the 2000s. Sassen (2007) argues that the global "inhabits" nation states and organisations, which offers a perspective that contrasts with theories of local-global duality or other binaries. Places where the global "touches down" on the local are considered as "frontier zones" or "liminal" spaces (Sassen 2007). They are spaces that take the form of borderlands, such as cities and workplaces, where "continuity and change could be observed most intensely" (Dürrschmidt and Taylor 2007: vii). Dürrschmidt and Taylor (2007) investigate liminal spaces or "hotspots of transition" within global cities through studies of Indian call centres. Their research reveals patterns of collective resistance to changes in the workplace. This resistance was brought about by the tension between (local) knowledges, histories and identities of workers, organisations and cultures, and global discourses of production, development and management supported by governments and corporations. It is in such liminal spaces or boundary zones that evidence of resistance to change, transgression and innovation is most likely to be found. The boundaries create the space for learning, action and transgression.

In contrast to research that presumes fixed boundaries, feminist and other post-structural research traditions foreground boundaries that are fluid, create permeable surfaces and enable transgression (Bowker and Star 1999; Haraway 2008). The idea of "transgression" is associated with movement across boundaries (Haraway 2008; hooks 1994). This movement becomes visible as transgression becomes visible, relative to particular social norms and identities. Foucault (1973) considers transgression in terms of power-knowledge relations that are adhered to or rejected as subjected identities resist or challenge established institutional regimes, traditions, systems and "truths". Challenges generally come from "foreign elements", interventions from outsiders, "others" who are "different" (Foucault 1973: 51). The "order of things" is disturbed when boundaries are crossed.

Transgression is identified as a positive action that is crucial to evolution (Haraway 2008). Symbiotic boundary-crossing processes bring about change in evolutionary development (Haraway 2008). Recognising the permeability of boundaries means boundaries are not always sharply delineated. Then it becomes difficult to know where one entity starts and another ends; the boundary becomes visible as a boundary zone or "borderland". This fluid notion of boundaries challenges the concept of "I" as a human being that is completely separate from other life forms, and also transgresses long-established "truths" about "humanity":

> I love the fact that human genomes can be found in only about 10 percent of all the cells that occupy the mundane space I call my body; the other 90 percent of the cells are filled with the genomes of bacteria, fungi, protists, and such, some of which play in a symphony necessary to my being alive at all.
>
> (Haraway 2008: 3–4).

The "transgression of sacred boundaries" in evolutionary processes troubles the idea of "human" and how humans connect to bounded spaces (Haraway 1997: 61).

This is a central theme in Haraway's extensive writing from the time of her seminal essay, "Manifesto for cyborgs: Science, technology, and socialist feminism in the 1980s" (1985). The cyborg transgresses boundaries between human and machine, the natural world and the world of science and technology. "Cyborg" describes alternative forms of political and social identity that do not conform to conventional models of identification, which rest on the familiar historical ordering of social spaces. Using "cyborg" as metaphor is a way of questioning prevailing categorisations and classifications of gender or race.

The cyborg world is about conceptualising things as "hybrid" or "material-semiotic", which challenges the theme of "purity of type". It is where "people are not afraid of their joint kinship with animals and machines, not afraid of permanently partial identities and contradictory standpoints" (Haraway 1991a: 154). In Western culture, the discourse of transgression is linked to immigration and racial differences on the grounds that transgressive boundary crossing "pollutes" lineages (Haraway 1997). Furthermore, Haraway argues that "racial purity fantasies and refusal to accept immigrants as full citizens actually drive policy now in the 'progressive' 'developed' world" (2016: 209). Critics of biotechnology also target the process of transferring genes between species as an "act that transgresses natural barriers, compromising species integrity" or purity of type (Haraway 1997: 60). By contrast, Haraway has long celebrated the transgression of boundaries in terms of "potent fusions" (1991a: 154). Responding to recent environmental debates about the planetary effects of anthropocentric processes, Haraway argues that "no species acts alone" in evolutionary processes (2015: 159). Haraway calls for a reconsideration of what we call "kin" to include "multi-species assemblages" and interactions which have been fundamental to evolution across vast space-times (2015: 160).

The idea of boundaries as permeable surfaces that can be crossed (Haraway 2008) suggests that boundaries are not fixed in space. The body has been conceptualised as a boundary formation but, as Haraway argues, it comprises many life forms, which raises questions about the body as a single and distinct entity. Haraway argues, "In the interconnection of embodied being and environing world, what happens in the interface is what is important" (2008: 249). From Haraway's standpoint, "boundaries" are culturally embedded and socially ordered, but are not impenetrable and can be transgressed or moved "through". Her ideas about boundaries and transgressing sacred boundaries suggest boundaries are crucial sites of innovation. Haraway's notion that cross-boundary interaction is seen to "pollute" lineages suggests cross-boundary work may be problematic in discipline-oriented cultures. There may be resistance to cross-boundary ways of working.

Accounts of transgression of boundaries help to explain why crossdisciplinary collaboration may be treated with suspicion and resistance when powerful disciplinary knowledge traditions and their boundaries are challenged (Land 2010). As Wenger and Snyder (2000) argue, in cross-disciplinary work where knowledge boundaries bump up against each other, the boundaries are *emphasised*, brought into sharp focus, at the same time as they are challenged. These ideas about disciplinary and knowledge boundaries are part of a long and ongoing debate that can be traced to Snow's (1959) lament about the distance between the sciences and the humanities in *The two cultures and the scientific revolution*. Gieryn (1983) explains how disciplinary distance has grown since the Industrial Revolution, along with increasing specialisation of occupations, and "demarcation" between them. Furthermore, the way we define ourselves, and our identities have long been tied to disciplines and occupations (Gieryn 1983): "I am a doctor", "I am a baker", and so on. However, from a post-structural feminist perspective, transgressive interaction between people who work together across knowledge fields, organizational and disciplinary boundaries (such as science and art) can contribute to knowledge building, transformation and can generate innovations.

## Science-arts differences and innovation

Ideas about cyborgs and transgression offer ways of connecting humans and technology, science and art, and their lineages through potent fusions. But considering the arts as a way of knowing, a form of reasoning or knowledge practice is mostly downplayed with reference to science in Western culture. The positivist paradigm of knowledge production and processes of inquiry privileged science as an epistemology that could test and prove propositions, using empirical scientific procedures as a means of generating meaningful knowledge (Bryman 2004). Relative to this paradigm, the arts were seen to be about emotions and valued for decorative rather than informative qualities (Eisner 2008).

Yet since the 1930s, critiques of positivist science have questioned these scientific processes of inquiry on the grounds that they do not necessarily yield finite facts or certainty (Eisner 2008). Because "knowledge" is always changing, Dewey (2005) used the idea of "journeying" to describe ways of working that produced knowledge through the arts as well as the sciences. He saw art as more about the expression of ideas and meanings whereas science focused on making definitive and objectively based statements of meaning and forming conclusions (Dewey 2005). The point is that artists' ways of working, as much as scientists', are a valid approach to investigating and knowing the world (Polanyi 1958, 1967; Berger 1979).

The distinctive character of "arts practice" is linked to what we understand or "know" of the world through taste, smell, or look that cannot necessarily be put into words (Eisner 2008). "Tacit" forms of knowing are identified in the creative arts, acknowledging informed guesses and imaginings that are seen to be part of exploratory and creative acts, which cannot necessarily be formally explained (Polanyi 1967). Words are tools, used to describe or explain what we "see". But as Berger argues:

> The relation between what we see and what we know is never settled. Each evening we see the sun set. We know that the earth is turning away from it. Yet the knowledge, the explanation, never quite fits the sight.
>
> (Berger 1979: 7)

In other words, art conveys more than can be seen. The power of an image lies in its particular form of communication across barriers of language (Berger 1979), and also time and space (Tolstoy 1955). The artist applies skilful understanding of certain materials and techniques to form structures, or representations that echo, or embody, feeling or experience (Eisner 2008). Objects made by artists can be powerful mediators of human feeling or experience across boundaries because arts perspectives and practices are grounded in, and also speak into, subjective human experience. These ideas about arts practice suggest that artists' ways of seeing, doing and knowing are different to those of scientists. This is because artists and scientists are differently embedded in the world and their situated knowledge means they see innovation and its human dimensions in different ways.

## Hotspots of innovation: arts interventions in organisations

The last decade has seen increasing interest in arts interventions in organisations which are seen to foster innovation. Artsbased methods have been used as a pedagogical approach to build learning capacity at individual and organisational levels in companies such as Airbus and GlaxoSmithKlein. These organisations perceive how arts ways of thinking and doing can help employees shift perceptions and look beyond the obvious to develop imaginative and creative ideas and approaches to work (Nissley 2010). These benefits are also reflected in Root-Bernstein, Bernstein and Garnier's study of scientists and their avocations, which indicates significant correlations between scientists with interests in the arts "and particular modes of thinking (especially visual ones)" and their professional impacts (1995: 115).

In their review of 205 publications on arts interventions in organisations, Berthoin Antal and Strauß identified impacts on strategic and operational areas (productivity, product development and marketing strategy), organisational culture, leadership and working climate. However, positive impacts are more often reported on collaborative ways of working and communication, extending relationships and personal development, and adopting "artful ways of working: dealing with unexpectedness and being open to the new" (Berthoin Antal and Strauß, 2013: 12). These were simultaneously physical and social spaces; environments where employees felt safe to "share even the wildest stories" (ibid.: 32). What was most valued by both managers and employees alike in organisations was the discovery of "new ways of seeing and doing things" which impacted on people's "willingness to act and engage in change" (ibid.: 3). The power of these interventions "resided in opening up spaces of possibility" in these "interspaces" (ibid.: 32–33).

Responding to changing and volatile environments in recent times of economic adversity, governments and institutions have called for people to be more innovative. Yet the first cuts in government funding and school curricula typically relate to the arts. For example, states across the US dramatically cut funding to the arts in response to the "global financial crisis" of 2008; for example, Florida (97 per cent), Ohio (47 per cent), and Arizona (54 per cent) (Nissley 2010). This is despite plentiful evidence that the arts generate innovation in both science and business (Nissley 2010). These examples are powerful indicators of the broader barriers and cultural ordering that constrains innovation.

## Learning through working

Issues of innovation and learning are often identified with STEM and STEM education. This perspective is problematic for theorists who see learning and "knowing" emerging from and co-produced through particular contexts (Dewey 1938). Space-times for learning unfold everywhere, including workplaces. But interest in learning for work and, therefore, workplace learning has become more significant as governments around the world have addressed the challenges of developing capacities for innovation in knowledgebased economies (James, Guile and Unwin, 2011).

The idea of "learning through working" identifies "working" as the context for learning and innovation. This notion suggests innovation is an effect of workplace organisation, culture and learning. The idea of learning through working is developed from ideas of "learning" as an emergent process that occurs "through" "working" in workplace learning theory and post-structuralist feminist theory (Somerville 2006; Haraway 2008), and considers the spatial and temporal dimensions of the concept. The word "through" foregrounds movement from one space and time to another. It acknowledges that learning takes place because the learner is no longer in the same position as before once something has been learned. "Learning-through-working", therefore, captures the situatedness of working with knowledges *across* disciplinary boundaries, and how learning unfolds with reference to time, both as a process of learning and as a process of recognising transgression.

Research on "embodied learning", and the influence of feminist theory on this work, has been the subject of literature in workplace learning, particularly since the mid-2000s. Somerville considers the learning body as a "borderland" that develops "in between" formal learning and expertise as people gain experience through their work. She traces these processes of learning through working amongst mine workers and aged care workers (Somerville 2006) and beginning teachers (Somerville, Plunkett and Dyson 2010). In a study of learning safety at work, Somerville (2006) documented the experiences of workers and then analysed their "storylines". She found that there was little relationship between formal, theoretical learning about safety and the "embodied" learning developed through experiences at work.

Somerville explains this contradiction – the disconnect that suggests the "body" is constructed and culturally separate from the mind – from a post-structural perspective (Somerville 2006). Somerville draws, in part, on Foucault's (1980) theories of how bodies are shaped by discourses "through the organisation and regulation of the time, space and movement of our daily lives" (2006: 39). She troubles the binary construction of mind and body, theory and practice, which creates problems in workplaces. Mine workers resisted the implementation of (paper-based) "safety at work" theory because it failed to consider their tacit knowledge that had become embodied over years of experience, and which they valued highly. Somerville and colleagues argued that our understanding of places (such as workplaces) emerges from the senses and "that a sense of embodied connection to place is fundamental to learning place and forming community" (2010: 42). In contrast to textual practices codified in competency-based training programmes, mine workers used what they described as "pit sense" to tell them whether their "bodies-in-place" were safe (Somerville 2006: 43). Pit sense included "sound, smell, touch . . . and other senses that have no name such as the sense of the heaviness of the air" (ibid.). Somerville's standpoint recognizes embodied learning as a valid way of knowing the world and situates the body at the centre of learning about place, rather than peripheral to it.

The storylines that Somerville examined reveal three insights into how learning emerges "through" the embodiment of practices. Firstly, the materialisation of learning taking form as practice either conform to established regulations and norms, or disrupt and transgresses those cultural orders. Secondly, specific places act as "contact zones" or "in-between" spaces. They are "the intersection of multiple, and often contested stories" (Somerville et al. 2010: 43). The "border work" of place learning in the "contact zone" comes at a cost because it requires negotiating difference. This work "involves precarious, risky and difficult emotional work" (ibid.) as power relations are played out. These ideas about the contact zone point to the power relations that add to the complexities of learning and working across disciplinary knowledge boundaries in these kinds of in-between spaces. Thirdly, learning is not fixed; it involves movement, unfolding with time and transformation as learning is gained "through" lived, embodied experience across time, which can generate change and innovation.

"Learning through working" offers a conceptual framework that identifies three key interconnecting dimensions of innovation. Firstly, the organisation of work and environments within and beyond the workplace can impact on innovation. Secondly, learning through the direct experience of "doing" work – learning in practice – supports innovation. Thirdly, learning emerges "through" the embodiment of practices in ways that often conform to established norms and cultural orders, but transgressing those normative frames of reference contributes to innovation. The case study introduced earlier is examined in relation to these themes in the next three sections.

## Making space for innovation

Henschke and Boland's *Synapse* project, *Lightbridge*, undertaken at Australian Synchrotron (Melbourne, Australia), illustrates the making of space that enables and constrains innovation. This case study was one site in a broader study of innovation and arts practice that investigated how artists and scientists worked together in three *Synapse* projects. Interviews shed light on people's experiences, understandings and practices that contributed to learning and innovation through cross-disciplinary work (White-Hancock 2017). The workplace where the synchrotron *Synapse* project occurred was a particular boundary zone: a "hotspot"

(Dürrschmidt and Taylor 2007) where knowledges flowed (Sassen 2007) and where continuity and change could be observed (Dürrschmidt and Taylor 2007). This borderland was a knowledge-sharing space of innovation that disturbed the traditional disciplinary boundaries between art and science. Investigating what happened in the borderland showed how the space of innovation unfolded through interactions across boundaries and transgressions that contributed to evolutionary development (Haraway 2008).

### Organisational and environmental spaces

A synchrotron is a physical, mental and social space. Its intertwined effects create an environmental space that supported *Synapse* project participants in their work together. Heiskanen and Heiskanen define "space" as a "network of relationships, which create conditions for human action and interaction" (2011: 2). "Physical" spaces are material facilities including artefacts and regulatory structures such as "budgets, electronic domains and work schedules" (ibid.: 4). Mental spaces refer to "the world of theory and meanings" and social spaces refer to social relationships (ibid.: 3). The authors argue that these spaces work together in a holistic way to create the conditions for human action and interaction, which can either support or constrain innovation in organisations. However, a discussion of spaces also means talking about boundaries because they locate things that occupy spaces. Physical spaces have boundaries that are often quite visible but social and mental boundaries are often invisible and only become visible when they are transgressed (ibid.).

## Physical spaces

The physical, mental and social spaces that located Henschke and Boland's *Synapse* project were established by the Australian Network for Art and Technology (ANAT) in 2004. ANAT offered funding to support artists in the development of their cross-disciplinary practice (ANAT 2016). *Synapse* project grants were awarded on the basis of artists' and scientists' cases for innovative approaches and projects in scientific organizations (ANAT 2011). Several salient features of the *Synapse* programme's organisation were seen to support and mediate project participants' work together. ANAT's role as the intermediary agency was critical in that it funded, organised and managed the programme. ANAT developed the structure and regulatory framework of the programme, the selection criteria for residencies and established terms and conditions for project acceptance. ANAT's "hands off" approach once residencies were granted afforded informants the freedom and discretion to conduct their work as they saw fit. Finally, Henschke pointed out that there was little expectation of product "outcomes" since the programme aimed to support artists in the conduct of their research. ANAT's approach is unusual because organisations funding grants to artists mostly require outcomes such as artworks, other products or exhibitions.

According to Boland, Australian Synchrotron operates 24/7 and is a hive of activity and interaction for a global scientific community. Since opening in

2007, the facility has hosted more than 3,000 researchers from 186 organisations in 27 countries (Australian Synchrotron 2013). Feeling part of this environment was important to Henschke. Responding to a question about the environment of the workplace that enabled his collaborative work at Australian Synchrotron, Henschke referred to the architecture of the space:

> It's all open and you can wander around and it's quite aesthetically designed for that kind of facility . . . gradually sticking up images of my work kind of all around the place, so now I'm sort of almost integrated visually into their whole corporate aesthetic.
>
> (White-Hancock, 2017: 126)

The modern, minimalist building reflects the round shape of the particle accelerator that it houses. The openness of physical spaces and having room to move about reflect ideas of freedom (Høyrup 2012) and openness (Curtin, Stanwick and Beddie 2011) in work practices which both Henschke and Boland felt supported their collaborative work. Putting his artwork around the space helped the artist feel more at home, giving a sense of ownership and being more a part of the Synchrotron community, which is extensive.

Henschke indicated that openness, intellectual freedom and freedom of access (Curtin et al. 2012) to human and physical resources including technologies, other artefacts and data in scientific organizations was critical to his work. However, while the 16-week time frame of *Synapse* projects was highly valued, time and access to resources and expertise within the scientific organisation were not always available to Henschke. Nevertheless, the grants and ANAT's approach to their management provided both physical and temporal spaces that supported the development of creative work and innovations. These organisational approaches provided space and time for exploration and experimentation, argued to be important in literatures on innovation (for example, Høyrup 2012).

## Mental spaces

Henschke has worked with scientists at Australian Synchrotron since undertaking a residency there in 2007. The artist had initially studied physics at the University of Melbourne in the 1980s. He went on to study geology and meteorology, then psychology, anthropology and film-making. However, his interest in emerging digital technologies redirected his career and led to his work teaching experimental film/video at RMIT University (Melbourne, Victoria). Henschke's work with Synchrotron was largely computer-based. The artist had also undertaken a residency at the *Conseil Européen pour la Recherche Nucléaire* (CERN) in Switzerland prior to the establishment of Australian Synchrotron in Melbourne. Earlier, the artist had been involved in a collaboration with a mathematician from Melbourne University as part of the Arts Victoria Innovation Program. The artist's profile establishes a professional history of cross-disciplinary work and point to an identity that is not strictly tied to one discipline or the other.

Boland had collaborated on the research at CERN and introduced Henschke to people at the Swiss facility. As Chief Scientist at the Synchrotron, Boland's work involved a layer of management and meetings. He had completed his PhD in photonuclear research (the University of Melbourne) and, later, helped to design, commission, build and operate the Australian Synchrotron. As scientist, he was recently awarded the 2014 Fulbright Professional Scholarship in Nuclear Science and Technology to conduct research at the SLAC National Accelerator Laboratory (at Stanford University, USA). Boland has an interest in the creative arts and likes to draw. His profile reflects the findings of Root-Bernstein, Bernstein and Garnier's (1995) study of scientists and their avocations which linked their professional impact/success to interests in the arts.

*Lightbridge*, the name of Henschke and Boland's project, foregrounds a phenomenon (light) that links different environments or bridges boundaries. It involved new ways of looking at and thinking about science, its practices and conventions, and making connections across disciplinary boundaries of art and science. Boland explained that the project was conceived of as "a kind of a portal where the data that's usually made available for scientists and then interpret in a very traditional scientific way" is shared with others (White-Hancock 2017: 137). He also spoke about how an artist's lens might "capture the side ghosts" or see something new that the scientists missed (ibid.: 142). In Boland's view, *Lightbridge* was innovative because it attempted to

> ... open up the data channels that are usually reserved and tightly guarded ... to open up an opportunity and to create this environment where people can do completely different things with it, but still use that concept and then come up with their own ideas as to how they want to use that data ... So, if you look at a plot you might come away with one thing, but if you have all your representation (audio, visual) you might have a different perception of that and you might notice something different.
>
> (Ibid.: 142)

Henschke acknowledged that his project involved adopting new practices in relation to the technology and in the ways that Synchrotron data was used. But it was his experience of the interior space of the particle accelerator itself that was of greater significance to the artist. The internal space of the machine is enlivened through Henschke's filmic representation which captures the electrons' look, movement and sound or "voice". The machine is a mass of wires, cables and racing electrons but, as Henschke explained, "even when it's off it's still kind of on" (ibid.: 143). It is as if the synchrotron has its own life, independent of the scientists who make it. Interpreted in this way, Henschke's innovative work transgresses boundaries as the embodiment of the synchrotron's life-form blurs distinctions, in Harawayan terms, between "living" and "non-living". In this way, the artist's thinking about the technology extended beyond the creative use of data generated by the machine. Henschke's thinking also embraced an experiential, embodied practice dimension that involved closer interaction with the machine, almost a kind of communion.

The artist considered that another aspect of his work relating to cross-disciplinary communication was both innovative and problematic: "Maybe the more . . . realistic innovation is just trying to work out how to work with these people." The artist felt that his efforts at communication with some scientists and people working in the scientific organisation were still the source of some frustration. The comment suggests that while the ideas of knowledge and data sharing sound straightforward in the innovation-collaboration rhetoric of government policies on innovation, in practice, the reality was quite different. The social space of innovation was emphasised.

## Social spaces

Henschke and Boland's partnership was characterised by a respectful working relationship, open communication and trust. Their ways of relating supported arguments about the importance of these features for collaborative learning through working and innovation (for example, Curtin et al. 2011; Felstead, Fuller, Jewson and Unwin 2009). The characteristic of openness contributed to a safe environment for work that involved risk as boundaries were challenged or disturbed (Quinlan, Farrell and Hogben 2010). As Henschke explained, in his experience of cross-disciplinary work, it was important to communicate well:

> I think that what it ultimately comes down to is the person you're working with, if you can kind of integrate with their sort of world view and vice-versa, then it'll work. And if you can't, it doesn't matter how much you try . . . it's just not going to get over the hurdle. [Boland's] . . . in some ways the most open-minded person I've met because I know he's so rigorously into the whole quantum physics straightjacket very empirical stuff, but then he can also understand how the other side works.
>
> (White-Hancock, 2017: 146)

Informal or "in-between" spaces (such as tearooms) also provided a safe environment and were places where physical, mental and social spaces of the workplace environment intersected. The importance of hybrid spaces in mediating workplace learning are discussed in literature to some extent (for example, Høyrup 2012), but surfaced as a critical issue for Henschke in this study. Interaction in these in-between spaces helped the artist to "fit in" to the project workplace, providing opportunities to open up lines of communication. It was necessary to find common ground, build trust, and break down disciplinary boundaries through "gentle", everyday interactions. However cultural orders and boundaries within the scientific workplace impact learning-through-working in significant and sometimes troubling ways.

## The culture-order that authorizes innovation

The synchrotron *Synapse* project illustrates how transgression becomes visible as social, mental and cultural boundaries are challenged (Heiskanen and

Heiskanen 2011. The idea of a "culture-order" is drawn from Hasse and Brandi (2012) and Foucault (1973). Hasse and Brandi define organisational culture as "what we do in organisations which teach employees certain cultural values, discourses, emotions, traditions and meanings of artefacts through a process of practicebased learning" (2012: 135). In Foucauldian terms, approaching organisational "culture" as the "orders" that "border" work in workplaces suggests "management" is a form of boundary work. Managers order the culture and "managing innovation" orders the work of innovation at government and organisational levels.

While Henschke found working with ANAT straightforward and unproblematic, he was challenged at times by the management of the Synchrotron facility. As he explained:

> On my first day of my first residency at the Synchrotron I had a meeting with the Director and Co-director of the place . . . The Co-director said, like totally serious, "So where's your easel and your paints, paintbrushes?" I was like, and the Director was like, "Yeah, this is what you're going to have to deal with. This is where we're at." So, upping the ante I said to them, well, I pointed at the giant particle accelerator and I said, "Well, you're right in a sense, but that is my paintbrush." The Co-director just got bright red in his face and stood up and went, "You're not going to go anywhere near that bloody thing. If you touch that thing, I'll come after you with a hammer." So that's the introduction. That actually did allow me to realise what I'm dealing with.
>
> (White-Hancock, 2017: 162)

The artist's introduction to Australian Synchrotron management was a confrontation that highlighted some of the challenges to collaborative art-science work. The Co-director perceived the need to "protect" or maintain control of the facility. "The artist" was not trusted to work with the machine. Seeing the Synchrotron as "paintbrush" was an idea that crossed the line, bringing the boundary between artist and scientist into sharp focus (Wenger and Snyder 2000; Heiskanen and Heiskanen 2011). The Co-director's reaction points to the perceived transgressive nature of the artist's work. The reaction also illustrates a disciplinary sensitivity and a certain defensiveness. Regulating access to data can be understood as issues of maintaining continuity of control over knowledge and protecting knowledge boundaries.

The confrontation also revealed the Co-director's stereotypical view of the artist and what artists do. The assumption was that all artists paint and use paint brushes and easels. This annoyed Henschke, prompting his reaction that the machine was his "paintbrush". The artist's story revealed that he was challenged by the disciplinary misconception, and also by being threatened with a hammer. This experience points to the disciplinary myths, assumptions and misconceptions which can serve to maintain the disciplinary divide and restrict learning in cross-disciplinary work. Henschke's story illustrates the "border work" of place learning in the boundary or "contact zone" that Somerville and colleagues (2010) write about, and the cost of negotiating difference and change. This work involved "risky and difficult emotional work" (ibid.: 43) as power relations were played out. The case illustrates how the human dimension of innovation is tensioned between continuity and change.

The example illustrates two arguments related to the effects of culture-orders on learning and innovation. Firstly, innovation was to some extent dependent upon the affordances of managers who ordered work in ways that maintained certain continuities (conventions, protocols) in their organisations (Felstead et al. 2009; Billett 2001). Secondly, Henschke's critical incident shows how his work was not recognised as innovation by management (Hasse and Brandi 2012). Without recognition or the affordances of management, Henschke's innovative work was initially restricted, caught between conflicting influences of continuity and change. Given these challenges, questions are raised about what is involved in "*doing*" art-science work in these in-between spaces, and what supported collaborators in their work which was tensioned between continuity and change.

### Learning in practice

The *Synapse* case reveals how an artist's intervention in the scientific organisation and the relationships challenges historically, socially and culturally embedded myths about differences between the disciplines. This was striking because literature reviewed tends to focus on disciplinary distance (for example, Snow 1959; Gieryn 1983) and "culture clash" (Berthoin Antal and Strauß 2013) rather than commonalities between art and science, whereas the interviews with Henschke and Boland surfaced the idea and the long tradition of the artist-scientist. While different aims and outcomes were acknowledged, shared sensibilities, and overlaps in the ways artists and scientists think and their methodological approaches became apparent by working together. Boland explained his understanding that when building knowledge:

> There are certain beliefs and principles and rules that you have to stick with . . . scientists are working in a framework where the fundamental philosophy is that there is an underlying truth that you're nutting out, and then in order to discover that, you can't go down a linear path. You have to be creative and go all over the place to find the trapdoor that will lead you into the next . . . there's a certain framework or certain mystery that you're trying to unravel as a scientist that requires similar techniques as an artist.
>
> (White-Hancock, 2017: 196)

Boland described his "suck it and see" method as common to scientific practice, and indicated that *not knowing* drives a great deal of scientific research, particularly in the arts. In each interview, I found myself asking: W*ho is the artist? Who is the scientist?* For Henschke, the process of journeying (Dewey 2005) involved having some initial ideas but allowing them to emerge and change from the process itself. At one point in his project, Henschke felt:

I've got to push it in a totally different direction. In almost a state of despair I started playing around with this different way to work . . . analyzing little slices of the images in a way that the scientists would break up the data. So, in a sense I was kind of using their process as a metaphor for my process. Then suddenly I was getting all this great stuff which I hadn't thought of before. And it was only through that moment of despair, "This is ridiculous, what am I doing?" that I . . . went, "Look, try anything. Hey, what about this? Look, it works."

(White-Hancock, 2017: 180)

Consistent with Fenwick's (2003) research, Henschke's learning through working involved intuition, improvisation and integration of seemingly unrelated concepts and processes. This new direction drew connections between scientific processes and Henschke's own process which transformed his work. Synchrotron data was also portrayed in a new way, given a "face", a "voice", a persona.

## Unexpected learning

Insights into commonalities between artists and scientists emerged from one of those tearoom conversations Henschke had with a scientist. The scientist unexpectedly told the artist that "I do my best thinking when I'm not thinking at all." Henschke elaborated:

Ultimately in scientific research as well as art it becomes this intuitive thing. [The scientist explained], "I just have a hunch and it's usually the right way. If I think about it too much I don't get anywhere. I have to go off and watch TV or do something different and not think about it and then the answer will just pop into my head." [Henschke replied], "That's like what I do." So, it was through that playful blah, blah, blah that I managed to get some really deep stuff out of them in a way that normally they probably wouldn't dare let on.

(White-Hancock, 2017: 196–197)

Henschke's story revealed similar approaches to problem solving and the role of intuition in the working processes of both artists and scientists. Again, the question arises: *Who is the artist? Who is the scientist?* The artist was elated with his discovery of common ground as well as understanding that the scientist had admitted to what might be considered an "unscientific", unobjective approach that relied on hunches and intuition. Yet Henschke felt that this approach was one that scientists "probably wouldn't dare let on" within the scientific community.

The tearoom was the space that mediated experience between artist and scientist. The tearoom is one of those spaces where people are working and not working at the same time. Unexpected and surprising insights into other disciplinary practices were gained and perhaps more willingly shared between people in this informal, in-between space. The story is consistent with research (such as Høyrup 2012) on the significance of "hybrid" or "in-between" spaces in workplaces where unexpected learning can occur when a diverse range of people meet socially and share ideas. Traditional forms of managerial control of work processes also are disrupted through informal interactions in these spaces.

Henschke spoke about how much he relied on the scientists; he couldn't make a move without their know-how. But his interventions also impacted on Boland personally and professionally in unexpected ways:

> Maybe it's opened up my mind, but how do you measure that or how do you really feel that? So maybe I am thinking more creatively now and maybe I am striving more for excellence. Maybe I'm more uncompromising now given that experience with Chris . . . it gave me this freedom to think in a different way rather than – because the main things that sort of come at you that dominate are the sort of management things, you know, budget, is it on time? So, that's the sort of constant hum in your ear – that sort of puts you on a certain path. Then to be able to step away from that and just not have that weighing on you, that changes the way you operate.
>
> (White-Hancock, 2017: 202)

Taken-for-granted, institutionalised work practices, norms and processes embedded in Boland's workplace that served to maintain continuity were brought into focus. The artist disrupted Boland's usual pattern and approach to work, which the scientist found inspiring to the point that he would find himself tapping away on his computer at 2 am, "nutting out" a problem on his project with Henschke. Management imperatives had driven the scientist to work in a certain way along a certain path, and this is likely how much scientific work, as well as much work in any field, is done. Understanding Henschke's approach enabled him freedom to think and work differently. Boland reconsidered management imperatives that drove daily activities and the need for outcomes which have the effect of restricting creative thinking and forcing compromises. The artist generated insights for the scientist about *how* his work was done and provoked a rethinking of his work practices.

## Learning how to do art-science work

Henschke's "hammer threat" story highlights how the Synchrotron *Synapse* project was a workplace tensioned by different discourses and cultural understandings that resulted from his intervention. Yet he hoped that some connection or learning to understand each other might result. Project collaborators had to learn how to deal with conflict and confrontation that challenged them at epistemic and ontological levels. Asked how he experienced working outside his "comfort zone" in the Synchrotron space, Henschke commented:

> At first, you're really excited, wow, this is great, it's amazing, and then after a few weeks all of a sudden like you just drop and you go, "This is ridiculous. What am I doing here? I shouldn't be here, I'm not a scientist." Then you sort of get re-inspired and go, "Yeah, I can do this." I'd go up to some of

these guys, the ones I could communicate with like Mark, and I'd go, "I don't know what I'm doing here. This is crazy. What's it got to do with me? I don't understand it. I've got no idea where I'm going, what I'm doing." They said, "That's how I feel every day when I come in." The knowledge that you share that kind of bewilderment and suffering with them even sort of helped in the difficult moments.

(White-Hancock, 2017: 191–192)

Henschke's response signifies the psychological and social dimensions of learning and working in what he described here as "weird social situations". The psychological rollercoaster from excitement to depression, bewilderment and confusion was reconciled by social interactions. Finding common ground and sharing experiences at an emotional level, and opening up provided crossing points which enabled communication and helped the artist to meet challenges, span boundaries and move on.

Confronting different standpoints and work practices was a challenging aspect of doing cross-disciplinary work. Henschke spoke of learning about "how to work with these people" and how to communicate in cross-disciplinary environments as an important part of collaborative cross-disciplinary work. The artist noted the need to establish an understanding of the workplace environment and adopted a respectful attitude toward the people who work in these spaces, their particular workplace conditions and their practices. Henschke and Boland spoke with immense respect for each other's deep disciplinary knowledge, skills and practices, and had developed a significant friendship as a result of their work together. At the same time, Henschke and Boland's experiences of "doing" art-science work together point to the issue of the need to learn *how* to work in cross-disciplinary spaces which are tensioned between continuity and change.

## Supporting transgressive knowledge practices: creating spaces of innovation

This chapter has examined human dimensions of innovation that are enable by cross-disciplinary collaboration. The study targeted collaboration in a cross-disciplinary context where an art-science project constituted a "workplace" that operated as a boundary zone that is tensioned between disciplines. Examination of this case produced a complex picture of innovation as an effect of transgressive practices that unfold through the interplay between physical, mental and social spaces of workplace organisation, culture-order and learning through working. Under certain terms and conditions of work, arts practice offers novel ways of navigating established disciplinary knowledges and organisational authority, and the tension between continuity and change, to produce innovation. The learning through working that materialises arts practice helps to clarify the human dimensions of arts-science partnerships and their effects that sometimes unfold over time and space in novel ways.

Rather than approaching artist and scientist on a lateral plane that sees a horizontal landscape where different knowledge practices collide at a boundary, this study has looked into the workplace and traced the unfolding relational space of knowledge and authority from a multidimensional perspective. This shift of orientation has two consequences. First, it made it possible to see how the place where artist and scientist collaborated is networked through knowledge spaces that border and order knowledge work in institutionally persistent ways. Social and mental boundaries became visible as they were transgressed. Henschke experienced the disciplinary divide as an issue of epistemic power and cultural ordering. Second, the multidimensional perspective made it possible to analyse the boundary zone where interactions between artist and scientist prompted mutual change and co-produced hybrid practices and identities that transgressed established patterns of work and learning.

Realizing innovation means disrupting or disturbing the prevailing knowledge and authority orders that delineate knowledge boundaries as social boundaries. As both artist and scientist said, the knowledge work that generates innovation is a kind of art, where individuals – like the *Synapse* project participants – can sometimes develop novel practices of working and learning which bridge boundaries by being informed by the other. This study points to the need for diverse cross-disciplinary education through activities that help build respect for different ways of knowing and doing, in recognition that no "species" acts alone in evolutionary development (Haraway 2015). Learning that comes from diverse collaborative assemblages offers a future time-space for innovation.

## Notes

1 ANAT is funded by the Australian Federal Government through the Australia Council for the Arts, and the State Government of South Australia.
2 The machine is used in many areas of R&D, including physics, biology, medicine and drug development, mineral exploration and processing, materials science, agriculture, manufacturing, new materials, nanotechnology, advanced electronic devices and sustainable energy (Australian Synchrotron 2013).
3 Albert Einstein and Nathan Rosen (1935) used the theory of general relativity to propose the existence of "bridges" or "wormholes" that link separate points in space-time (Lindley 2005).
4 The "Ricci tensor" is a term used in relativity theory that describes the part of the curvature of space-time that influences how matter converges or diverges in time (Chow and Knopf 2004).
5 To view this 12-second film, go to http://henschke2010.anat.org.au/files/2010/09/lightcurve-fraction.mov.

## References

ANAT (Australian Network for Art and Technology). (2011). 2011 Synapse Residency Program. Retrieved February 21, 2011 from: www.anat.org.au/2011-synapse-residency-program/.
ANAT (Australian Network for Art and Technology). (2016). Current program. Retrieved March 12, 2016 from: www.anat.org.au/current-programs/.
Australian Synchrotron. (2013). About us: Welcome. Retrieved November 18, 2013 from www.synchrotron.org.au/about-us/welcome.

Berger, J. (1979). *Ways of seeing.* London: Penguin.

Berthoin Antal, A. and Strauß, A. (2013). *Creative clash – Artistic interventions in organisations: Finding evidence of values added.* Berlin: WZB. Retrieved June 4, 2014 from www.wzb.eu/sites/default/files/u30/effects_of_artistic_interventions_ final_report.pdf.

Billett, S. (2001). *Learning in the workplace: Strategies for effective practice.* St. Leonards, NSW: Allen & Unwin.

Bowker, G. and Star, S. L. (1999). *Sorting things out: Classification and its consequences.* Cambridge, MA: MIT Press.

Bryman, A. (2004). *Social research methods.* Oxford: Oxford University Press.

Chow, B., and Knopf, D. (2004). *The Ricci Flow: An introduction.* Providence, RI: American Mathematical Society.

Curtin, P., Stanwick, J. and Beddie, F. (Eds.). (2011). *Fostering: The innovation and skills nexus – Research readings.* Adelaide, South Australia: National Centre for Vocational Education Research.

Dewey, J. (2005). *Art as experience.* New York: Perigee Books (original work published 1934).

Durkheim, E. (1965). *The elementary forms of religious life.* New York: Free Press.

Dürrschmidt, J. and Taylor, G. (2007). *Globalisation, modernity and social change: Hotspots of transition.* New York: Palgrave Macmillan.

Einstein, A. and Rosen, N. (1935). The particle problem in the General Theory of Relativity. *Physical Review, 48*(1), 73–77.

Eisner, E. (2008). Art and knowledge. In J. Knowles and A. Cole (Eds.). *Handbook of the arts in qualitative research: Perspectives, methodologies, examples, and issues* (pp. 3–14). Los Angeles, CA and London: Sage.

Felstead, A., Fuller, A., Jewson, N. and Unwin, L. (2009). *Improving working as learning.* London: Routledge.

Fenwick, T. (2003). Innovation: Examining workplace learning in new enterprises. *Journal of Workplace Learning, 15*(3), 123–132. doi: http://dx.doi.org/10.1108/ 1366 5620310468469.

Foucault, M. (1973). *The order of things.* New York: Random House.

Foucault, M. (1980). *Power/knowledge: Selected interviews and other writings, 1972–1977,* ed. and trans. Colin Gordon, Brighton: Harvester Press.

Gieryn, T. F. (1983). Boundary-work and the demarcation of science from non-science: Strains and interests in professional interests of scientists. *American Sociological Review, 48*(6), 781–795. doi: 10.2307/2095325.

Haraway, D. (1985). Manifesto for cyborgs: Science, technology, and socialist feminism in the 1980s. *Socialist Review, 80,* 65–108.

Haraway, D. (1991a). A cyborg manifesto: Science, technology and socialist-feminism in the late twentieth century. In *Simians, Cyborgs and Women: The Reinvention of Nature* (pp. 149–181). New York: Routledge (original work published as *Manifesto for cyborgs: science, technology, and socialist feminism* in 1985).

Haraway, D. (1997). *Modest_Witness@Second_Millennium.FemaleMan_Meets_ OncoMouse™: Feminism and technoscience.* New York and London: Routledge.

Haraway, D. (2008). *When species meet.* Minneapolis: University of Minnesota Press.

Haraway, D. (2015). Anthropocene, capitalocene, plantationocene, chthulucene: Making kin. *Environmental Humanities, 6,* 159–165.

Haraway, D. (2016). *Staying with the trouble: Making kin in the Chthulucene.* Durham, NC: Duke University Press.

Hasse, C. and Brandi, U. (2012). Employee driven innovation: From spontaneous idea generation to new collective practices. In S. Høyrup, C. Hasse, K. Møller, M. Horst and

M. Bonnafous (Eds.). *Employee-driven innovation: A new approach* (pp. 127–149). New York: Macmillan.

Heiskanen, T. and Heiskanen, H. (2011). Spaces of innovation: Experiences from two small high-tech firms. *Journal of Workplace Learning, 23*(2), 97–116. doi: http://dx.doi.org/10.1108/13665621111108774.

Henschke, C. (2010). Lightbridge Project: Chris Henschke @ the Australian Synchrotron – 2010 Synapse residency program. Retrieved from http://henschke2010.anat.org.au/ 8 October 2012.

hooks, b. (1994). *Teaching to transgress: Education as the practice of freedom.* New York: Routledge.

Høyrup, S. (2012). Employee-driven innovation: A new phenomenon, concept and mode of innovation. In S. Høyrup, M. Bonnafous-Boucher, C. Hasse, M. Lotz and K. Møller (Eds.). *Employee-driven innovation: A new approach* (pp. 3–33). New York: Palgrave Macmillan.

James, L., Guile, D. and Unwin, L. (2011). From learning for the knowledge-based economy to learning for growth: Re-examining clusters, innovation and qualifications. Retrieved March 3, 2013 from: www.llakes.org/wp-content/uploads/2011/07/29.-James-Guile-Unwin-reduced.pdf.

Lamont, M. and Molnár, V. (2002). The study of boundaries in the social sciences. *Annual Review of Sociology, 28,* 167–195. doi: http://dx.doi.org/10.1146/annurev.soc.28.110601.141107.

Land, R. (2010). Threshold concepts and issues of interdisciplinarity. Paper presented at the Third Biennial Threshold Concepts Symposium, 1–2 July 2010, University of New South Wales, Sydney.

Lindley, D. (2005). The birth of wormholes. *Physical Review Focus, 15*(11). Retrieved March 25, 2015 from: https://physics.aps.org/story/v15/st11.

Marx, K. (1948). *The eighteenth brumaire of Louis Bonaparte.* Moscow: Foreign Language Publishing House (original work published 1852).

Nissley, N. (2010). Arts-based learning at work: Economic downturns, innovation upturns, and the eminent practicality of arts in business. *Journal of Business Strategy, 31*(4), 8–20. doi: 10.1108/02756661011055140.

Polanyi, M. (1958). *Personal knowledge: Towards a post critical philosophy.* London: Routledge.

Polanyi, M. (1967). *The tacit dimension.* New York: Anchor Books.

Quinlan, A., Farrell, H. and Hogben, P. (2010, 1–2 July). Attending to liminality: Constructing an identity as a student of architecture through experiential learning. Paper presented at the Third Biennial Threshold Concepts Symposium, University of New South Wales, Sydney.

Root-Bernstein, R. S., Bernstein, M. and Garnier, H. (1995). Correlations between avocations, scientific style, work habits, and professional impact of scientists. *Creativity Research Journal, 8*(2), 115–137. doi: 10.1207/s15326934crj0802_2.

Sassen, S. (2007). *Sociology of globalization.* New York: Norton & Co.

Snow, C.P. (1959). *The two cultures and the scientific revolution.* Cambridge: Cambridge University Press.

Somerville, M. (2006). Subjected bodies, or embodied subjects: Subjectivity and learning safety at work. In S. Billett, T. Fenwick and M. Somerville (Eds.). *Work, subjectivity and learning* (Vol. 6) (pp. 37–52). Netherlands: Springer.

Somerville, M., Plunkett, M. and Dyson, M. (2010). New teachers learning in rural and regional Australia. *Asia-Pacific Journal of Teacher Education, 38*(1), 39–55. doi: 10.1080/13598660903474130.

Tolstoy, L. (1955 [1897]). What is art? (A. Maude, trans.). In A. Maude (ed.), *What is art? and essays on art by Leo Tolstoy* (pp. 70–289). London: Oxford University Press.

Weber, M. (1978). *Economy and society* (Vol. 1). Berkeley: University of California Press.

Wenger, E. and Snyder, W. (2000). Communities of practice: The organizational frontier. *Harvard Business Review, 78*(1), 139–145.

White-Hancock, L. (2017). *Innovation and arts practice: Work, learning and transgression.* Melbourne, Australia: Monash University. Retrieved 15 April 2017 from: https://figshare.com/articles/Innovation_and_arts_practice_Work_learning_and_transgression/4892108.

# Section II

# Troubling temporalities

# 8 Digital classrooms and the reconfiguration of the space-times of education

## On transient images, ephemeral memories, and the challenges for schooling

*Inés Dussel*

## Introduction

There is much talk today of how digital media are transforming schools, and more generally our modes of knowing and sensing the world, to the point that it has become, in Isin and Ruppert's words, "a cliché that does not need repeating" (2015:1). Yet, in these diagnoses there are several assumptions about what changes and what remains stable, or even about what social change is (McLeod and Thomson, 2009), all of which would need further exploration in order to move beyond what the celebratory rhetoric is saying about present and desirable school change.

In this chapter, I would like to present some reflections on my current research on digital media in secondary schools and discuss how and to what extent these media are reconfiguring the space-times of education. Broadly speaking, digital media have been associated with a reorganization of time, or a re-orchestration of temporalities (Mongin 1993), which has been defined variously as an acceleration (Virilio 2006), liquidification (Bauman 2000), or compression (Harvey 1989) of time. In the educational realm, it has been said that the introduction of these media in classrooms has produced new chronotopes of teaching and learning (Lemke 2004), that is, the emergence of different paces, rhythms and durations that expand or shrink the experience of time for teachers and students, and that negotiate with the rigidity of school schedules and curriculum through local arrangements.

However, this acknowledgment of a changing school space-time is, in several cases, based on notions of time and space that still hold them as homogeneous and linear systems. It is as if the major change consisted of the increased speed and mobility of rather stable conditions of living for human beings, or was the product of the clash between two closed systems, those of the modern temporality of schooling and the "post" temporality of digital media. In this dichotomy, the space-times of schooling and digital media are not problematized; heterogeneity is attached to one particular strand that moves at a different pace, or is the effect of an external force. But what if the space-times of digitalized schools were to be approached differently? How would they look if the movement was not "outside" school walls, or even if the notion of clear boundaries was to be questioned? What if institutional arrangements were less stable, and were made of different temporalities? What if digital classrooms were conceived as the intersection of multiple trajectories, "the meeting up of stories" that is both a dense "here" and a dense "now" (Massey 2013: 118)?

It has to be noted that this meeting-up of multiple trajectories has frequently been thought of as the result of what the students' and teachers' bodies and affects bring to the schools. Less often do we hear about how technological devices are also adding their own dense temporality to these encounters, bringing in and opening up different trajectories from the ones that were brought up by textbooks or blackboards. For example, the "virtual windows" of the digital screens have some points in common with Renaissance perspective framework (Friedberg, 2006), but also depart in other directions from the ones that used to be bounded, even if precariously, by the materiality of schooling until mid-twentieth century (Lawn and Grosvenor 2005; Dussel, in press). Orit Halpern argues that, while seated in front of multiple screens and staring at interfaces, we "no longer aspire to go out and explore the world": "We have come to assume that the world is always already fully recorded and archived; accessible at a moment's notice through the logics of computational devices" (Halpern 2014: 13). It seems that, in schooling, the shifts in archiving and knowing are more encompassing, more wide-ranging than the change from encyclopedias to Wikipedias, from handwritten to digitalized texts, or from physical to virtual classrooms, which often appear to be the main concern of educators. Thus I would like to claim that digital media involve a reconfiguration of temporality and truth, and of the régimes of attention and distraction, and that reformulates the space-times of schooling beyond its physical territories and time schedules. This reconfiguration has powerful effects on teachers' and students' identities, as will be discussed later.

To analyze the trajectories that are brought by digital media to this encounter of "unfinished stories," as Doreen Massey calls them (2013: 118), I will rely on some strands of social theory that have reconceptualized space and time (Thrift 2006; Massey 2013; Galison 2003). I will also draw from historical and sociological reappraisals of the materiality of life and the connections and entanglements of humans and non-humans (Ingold 2015; Latour 2005; Daston 2006). Another important theoretical grounding of my project is the work done by historians of visual media and particularly of digital media (Doane 2002; Gitelman 2008; Friedberg 2006; van Dijck 2013; Halpern 2014; Mirzoeff 2015), who are studying media change as part of major epistemological, aesthetic, and political transformations. Many among them are inspired by Walter Benjamin's approach to the human sensorium and aesthetics as technohistorical constructs, deeply enmeshed in a history of the sensibilities and of artifacts, of political authorities and cultural icons (Benjamin 1999). These different strands of social theory help me to unpack what is presented as change in digitalized schools, and to contribute to the reflections on the uneven space-times of education that are presented in this volume.

The chapter is organized in four sections. The first one presents the theoretical framework on media and their space-times, analyzing its relevance for producing more complex understandings of schooling. The second one discusses the specificities of digital media as time-based media, and the new space-times of a 24/7 world – referring to Jonathan Crary's metaphor to speak about a hyperconnected world where availability and alertness are required all the time. The third one introduces some reflections on the space-times of digitalized schools, focusing on the archival practices and the new functions of images in these regimes, their relationship to truth claims, memory, the representability of the real, and the politics of images. In the closing section, I pose some questions about the value of physical space-times for schooling, and about the kind of pedagogies that might be needed to make room for an encounter with difference and otherness, an experience of duration that might not be easily available in today's hyperconnected life, dominated by the serialized production of the same.

## Space-times, technologies, and media: multiple trajectories within schooling

> If you were really to take a slice through time it would be . . . full of holes, of discontinuities, of tentative half-formed encounters: space being made.
>
> (Massey 2013: 122)

How to approach the uneven space-times of education, and particularly of schooling, in digital times?[1] I will take a leap back in order to approach this question. Education has been defined as a space of encounter between generations that bring in the past, the present, and the future (Arendt 1961). If traditionalists have always emphasized the importance of the past in order to equip the new generations with tools and resources to make their own path, modern reformers have tended to side with the promise of renewal that is brought by breaking ties with the past, probably echoing the Marxian dictum of the unbearable weight that the dead past has on the shoulders of the living and of the need to leave it behind. One fine example of this kind of argument can be found in Walter Benjamin's early writings, in which he criticized schools' fixation with the past that led to a "desiccated humanism" (Benjamin 2011: 96). He advocated for an educational reform that would make room for a historical awareness of the cultural and historical relevance of the present (ibid.: 113). Whether he was already posing a new relationship with temporality and memory in these 1912–13 texts is not clear, but what comes forth in them is that school has to bring in other temporalities in order to be more relevant, and come back to life again.

If I return to these early twentieth-century writings, it is because I find resonances with current mainstream debates on digital media and schooling. In them, new media is presented as the future, even more than the present; the "rhetorics of inevitability" of technological change (Nespor 2011: 2) is set against schools, which are posited as being a force of the past, of conservativism. The opposition is simple and the solution clear-cut: schools have to cut loose from the past (epitomized in disciplines, exercises, memory) and embrace the future (represented by competences, soft and flexible skills, connected media, fluid identities). It has already been well established that the new language of cyber reform picks up on the counterculture of the 1960s and earlier (Turner 2006), but evacuates its radical politics and collective horizons. What is interesting for my argument is that propositions concerning technological changes in schools mostly persist with an orderly vision of time and space that sees them as discrete dimensions that have to be traversed more quickly – as in the acceleration of time or the shrinking of distance. It is a matter of setting in motion a predefined and homogeneous quality.

Yet, this mainstream perspective neglects the extent to which the linear vision of time is unhelpful to understand contemporary transformations – or prior ones, for that matter. I would like to present some other approaches that might allow a reconsideration of the making of space in time and of the spatial condition of temporality in schooling. One good guide in that path is the work of Doreen Massey, who argued that the multiplicity is both ways: space gives us the gift of the coexistence of difference, of the simultaneous existence of multiple conditions, and time speaks of journeys, trajectories, incomplete stories, and loose ends (Massey 2013). A non-linear approach to time and space should make room for multiple becomings, and depart from the notion of a single, linear movement from modern temporality to postmodern instantaneity.

This multiplicity of becomings, however, is not infinite. What we can become has to do with the particular entanglements in which we live, conditioned by available technologies, objects, agents, and affects. In this respect, our conceptions of time need to be historicized too, and made more spatial and material, attentive to the coevalness of knowledge, artifacts, and people. I turn here to Peter Galison's history of synchronous, mechanical time, which illuminates the many strands of which the notion of time – homogeneous, uniform, linear, divisible – was made in the early twentieth century. Galison remarks that while Newton had been guided by God's sensorium, and Galileo measured distance in heartbeats ("heart clock"), Einstein was inspired by trains, telegraphs, and his work at Bern's patent office: "When we read Einstein's and Poincaré's many discussions of the new ideas of time and space cast in the lexicon of automobiles, telegraphs, trains, and cannons, we are seeing the conditions under which these questions became commonplace" (Galison 2003: 313).[2]

This combination of technical, philosophical, and scientific trajectories in how time is conceived is also evident in the contemporary shifts brought forth by and through digital media. For Galison, if Einstein used the coordinated clocks, electric signals, and trans-oceanic telegraphs to dismantle the "old order of time" and instead create the "*times* of relativity," the current "informational revolution" provides another example of the combination of abstraction and concrete materials and technologies. In the intersection of cybernetics, computer science, and cognitive science "converged the dense histories of wartime feedback devices that tumbled out of weapons production, alongside the more arcane trajectories of information theory and models of human mind" (Galison 2003, 321). Orit Halpern (2014) brings this conceptualization closer to our present. In her study of Norbert Wiener's cybernetics during and after World War II, she analyzes how it helped to transform the reason of Enlightenment into a machinic rationality, a change in which cognitive science (with strong links to current cognitive psychology and mainstream educational research) played a significant part. The work of cognitive psychologists, designers, and computer engineers made space into a sentient, smart, and efficient organization, and knowledge into a data set that had to be managed, produced, and made visible in elegant and persuasive ways (commodified, algorithmic, discrete and definitive, fast and economic). The senses started to be treated as commodities, technologies, and infrastructures; they were subjected to "new models of sense, measure and calculation" (Halpern 2014: 29) that produced particular ways of governing.

These readings make it clear that the space-times of digital media, then, are considerably different from the ones dominant sixty or seventy years ago, and not just because they are quicker or more expansive. History and time are inextricably related to media and to particular spatializations, and change with them, because media are important vectors through and in which our relationships and experiences with time and space are constituted; it is not the same to think and experience time while looking at trains, as Einstein did, than while looking at retina screens that promise hyperreal images, instantaneity, and immaterial communication.[3] This affects the space-times of schooling, considering that the media and the records of culture that are part of schooling draw in these new conceptualizations of time and the new simultaneity of real-time streaming. Schools cannot be, and are not, left on the margins of these changes, as critics of its conservativism claim: they are crisscrossed by these trajectories, whether the devices are present or not.

There is a trait of digital media that is utterly relevant for understanding these changes, and that is their capacity for archiving culture and disseminating its records. If schools are, as claimed at the beginning of this section, a space-time encounter with multiple temporalities, these are brought not only by teachers and students but also by the objects and artifacts that are archives of culture. Books, wall charts, maps, portraits, desks, buildings, all contain traces of the past that become active in each new encounter. At its turn, this encounter produces new intersections in which these objects or artifacts gain other meanings, or tell other stories, as Massey argued. But this possibility of relating to records of culture has changed overtime. One of the most significant transformations in this realm was brought out by the emergence of mechanical visual media, of which digital media is the latest heir.

How have mechanical visual media such as photography and cinema produced such a sea change? While images have always given "a visible form to time" (Mirzoeff 2015: 22), the emergence of photography, a medium that defines its images by the length of time that the film or digital sensor is exposed to light, caused an earthquake in an era that was preoccupied with the debates on geological time and the evolution of species. "The brief exposure of Daguerre's shutter contrasted dramatically with the millennia of geological time and revealed the new human power to save specific instants of time" (ibid.: 23): from then on humans were able to record, condense, or capture time or, more precisely, an instant of time, a slice of time, and archive it for future viewers. This change addressed deep issues about the mortality of human beings and set a whole new horizon and way of thinking about time, its representability and its archivability.

But film dug deeper than photography on the pathway of archiving time. For Mary Ann Doane, one of the most sophisticated historians of cinema as a time-based media, "Photography presented itself as the indexical tracing of space; the cinema went further to claim that it was the indexical tracing of both space and an unfolding time" (Doane 2002: 229). Photography could make a past event simultaneous, but film set the past in motion, making it more durable and expanding our senses of time. Cinema mimicked life with its mechanical ability to project movement, with an increased indexicality (that is, its fidelity to its referent).[4]

Yet there was one more trait that made it the central medium of the twentieth century: its relationship with contingency, which constitutes, according to Doane, cinema's main contribution to contemporary configurations of time. As a medium, cinema made duration archivable, and had an "apparent capacity to perfectly *represent* the contingent, to provide the pure record of time" (ibid.: 22). Cinema could capture, in better ways than other media, modernity's excesses, that which goes beyond rationalization and includes change, chance, the ephemeral, and contingent (e.g., Marx's famous phrase that "all that is solid melts into air," see Berman 1982). Film helped to produce contingency and ephemerality "as graspable, representable" (Doane 2002: 32), but also as the site of emergence of freedom, newness, difference. Cinema offered both an evidence of "the rationalization of time and an homage to contingency" (ibid.: 32); through cinema, "[a] ccident and chance become productive" (ibid.: 11), pleasurable, enjoyable. This runs parallel to the emergence of statistics and the "epistemologies of indeterminism" that made the contingent legible and manageable (Hacking 1990), which became a powerful source for social stability during the twentieth century (which, it has to be said, was never achieved fully or completely). But contingency also opens up to the utopian, to non-deterministic views of technology and its politics: it is "a witness against technology as inexorability, a witness that it could have been otherwise" (Doane 2002: 232). Cinema contributed to the spread of the "pressures [and pleasures] of contingency," and of the "ideologies of instantaneity, of temporal compression, of the lure of the present moment" (ibid.: 19–20) that became so central to visual technologies in the twentieth century – including, as will be seen later, digital technologies.

The knowledge effects of these new time-based media are also very relevant for the space-times of schooling. Among these effects, there are the new standards of "accuracy, memory, knowability" (ibid.: 24) for any record of culture, but also the expansion of the archival impulse, of the pressure to record life, and to store it as a separate unit – a sort of unbounding of the archival desire, that will continue to expand with digital media. It is no surprise, then, that some educators gave a warm welcome to cinema as the possibility of enlargening the experience of their students, of bringing "the real world" and "real life" to the classroom (Curtis 2009).

Cinema marked a new threshold for the accuracy of the archives of culture with which schools worked, although its relationship with contingency and its contribution to the erosion of the old order of time produced uneasiness among more conservative educators (Dussel 2014). This uneasiness was related to the multiple temporalities with which the filmic image engages, drawing in the temporality of the apparatus/camera (mechanical or machinic), of the scene or the time represented by the image (diegetic time), and of the reception or projection (Doane 2002: 30). If the record ineluctably becomes the past at the moment in which it is stored and archived, when it is screened it becomes a presence, although that presence is that of the screening and not of the original moment and thus is "a presence haunted by historicity" (23). That is why time-based media images, and particularly filmic ones, are always already images of a contingent, temporally dense time, and make the "here-and-now" of media an intersection of disjuncted temporalities, of presences that carry traces of the past and promises for the future, but also extend the pleasures and openness of the present. Going back to Benjamin's writings from the beginning of the twentieth century, it seems clear why these disjunctures and openness would cause discomfort to educators who thought that their role was to police the relationship between past, present, and future, and who saw in cinema a "desiring machine" that escaped their control.

## The space-times of digital media

If cinema brought a new sense of time and contingency, digital media seems to have moved even further on the same road. Media scholars have debated whether this is a change in quantity or quality. Mary Ann Doane is among those who believe that there is no rupture between old and new media: "what is still very much at stake is the attempt to structure contingency," a shared "tension between the desire for instantaneity and an archival aspiration" (Doane 2002: 29).

Yet other scholars emphasize that digital texts, and particularly images, imply new archival practices and a new temporality. For example, for Nick Mirzoeff in the digital era, "Time-based media are newly ascendant, creating millions upon millions of slices of time, which we call photographs or videos, in what seem to be ever-shrinking formats like the six second-long Vine" (Mirzoeff 2015: 26). Joan Fontcuberta, a historian of photography, also claims a big breakthrough with digital photography: its indexicality and truth claims are played out in a totally different way than in analog photography (Fontcuberta 2016), an argument that will be discussed in the next section. Perhaps more significantly, these days digital devices are producing records and traces of almost every move made by their users. While this can be seen as an extension of the archival impulse of early twentieth-century visual technologies, these data records are cut loose from the tradition of archival images, no longer to be managed or preserved as a record of time and memory, but fully swallowed by the circuits of commodities and automated data processing.

Jonathan Crary reflects on these changes in *24/7*, an essay on the present conditions of existence as "a time of indifference . . . a non-social model of machinic performance and a suspension of living that does not disclose the human cost required to sustain its effectiveness" (2013: 9). In a rather gloomy picture of the space-times of our era, *24/7* makes reference to the pressure to be available and alert all the time, the whole week, the whole life; it denounces capitalism's intentions to colonize sleep as the last frontier of unproductive time, and to achieve a "perpetually illuminated" world that seeks to exorcize "the otherness that is the motor of historical change" (ibid.). As instantiated before with Einstein's clocks, these changes are made of many more trajectories than media and visual technologies, but are undeniably held and propelled by them.

There are three traits of technological devices in Crary's analysis of the new temporalities of current conditions that are particularly interesting for rethinking the space-times of digitalized classrooms. While they are perhaps too general and make no room for the asymmetrical and uneven ways in which these transformations are taking place, they nonetheless point to traits and trends that make up the qualities of which our space-times are made.[5] One is the rhythm of renewal and change of the devices, which makes it very difficult to become familiar with and fluent in them. Beyond particular apparatuses, the experience and perception of duration and of time are changed by "the rhythms, speeds, and formats of accelerated and intensified consumption" (ibid.: 39). Crary seems to agree with Doane that this was already present in the archival impulse of photography and cinema, yet now its speed is being set more explicitly against the fragility of human life, unable to cope with this pace. The second trait is related to its seriality. Quoting Jean Paul Sartre's criticism of the "practico-inert", Crary retrieves the key term of *seriality* as a combination of activity and animation with inertia. For Crary, the "desultory electronic activity and exchanges" in social media is "the numbing and ceaseless production of the same" (ibid.: 117), which leads to loneliness and a loss of collective and community horizons. The third trait involves "the delusion of a time without waiting, of an on-demand instantaneity" (ibid.: 124). The rhythm and pace of this 24/7 life, and its seriality, lead to an atrophied patience, something critical for democracy: without patience, affording the time "to listen to others [or] to wait one's turn to speak" (ibid.: 124), public life will be severely curtailed.

These traits seem especially challenging for the space-times of classrooms, however uneven they might be. Accelerated speed and consumption, instantaneity and undisciplined seriality seem to go against the grain of routines, predictable and homogeneous timetables, and long durations and sequences that characterizes modern schooling. On the other hand, the time-without-waiting and the impatience that it nurtures defy schools' potential to suspend a space and a time to share specific questions and procedures about knowledge with others (Masschelein and Simons 2013). It can be said that, in the space-times of the instantaneous and im-mediacy, the possibility of having the experience of the simultaneity of difference, of having a space-time for the other, seems increasingly scarce. This will be discussed more thoroughly in the next section.

## Truth, memory and the archival impulse in digital classrooms

I would like to present now some reflections based upon recent research conducted on the use of digital media in secondary school classrooms. The research was concerned with how digital devices, whether part of technology-intensive federal programs or of bring-your-own-device situations, were being introduced in schools. Research questions included the local policies that were effected for their regulation (if any) and the type of activities and teaching strategies that were set in motion; how space and time were being redefined, and what counted as school knowledge and as legitimate school texts in the new media ecology and material life of classrooms. Based on a broad corpus of observations and interviews,[6] I will present four sets of reflections that speak to the effects of new media on school knowledge and on schools' capacity to organize a space of encounter or become a public arena. These reflections refer to the new regimes of truth and their relation to new forms of indexicality in digital media; the archival practices in digitalized classrooms; the representability of time and culture through mechanical and bodily technologies, and the overwhelming presence of ephemeral and transient images (Freedman 2011). They are brought together to help me build an argument about the new trajectories and journeys that are intersecting in digitalized schools. While they are not directly about teachers' or students' identities, they undoubtedly are part of them, providing the texts and materials with which their stories are told and lived.

First, some comments on the new regimes of truth and indexicality. Drawing on Michel Foucault's analysis of régimes of truth as the rules or justifications that bring forth some forms of subjectivity, object domains, types of knowledge and truth claims (Foucault 1983), the relationships with truth that emerge in digital classrooms can be interrogated. These issues relate to current debates on post-truth,[7] particularly considering that digital media seem to be an important drive for the erosion of factual, scientific truths and the adoption of popularity and emotional appeal as new criteria for judging a given statement's value (Boltanski and Thévenot 2006). This erosion is linked to the blurring boundaries between entertainment and information, "all overridden by a compulsory functionality of communication that is inherently and inescapably 24/7" (Crary 2013: 76), and that proclaims the de-disciplinarizing and de-specialization of spaces and activities.

The lack of specialization and the privileging of emotional appeal over truth criteria are visible in the digital classrooms observed over the last few years. These classrooms seem to have lost their distinctive characteristics in terms of bodily dispositions, regulation of speech and silence, and specialized language. Of course, these changes are not only due to digital media but are related to broader processes of informalization of manners and relationships in the twentieth century (Wouters 2007), the spread of soft or horizontal pedagogies in schools and other pedagogical discourses (see Dussel, in press). However, the presence of digital artifacts introduces other trajectories into the interaction between students, teachers, and the materiality of devices and school materials. In classrooms, students' bodies are generally relaxed, their eyes are set on the screens and not on the blackboard, and there is a significant noise and heightened conversation during class time. Quite frequently, students ask for the teacher's permission to use their headphones to listen to music while they read or write pieces, and again frequently teachers agree, convinced that they have to replicate the domestic setting in classrooms so that their students engage more willingly in schoolwork. The classroom's appearance, then, is not different from other public spaces where young people are plugged in to their own devices, and in privileged schools or universities, they seek to imitate airport lounges or cafeterias. As Orit Halpern said, space has to become smart and sentient, homely, and warm (something that was already present in pedagogical discourses since the early 1900s, particularly for kindergartens). The demands on activities and dispositions are also becoming increasingly similar, all leading to well-being and personal satisfaction; routines and exercises are to be avoided or disguised as creative moments. One of the repeated mantras of the teachers interviewed is that digital media is good because students feel good, engaged, active: there is a notorious confluence between the corporate language and the pedagogical discourses that seek to renew educational practice.

A particular note can be made about the use of images for schoolwork, which is also telling of the shift from one regime of truth (scientific or based on the authority of the teacher and the curriculum) to another one, more concerned with emotional impact and motivation, a shift that has powerful effects on the identities of students that are now framed as flexible, ubiquitous, and creative learners (Biesta 2006). In observations and interviews, teachers and students valued and promoted an increased use of images in school subjects, and their justification was the potency of images to shock or capture students' attention (a trait related to their contingency: Doane 2002). However, few teachers work through and with the images, which are generally taken as an illustration or example of a verbal argument. Films – fictional or documentary – are used as documents in history, social sciences, or psychology; photos are used in geography and natural sciences to instantiate categories or species; simulations are rarely used, and mostly in physics or chemistry, in which they are assumed as indexical representations of natural processes. In almost all the classrooms observed, no comments were made on the problematic status of their indexicality, or on how they were produced or circulated. On the one hand, it was evident that images were mostly taken as neutral or transparent texts that were subordinated to the argument provided by the teachers, and thus they seemed to reinforce the authorial voice of the teacher (that is, an "older" regime of truth). On the other hand, the lack of work upon the image itself, its neutralization as a specific sign or artifact, and its use as a strategy of shock and awe, also speaks of the erosion of the critical intellectual operations that schools were supposed to perform upon texts, and of the dominance of their emotional, motivational value, aligned with the demands of the entertainment industry.[8]

Second, the archival impulse seems to be at large in schools, expanding *ad infinitum* the collections of texts and images that are available. For example, students are asked to perform searches on almost every topic, and very often they take pictures or produce videos that are graded and considered as relevant schoolwork. But these records do not seem to accumulate in a particular memory, be it the school curriculum or the student's. Joan Fontcuberta, speaking about digital photography, says that the current wave of digital devices has led to a discrediting of memory: "post-photography is indifferent to the mnemonic function and to the responsibility for remembering" that analog photography kept (Fontcuberta 2016: 74).[9] The lack of accumulation can also explain the decline of narrative in favor of the shock and awe of instantaneous images, and also the weakening of its utopian side, as events do not follow a line that can be challenged or seen otherwise.

Evidently, questions about the ownership and authorship of texts in schools are not new (i.e., whose writing was it in school written exercises or notebooks?), but the digitalization of the archive seems to extend this trait to a new level, that of the numb seriality described by Crary. In Mexican schools, for example, the use of digital platforms in secondary schools leads in many cases to more fragile records, uploaded for grading but not stored or kept as separate units that can be retrieved later, or accumulated in sequential series by the students. The situation seems to be far away from the dessicated humanism that Benjamin described in 1913, but it is also far away from his proposal of finding a particular relevance for the present in the history of culture. Also, the de-disciplinarization mentioned above can be read in Foucaultian terms: the current movement seems to be shifting from the disciplinarian techniques that individualized the student into the grid of school power, giving her or him a name and a position, to another situation in which what counts is the series in flux. The student seems to be fragmented in tasks and activities, no longer a stable, unified site of teaching and learning.

The fragility of the accumulation of experience speaks of a paradox: this era saturated with serialized records and registers is also considered the era of amnesic recording: "while all information and communication is preserved and recorded on servers and hard drives, at the same time, by its transformation into data, everything somehow seems to vanish" (Berrebi 2014: 218). A clear example of the amnesic recording are Snapchat pictures, an application that was introduced in 2012 and is based on the ephemeral circulation of photos that have a very short life after being viewed. One of the most popular apps among young people, Snapchat is built upon the fragility of evidence, but instead of being worried about it, its main affordance is to exploit and commodify this evanescence and make it ever more playful, with new technical possibilities for intervening the photos that are thrown into the market almost permanently. While they can offer opportunities for "gleeful appropriation" (van Dijck 2013: 155), the observations of young people's uses of this and other platforms points to a serialized activity that stays within the limits of what the apps propose and that only occasionally shows signs of unpredicted, out-of-the-box uses.

A third comment is on the representability of the real, which is telling of the ambivalences of these space-times. In several schools, students spoke about the pleasure they find in drawing, much more than in taking pictures. It seems that, in the age of mechanical reproduction, drawing acquires a different value. Drawing appears associated with ways of representation that are more "humane" and closer to reality, and touch upon issues of indexicality and truth as well.[10] Mechanical images are seen as fake; human drawing captures the spirit and the climate in more accurate ways. For example, an Argentinean student who was an avid collector of photos and fan art on Harry Potter, with over 8,000 pictures on her computer, selected as her favorite piece a drawing by a US fan artist, because it was, for her, the image that best captured the characters of the books. In a Mexican school, students who were to produce a video on animals in danger of extinction for their Biology class decided to film one classmate while he was drawing these animals because it was "realistic," and also because "we haven´t seen that in other videos, you have a talent and you are showing it." Despite the millions of photos of endangered species that they could find on the Internet, what these students considered as real was a human body and a human hand producing singular, original registers, and showing their talents and abilities.[11] It can be seen, then, that a particular question about the limits of the mechanical and machinic representation of the real is still there for many students, although it is not something that is raised in the curriculum or discussed by their teachers. In relation to questions of identity, these examples speak about the effects that digital media are having on subjectivities, of the troubles and uneasiness with the machinic production of the real, and of the different ways in which young people are positioning themselves regarding the new conditions for knowledge and reality.

The fourth and final comment is related to the overwhelming presence of images, which are increasingly ephemeral and transient. Classroom pedagogies appear to be more concerned with promoting curatorial projects in which learning becomes "scanning" a multitude of images, than with providing students with a canon of images that they have to master.[12] In this pedagogy, both teachers and students assume the role of the curator; seeing (and orally discussing the meaning of what they see) is part of a method that privileges vision over other activities that used to be highly regarded, such as writing or reading texts. Asking students to produce visual presentations and videos is an increasingly popular strategy among teachers, but as noted above, these images are not worked through or questioned in their knowledge value or their iconicity. Also, there is a tension and a paradox between the production of visual records and the expansion of visual archives and their ephemeral quality.[13]

An important dimension of ephemeral images is the politics of their management and circulation, a critical point in collections that are para-human in their size. Fontcuberta says that "There is a phenomenon of massive substraction of images in its apparent abundance. The politics of the image are linked, more than to its excess, to the ability to discard, substract, or censor them" (2016: 32). Considering the seriality and automatization of picture-making, what becomes decisive is "who manages the life of the image" (ibid.: 67), who gets to stabilize its meaning, and who controls its circulation through spreadable media (Jenkins, Ford and Green, 2013). This is particularly visible in the images that students produce for themselves. In the interviews, many students shared that they took hundreds of pictures at social events, but the only ones that they cared about, edited, or censored were the ones in which they appeared. The regulation of the impact that they want to produce on other people, the control of their public image, is a privileged space of intervention, or even the only one they decide to occupy in relation to the images they produce. Their images are inscribed in circuits of circulation that seem to be narrowly defined by dominant rules on how the self can be presented (sexy, playful, ironic, etc.), and also by the imperative of sharing all archives, an imperative that social media corporations have successfully imposed on public interactions (van Dijck 2013).

These differences between what is done with images related to school content and images for personal consumption can be linked to a different thread on the circulation of pictures. In 1995, Don Slater said that "*Taking* pictures is a taken for granted part of leisure activities; but *looking* at them is marginal" (emphasis added). However, social media platforms and portable devices have changed that: images are to be looked at, and the act of sharing them and reacting to them is critical to current uses of photography. They are "tools for conversation and circulation" (Fontcuberta 2016: 120), no longer a conversation *about* the photo but a conversation *through* photos. These pictures are not important because of who took them (and in that sense, this is a reminder of the seriality and automatism that Sartre spoke about, and of the decline of authorship); the photograph's most relevant feature is to be found in the number of conversations it enters, in the digital traces it leaves, conversations that are increasingly operating as markets for branding the self and achieving a commodified popularity in social media (Banet-Weiser 2012; van Dijck 2013). This is perhaps a realm in which the effects of digital media on subjectivities are felt the most: identities are reduced to self-images that have to be carefully monitored and tailored in order to gain popularity and value in social media. The presence of images, then, brings many more dynamics and problematics than those implied by the metaphor of new literacies: images are not only a linguistic code, but part of social experiences and practices that open in several directions that need to be considered and worked pedagogically.

## Concluding remarks

Throughout this chapter, I have tried to understand the space-times of digital schooling, questioning the metaphor of the clash between two closed systems (modern schooling as representative of the past and digital media as the future), and instead analyzing these space-times as heterogeneous entanglements, as a "space of intersecting trajectories and of the simultaneity of stories so far" (Massey 2013: 121). The uneven space-times of schooling are such not only because of the different territories in which they take place; their unevenness is related to the multiple temporalities and spatialities that knowledge, media, and people bring to it.

Among these multiple trajectories, I have taken a close look at digital media. I have tried to show that the changes in the digital space-times of schooling go well beyond the decline of handwriting or the use of Wikipedia, and involve new relationships to truth, to the real, to memory, and to the politics of the visible. I have tried to approach these transformations based on media and visual studies and social theories that are reconceptualizing space and time, and I have sought to understand their effects on school knowledge and subjectivities.

I have focused, first, on the space-times of digital media, discussing how they build upon older media such as photography and cinema and their archiving of time. Following historians of photography and cinema, I have argued that the archivability of the past crossed a threshold with cinema, with its ability to represent movement through montage, and to bring, through projection, several temporalities together (that of the apparatus, that of the moment recorded, and that of the scene of screening). Cinema's relationship to contingency is particularly important, as it is both tamed or managed through cinematic narrative and at the same time made pleasurable and enjoyable, as a testimony that things could be or can be otherwise, thus carrying a utopian possibility. These features deeply marked the twentieth-century relationship to time and to the representability of the real.

I have then examined the ways in which digital media are continuing with but also departing from these archival impulses and practices, particularly in their relationships with indexicality and reality, and their effects on knowledge practices. I have remained ambivalent about their novelty; many of these trends precede the emergence of the Internet and can be traced back, in a Benjaminian sense, to the age of the mechanical reproducibility of images, that is, of time-based media. But there are also new traits that are taking the trends to new levels: the rhythm and pace of technological renewal, the seriality of social life, and the pressure for instantaneity are producing what some call amnesic recordings, in which the ephemeral becomes more and more salient.

In the third section, I have followed some threads to analyze the space-times of digital classrooms: how digital media are forcing a tension in the relationship between indexicality and truth, and indexicality and memory; how the representability of the real is played through and with mechanical and machinic representations; and how the new politics of the image is taking place amidst young people's participation in social media but also in school homework, both inscribed in the context of a saturation of the visual and archival records.

Throughout my analysis, I have stayed closer to what digital media are bringing, and more distant to other dynamics of schooling that might be equally important to understand contemporary transformations in the space-times of schooling, such as school curriculum and organization, local arrangements and micropolitics. Doreen Massey said that "'Here' is not a place in a map. It is that intersection of trajectories, the meeting-up of stories; an encounter. Every 'here' is a here-and-now" (Massey 2013: 118). In the dense "here" and dense "now" of schooling, I have tried to emphasize the importance of including the trajectories that are being defined by digital media, that are not reduced to the devices or to the teachers or students that bring them into the classroom. I argue that paying attention to the "deep time of media" (Zielinski 2008) is crucial for understanding the epistemic, ethical, and political challenges that these media are posing to schooling.

However critical I am of some of the directions that digital media are taking, it is important to stress that there are tensions and ambivalences in these space-times. For example, the appeal of drawing speaks of old and new questions about the real; the impulse to archive is in conflict with lives that are always contingent, and also with the contemporary pressure to interact, transform, and create new records. Young people find ways to resist or creatively engage with these media, for example, in their negotiation of privacy, or the use of memes for critical politics. Yet the observations and interviews point to the weak problematization of these trends in school pedagogies, and to the implicit alignment with the demands of the entertainment industry, for example, when teachers do not interrupt the circuits of circulation and consumption of images, or when they do not contribute to deeper discussions about the representability of the real and the marketization of identities.

There are several loose ends to follow in future research and writings, beyond what I have been able to consider here. But I would like to conclude these reflections with a note on the space-times of schooling, as the possibility of an encounter that exceeds the logic of the market and of the commodification of personal life. Schools can offer opportunities for waiting and learning to be patient; they can be the experience of a particular duration that goes beyond the instantaneity and the compulsion to record everything, even if these registers are soon to be forgotten.

Masschelein and Simons (2013) have written a manifesto for schools as spaces and times of suspension, of an interruption of current trends in contemporary life, where other journeys can be opened. In line with their thought, I believe that disrupting the seriality, producing another duration, making visible the density of the here-and-now in which schooling takes place, is a central task for contemporary school pedagogies. It is important that schools think 'stratagems' to resist the current state of affairs, but at the same time avoid indulging in nostalgia (Zielinski 2008: 10). Maybe schools have to work much more clearly and explicitly on problematizing what is today considered as truth or memory, and to make visible the complex relationship of knowledge signs to the real, that is, their indexicality. In particular, I believe that schools might need to become venues where the politics of the image can be discussed, so that in the pedagogical encounter students and teachers are able to meet with stories and knowledge paths that might not be immediately available or visible for them. It is very likely that this encounter has to be, at least at some point, an encounter of bodies, of faces, where the other in its irreducible corporeality comes forth. But above all, in the space-times of digital culture, schools should be concerned with creating pedagogies that emphasize the possibility of new encounters with difference, that keep seeing stories as unfinished and that refuse to endorse the serialized repetition of the same gestures and journeys. It is not, then, a question of whether there should be more or less digital devices in classrooms, but of deciding to critically intervene in how schools inhabit these digital space-times and how they make room for other openings.

## Notes

1  I follow here David Hamilton's distinction between education as related to the accumulation, transmission, and codification of experience, and schooling as concerned with the distribution of experience via institutions and specialized personnel. Schooling is not, as it has been conceived, a more formalized or systematic version of education, but a rather idiosyncratic activity that has to do with making available or making public particular knowledge (see Hamilton and Zufiaurre 2014).
2  "Time was indeed felt – as a weight, as a source of anxiety, and as an acutely pressing problem of representation . . . Modernity was characterized by the impulse to wear time, to append it to the body so that the watch became a kind of prosthetic device extending the capacity of the body to measure time" (Doane 2002: 4). These reflections can be extended to current technological gadgets that are to be worn or implanted on the body, and also of mobile phones that act as extensions of the limbs.
3  This has been extensively analyzed by German media theorists such as Kittler (1999) and Zielinski (2008), but also is worked by Derrida (2005) and Stiegler (2010). This includes analog media such as cinema and television, as is discussed below, but also other media or technologies that produce inscriptions of culture like print, pencils, typewriters, drawing tools, etc. One notorious example, studied both by Derrida and Kittler, are Nietzsche's reflections regarding his typewriter: "our writing tools are also working on our thoughts" (quoted in Kittler 1999: 200).

4  Indexicality is a complex notion that comes from Charles Peirce's semiotics and refers, broadly speaking, to the relation between the sign and the referent, and to the truth claims of the sign (the fidelity or accuracy with which the referent is represented by the sign). I refer to Tom Gunning's work on the indexicality of digital photographies for a lucid discussion on the adequacy and relevance of the term for contemporary debates on truth and representability (Gunning 2008).

5  An ethnographic account of digital media in different locations would point to other traits (see, for example, Burrel 2012).

6  Four research projects were developed in Argentina and Mexico between 2011 and 2016, which included classroom observations in public secondary schools, in-depth interviews with teachers and students, and analysis of school homeworks that involve digital media (videos, documents, visual presentations). In Argentina, the research was carried out with a group of colleagues: Patricia Ferrante, Julieta Montero, Delia González, Ariel Benasayag, and Jaime Piracón, at FLACSO (Latin American School for the Social Sciences) and the Universidad Pedagógica. Overall, more than 40 classes were observed in the different projects, including different disciplinary subjects; 82 students and 64 teachers were interviewed in depth, on occasion twice or three times; the research corpus includes over 60 audiovisual texts made by students that were subjected to a socio-semiotic and genealogical analysis.

7  In 2016, the OED has proclaimed "post-truth" as the word of the year, defined as "relating to or denoting circumstances in which objective facts are less influential in shaping public opinion than appeals to emotion and personal belief". See "Word of the Year: Post-Truth, Oxford Living Dictionaries: English." Retrieved February 2, 2017 from: https://en.oxforddictionaries.com/word-of-the-year/word-of-the-year-2016.

8  This weakness of the intellectual operations that schools are supposed to perform upon knowledge precedes the expansion of digital media, and is related to many other dynamics and trajectories. However, what might be new is the pressure to accommodate school routines and interactions to the model of the entertainment industry and particularly to the pressures of contemporary social media.

9  Fontcuberta says that "Kodak promised to preserve the fleeting moments of our lives; the iPhone sets us in an enlarged 'now' as life experience" (2016: 115).

10  John Berger wrote "Drawing . . . has less to do with the sense of sight than with the sense of touch, with touching the substance and energy of things, with touching the enigma of life without thinking about eternity . . ." (Berger 2013: 143).

11  The example of the Biology video is taken from Blanca Trujillo's PhD thesis (see Trujillo, in progress). The connection between the amateur videos and the tradition of the vaudeville in the nineteenth century, where everyone could show their own talents, was made by Jenkins (2007). It also relates to the opposition between painting and photography in the nineteenth century: William Fox Talbot (1800–1877), one of the early photographers, said that photography was "a mechanical aid for those who lack drawing talent" (Gunning 2008: 27).

12  I follow here Orit Halpern's analysis of design education in the 1950s and 1960s, which seems to have extended to mainstream school pedagogies in the last decades (Halpern 2014: 88).

13  This paradox should be investigated further. The images that students mobilize for their homework are increasingly reduced to stereotypes, a replication of the most popular result in the search engine or of the tropes and motifs of the entertainment industries. The stereotyping and repetition could speak of a certain collective visual memory; yet, as far as we could observe in our research, students do not seem to relate to them as signs of memory, and tend to easily forget the content or meaning of the images that they used. Images in digital schoolwork appear to be another ephemeral sign in a permanent circuit of consumption.

# References

Arendt, H. (1961). The crisis in education. In H. Arendt, *Between past and future: Six exercises in political thought* (pp. 173–226). Cleveland, OH: Meridian Books.

Banet-Weiser, S. (2012). *Authentic™: The politics of ambivalence in a brand culture*. New York and London: New York University Press.

Bauman, Z. (2000). *Liquid modernity*. London: Polity Press.

Benjamin, W. (1999) *The arcades project* (H. Eiland and K. McLaughlin, Trans.). Cambridge, MA: The Belknap Press of Harvard University Press.

Benjamin, W. (2011). *Early writings (1910–1917)* (H. Eiland, Trans.). Cambridge, MA: The Belknap Press of Harvard University Press.

Berger, J. (2013). *Understanding a photograph* (G. Dyer, Ed.). New York: Aperture.

Berman, M. (1982). *All that is solid melts into air*. New York: Simon & Schuster.

Berrebi, Sophie (2014). *The shape of evidence: Contemporary art and the document*. Amsterdam: Valiz.

Biesta, G. (2006). *Beyond learning: Democratic education for a human future*. New York: Paradigm Books.

Boltanski, L. and Thévenot, L. (2006). *On justification: Economies of worth*. Princeton, NJ: Princeton University Press.

Burrel, J. (2012). *Invisible users: Youth in the internet cafés of urban Ghana*. Cambridge, MA: MIT Press.

Crary, J. (2013). 24/7: *Late capitalism and the end of sleep*. London and New York: Verso.

Curtis, S. (2009). Between observation and spectatorship: Medicine, movies and mass culture in imperial Germany. In K. Kreimeier and A. Ligensa (Eds.). *Film 1900: Technology, Perception, Culture* (pp. 87–98). Eastleigh and Bloomington: John Libbey/ Indiana University Press.

Daston, L. (2006). *Things that talk. Object lessons from art and science*. New York: Zone Books.

Derrida, J. (2005). *Paper machine* (R. Bowlby, Trans.). Stanford, CA: Stanford University Press.

Dijck, J. van (2013). *The culture of connectivity: A critical history of social media*. Oxford: Oxford University Press.

Doane, M. A. (2002). *The emergence of cinematic time: Modernity, contigency, the archive*. Cambridge, MA: Harvard University Press.

Dussel, I. (2014). Usos del cine en la escuela: Una experiencia atravesada por la visualidad. *Revista Estudos da Língua(gem)*, Brasil, *12*(1), 77–100.

Dussel, I. (in press). *Sobre la precariedad de la escuela* (On the precariousness of schooling). In J. Larrosa (Ed.), *Elógio da Escola* (In Praise of the School). Belo Horizonte, Brazil: Editorial Autêntica.

Fontcuberta, J. (2016). *La furia de las imágenes: Notas sobre la postfotografía* (The fury of images: Notes on post-photography). Barcelona: Galaxia Gutenberg.

Foucault, M. (1983). *La verdad y las formas jurídicas* (Truth and its juridical forms) (E. Lynch, Trans.). México: Editorial Gedisa.

Freedman, E. (2011). *Transient images: Personal media in public frameworks*. Philadelphia, PA: Temple University Press.

Friedberg, A. (2006). *The virtual window: From Alberti to Microsoft*. Cambridge, MA: MIT Press.

Galison, P. (2003). *Einstein's clocks: Poincaré's maps: Empires of time*. New York: W.W. Norton & Co.

Gitelman, L. (2008). *Always already new: Media, history and the data of culture*. Cambridge, MA: MIT Press.

Gunning, T. (2008). What's the point of an index? Or, faking photographs. In K. Beckman and J. Ma (Eds.). *Still moving: Between cinema and photography* (pp. 23–40). Durham, NC and London: Duke University Press.

Hacking, I. (1990). *The taming of chance*. Cambridge: Cambridge University Press.

Halpern, O. (2014). *Beautiful data: A history of vision and reason since 1945*. Durham, NC and London: Duke University Press.

Hamilton, D., and Zufiaurre, B. (2014). *Blackboards and bootstraps: Revisioning education and schooling*. Rotterdam: Sense Publishers.

Harvey, D. (1989). *The conditions of postmodernity: An enquiry into the origins of cultural change*. London: Blackwell.

Ingold, T. (2015). *The life of lines*. New York and London: Routledge.

Isin, E. and Ruppert, E. (2015). *Being digital citizens*. Lanham, MD: Rowman & Littlefield.

Jenkins, H. (2007). *The wow climax: Tracing the emotional impact of popular culture*. New York and London: New York University Press.

Jenkins, H., Ford, S. and Green, J. (2013). *Spreadable media: Creating value and meaning in a networked culture*. New York: New York University Press.

Kittler, F. (1999). *Gramophone, film, typewriter* (G. Winthrop-Young and M. Wutz, Trans.). Palo Alto, CA: Stanford University Press.

Latour, B. (2005) *Reassembling the social*. Oxford: Oxford University Press.

Lawn, M. and Grosvenor, I. (Eds.). (2005). *Materialities of schooling: Design, technology, objects, routines* (pp. 1–15). Oxford: Symposium Books.

Lemke, J. (2004). Learning across multiple places and their chronotopes. Paper presented at AERA 2004, April 12–16, San Diego, CA. Retrieved March 14, 2015 from: www-personal.umich.edu/~jaylemke/papers/aera_2004.htm.

Masschelein, J. and Simons, M. (2013). *In defence of the school: A public issue* (J. McMartin, Trans). Leuven: Education, Culture & Society Publishers.

Massey, D. (2013). Some times of space. In A. Groom (Ed.), *Time: Documents of contemporary art* (pp. 116–122). Cambridge, MA: MIT Press and The Whitechapel Gallery.

McLeod, J. and Thomson, R. (2009). *Researching social change*. London: Sage.

Mirzoeff, N. (2015). *How to see the world: A Pelican introduction*. London: Penguin Books.

Mongin, O. (1993). *El miedo al vacío: Ensayo sobre las pasiones democráticas*. Buenos Aires: Fondo de Cultura Económica.

Nespor, J. (2011). *Technology and the politics of instruction*. New York: Routledge.

Slater, D. (1995). Domestic photography and digital culture. In M. Lister (Ed.). *The photographic image in digital culture* (pp. 129–146). London: Routledge.

Stiegler, B. (2010). *Taking care of youth and the generations*. Palo Alto, CA: Stanford University Press.

Thrift, N. (2006) Space. *Theory, Culture & Society*, *23*(2–3), 139–55.

Trujillo, B. (in progress). *Tareas escolares en la cultura digital. Transformaciones y tensiones en el ensamblaje de la escolarización* (School homework in digital culture. Transformations and tensions in the assembling of schooling). Doctorado en Ciencias en la Especialidad de Investigaciones Educativas, Departamento de Investigaciones Educativas del CINVESTAV, México.

Turner, F. (2006). *From counterculture to cyberculture: Stewart Brand, the Whole Earth Network, and the rise of digital utopianism.* Chicago, IL and London: University of Chicago Press.

Virilio, P. (2006). *Speed and politics: An essay on dromology* (M. Polizotti, Trans.) (2nd. ed.). New York: Semiotext(e).

Wouters, C. (2007). *Informalization: Manners and emotions since 1890.* London: Sage.

Zielinski, S. (2008). *Deep time of the media: Towards an archeology of hearing and seeing by technical means.* Cambridge, MA: MIT Press.

# 9 The affective-discursive orthodoxies of the "I don't forget" education policy in Cyprus

*Michalinos Zembylas*

In this chapter I focus on a corpus of circular and curriculum documents collected between 1996 and 2016 concerning the education policy of "I don't forget and I struggle" (*Δεν ξεχνώ και αγωνίζομαι*) (henceforth "I don't forget") in Greek-Cypriot schools. The educational policy of "I don't forget" became prominent in the Greek-Cypriot national curriculum in the years after the Turkish invasion of 1974 that divided the country. This policy aimed at teaching Greek-Cypriot children and youth to preserve history, memory and identity so that they would never forget the territories occupied by Turkey and that they would care enough to carry on the struggle to liberate those territories. My analysis focuses on the affective life of these circular and curriculum documents and particularly how time and history might be connected to the assembling of affective-discursive orthodoxies (Wetherell 2012; Wetherell, McCreanor, McConville and Moewaka Barnes 2015) that construct children and youth as emotional subjects who formulate and express canonic emotions. In other words, I am interested in "historicizing" the production of these documents and their formulation into an "emotional archive" that has important implications for the processes of subjectivity and memory. First let me define my terms.

By "historicity" I mean both a "sociohistorical process" and the "narrative constructions about that process" (see Trouillot 1995: 22–29). In Trouillot's words: "Human beings participate in history both as actors and as narrators, yet the boundaries between these two sides of historicity, necessary as they are as heuristic devices, are themselves historical, and thus fluid and changing" (2003: 12). Of particular importance to this conceptualization of historicity is how subjects are actively involved in this process and the narrative construction of its representation. I hope to show, then, that emotions are pivotal to understandings of history and the formation of historicity (see also Hermann 2005). In particular, the "I don't forget" policy is an interesting case for investigating how the nation-state mobilizes the affective-discursive in educational policy-making to communicate to children and youth what Kenway and Fahey call "the emotional archive of the nation-state" (2011a: 190). The emotional archive of the nation-state, according to Kenway and Fahey, includes the feelings stored over time in both the body politic and the national culture. Importantly, a consideration of the emotional archive of the nation-state through the journey of an education policy in a specific geopolitical time/place shows not only the historicity of affects and the politics of memory, but also how the nation-state imagines its children and youth participating in history as actors and narrators. Collectively, then, the "I don't forget" policy over the years constitutes a sociohistorical archive, a repository of emotions, coded not just in its content but also in the practices that are employed in its production, reception, and eventual expression by children/youth-as-emotional subjects (see Cvetkovitch 2003).

The chapter unfolds as follows. First, I briefly discuss some theoretical considerations concerning the affective-discursive entanglements to show how they have guided my analysis and how they are explicitly connected to the themes of time, history, and memory. Then, I provide a genealogy of the "I don't forget" policy to demonstrate the affective-discursive positions of the circular and curricular documents analysed, focusing in particular on the last twenty years – that is, from 1996 (which marks the official appearance of the "I don't forget" as a school subject in the national curriculum) until the present. The third part of the chapter identifies the affective-discursive patterns of the emotional archive of the nation-state, as they are emerging from these documents, and discusses what kind of emotional subjects and what kinds of repertoires "populate this canon" (Wetherell et al. 2015: 61). Finally, the chapter ends with discussing some implications in relation to investigating the entanglement of educational policies with the emotional archive of the nation-state.

## Theoretical considerations

The complex intertwining of emotion, time, and memory has received increased attention in recent years, especially from the perspective of looking at the politics of memory, that is, the political dimension of remembering, recording, or forgetting a particular event by different groups of people. As Ahmed writes:

> Emotions tell us a lot about time; emotions are the very "flesh" of time. They show us the time it takes to move, or to move on, is a time that exceeds the time of an individual life. Through emotions, the past persists on the surface of bodies. Emotions show us how histories stay alive, even when they are not consciously remembered; how histories of colonialism, slavery, and violence shape lives and worlds in the present.
>
> (Ahmed 2004: 202).

Understanding the politics of memory as more than struggles over legitimate representations of the past, it is argued that these struggles are always *performed* and *felt* and thus always work through entangled forces of emotion, time, and memory (Curti 2008). As Curti explains:

> The role of emotion as an adhesive of experience cannot be separated from that of memory: it is not *either* memory or emotion that adhere together blocs of experiences in (re)creations of identity, but *both together* working through a reflexive embodied symbiosis.
>
> (Curti 2008: 107; original emphasis)

Fights over representations of the past "are always performed and felt between, in and through bodies and thus always work through entangled forces of emotion, affect and memory" (ibid.: 108). For instance, the perception of the Berlin Wall, or the West Bank separation wall, or the walls that separate Catholics and Protestants in Belfast neighbourhoods, exists emotionally and performatively through the memories, bodies, and identities of the people who live(d) on both sides of the wall, albeit in very different ways. How this wall is *felt* within a society is very much relevant to the ways in which it functions – in time and history – as an affective-discursive practice. Knowledge of the past is both product and source of historicization – namely, how people perceive emotionally the past and narrate past events (Hermann, 2005). The implications of this intertwining among emotion, history, and memory are particularly important for educators and schooling.

First of all, schooling has always functioned as an important arena for cultivating certain memories of the past together with certain emotions (Bekerman and Zembylas 2012) The term "schooling of emotion" (Worsham 2001) reflects the idea that schools perform certain pedagogies of emotion, and as such they are effective ways of anchoring students in a particular way of life. For example, schools in conflict-troubled societies are seen as prime sites in which the traumatic experiences that shape collective historical narratives are re-created, passed on to future generations and used to strengthen dichotomies between *we* and *they, victims* and *perpetrators* (Bekerman and Zembylas 2012; Davies 2004). The schooling of emotion, then, may establish, assert, challenge, or reinforce particular "emotional hegemonies" (Jaggar 1989) or canonic emotions about what students *should* feel. Despite the evidence of this process taking place, there have been very few sustained investigations in educational policy making focusing on *how* exactly the entanglement of emotion, time, and memory takes place in curricular documents and what kind of emotional subjects are invoked in these policies. More importantly, it is valuable to explore what it would take to break down these emotional hegemonies and encourage the interrogation of canonic emotions.

Pursuing this line of analysis, this chapter draws on two main ideas to analyse the circular and curricular documents of the "I don't forget" policy in the Greek-Cypriot educational system; first, the notion of "affective-discursive entanglements"; and, second, the concept of "emoscape". The first idea is grounded in Wetherell's "social practice approach" (2012; Wetherell et al. 2015) – namely, that every social practice has affective and discursive dimensions that are entangled. Social practice is understood here as both doings and sayings, that are space and time bounded (Reckwitz 2012); this notion includes manifestations of everyday life from social events to media and texts. This approach, then, focuses on the analysis of patterns of affective-discursive material as evident in social practices. For example, it would be interesting to explore the temporal dimensions of affective-discursive entanglements, namely, how time may change what Wetherell and colleagues (2015) call the "affective-discursive canon" or "emotion canon" found in texts such as circular and curricular documents. "By 'affective-discursive canon'," they write, "we mean the established, immediately familiar and orthodox procedures for emoting and making sense" (ibid.: 60) found in different manifestations of social practice.

In reference to the specific geopolitical time/place of Cyprus and the perceived role of education over time, for instance, it would be valuable to identify the affective-discursive orthodoxies that are present in a corpus of circular and curricular documents over a certain time period.

The second analytic concept that guides my exploration of the emotional patterns in the "I don't forget" policy is the notion of emoscape (Kenway and Fahey 2011a, 2011b). As Kenway and Fahey (2011a, 2011b) argue, the term "emoscape" adds another potential "scape" to Appadurai's (1990) original list of the "ethnoscapes", "ideoscapes" and "mediascapes". The suffix "-scape" denotes that these terms are situated within historical, cultural, and political spaces. As they explain:

> By this [emoscape] we mean the movement of emotion across various spatial scales. In proposing this notion, we clearly reject the view that emotion only moves *within* individuals' psychology or psyche. Instead, we draw on the views above that understand emotions as processes, involving intersections of the social, cultural, spatial and psychic realms. We see emotions as mobile, mobilized and mobilizing. Emotions move individuals, but they also operate in a realm beyond the personal and interpersonal. Emotions are on the move on a global scale via different technologies. They are mobilized by various discourses. It is these discourses that create a cultural context for certain ideas. And, finally, emotions are mobilizing as they motivate people to act. These actions then work to move other people and thus we come full circle.
>
> (Kenway and Fahey 2011b: 169; original emphasis)

Clearly, then, the notion of emoscape, in Kenway and Fahey's view, refers to the *spatial* flow of feelings between people and places, emphasizing not only the movement of emotion within an individual or between individuals, but also in relation to particular historical, political, social, and cultural landscapes. However, there is another dimension that is not highlighted as much by Kenway and Fahey and seems to be lost in their emphasis on spatial scales: the temporal scale. In other words, the notion of emoscape seems to rely on temporal processes of affective-discursive entanglements as much as it depends on spatial ones. The temporal scale becomes more evident in the second analytic concept I employ here.

Kenway and Fahey's "emotional archive of the nation state" (2011a) refers to the historical flow of emotions within the nation-state. This archive functions as a repository of emotions (Cvetkovitch 2003) associated with important historical and social events of the nation-state that are "written" in its consciousness, creating particular emoscapes. In this way, texts such as education policies are viewed as "archives of feelings" where the traces of technologies of power can be identified, both at the micro- and macro-levels. In highlighting the entanglement between the micro- and macro-levels, Kenway and Fahey (2001a) use Hochschild's (1983) notion of "feeling rules": to emphasize how certain rules and codes at the macro (national) level are manifested at the everyday (micro) level of individuals, navigating certain emotional behaviours. Education policies, then, are interesting not only for their content but also constitute temporal and spatial practices that are employed to produce particular students-as-emotional-subjects. The notions of "affective-discursive entanglements" and "emoscape", then, are helpful here in that they draw analytic attention to the affective, spatial, and temporal features of policies and show how these features could constitute powerful technologies of power to drive students' emotions toward particular orientations.

The next part of this chapter utilizes these two analytic concepts – namely, the notion of affective-discursive entanglements and the concept of emoscape – to engage in a genealogy of the "I don't forget" policy in the Greek-Cypriot educational system. But, before doing so, it is helpful to note a few things about the wider historical and political context of education in Cyprus.

## Genealogy of the "I don't forget" policy[1]

Greek-Cypriot society and its educational system have been deeply marked by the so-called "Cyprus Issue", which refers to the strife between the island's two main ethnolinguistic communities: the Greek-Cypriot majority (about 80 per cent) and the sizeable Turkish-Cypriot minority (about 18 per cent). Following a period of inter-ethnic violence in the 1960s, the conflict culminated in 1974 with a Greek-Cypriot coup staged against President Makarios and Turkey's reaction, which was to invade Cyprus. The Turkish invasion dealt heavy Greek-Cypriot casualties (thousands of dead and missing) and divided the island, forcing 200,000 Greek Cypriots (one-third of the total population) to be displaced from their homeland and move to the south of the island (Hitchens 1984; Mallinson 2005). In addition, 45,000 Turkish Cypriots (one-fourth of Cyprus's total population) were displaced to the north of the island. Since then, the country has been divided *de facto* into two ethnically homogenized parts: the Cyprus Republic, which controls the southern part and is practically dominated by the Greek-Cypriots, and the "Turkish Republic of Northern Cyprus", established in 1983 – a formation that has been declared legally invalid by the United Nations and is recognized only by Turkey. Despite the ongoing negotiations for a settlement under the auspices of the UN, the partition of the island still remains in place. However, since 2003, the opening of a few checkpoints in the buffer zone has allowed relative freedom of movement across the dividing line.

What is known as the policy of "I don't forget" became prominent in the Greek-Cypriot school curriculum soon after the Turkish invasion of 1974, and for more than four decades has aimed to teach students about the disastrous consequences of the invasion and to transmit information about the occupied territories and pre-1974 Greek-Cypriot life there. The "I don't forget" slogan in the Greek-Cypriot community has become the symbol of the communal trauma and suffering from the Turkish invasion of 1974 (Roudometof and Christou 2011). As Bryant has aptly written: "In Cyprus, as in many ongoing conflicts, memory has been institutionalized as wound, visible in the rupture of partition as well as in politicized personal suffering" (2012: 340). The following genealogy focuses on demonstrating the affective-discursive positions of the circular and curricular documents analysed, covering in particular the last two decades (1996–2016).

### The early years

The first educational publication on the topic of "I don't forget" was the textbook *Our Enslaved Land* (*Η σκλαβωμένη γη μας*) (Anastasiadis, Sarantis, Kougialis and Theofilaktou 1978), which was used as a textbook for literacy lessons in primary school and contained a selection of texts on related topics (e.g., refugee life, missing persons, occupied places, etc.), accompanied by language exercises. However, according to Aristodemou (2004), the slogan "I don't forget" had not appeared in that publication, as hopes for a settlement that would make the return to the north possible were still very strong at the time.

The slogan "I don't forget and I struggle" was introduced as an educational policy with its related practices a decade after the dislocation of 1974, with the aim of producing for the younger generations *unlived* collective memories of the war and the occupied territories in the north (Aristodemou, 2004). Before making its way into educational policy, however, the phrase "I don't forget" had previously been already established as a slogan in Greek-Cypriot society.[2] Papadakis describes the meaning of this slogan as follows:

> The Greek Cypriot official reference to social memory is encapsulated [in the slogan] "I Don't Forget (*Δεν Ξεχνώ*)". This refers to 1974 and the refugees who "don't forget their homes and villages in the occupied areas" . . . The focus of Greek Cypriot social memory is 1974 and the suffering brought about by the Turkish military offensive . . . .
>
> (Papadakis 2006: 7)

Bowman (2006) also describes how the "I don't forget" policy, especially a few years after the events of 1974, had permeated all facets of Greek-Cypriot society:

> "I Don't Forget". These words were a symbol found everywhere in Cyprus. They were on school exercise books and on photos of villages under occupation. Children saw them every day they went to school, every time they had to write. Every night, before the main evening news, the photo of an occupied village was shown with "I Don't Forget" underneath. What should not be forgotten was so clear that there was no need to say more. "The memories of our occupied villages, our ancestral hearths, our graveyards, our occupied churches, our occupied homes, our gardens, our orchards."
>
> (Bowman 2006: 122)

By the mid-1980s, the slogan "I don't forget" dominated Greek-Cypriot educational culture through abundant photographic displays in educational spaces[3] of locations in the north, profuse references to the losses of the war, and regular commemorations of the "lost lands" on given occasions. As my ethnographic study of memorial ceremonies in Greek-Cypriot schools has shown (Zembylas 2013), the "hegemonic" model of "I don't forget" has emphasized the emotional themes of heroism and victimhood. This model has stressed emotional identification with victimhood and the emulation of heroes who sacrificed their lives for the country; in addition, it has reinforced past-oriented hero/victim discourses and practices of grief. For example, there are many symbolic messages grounded in the emotional distinction between "we-the-good" and "they-the-evil". By focusing exclusively on the feelings of victimhood for the Greek-Cypriot community, while ignoring the pain of the "other" (i.e., Turkish Cypriots), the emotion discourses floating around reaffirm the linkage between national memory and the emotional canon.

### The 1990s

In the early 1990s, the Ministry of Education produced a series of three more primary-school textbooks with the topic of "I don't forget", which provided rich textual and photographic material for cross-curricular use. The first two textbooks came with the title *I Don't Forget and I Struggle* (Δεν ξεχνώ και αγωνίζομαι) (1990, 1992), while in the third, the title was changed to *I Know, I Don't Forget and I Struggle* (Γνωρίζω δεν ξεχνώ και αγωνίζομαι) (1994). The textbooks' titles – and the Ministry's discourses that accompanied them – signify the initiation of a new phase in the policy of "I don't forget" in the early 1990s. More than fifteen years after the dislocation of 1974, the purpose of "I don't forget" had to be redefined towards the *construction* – rather than the preservation – of "collective memories" of the northern territories, since the younger generations neither had lived before the war of 1974, nor could they visit the occupied areas (access was prohibited by the Turkish-Cypriot authorities until 2003). The expansion of the "I don't forget" slogan to "I know, I don't forget and I struggle" renders explicit both the cognitive ("knowing", "remembering") and the prescriptive ("struggling") aspects that the policy had acquired. According to Philippou (2007: 252), the addition of the verb "I struggle" came as a response to concerns expressed by teachers that for students who don't have actual memories of the war and the north, "I don't forget" remains vague and "they [have] no clear understandings of how they could actively contribute to the political problem." The preface written by the general director of primary education in the 1992 volume captures clearly the intended social and political functionality of the "I don't forget" policy:

> This book is yet another attempt to deal with the consequences of the Turkish invasion in Cyprus, based on the awareness of our homeland's amputation ... The invader attempts to obliterate memory, to change place names, to load the occupied territories with settlers ... Yet, we want our children to be rememberers of their fathers' land and fighters for the restoration of justice. In this respect, this book with its pictures, maps and texts is a strong weapon in the hands of students and teachers. I am sure that teachers, as genuine Cypriot Greeks, do not need further incentives to take advantage of this excellent book ... I hope that the militancy of each of us is constantly escalating until the just solution of our problem.
>
> (Ministry of Education and Culture 1992: 7)

Evidently, this preface creates a strong link between cognition and social action, reflecting the belief that education should be at the forefront of national struggles. The excerpt very consistently interweaves the need to know and remember lost homelands – "awareness of our homeland's amputation", "rememberers of their fathers' land", "the invader . . . obliterates memory" – with the need to fight for justice and vindication. A series of lexical choices reinforces a pervasive sense of "being embattled" – "invader", "fighters", "weapon", "militancy") – which justifies the need to assign to education the duty to evoke patriotism ("as pure Greek-Cypriots") and, ultimately, instigate actual struggle against the invader. This text deploys the familiar rhetoric of "we" along with the "proper feelings" and relations that are clearly prescribed to formulate "proper" history: A collective "we" is imagined, supplied with cognitions and knowledge ("the invader attempts to obliterate memory"), ways of organizing our behaviour ("we want our children to be rememberers"), and, crucially, with emotions, evaluations, and motivations ("as genuine Greek Cypriots . . . the militancy of each of us . . .").

More importantly, the inclusion of the slogan "I know, I don't forget and I struggle" as a separate school subject in the new curriculum of 1996 marks an important step in normalizing it within educational policy and school life, and transferring the traumatic memory of 1974 to the new generation (Routometof and Christou 2011). The idea, as Roudometof and Christou explain, is not to add another school subject but instead infuse the whole curriculum from kindergarten to the last year of Lyceum (ages 4–17) with references to the problem of Turkish occupation. In the section of the curriculum devoted to the subject "I know, I don't forget and I struggle" (Ministry of Education 1996: 93–97), the emotional tone is rather strong and indicative of the affective-discursive practices of grievance for the injustices and sufferings that continue to trouble the Greek-Cypriot community. For example, the following excerpt from the 1996 curriculum shows how "I don't forget" aims explicitly to *nationalize* children's and teachers' emotions about refugees:

> [The students need] to mention and justify the elements that keep refugees and generally the [Greek-Cypriot] people emotionally tied to their land . . . to become emotionally moved through experiencing customs and traditions of our occupied land . . . to learn about the living of the inhabitants of occupied Cyprus before and after the invasion, and to collect information that shows nostalgia for return from those who were uprooted.
>
> (Ministry of Education and Culture 1996: 96)

The nationalization of emotions aims to invest students and teachers with national norms that reify particular perceptions, e.g., the "Greekness" of the land, the emotional ties of refugees with their land, the need to be emotionally moved and committed to the struggle for liberating Cyprus, and so on (for more details, see Zembylas 2015; Zembylas, Charalambous and Charalambous 2016).

### The 2000s

A new reform of the policy of "I don't forget" came in 2001, aiming to substantially "upgrade" and "prioritize" it as an educational objective in Greek-Cypriot primary schools. The circular F:7.11.13.3 (October 2001), came with the acknowledgement that recently "students' knowledge and interest in the occupied territories and in various aspects of our national problem has diminished and became attenuated." According to this circular:

> We expect that the correct development of our students is based on the cultivation and invigoration of their national and fighting spirit; on their knowledge of the occupied territories and the preservation of their memory of them; and on the realization of their obligations and rights in a semi-occupied homeland with European orientations and away from intolerance.
>
> (Circular F:7.11.13.3, October 2001)

Ethnographic research (Christou 2006, 2007) conducted in Greek-Cypriot secondary schools around the same time (2000) confirmed students' diminishing knowledge and interest. The research showed that although the cognitive aims seemed to be achieved – students seemed to know about and "remember" the occupied areas – the policy's prescriptive section, evoking patriotism and instigating struggle, did not appear particularly effective in practice. According to Christou (2006), the policy of "I don't forget" failed to construct an imagination of what the future could look like in a reunified federal Cyprus, thus leaving the goal for national struggle "discursively empty". To cover for what remained unsaid, students resorted to the familiar cultural resources of the predominant discourse – and its underlying irredentist origins – and tended to define this struggle as a "return to the occupied part of the island and to past glories", from "a time when Greek-Cypriots had more specific and lofty national goals" (Christou 2006: 286).

Nevertheless, since the opening of the checkpoints in April 2003 and for the following decade (until September 2013), the policy of "I don't forget" was considerably toned down in terms of both its patriotic militancy (Christou 2006: 302) and its demands for implementation (Zembylas 2015). Although still active in forming a policy framework, the Ministry of Education and Culture refrained from issuing any further circulars and instead restricted itself to scattered references only to the 2001 circular. The potential for new generations to actually visit the northern part of the island might have somewhat diminished the urgency to encourage students to "know" the occupied territories, while other developments such as the EU accession could have heightened a sense of the policy being dated and ineffective.

The latest development in the "I don't forget" policy involved a further revival of the policy under a new government. The Ministry of Education and Culture reframed the policy as "I know, I don't forget and I contest" (*Γνωρίζω, δεν ξεχνώ, διεκδικώ*, in Circular F. 7.11.09/12, 5.13.04.3), and set it as the primary objective for the school year 2013–14 (reiterated in upcoming school years, including 2016–17).

For example, the latest circular issued by the director of primary education, and addressed to school principals and teachers, includes the following excerpt regarding this objective:

> Another school year begins while a large part of our homeland continues to be occupied. The fact that during this school year we are going through the 43rd year of occupation of half of our land steels our determination and our faith for liberation and reunification of our homeland . . .
>
> The main parameters of this objective are three: (a) I know my homeland; (b) I don't forget my occupied land, and (c) I contest the liberation and reunification of my homeland.
>
> (F. 7.11.09/15, 5.13.04.3, August 3, 2016: 56)

Interestingly, the reference to this objective – a mere two pages long (56–57), buried in a long text of 93 pages, with instructions about other issues for the beginning of the new school year – is copied and pasted from the text that appeared in 2013–14. A brief explanation of each of the three parameters (again copied and pasted from the earlier text) is provided, including references to: "the necessity that our students know the history, traditions . . . of both our free and our occupied homeland"; "A dominant place in our educational system is the effort to maintain as inextinguishable the memory of our occupied villages and towns", and "Contesting the liberation and reunification of our homeland . . . is expressed with peaceful means and on the basis of basic human rights."

## Patterns of the emotional archive of the nation-state

I argue here that the emotion canon evident across my circular and curricular sample is composed from four main affective-discursive threads. These affective-discursive threads show the temporal and time manifestations of emotion, history, and identity over a period of two decades. The circular and curricular archive constitutes a repository of emotions about history, memory, and identity in Cyprus; this repository is employed with the aim of producing particular students-as-emotional-subjects. To put this differently: the affective-discursive entanglements and the emoscapes emerging from this archive mobilize the affective-discursive canon in Greek-Cypriot narratives of history, identity, and memory. Each of these four threads is briefly discussed below.

The first affective-discursive thread is feelings of victimhood and loss, especially in the early years following the 1974 Turkish invasion. The slogan "I don't forget" implored Greek-Cypriot children and youth to remember the community's losses and victimhood, while silencing the traumatic experiences of the "Other" (i.e., Turkish Cypriots), what has become known in the literature as one-sided victimization narrative (Bekerman and Zembylas 2012). The policy framework of "I don't forget" provided the platform to imbue love for the homeland and the need to cultivate remembrance for the occupied territories. Yet this discourse disallowed, for the most part, any representations of victimization experienced by the

"Other" and conveyed a sense of embattlement which called for militancy in the struggle for justice. The two repertoires utilized – namely, "we-the-good", on the one hand, and "they-the-evil", on the other – mobilized clear affective-discursive subject positions for Greek-Cypriot students: Greek Cypriots are patriotic people who fight for justice, while the "other" side is positioned as unjust and apathetic to Greek-Cypriot suffering.

The second affective-discursive thread is feelings of bitterness and resentment. Bitterness and resentment become part of an affective-discursive position in all aspects of everyday life (including education) that constitutes Greek Cypriots as eternal "victims" of Turkish expansionism (Papadakis 2008); these feelings become integral and "stuck" to Greek-Cypriot consciousness. This stickiness works through discursive rituals to render bitterness a justifiable emotional response as a result of trauma, loss, and perceived injustice. The commitment to the idea of returning to the land now occupied by Turkish troops, then, is galvanized by a range of feelings about displacement such as fear, anxiety, depression, vulnerability, helplessness, resentment, and bitterness (see Loizos 1981, 2008; Zetter 1991, 1999). Return, in particular, as a prominent slogan in the "I don't forget" policy, has dominated the domestic and international agendas of Greek Cypriots. As Zetter writes: "Frustration and even disbelief are exacerbated by protracted exile of the Greek Cypriots, but the intention, aspiration and the right to reclaim what has been lost is never disputed" (1999: 6). However, as Zetter argues, a myth has been constructed around return. What is mythologized and idealized is the extent to which the physical and symbolic past can ever be reclaimed. Yet, this affective-discursive position and repertoire of suffering – which is often portrayed as an "open wound" – remains prominent in the "I don't forget" over the years.

The third affective-discursive thread is a feeling of nostalgia for what was lost in the occupied territories – a feeling that was more prominent in the 1990s. The affective-discursive position constructed in this thread suggests that through the concept of "I don't forget", the new generations could keep alive an idea of a pre-1974 "homeland" in which the Greek Cypriots have flourished in the lands of their ancestors. In these narratives, there is a sense of nostalgia that intrudes the present to mourn for the loss of a past place and time. This nostalgia was essentially mediated by "postmemories" (Hirsch 2001, 2008; Hirsch and Spitzer 2002). Postmemories are memories which do not refer to or draw on a person's actual past experiences, but rather memories generated through the lens of a preceding generation marked by trauma. As Hirsch explains, postmemories describe "the relationship of the second generation to powerful, often traumatic experiences that preceded their birth but were nevertheless transmitted to them so deeply as to seem to constitute memories in their own right" (2008: 103). The "I don't forget" policy was then an attempt to transmit "unlived" memories to children and youth for a place or time that no longer exists, or never existed because it was idealized.

Finally, the fourth affective-discursive thread expounds feelings of hope and perseverance. The repertoire of hope constructs liberation of the occupied territories and reunification of the homeland as achievable, despite the difficulties over the years. This repertoire is considerably different from the other three, in that there is a "positive" emotional outlook that is not always present in the others. This emotional repertoire constructs liberation as compatible with the students' own emotions, and it can be identified in two distinct versions: one expresses a controlled optimism about the prospects of liberation, acknowledging its value, despite the many difficulties cited; the other is combined with the affective-discursive position of perseverance, namely, the necessity that students adopt feelings of determination and a fighting spirit.

The four threads of affective-discursive positions and repertoires about "I don't forget" show how circular and curricular documents over the years have included powerful affective registers aiming at shaping students' emotional subjectivities; however, these affective registers include internal contradictions, paradoxes, and ambivalences about the potential effectiveness of the policy measures that are promoted, as time goes by and the division of Cyprus continues. As Roudometof and Christou (2011) have argued, the "I don't forget" objective is paradoxical because it demands that new generations identify with the memory and suffering of events not personally experienced. It is not surprising, then, that some of the affective-discursive positions seem to have toned down over the years (Christou 2006, 2007; Zembylas 2015).

Another ambivalence identified in these affective-discursive positions and repertoires emerges from what Bryant (2012) calls "the temporality of the wound". In Greek-Cypriots' institutions of memory, she writes, "a sense of temporariness is created by emphasizing that Turkey is an occupying invader that has unjustly seized their lands and so must leave" (ibid.: 344). Although this sense of temporality is imbued with the emotional language of hope and perseverance that occupation will eventually end, there is simultaneously a feeling of disappointment and bitterness that time is passing by and nothing changes. This entanglement of hope and disappointment, suggests Bryant, has had a negative impact on the slogan of "I don't forget" – something that has been reflected in the fading of the emotional language used in recent years, compared to the early years, namely, the 1980s and the 1990s:

> Originally a slogan of struggle, many had gradually come to see the call for people to remember their villages as simply a nostalgia for a lost past . . . Slogans such as "I do not forget" have not fully disappeared, but have instead taken on new meanings. Whereas before 2003 "Den Xechno" referred to an anticipated revival and recreation of a lost life that would take place at the moment of return, the slogan's more abstract meaning is now emphasized, reminding refugees not to forget about the violation of their rights.
>
> (Bryant 2012: 353)

The toning down of the affective-discursive positions marked by space/time is not irrelevant to invoking an "instrumental" sentimentality to students about their occupied homeland. On the one hand, the aim of the policy is to align students' feelings with the trauma of their homeland. The emotional distress or inspiration that accompany this alignment grounds the claim for students' political transformation and their commitment to keep the traumatic event of 1974 open, which means communicating it in a way that keeps it traumatic for them (Berlant 2001). On the other hand, however, as Berlant (2000, 2001) warns us, not only is this alignment far from implying any identification with trauma experienced by others (e.g., the students' parents and grandparents), but also it may lead to the trauma being fetishized, which thereby condenses the trauma in self-repetition and habituated banality. That is, there is the danger not only to an impasse in terms of connecting with trauma not experienced, but also it threatens to diminish the implications of trauma – which seems to be acknowledged by the circular and curricular documents of "I don't forget" as time goes by, especially since 2001.

To sum up, these affective-discursive positions project the dominant emotional archive consisting of feelings of victimhood, bitterness, nostalgia, and hope, emerging from historical and political positions prescribing certain feeling rules for the new generation. I have shown that the historicization of the policy's framings indicates a sentimentalized shift. In doing so, I have identified the important role that emotions play in the landscape of national memory and identity. As Roudometof and Christou (2011) have pointed out "The focus of this curricular goal is *decidedly emotional* rather than anything related to the specific events preceding or following the 1974 Turkish invasion" (172; emphasis added). Thus, political emoscapes connect with the emotional goals of educational policies, mobilizing a national emotional temper to work for policy purposes with regard to memory, identity, and trauma. A consideration of the emotional archive of this particular education policy shows how time, space, history, and historicity are all intertwined and have important implications for how affective-discursive entanglements are integral to education policies. A greater attention to the emotional archive and affective-discursive entanglements for education policy will also provide opportunities to critically examine and challenge the affective-discursive canon and its intelligibility. Without identification of how this canon is mobilized, as it is marked by time and space, it would be less likely to be able to interrogate its workings.

## Conclusion

This chapter has described the main affective-discursive practices identified in the policy of "I don't forget" in the Greek-Cypriot educational system over the years. I attempted to show the affective-discursive orthodoxies set up and demonstrate how emotions are constitutive components of the national emotional archive involved in processes of (re)construction of national memory, history, and identity in schools. Though it is impossible to fully describe all the nuances of the entanglements between affects and discourses in an educational policy over such a long period, nevertheless, it is important to recognize that emotions in educational policies are powerful forces involved in the reproduction of national memory, history, and identity, and as such, in the maintenance of particular hegemonies. At the same time, emotions are not only involved in the reproduction of hegemonic national memory; they are also involved in processes of resisting and rupturing such memory – often unexpectedly and unintentionally. Thus, as it has been identified, the instrumental sentimentality emerging in the policy of "I don't forget" over the years seems to have subverted the process of cooptation of national memory, with the result that the power of the policy has faded. The historicity of the policy, then, indicates the ambivalent ways in which matters of time/space, history, and affect traverse macro-and micro-politics and processes of subjectivity and memory.

Therefore, as educational theorists, we need to recognize the importance of micro-level aspects recounted in the emotional archive of specific educational policies. The micro-level context has to do with the emotional elements of the policy and the emotional *power* upon its recipients *to* achieve desired ends regarding national memory and its interpretation. This *power-to* (Heaney 2011) is a capacity that structures and is structured by both the macro-political context (emoscape) and the micro-level of affective-discursive practices. The analysis of the "I don't forget" policy confirms the theoretical usefulness of a pragmatic approach on emotions, nation-state, trauma, and memory that shows how social processes constitute powerful technologies of emotion in everyday forms of nationhood.

Therefore, the task of educational theorists, policymakers, and practitioners regarding educational policies is to identify the emoscapes that "govern" students and teachers. In this sense, examining how the emotional archive of a nation-state both constructs and disrupts (unintentionally) particular students' subjectivities becomes of particular interest. Emoscapes are methodically established through affective-discursive practices. Therefore, this analysis is of crucial importance to educational theorists and practitioners, because it enables them to see educational policies in a new light and ask provocative questions such as: What rules, performances, and practices act to govern the emotions of students and teachers through specific educational policies, and to direct their emotional communication and subjectification along particular lines? What would it take to resist canonic emotions and pinpoint the technologies of power and the spaces within which alternative affective-discursive practices may emerge?

To conclude, it seems that any analysis of educational policies that doesn't consider emotion and its constitution through feeling codes, roles and rules misses an important element. Methodologically, this proposition has significant implications for how sociological studies of education are imagined and enacted, or the types of questions that are enabled. It is important, therefore, to deepen the exploration of how affective-discursive practices are implicated in the temporal and spatial processes of identity, memory, and history in schooling.

## Notes

1 The discussion in this section builds on and extends the analysis of Chapter 3 in Zembylas, Charalambous and Charalambous (2016).
2 According to Christou (2006: 302 fn.), "The phrase 'I don't forget' under the image of the island's shape with the northern part red and bleeding was conceived by the Greek author Nikos Dimou on August 14, 1974, the day of the second wave of the Turkish military offensive. Dimou, who owned an advertising agency, instructed his art director

Dimitris Georgiopoulos to design and print a few thousand stickers and send them out to the media. The symbol swiftly dominated Greek-Cypriot popular culture and social imaginary, and such stickers can be still found today, especially along the Green Line."

3　Photographic material of the occupied territories produced by the Ministry of Education with the caption "I don't forget" was circulating widely in school spaces (e.g., as decoration on classroom walls, notice boards, and the front cover of all primary school notebooks); much of this still remains in place.

## References

Ahmed, S. (2004). *The cultural politics of emotion*. Edinburgh: Edinburgh University Press.

Anastasiadis, A., S. Sarantis, B. Kougialis and Theofilaktou, P. (1978). *Η σκλαβωμένη γη μας (Our enslaved land)*. Ministry of Education: Nicosia, Cyprus.

Appadurai, A. (1990). Disjuncture and difference in the global cultural economy. *Public Culture*, *2*(2), 1–24.

Aristodemou, N. (2004). *Διατήρηση μνήμης κατεχομένων, δημιουργία αβίωτης μνήμης και εθνικής συνείδησης μέσα από τις κυπριακές εκδόσεις για τα δημοτικά σχολεία: 1974-σήμερα*. (Preserving the memory of occupied territories, creating unlived memory and national consciousness through the Cypriot publications for primary schools: 1974 – Today) (Unpublished MA assignment), Department of Education, University of Cyprus.

Bekerman, Z. and Zembylas, M. (2012). *Teaching contested narratives: Identity, memory and reconciliation in peace education and beyond*. Cambridge: Cambridge University Press.

Berlant, L. (2000). The subject of true feeling: Pain, privacy, and politics. In S. Ahmed, J. Kilby, C. Lury, M. McNeil and B. Skeggs (Eds.). *Transformations: Thinking through feminism* (pp. 33–47). London: Routledge.

Berlant, L. (2001). Trauma and ineloquence. *Cultural Values*, *5*(1), 41–58.

Bowman, J. (2006). Seeing what's missing in memories of Cyprus. *Peace Review: A Journal of Social Justice*, *18*, 119–127.

Bryant, R. (2012). Partitions of memory: Wounds and witnssing in Cyprus. *Comparative Studies in Society and History*, *54*(2), 332–360.

Christou, M. (2006). A double imagination: Memory and education in Cyprus. *Journal of Modern Greek Studies*, *24*, 285–306.

Christou, M. (2007). The language of patriotism: Sacred history and dangerous memories. *British Journal of Sociology of Education*, *28*(6), 709–722.

Curti, G. H. (2008). From a wall of bodies to a body of walls: Politics of affect | Politics of memory| Politics of war. *Emotion, Space and Society*, *1*, 106–118.

Cvetkovitch, A. (2003). *An archive of feeling: Trauma, sexuality, and lesbian public cultures*. Durham, NC: Duke University Press.

Davies, L. (2004). *Education and conflict: Complexity and chaos*. New York: Routledge.

Heaney, J. (2011). Emotions and power: Reconciling conceptual twins. *Journal of Political Power*, *4*(2), 259–277.

Hermann, A. (2005). Emotions and the relevance of the past: Historicity and ethnicity among the Banabans of Fiji. *History and Anthropology*, *16*(3), 275–291.

Hirsch, M (2001). Surviving images: Holocaust photographs and the work of postmemory. *Yale Journal of Criticism*, *14*, 5–37.

Hirsch, M. (2008). The generation of postmemory. *Poetics Today*, *29*, 103–128.

Hirsch, M. and Spitzer, L. (2002). "We would not have come without you": Generations of nostalgia. *American Imago*, *59*, 253–276.

Hitchens, C. (1984). *Cyprus*. London: Quartet Books.

Hochschild, A. R. (1983). *The managed heart: Commercialization of human feeling.* Berkeley: University of California Press.

Jaggar, A. (1989). Love and knowledge: Emotion in feminist epistemology. In A. Jaggar and S. Bordo (Eds.). *Gender/body/knowledge: Feminist reconstructions of being and knowledge* (pp. 145–171). New Brunswick, NJ: Rutgers University Press.

Kenway, J. and Fahey, J. (2011a). Getting emotional about 'brain mobility'. *Emotion, Space and Society, 4*(3), 187–194.

Kenway, J. and Fahey, J. (2011b). Public pedagogies and global emoscapes. *Pedagogies, 6*(2), 167–179.

Loizos, P. (1981). *The heart grown bitter: A chronicle of Cypriot war refugees*. Cambridge: Cambridge University Press.

Loizos, P. (2008). *Iron in the soul: Displacement, livelihood and health in Cyprus.* Oxford and New York: Berghahn Books.

Mallinson, W. (2005). *Cyprus: A modern history*. London: I. B. Tauris.

Ministry of Education and Culture. (1990). *I don't forget and I struggle. For grades fifth and sixth.* Nicosia: Cyprus Ministry of Education, Department of Primary Education (in Greek).

Ministry of Education and Culture. (1992). *I don't forget and I struggle. For grades third and fourth.* Nicosia: Cyprus Ministry of Education, Department of Primary Education (in Greek).

Ministry of Education and Culture. (1994). *I know I don't forget and I struggle. For grades first and second.* Nicosia: Ministry of Education and Culture, Department of Primary Education (in Greek).

Ministry of Education and Culture. (1996). *Curriculum for primary education – in the framework of 9-year education.* Nicosia: Department of Primary Education, Curriculum Development Unit (in Greek).

Papadakis, Y. (2006). Nicosia after 1960: A river, a bridge and a dead zone. *The Global Media Journal: Mediterranean Edition, 1*(1), 1–16.

Papadakis, Y. (2008). Narrative, memory and history education in divided Cyprus: A comparison of schoolbooks on the 'History of Cyprus'. *History & Memory, 20*(2), 128–148.

Philippou, S. (2007). Policy, curriculum and the struggle for change in Cyprus: The case of the European dimension in education. *Journal of International Studies in Sociology of Education, 17*(3), 249–274.

Reckwitz, A. (2012). Affective spaces: A praxeological outlook. *Rethinking History, 16*(2), 241–258.

Roudometof, V. and Christou, M. (2011). 1974 and Greek Cypriot identity: The division of Cyprus as cultural trauma. In R. Eyerman, J. Alexander and E. Butler Breese (Eds.). *Narrating trauma: On the imapct of collective suffering* (pp. 163–187). Boulder, CO: Paradigm Publishers.

Trouillot, M-R. (1995). *Silencing the past: Power and the production of history*. Boston, MA: Beacon Press.

Trouillot, M-R. (2003). *Global transformations: Anthropology and the modern world*. New York: Palgrave Macmillan.

Wetherell, M. (2012). *Affect and emotion: A new social science understanding*. London: Sage.

Wetherell, M., McCreanor, T., McConville, A. and Moewaka Barnes, H. (2015). Settling space and covering the nation: Some conceptual considerations in analyzing affect and discourse. *Emotion, Space and Society, 16*, 58–64.

Worsham, L. (2001). Going postal: Pedagogic violence and the schooling of emotion. In H. Giroux and K. Myrisides (Eds.). *Beyond the corporate university* (pp. 229–265). New York: Rowman & Littlefield.

Zembylas, M. (2013). Memorial ceremonies in schools: Analyzing the entanglement of emotions and power. *Journal of Political Power*, 6(3), 477–493.

Zembylas, M. (2015). *Emotion and traumatic conflict: Re-claiming healing in education.* Oxford: Oxford University Press.

Zembylas, M., Charalambous, C. and Charalambous P. (2016). *Peace education in a conflict-troubled society: An ethnographic journey.* Cambridge: Cambridge University Press.

Zetter, R. (1991). Labelling refugees: Forming and transforming a bureaucratic identity. *Journal of Refugee Studies*, 4(1), 39–62.

Zetter, R. (1999). Reconceptualizing the myth of return: Continuity and transition amongst the Greek-Cypriot refugees of 1974. *Journal of Refugee Studies*, 12(1), 1–22.

## Bibliography

### *Primary Sources*

Circulars cited (the information includes protocol file numbers, publication dates, titles, and online access):

1   F: 7.11.13.3, 15 October 2001, Upgrade of the objective 'I know, I don't forget and I struggle" in primary schools.
2   F: 7.11.09/12, 5.13.04.3, August 26, 2013, Beginning of 2013–14 school year, accessed online at http://enimerosi.moec.gov.cy/archeia/1/dde3802a.
3   F: 7.11.09/15, 5.13.04.3, August 3, 2016, Beginning of 2016–17 school year, accessed online at http://enimerosi.moec.gov.cy/archeia/1/ypp4418a.

# 10  Animating animus

Viscosities of school reform movements and public feelings toward teachers

*Nancy Lesko and Alyssa Niccolini*

This chapter focuses on the feelings about teachers that the US standards movement evokes and the affects this movement captures, flows within, and amplifies. We see school reform agendas as "*machines for generating affect*" (Shaviro 2010: 3; emphasis in original) that contribute to public feelings about education. In the decades since *A Nation at Risk* (*ANAR*) (1983) was published, its sentiments got "hooks into the flesh" (Massumi 2015: 85) as teachers drew antipathy, indicated by limits to collective bargaining by teachers' unions, increased testing of students, and value-added measurements of teaching quality. We argue that this animus congealed teachers within what Arun Saldanha calls a *viscosity*, "bodies gradually becoming stick[y] and clustering into aggregates" (2005: 10), and that this positioned teachers as separate from and at odds with "the public". This viscosity gained a thickness through affect, with teachers becoming a space of social belonging onto which anxiety, disagreeability, and fears about national progress found an anchoring point. In addition, this viscosity was positioned as jarring with the pace of the nation; it was perceived as recalcitrant and slow compared to the bold and fast reform measures gathering speed over the years.

We offer Saldanha's notion of viscosity as a useful figuration for thinking through the *space-time-matterings* of education since it is both a "spatial and temporal event" (2007: 106). Viscosity marks a mobile notion of materiality signalling when bodies aggregate over time into collectivities (imagined or actual) that become resistant to mixing. Saldanha elaborates:

> To evoke the continuous but constrained dynamism of space, I want to propose the figure of *viscosity*. Neither perfectly fluid nor solid, the viscous invokes surface tension and resistance to perturbation and mixing. Viscosity means that the physical characteristics of a substance explain its unique movements. There are local and temporary thickenings of interacting bodies, which then collectively become sticky, capable of capturing more bodies like them: an emergent slime mold. Under certain circumstances, the collectivity dissolves, the constituent bodies flowing freely again. The world is an immense mass of viscosities, becoming thicker here, and thinner there.
>
> (Saldanha 2006: 18)

Set in India, Saldanha's 2007 study looks at the ways racial dynamics take shape in Goan dance culture, with white European tourists thickening into a social viscosity each night that eventually excluded local Indians from the dance floor and re-entrenched dominant power geometries. Saldanha's 2007 study shows how viscosities are temporal in addition to spatial, as they are not permanently fixed or solid, but accrue (or "thicken") by aggregating bodies in social space over time (for example, the white European bodies gaining number and influence each night on the dance floor) and dissipate (or "thin") over time by disaggregating bodies as social collectives (such as the forced dispersal of Indians from the dance floor as morning approached).

A viscosity is also an affective social event since "[v]iscosity is about how an aggregate of bodies hold together, how relatively fast or slow they are, and how they collectively shape the aggregate . . . Viscosity is also about how this holding together is related to the aggregate's capacities to affect, and be affected, by external bodies" (Saldanha 2007: 50). These material-temporal-spatial movements have social and political effects. As Saldanha (2007) puts it, "[a]n ontology of the viscous in the human realm directly entails ethics and politics" (52). For example, in this chapter we trace how teachers thickened into an imagined aggregate separate from and inimical to the public and how, in turn, their capacity to affect public policy and educational reform measures eroded.

While Saldanha's study hones in on the social viscosities forming and dissipating in the span of a single night, we argue that his model provides a vibrant means of understanding the slower temporal shifts (occurring over decades) in how teachers were viewed in US reform movements. Beginning around the Civil Rights Movement and extending to the present day, this shift in social positionality saw teachers gradually accrue a "thickness" as a group and established them as a social space apart from the public. Like a bead of oil in water gathering a separate integrity from a larger bubble, teachers moved from being considered guardians of the public interest, as imagined in the early Common School movement, to being opposed to the public's sentiments, politics, and very interests. As two educators working as and with public school teachers in New York City over the last decade, we have intensely felt the waves of teacher-animus moving through deskilling measures such as the narrowing of the curriculum, the surveillance of teacher-educators and teachers-to-be in more stringent accreditation mandates, and the emergence of a political climate dominated by corporate models of education reform. Public school teachers recognize the disgust towards them and their students.

These processes have been at times slow and gradual and at others swift and unexpected. In an attempt to dwell in these contradictory space-times, we move about through history in this chapter. We start by going back to 1983's *A Nation at Risk* and then jump ahead to its resonances in more contemporary events. We see the modulation of affects around teachers as a form of political power (Massumi 2002: 232) that urged this new social viscosity to take shape. While the standards and accountability movement has received stiff criticism from educational progressives and activists, it rolls on and its momentum is, in large part, affective.

Brian Massumi (2002: 232) argues that power has mutated from a normative, disciplinary form to an affective one: "The legitimization of political power . . . no longer goes through the reason of state and the correct application of governmental judgment. It goes through affective channels." Government and media exert control via the "ability to modulate the affective dimension". This chapter explores the modulation of affects toward teachers among both conservatives and liberals beginning with *A Nation at Risk* and how these modulations gradually thickened viscosities that separated teachers as antithetical to public interest.

The primary questions for the study are: *What affects towards teachers and teaching are mobilized in reports, legislation, and media coverage? How do these feelings aggregate bodies into particular collectivities (i.e., viscosities) with varying social and political effects? How do the viscosities forming around teachers get "hooks" into the social flesh, reworking its dimensions and divisions? And, if teachers gain a thickness set against the flesh of the public, how are their capacities for movement – enacted through such political practices as collective bargaining, impact on educational policy decisions, and influence on reform measures – enhanced or diminished?*

Some historical events bolt us into a sense that "everything changed", but suspicions toward teachers have sedimented slowly (Kumashiro 2012; Taubman 2009). While the standards and accountability reforms have a national scope, their affective intensities are most recognizable in specific people and groups in particular locations and times, such as Michelle Rhee in Washington, DC, and Scott Walker's policies as governor of Wisconsin. Our analysis attempts to highlight these temporal and spatial dimensions of public feelings on education.

## "A disagreeable thing": *A Nation at Risk* and genres of crisis

Historian of education and standards movement supporter-turned-critic Diane Ravitch (2010) identifies the report *A Nation at Risk* (*ANAR*) (National Commission on Excellence, 1983) as the starting point for the standards movement: "Where did education reform go wrong? Ask the question, and you'll get different answers, depending on whom you ask. But all roads eventually lead back to a major report released in 1983 called *A Nation at Risk*" (Ravitch 2010: 22). Jal Mehta locates *ANAR* as the third standards and accountability movement, following those of the 1890–1930 and the 1950–70 periods. School accountability repeatedly brought together the left and the right (Mehta 2013: 16) in ways that teachers and teachers' unions have been unable to effectively resist. As we will see, *ANAR* mobilized a broad array of elites and a sticky nexus of charged feeling at the public level.

Many commentators have highlighted the melodramatic rhetoric of *ANAR* in which "the nation is at risk" from a "rising tide of mediocrity", since schools and teachers have gotten slack. This slackness, like an atrophied muscle, positions the body of the nation as no longer able to compete globally, no longer to be number one, if students are not educated well. The threats are explicitly linked to being physically vanquished: "If an unfriendly foreign power had attempted to impose on America the mediocre educational performance that exists today, *we might well have viewed it as an act of war.* As it stands, we have allowed this to happen to ourselves" (National Commission on Excellence, 1983: 5; emphasis added). The language and imagery of *ANAR* communicate fear of middling and slackness – of being weakened by mediocrity and preyed upon by superior (stronger) nations. There is, in turn, a threat of punitive measures if US schools do not improve; the first line of the sub-section "The Risk" is "History is not kind to idlers" (National Commission on Excellence, 1983: 6). A laziness, or slowness, is implied to be taking over the American social body – a dangerous lethargy we will see associatively slide to teachers. While some scholars have dubbed this standards movement a "manufactured crisis" (Berliner and Biddle 1995; Stedman 1996), then Secretary of Education Terrel Bell recollected that in the 1970s and 1980s, teachers were demoralized, teacher pay was terrible, and "respect for teachers was commensurate with their salaries" (1988: 77). "Our schools' performance deficiencies could be traced directly to the pitiful standing of teachers in American society", for "teaching is a dead-end job" (ibid.: 77–78). Teachers lacked verve, alacrity, and motivation and consequently garnered a "pitiful standing" in American society.

ANAR told a "powerful story of decline that resonated with policymakers and the public . . . The report contained an identifiable narrative arc that made it both memorable and resonant . . . a story of decline and fall . . . supported by dropping SAT scores", and lower enrolments in advanced high school courses (Mehta 2013: 90–91). ANAR also played off "hard" and "soft" visions of educational reform – with teachers, like an atrophied body, being too soft. The trope of hard over soft appealed to "anyone who thought that the 1960s had unleashed a soft self-indulgence that needed to be countered with discipline, rigor, and a drive for excellence" (ibid.: 91). Journalist Meg Greenfield was struck by how much

> . . . the political antipermissiveness crowd [the hard educational reform-ers] . . . implicitly view[s] education as a *disagreeable thing* . . . as between a medicine and a punishment that must be administered to its unwilling little subjects for their own good no matter how they howl. It is not supposed to be fun . . . and children cannot be expected to like it – whatever happened to our moral fiber, and so forth.
>
> (Mehta 2013: 91–92; emphasis added)

At a time when "family values" also reigned, a "strict-father" family model pulled "soft" schools and teachers back into line not with carrots but with a stick (Kumashiro 2012: 30–33; Lakoff 2004: 7–10). The combination of a "hard" approach to reform enacted by "strict-father" policies and tools animated animus toward teachers, especially toward those deemed recalcitrant. Teachers began to gel into a social viscosity separate from national, and particularly, public interests. As unions pushed back against hard and soft reform approaches, the mediocrity and disagreeability associated with education slid like a "slime mold" (Saldanha 2006: 50) to educators. While much of the standards and accountability move-ment rationales are sanitized, deep into Bell's autobiography we find rewards for excellent teachers via merit pay accompanied by the will to punish mediocrity. Despite the low educational performance being attributable to "the pitiful stand-ing of teachers", schools have "doggedly refused to reward excellence and *punish mediocrity in teaching*" (Bell 1988: 78, emphasis added). This "dogged refusal" marks the teaching body as recalcitrant and stubborn. While advocates of teacher improvement regularly highlight higher salaries for outstanding teachers, *punishing mediocre teachers* is usually edited out. As we will see in a later section, Michelle Rhee burst on the national stage in large part for her eager punishment of what were deemed less-than-excellent teachers.

Marking a shift in intensity, *ANAR* also altered the relative importance of education on state and national agendas, the terms of the debate, and actors in the policy arena (Mehta 2013: 93). This stoking of intensity helped affectively mould the viscosity that enveloped teachers as separate from the public. For example, voters gave education increased priority almost simultaneously with *ANAR's* release. In 1968 and 1972, education was last on agendas of important issues at the state level; by 1984 it had moved to the top third of issues, and by 2000 it became "voters' single most important issue" (Mehta 2013: 96). Mehta also documents the rise of education as an issue at the federal level: "Education's rising agenda status at the federal level was also sparked by *ANAR*, as the issue shifted from 23rd out of 41 issues in 1980, to 17th of 51 in 1984, to 5th of 24 in 1992, and then to 1st of 11 in 2000" (ibid.: 233). *ANAR* succeeded in making education important to voters through linking it to the "decline and fall of the US" narrative and to an explicit "education-economy link". If education is a "disagreeable thing", its too-soft teachers are harbingers of literal *disagreement* with neo-liberal sentiments. As the most densely unionized labour force in the US and generally liberal leaning, teachers became a viscous space of vaguely anti-capitalist sentiment that had to be positioned outside of a national progress that valorizes individual actors, freedom to follow self-interest, and minimally regulated markets.

*ANAR* aligned both Republicans and Democrats with the "strict-father" view of teachers and schools. No national Republican leader had embraced a significantly expanded federal role in education until G. W. Bush did so in the run-up to the 2000 presidential election. A majority of the Republican leadership fell in behind Bush. By 2000, both political parties converged on test-based accountability to "fix" education. An exception was Senator Paul Wellstone from Minnesota, who wrote that without additional resources, "more testing would simply set up poor children to fail" (Mehta 2013: 234). But even liberals like Senator Edward Kennedy took the strict father stance toward giving schools additional resources, slowly shearing teachers from their political alignment with even the left, helping to "thicken" the separate viscosity they were becoming. "Support for accountability among legislators of both parties was strengthened by the prevailing analysis that the 1994 ESEA [Elementary and Secondary Education Act] reforms were not uniformly implemented" (ibid.: 235). Thus, educators' recalcitrance on past reforms encouraged a "harder" line, and by 2000 the strict father model on accountability was endorsed by Republicans and Democrats.

In addition to this strict father assault on "mediocre" and "too-soft" teachers, widespread racism also converged to spur anti-teacher animus. If the 1960s had been permissive, the Civil Rights Movement and school desegregation were central components of that "disordered" decade. The "Great Society" of President Lyndon Johnson had enacted state empathy and amelioration of inequity in civil rights legislation and *Brown* v *Board of Education*. By 1983, integrated schools were the law (although never really implemented). So, when *ANAR* decried the "mediocrity" of schools, students of colour were spotlighted, despite the colour-blind language (Alexander 2012). Sociologists of education have noted that teachers are linked with the status of their students; if teachers work with Advanced Placement students, they share in the students' positions at the top of the academic hierarchy. Teachers of students labelled "remedial" are often viewed as having less status. Therefore, as the public school population shifted and became increasingly racialized, the teachers' status likewise moved. While Mehta (2013) emphasizes that teacher unionization, strikes, and collective bargaining lowered teachers' status, he omits the increasing percentage of students of colour in public schools. If racial animosities were directed at activists such as the Little Rock Nine, their public school teachers also invoked feelings of enmity helping to firm up a social viscosity where teachers gathered animus.

Helping to shore up the perception of teachers as an aggregate at odds with the public interest was "a declining view of educators. Educators were not seen as professionals who should be left in charge of their own domain; rather, they were viewed with skepticism, and their ability (or even motivation) to meet the desired standards was distrusted" (Mehta 2013: 98). For the strict father, "A moral person is someone who is disciplined enough to be obedient, to learn what is right, do what is right and not do what is wrong, and to pursue her self-interest to prosper and become self-reliant" (Lakoff 2004: 8). But the bad child, or "disagreeable" teacher, "does not learn discipline, does not functional morally, does not do what is right, and therefore is not disciplined enough to become prosperous. She cannot take care of herself and thus becomes dependent" (ibid.: 8). The strict father version of family values means that social programs are unethical: "It is immoral to give people things they have not earned . . . . Social programs are immoral because they make people dependent. Promoting social programs is immoral" (ibid.: 9). The strict father model links morality with prosperity, further marking teachers as a viscous aggregate separate from the moral fibre of the American nation/public.

## Bad teachers: "hard" and "soft" visions of education reform

"Teachers can't teach," read *Time* magazine's 1980 cover. This generalized public sentiment undergirded "hard" versions of educational reform that involved "compassionate conservatism", a focus on test-based accountability, and a willingness to go after mediocre teachers and their protective unions. Hochschild (2016) writes that part of the anger of poor whites in Louisiana was the belief that government workers are overpaid. Certainly teachers and teachers' unions received the same charges; while student test scores plummeted, teachers – good, bad, indifferent, and almost always positioned as "disagreeable" to any contract changes – received scheduled raises. Soft versions of educational reform involved concern for students' backgrounds and differences, attention to multicultural curricula, and teacher training for working with diverse students.

Terrel Bell, Secretary of Education and the convener of the Committee on Education Excellence, which authored *ANAR*, wrote in his autobiography about the low status and morale of teachers in the middle decades of the twentieth century:

The heart of education is its teachers. If [educational] reform was to get underway, it made sense to begin with the teachers . . . I wanted to promote performance based salaries for teachers. The profession was sinking along with student SAT scores . . . Our schools' performance deficiencies can be traced directly to the pitiful standing of teachers in American society. Many people claim that the teachers are to blame . . . Teacher unions force taxpayers to raise the salaries of the worst at the same rate as the best in order to pay the best what they are worth.

(Bell 1988: 76–78)

Comparing universities with assistant and associate professor ranks, "public and private elementary and high schools have doggedly refused to reward excellence and punish mediocrity in teaching" (ibid.: 77). Usually, merit pay reforms emphasize the importance of rewarding excellence, but Bell revealed the strict father component of the reform: to punish mediocrity in teaching.

Michelle Rhee might be seen as the bad cop to Bell's good one. Bell was a lifelong educator, while Rhee is a media celebrity, entrepreneur, and, most recently, a short-lived candidate for Secretary of Education in Donald Trump's administration. She amplifies cable television viewership, but may now be too controversial for policy positions. In her autobiography, she condemns teachers' unions for controlling the educational agenda, which has resulted in neglected students. Her foundation, *StudentsFirst*, aims to correct the situation by placing an excellent teacher in every classroom, for "great teachers can inspire regardless of that child's circumstances" (Rhee 2013: xii). She enacted this reform agenda in a three-year stint as Superintendent of Schools for Washington, DC. In 2008, the cover of *Time* magazine proclaimed "How to fix America's schools", with a photo of Rhee holding a broom, signalling her tough program to get rid of "incompetent" teachers.

## Teachers versus the public

Mehta argues that standards, testing, and accountability offer a "thin theory" of how to actually improve practice (2013: 311, fn. 3). Despite this thinness, standards and accountability have gotten hooks into US flesh. This thinness has in turn created a *thickness* in a gelling of teachers into a separate viscosity from the imagined public interest. We can feel a surface tension gradually, but persistently shore up historically, as, rather than part of education's progress, teachers' lack of motivation, disagreeability, and softness are positioned as the reason for its stagnation. If teachers are to blame, the public must put its faith in the state to keep that viscosity under wraps, spurring increased reform efforts. During the 1990s, "teacher quality" echoed in school reform circles, indicating that teachers were a critical influence on what and how much students learned (Cochran-Smith and Lytle 2006), yet no one could agree on a definition of teacher quality. The 2002 legislation and supplementary materials tethered teacher quality to following "what works" guidelines, scientifically based research findings, using data to inform classroom decision making, and raising students' test scores. Teachers' unions parted ways, emphasizing educational credentials, tenure, and seniority in rewarding teachers.

Bespeaking the culmination of the social viscosity pitting teachers against the interests of the public, a volume focusing on the gulf between teachers' views and those of "the public" was published by the Brookings Institute in 2014. *Teachers versus the public* (Peterson, Henderson and West 2014) inflamed the sense of isolation and self-interest of the "educational establishment" (teachers' unions, Department of Education bureaucrats, and educational researchers) and of teachers as a separate interest group. Teachers were accused of clinging to antiquated views that are out of touch with public sentiment. The survey data presented are especially cleaved on the topics related to "teacher policy", such as merit pay,

*Table 10.1* Documenting the gulf between the public's and teachers' opinions on selected educational issues

*Percent*

| *Issue/opinion* | *General public* | *Teachers* | *Difference between public and teachers* |
|---|---|---|---|
| *Teacher policy* | | | |
| Use merit pay | 66 | 16 | −50* |
| Use merit tenure | 76 | 29 | −46* |
| Allow flexible hiring | 58 | 30 | −28* |
| Eliminate tenure | 72 | 35 | −37* |
| Teacher unions are harmful | 57 | 32 | −25* |
| *School choice* | | | |
| Expand choice with universal vouchers | 65 | 38 | −27* |
| Use government funds for mean-tested vouchers | 51 | 27 | −24* |
| Allow charter schools | 71 | 54 | −17* |
| Allow tax credit-funded scholarships | 71 | 51 | −20* |
| Allow online courses | 65 | 56 | −9 |
| *Accountability* | | | |
| Require annual testing | 89 | 65 | −24* |
| Use common standards/test | 72 | 60 | −12* |
| Use test for grade promotion | 86 | 72 | −15* |
| Require graduation test | 86 | 77 | −10* |
| *Taxes and spending* | | | |
| Increase spending | 64 | 71 | 6 |
| Raise taxes | 35 | 49 | 14* |
| Raise teacher pay | 54 | 80 | 26* |
| Increase teacher share of benefit costs | 66 | 29 | −37* |
| *Cultural issues* | | | |
| Allow single-sex schools | 59 | 71 | 12* |
| Grant principal final disciplinary authority | 40 | 57 | 17* |
| Allow time for silent prayer | 69 | 58 | −11* |
| *Diversity* | | | |
| Use family income to assign students | 37 | 37 | 0 |
| Separate classes for disturbed students | 65 | 67 | 2 |

Source: Petersen, Henderson and West, 2014: 19.

Notes: a  Boldface type indicates that among those with an opinion on the question, a majority of teachers and a majority of the public were on opposite sides. See appendix B for the wording of the questions. Questions are the national, not the local, wording options given in the appendix. Questions on principal's authority and school prayer were posed in 2008. Differences are rounded to the nearest whole number.

*  Statistically significant at the 0.05 level

tenure, hiring practices, and unions (see Table 10.1, category at the top). Merit pay and tenure provoked the largest differences of support from the public and teachers, indicating the teaching body's recalcitrance to reform measures.

In the middle, nowhere, failing to be excellent or outstanding, they were socially suspended and affectively cast as outside of US exceptionalism and narratives of progress. Teachers had begun to be associated with the term that reverberated from *ANAR: mediocrity*. New York City Schools Chancellor Joel Klein castigated the entire system as mediocre: "The whole education system is built on three pillars of mediocrity: lockstep pay, life tenure, and seniority" (Whitmore 2011: 59). Klein prophesied that a new foundation for success would rest on performance, accountability, and excellence, which required disruptive strategies to enact.

## Animating accountability: fast reform and sluggish bodies

Terrel Bell (1988) recalled how President Ronald Reagan had advocated for the importance of improving education and helped focus national attention on *ANAR* during his re-election campaign leading up to 1984. Once re-elected, Reagan made it clear that his second administration would return to its priority of getting the federal government out of education, and Bell promptly resigned from his Cabinet position (see Chapter 11 of Bell 1988: 144–159).

Two decades later, and with much more public concern over education, Michelle Rhee came to national attention as the superintendent of the Washington, DC, public schools, despite little experience in teaching and no experience running schools. She rode into her position on the standards and accountability movement and tried to lead the District of Columbia educators into placing "students first". Her version of placing students first, between 2007 and 2010, was to establish merit pay, fire educators who were mediocre, and replace the seniority system of teachers' unions (based on experience and advanced degrees) with "excellence". Teachers, then, were socially suspended as separate from the recognizable "excellence" fostered by new leaders.

In his semi-authorized biography of Rhee, Richard Whitmore's (2011) descriptions of her provide important dynamics in her championing students and ridiculing teachers. In the early pages of the book, Rhee "never flinched", had a "no nonsense glower" on the cover of *Time*, and humiliated teachers by telling them they were wrong and poking them in the eye too. Picking up one of Rhee's favourite words, *crazy*, Whitmore writes, "it takes a *crazy* person to produce results under the conditions Rhee found [in DC schools]" (ibid.: xiv; emphasis added). In later chapters, Rhee was "shredding common thinking about reforming a district" (ibid.: 6) and she was a "bomb thrower" (ibid.: 58). Rhee never wasted a moment and, like teachers whom he had observed in a KIPP (Knowledge is Power Program) school, had "snap", which he defined as "a quick twitch in their bodies, urgency in their moves, and devotion to pursuing a measurable goal" (ibid.: xiv). The animated bodies and movements of these "exceptional" teachers were deemed vulnerable to the sluggish viscosity of soft and dispirited teachers fettered by the teachers' union, a lack of motivation, and resistance to change.

Rhee further animated animus – charges of mediocrity and neglecting students – with her own affective style, and her physically charged movements and interactions became a foil to the soft and slow teacher image: she is repeatedly described as *throwing bombs, never flinching, rubbing a point in someone's face, shredding conventional practices*, and having *"snap"* in her non-stop, waste-free, *nerve-ful* body. Unlike the sluggish and demoralized viscosity enveloping teachers, Rhee has nerve and an "iron will", and was inclined to fast, drastic changes and reckoning later with the controversy. While she reiterated the need to put students first, her path to accomplishing that was to demean, shame, and remove teachers. These quick and frenetic movements, evocative of the slash-and-burn styles of many education reformers, further marked teachers as slow-moving and loath-to-change viscosity, a "slime mold", to use Saldanha's (2007) words, that lacked verve and energy.

Diane Ravitch claims that "more than anyone else Michelle Rhee is the face of the corporate reform movement" (2013: 145), a model based on free market values. This vision of education follows neo-liberal sentiments of choice, privatization, and the swift and unpredictable fluctuations of markets. Such rapid shifting valorizes thin viscosities – brief and temporary coalitions of bodies – whereas teachers had coalesced into a thick viscosity resistant to thinning. Rhee also animates animus toward teachers as she combines confidence, indignation, accepts no excuses, and asserts that policies established by teachers' unions work against students. Rhee's frenetic affective repertoire and fast reform is representative of the public's interest in a global age, while teachers' "disagreeability" to change is positioned as affectively at odds with the economic demands of a rapidly changing America. She presents a feminized version of the "strict father": her biographer chronicles her eating a bee to get respect from her students; a PBS documentary shows her firing a principal on camera; she shames teachers who cannot raise the scores of their students "for using poverty as an excuse". She repeats again and again, that there are "no excuses" for not having an "exceptional" teacher in every classroom. Teachers, on the other hand, are imagined as always having excuses, as slow to change, and unwilling to accept accountability. Her narrative of teaching adheres to the "great teacher image", in which superior teachers can correct all ills and overcome all obstacles (Cochran-Smith and Lytle 2006). These classroom saviours are lone actors, but are threatened by a "tide of mediocrity" (National Commission on Excellence, 1983). Evocative of a cheesy horror movie, they are vulnerable to being swallowed within the thick, sticky viscosity of "disagreeable" teachers.

## Under the flag of compassionate conservatism

The triumph of accountability arrived with the No Child Left Behind (NCLB) legislation in 2002. President G. W. Bush had championed accountability-based school reform as the centrepiece of his claim to be a "compassionate conservative" in his run for president (Mehta 2013: 133). What is compassion when it is linked with conservatism?

The compassionate person sympathizes with misfortunes that she did not cause and that would not otherwise touch her life . . . Any intervention that she undertakes from compassion, beyond expressing condolence, will involve generosity or kindness . . . [and will be] beyond the limits of responsibility. While it's good to help strangers now and then, you do not *owe* aid and comfort to particular strangers.

(Vogler 2004: 30; original emphasis)

This absence of obligation is important. According to Berlant, "Compassion implies a social relation between spectators and sufferers, with the emphasis on the spectator's experience of feeling compassion and its subsequent relation to material practice" (2004: 1). She continues: in the contemporary US

. . . the word *compassion* carries the weight of ongoing debates about the ethics of privilege – in particular about the state as an economic, military, and moral actor that represents and establishes collective norms of obligation, and about individual and collective obligations to read a scene of distress not as a judgment against the distressed but as a claim on the spectator to become an ameliorative actor . . . [The] grand gestures of the Great Society have been replaced by the melodrama of the overtaxed and the underemployed, those whose dignity must be returned to them by tax cuts and welfare-to-work programs . . . The compassionately conservative state wants to limit technologies of amelioration and to shift its economic obligations from redressing poverty to protecting income by taking less from and giving less back to workers and citizens. Compassion can be said to be at the heart of this shrinkage.

(Ibid.: 1–2)

Kathleen Woodward writes that for conservatives, "compassion is deployed predominantly as an adjective, one that characterizes an ideological stance, policy, or program. Bush not only ran on a platform of compassionate conservatism, he has described his budget as compassionate." She continues, that while it is detached from people, "compassion is attached to policies and practices. In the mouths of conservatives, compassionate has no referent to a feeling at all . . . It is merely a word that refers to economic conservatism" (2004: 73). Woodward concludes that compassionate conservatism is emptied of sympathy for others.

While Michelle Rhee enacts a snappier reform effort, animus toward teachers is also carried in budgets and legislation that shrink public responsibility for the education of children and young people, which in turn further position teachers as a viscous aggregate affectively at odds with and outside of the "compassion" of the state. The strict father model, as Lakoff reminds us, makes it a moral principle to withhold resources from citizens who are not self-disciplined. "It is immoral to give people things they have not earned" (2004: 9) and, therefore, the handouts to mediocre teachers must be clawed back.

## Teacher shrinkage and accountability

Evoking a battle against a stubborn "slime mold", teacher "shrinkage" is an apt moniker for reformer battles against the perceived thick, slow viscosity of the teaching body. In these pages, we have evoked some of the sentiments that the standards and accountability advocates have stoked and directed toward teachers. These are largely produced through a mismatching of speeds – the swiftness of reformers acting against the perceived sluggishness of the teaching body. Starting with *ANAR*, charges of mediocrity and neglect have swarmed, and teachers' unions have only weakly responded, firming up views of teachers as an effete body lacking verve and "snap". While education has surged in importance at state and federal levels, teachers' unions and critics of standards and accountability have not gained much support. Mehta (2013) reminds us that neither teachers' unions (AFT or NEA) ultimately opposed NCLB: "Although the teachers' unions were the most powerful forces in elementary and secondary education, they couldn't fight the spirit of more accountability" (2013: 237). This "spirit" was largely an affective ethos of speed and snap, "thin" alliances, and individual accountability.

According to the strict father model, such individual accountability will re-establish moral authority and order by "starving" those who are dependent. Teachers will have to perform in ways evaluated as "excellent" or be humiliated and driven from schools. Younger, "snappier" teachers will follow the dictates of research-backed programs, raise test scores, and produce better results each year. This new generation of teachers will not look to the slow, sedimented traditions of union-backed tenure, seniority, or credentials raises. In a lean and mean future, performance will bring success and merit individual rewards.

Michelle Rhee's vigour and freneticism entertain and grab headlines, as do the controversies surrounding her. But we think it is important to ask what remains veiled for the public to take satisfaction, and invest fascination, in swift-turnaround success stories? As enmity and ill will, along with charges of mediocrity and laziness are directed at teachers, and as teachers become imagined as a recalcitrant viscosity resistant to change and opposed to the public's interest, the idea of a public good and public responsibility, in turn, thin. Teaching and social responsibility shrink in accountability's imagined future (Anderson 2015). The strict father's aim is to catch teachers who are not earning their salaries – who are, in effect, stealing from the public, the tax-payers. The banner of "students first" seems to value schooling and students who have been left behind, but instead really values taxpayers holding onto their dollars.

The neo-liberal effects of accountability, demands for teachers' excellence, and monitoring students' constant testing narrow teacher subjectivities (Berlant 2004: 5; Cochrane-Smith and Lytle 2006). At the same time, "the public" takes pleasure in seeing teachers humiliated and stripped of collective bargaining and teachers are firmed up as a separate, and dangerously sticky, social viscosity. Saldanha argues that:

One important thing to remember about human viscosity is that actual speed on one scale can "slow down" the abstract machine of a web of relation on a higher scale. The fluidities of finance capital, missiles, business travel, advertising, and telecommunications serve to consolidate the topological power of the capitalist system. Conversely, the movements of refugees mainly strengthen state borders and the inequalities between those with and without property . . . Movement always relates to power relations on a variety of often contradictory scales.

(Saldanha 2007: 52)

Here, we've mapped the reverse process – how the brisk and sharp affects that mobilize "snap" and crazy-fast reform strategies at the macro level of politics have congealed the slow and unglamorous work of teaching at a more micro level. While teachers have been stalled and congealed within an oppositional viscosity to the public, this is not to say that all teaching bodies move within that space with uniform speeds. Another study could zoom in, for example, on the differential way that race, class, and gender, among other identity registers, further impede and impel movements of particular teaching bodies. But as a sum aggregate, the body as disagreeable "stuff" has gotten its hooks into flesh, into policy, and into the very organization of social space. In essence, reform measures, like the late capitalist ethos they are largely founded on, champion thin and easily divertible alliances (to swiftly changing markets, commodities, pitches, and products), over thick and more enduring alliances. As such, thin viscosities become the rule; the potential for new alliances and thickenings, vital for the complex negotiations necessary for meaningful school reform as well as the slow work of teaching and learning, become ever more difficult to take shape.

## References

Alexander, M. (2012). *The new Jim Crow: Mass incarceration in the age of colorblindness.* New York: The New Press.

Anderson, B. (2015). Neoliberal affects. *Progress in Human Geography, 40*(6), 1–20.

Bell, T. (1988). *The thirteenth man: A Reagan cabinet memoir.* New York: Free Press.

Berlant, L. (Ed.). (2004). *Compassion: The culture and politics of an emotion.* New York: Routledge.

Berliner, D. and Biddle, B. (1995). *The manufactured crisis: Myths, fraud, and the attack on America's public schools.* Reading, MA: Addison-Wesley.

Cochran-Smith, M. & Lytle, S. (2006). Troubling images of teaching in No Child Left Behind. *Harvard Educational Review, 76*(4), 668–697.

Hochschild, A. R. (2016). *Strangers in their own land: Anger and mourning on the American right.* New York: The New Press.

Kumashiro, K. K. (2012). *Bad teacher! How blaming teachers distorts the bigger picture.* New York: Teachers College Press.

Lakoff, G. (2004). *Don't think of an elephant: Know your values and frame the debate.* White River Junction, VT: Chelsea Green Publishing.

Massumi, B. (2002). *Parables of the virtual: Movement, affect, sensation.* Durham, NC: Duke University Press.

Massumi, B. (2015). *Politics of affect.* Malden, MA: Polity Press.

Mehta, J. (2013). *The allure of order: High hopes, dashed expectations, and the troubled quest to remake American schooling.* Oxford: Oxford University Press.

National Commission on Excellence in Education. (1983). *A nation at risk: The imperative for educational reform. An open letter to the American people. A report to the nation and the Secretary of Education.* Washington, DC: U.S. Department of Education.

Peterson, P. E., Henderson, M. and West, M. R. (2014). *Teachers versus the public: What Americans think about schools and how to fix them.* Washington, DC: Brookings Institution Press.

Ravitch, D. (2010). *The death and life of the great American school system.* New York: Basic Books.

Ravitch, D. (2013). *Reign of error: The hoax of the privatization movement and the danger to America's public schools.* New York: Knopf.

Rhee, M. (2013*). Radical: Fighting to put students first.* New York: HarperCollins.

Saldanha, A. (2005). Vision and viscosity in Goa's psychedelic trance scene. *ACME: An International E-Journal for Critical Geographies, 4*(2), 172–193.

Saldanha, A. (2006). Reontologising race: The machinic geography of phenotype. *Environment and Planning D: Society and Space, 24,* 9–24.

Saldanha, A. (2007). *Psychedelic white: Goa trance and the viscosity of race.* Minneapolis, MN and London: University of Minnesota Press.

Shaviro, S. (2010). *Postcinematic affect.* Hants: Zero Book.

Stedman, L. C. (1996). The achievement crisis is real: A review of *The Manufactured Crisis. Education Policy Analysis Archives, 4*(1), 1–12.

Taubman, P. M. (2009). *Teaching by numbers: Deconstructing the discourse of standards and accountability in education.* New York: Routledge.

Vogler, C. (2004). Much of madness and more of sin: Compassion, for Ligeia. In L. Berlant (Ed.), *Compassion: The culture and politics of an emotion* (pp. 29–58). New York: Routledge.

Whitmore, R. (2011). *The bee eater: Michelle Rhee takes on the nation's worst school district.* San Francisco, CA: Jossey-Bass.

Woodward, K. (2004). Calculating compassion. In L. Berlant (Ed.), *Compassion: The culture and politics of an emotion* (pp. 59–86). New York: Routledge.

# 11 Modernity, identity, and citizenship

## Rethinking colonial situations and their temporal legacies

*Hannah M. Tavares*

## Introduction

In the Afterword of *The Darker Side of the Renaissance: Literacy, Territoriality, and Colonization*, Walter Mignolo discloses how he was drawn to Perry Anderson's enthusiasm about an immensely influential description of modernity that had been written by Marshall Berman. But that initial excitement soon turned into disappointment. His let-down appears to stem from Berman's insensitivity to what Mignolo described as the "darker side" of modernity (1995: 320). As explained by Mignolo:

> I was already well into the ideas that shaped this book [*The Darker Side of the Renaissance*]. In Berman's description of "modernity" I missed its darker side, the differential experiences of space and time, of speech and writing, "shared by men and women all over the world" who lived in peripheral colonial and postcolonial situations. Even if one can accept that there are few remaining areas of the globe untouched by the expansion of the West, this does not mean that whoever is touched by Western expansion becomes automatically a Western person who experiences space and time, speech and writing in Kerala or in the Andes in the same way that a person experiences them in Paris, Bombay, or Buenos Aires.
>
> (Mignolo 1995: 316–317)

Further along the same page, Mignolo goes on to add the need and value of generating and sustaining a conception of colonial situations for addressing contemporary issues:

> Modernity is a period, in the history of the West, in which contact and domination between human cultures reached their peak. Thus, reflections on colonial experiences are not only corrective exercises in understanding the past but helpful tools in speaking the present. Critical perspectives on Western values and ways of thinking have much to gain from understanding colonial situations: the darker side of the European Renaissance and Western modernity, perhaps, but also the brighter side of a utopian future.
>
> (Ibid.: 317)

I am drawn to Mignolo's argument because of the questions it poses for thinking the temporal legacies of colonial situations on the problem of identity and citizenship. Hawai'i, an archipelago of commercial and militarily strategic islands, geopolitically situated within the American polity and enmeshed in the dynamics of ongoing resistance to settler occupation, expansion and influence, is a fitting locale for engaging with such questions. I am particularly interested in the proposition that the European Renaissance is a significant marker in the *idea* of modernity, culminating in what Sylvia Wynter, citing Foucault, calls the "episteme/organization of knowledge that was put in place in the nineteenth century" (1984: 20). The episteme to which Wynter refers, and which surfaces in relation to the symbolic-cultural category of the "indolent" that was used to represent the indigenous peoples of Hawai'i, enables us to reflect on the mournful side of modernity which Mignolo references. This allows us get a sense of the cultural norms and assumptions embedded within the operations of writing and observing and the ramifications of their circulation in the present. Indolence is not an *a priori* quality of Hawaiian people but an achievement of non-Native accounts. That is to say, it is an effect of the role of temporal and spatial orientations associated with modernity, in which identity and citizenship are partially made.

For Mignolo, the basis of the idea of modernity commences toward the end of the fifteenth century with the European "discovery" of a "New World" (1995: xi). As he puts it, "frontiers were constructed not only in geographical terms and related to the extensions and the limits of the Atlantic Ocean but also in terms of the boundaries of humanity" (1995: xi). Mignolo's claim about the project of modernity, which builds on the work of philosopher Enrique Dussel, not only departs from the paradigmatic example, and what Stephen Toulmin calls "received wisdom" about the emergence of modernity (1990: 13–14), with its characteristic focus on a commitment to new rational methods of inquiry established among European natural philosophers during the seventeenth century. His claim also seeks to advance an ethic and an approach for theorizing colonial situations that will foreground conceptualizations of space and time that might reveal and recover forgotten spatio-temporal worlds. *The Darker Side of the Renaissance* does precisely that, excavating evidence of the presence of a diverse set of temporalities that were not yet ordered into an ostensibly neutral single system of explanation.

The ordering of life-worlds into a single horizon and single-point perspective is what Elizabeth Deeds Ermarth (1995) proposes as belonging to the "convention of historical time" and what Wynter (1995) refers to as "our present single world order and single world history". Ermarth's writings on time and Wynter's work on episteme underscores a difficult challenge for the inheritors such as myself of those intellectual conventions. Mignolo approaches the archival erasure of the plurality of temporalities and life-worlds as an "ethical obligation". His approach is to unearth, as he put it, the "incommensurable conceptual frameworks" and start the

... hermeneutically difficult task of re-establishing the lost equilibrium between what, at one level, were alternative conceptual frameworks and, at the other, became organized in a hierarchy of values established by those who were at the same time participants and observers.

(Mignolo 1995: 328)

Such a task, which would put forgotten temporalities and the conceptual frameworks by which the boundaries of humanity were constructed in the forefront, unsettles the conventional horizon of the "sociological imagination". This is because the key disciplinary objects associated with social life, for example, institutions, inequalities, and identity, are rarely treated in relation to the constitutive forces of temporal orientations. The issue, however, is not simply to recover those forgotten temporalities but to be aware of the explanatory grids to which they are subject.

For example, Elizabeth Ermarth in her essay *Time and Neutrality* notes very insightfully that contemporary discussions of time and history often take those terms for granted. Ermarth's concern is that the analysis of time is done without an analysis of the conventions by which the construct is maintained. Clarifying this point Ermarth states:

Looked at historically in terms of the invention and development of cultural grammars, "time" in the sense we assume it – as a neutral, homogeneous medium extending infinitely and "in" which mutual relevance can be measured – belongs to a fairly unique phase of Western culture: one in which European humanism underwrote empirical science and its technologies, just as it underwrote representation in politics and in art.

(Ermarth 1998: 356)

She goes further and says, "in Anglo-American traditions, the word 'time' functions insistently in its humanist construction only – time as a common denominator ... a basis for linkage and mediation" (ibid.: 357). Scholars, particularly Western academics who point out different *kinds* of time such as "linear time, cyclic time, ritual time, women's time", she argues, still take for granted a humanist construction of time. On this point, she has held that contemporary discussions of time "routinely invoke" linearity, or chronology, or sequence, or causality as a way to show that these temporal orientations are unique to our humanist, historical time (ibid.: 362). Yet Ermarth argues that "all kinds of cultural narratives can accommodate the linear, the sequential, the chronological, even the causal, and can still lack the neutrality characterizing the time of modernity" (362). As she emphatically put it, "*Neutrality* alone distinguishes the time of modernity" (ibid.: 362; emphasis original). Thus, Ermarth's interest is not "time" per se or to claim heterogeneous temporalities. Her interest, as she has put it, is in "the particular construction of temporality that makes time neutral" (1995: 93).

Ermarth insists that this convention of time as neutral has undergone many challenges in political and social theory, science, painting, and narrative, and that different writers have experimented with reshaping its humanist heritage by treating time as finite (1998: 362). The new cultural order within which many of these experiments are situated can be characterized by their temporal specificity rather than their neutrality. Referencing numerous authors as examples, she concludes: "In these post-Einsteinian texts, the inconvenient fact is that there is no common denominator between one time frame and another: no consensus on the fundamental terms for describing the world and operating in it" (1995: 94). The term she gives to what she regards as an alternative construction of temporality is "ph(r)ase time", which she draws from two different fields of study: Lyotard's (1988) *The Differend: Phrases in Dispute* and chaos theory. What Ermarth finds significant about Lyotard's book for her own argument of temporality is the proposition that the world of discourse can exist without "*any* mediating common denominator, especially the possibility of historical time" (1995: 95; emphasis original). For Lyotard, as Ermarth explains, a phrase has no determinate structure and is thus always contested (ibid.: 96). As put by Lyotard: "A phrase, which links and which is to be linked, is always a *pagus*, a border zone where genres of discourse enter into conflict over the mode of linking" (1988: 151). Viewed in this way, a phrase is both subject to limitations and has no limits or borders. What is pertinent here are the resemblances to Lyotard's ungrounded phrases in dispute and physicists' descriptions of chaotic processes. Ermarth says: "Within the so-called 'chaotic' sequence sets of regularity exist – what one physicist calls 'transient intervals of order'". The temporal dimension of chaotic processes, she adds, "is the unpredictable period during which certain regularities or periodicities hold" (1995: 98). Ermarth's essay is, of course, far too extensive and complex to adequately capture here, but a key point that can be drawn from the term "ph(r)ase time" is the undoing of the convention of historical time or neutral time by the challenges brought on by postmodern narrative and chaos theory (ibid.: 108). Perhaps even more critically, ph(r)ase time is the name given to the new kind of time that makes linguistic difference a crucial matter in understanding temporal orientations.

Having set out some key ideas and challenges since the late 1980s on language, space, and time, I want to now turn to how they help illustrate the approach I take here to the problem of identity and citizenship. Importantly, I want to consider the political consequences of the humanist legacy discussed above. To assist in this endeavour, I have organized the rest of this chapter into two parts. The first part includes two sections and focuses on the spatial-temporal practices introduced in a particular colonial situation and how those practices began to symbolically fasten the original peoples of the Hawaiian Islands to identifiable conduct within a hierarchy of social and moral value. For this part, the focus of my analysis relies primarily on two sets of sources. The first includes a historical ethnography titled *Anahulu: The Anthropology of History in the Kingdom of Hawaii*, published in 1992 by Patrick Kirch, a leading archaeologist of Oceania, in collaboration with the eminent social anthropologist Marshall Sahlins. I select this particular text because it is widely considered to be an invaluable reference on the Hawaiian symbolic order up to the nineteenth century. What is more, the book aims to show not only the colonizing forces of commerce and American settler Christianity, but also how these global forces, with their temporal order, became integrated into the Hawaiian cultural order.

The second set of sources comes from social theories that analyse the contemporary legacies of colonial situations that continue to structure the everyday lives of Native Hawaiians and their relations to others. I focus on a particular policy, the 1921 Hawaiian Homes Commission Act (HHCA), which put in place a narrow and functional conception of "Hawaiian" identity based on blood quantum. I highlight the temporal orientation of the policy through the recurring figure of the indolent Hawaiian. The concept of blood quantum was introduced in the nineteenth century by the United States federal government to measure the *degree* of Indian blood in Native Americans, in order to determine their tribal status. Blood quantum is one of a number of different methods that is used by government agencies to determine an individual's membership of a tribal nation. However, as Brooke Jarvis maintains, it was not a measure that tribal peoples used nor something that they kept track of (Jarvis 2017). In his essay, "The Disenrolled", Jarvis noted that the techniques for determining the percentage of blood shifted, depending on the changing goals of the colonial government. Government agents in the 1800s, for example, often simply guessed at the percentage of American Indian blood. Jarvis points out that "anthropologists used feet and hair width as a 'scientific' test of blood degree in indigenous tribes" (ibid.: 54). More recently, DNA tests are being touted as a more scientific method in determining blood quantum. In the case of Native Hawaiians, a state agency, the Department of Hawaiian Home Lands (DHHL), began enacting new rules to allow the use of DNA as admissible evidence for authenticating Hawaiian ancestry (Tavares 2017; Kelleher 2015).

The last part of the chapter brings together the complex historical relations of the region, in order to reflect on contemporary issues surrounding Hawaiian identity and its relationship to indigenous self-determination. In this section, I attempt to reconceptualize the study of identity and citizenship in relation to an understanding of temporal orientations. Although my chapter is necessarily constrained by word limits, I hope to provide some initial starting points to explore what an inquiry into conflicting spatial-temporal practices in colonial relations might entail, and to consider their broader implications for postcolonial theorizing of education. I am thinking here of the difficult task of elaborating the nexus between manifestations of abstract structures and micro-local expressions of what might appear to be insignificant. I am well aware that the object "blood quantum" does not fall within the conventional purview of educational studies and concepts related to identity or citizenship. Yet, the practice of measuring blood was and continues to be relevant to the efforts to define Native Hawaiian identity and the interrelated discursive and administrative processes of race-making and racial learning. Moreover, analysing the entanglement of blood quanta with these processes offers insight into the politics of the present and the real difficulty of seeking "the brighter side of a utopian future" (Mignolo 1995: 316) – thereby creating alternative registers that might elude the burden of modernity and persistent beliefs concerning time as neutral and universal. In other words, perhaps the challenge for education scholars is to show not only how the neutrality of time is, as Ermarth suggests, constantly reinscribed, but also to investigate existing temporal tensions that might convey the historical and social complexities of change and social transformation.

## Time and indolence

European observers in the late eighteenth and early nineteenth centuries stimulated and circulated a remarkably consistent portrait of the temporal practices of the original peoples of the Hawaiian Islands. Patrick Kirch and Marshall Sahlins observed in their historical ethnography that, as early as 1793, the explorer Lieutenant Peter Puget of the Vancouver Expedition had noted that the islanders were endowed with a "natural Indolency of Disposition". Other Europeans made similar observations, including Ebenezer Townsend, who wrote in 1798: "Those who work make it an exercise rather than labor . . . for they only work in the cool of the morning and evening, returning to the shade whenever the sun becomes uncomfortable" (cited in Kirch and Sahlins 1992: 29). John Whitman, who visited the islands from 1813 to 1815, made the following observation:

> They are of a lively and playful disposition, fond of sports and athletic exercises, but generally averse to hard labour, and seldom work, more than four, or five hours at a time, unless on some important occasion, as when working for the King.
>
> (Cited in Kirch and Sahlins 1992: 29)

Kirch and Sahlins found that missionary reports, beginning in the 1820s, circulated comparable observations about the purported indolence of Hawaiians. For example, Reverend Stewart had said, Hawaiians "sleep and lounge away more than half their time, while much of the remainder is given to amusement and pleasure" (ibid.). Officials of the kingdom expressed a similar viewpoint to those contained in many of the missionaries' reports. In 1846, R. C. Wyllie, minister of foreign relations, wrote to the French consul Dudoit:

> It may be safely asserted that the whole labour of the entire able-bodied population, does not amount to four hours per day, during the year, even including the labour days for the King and Landlord which amount to six per month. The natives spend the greatest part of the time in indolence and sleep.
>
> (Ibid.)

The observations circulated by European and American newcomers and settlers about Hawaiians' "indolence" or lack of industriousness are indicative of a visual point of reference and grammar derived from a specific temporal-spatial symbolic order. This symbolic order and its travelling temporal-spatial practices shared by the accounts of explorers, missionaries, and government officials, among others, insert temporal boundaries that construct Hawaiians in a morally and socially inferior time-space of humanity. As Wynter (1984) assiduously has shown, what constitutes "humanity" is far from transparent. It too is generated from a symbolic order and temporal frame that orients bodies in social and racial hierarchies.

Kirch and Sahlins provide a plethora of examples, which challenge the negative viewpoint that circulated in explorers' journals, missionaries' reports, and officials' questionnaires, by showing the productivity of Hawaiian agricultural practices and its appropriateness to what was required for their subsistence (1992: 30). The authors aim to demonstrate, albeit indirectly, the temporal orientations that are generated in specific historical processes. Their aim is not to suggest that Hawaiians shared the same temporal order with the newcomers and settlers; rather, it is to illustrate another experience of time. Though their study is not focused on the spatialization of time that occurs in colonial situations, what they do show is another symbolic order at work and how Hawaiian cultural practices and rhythms of work were appropriate to that order.

Accessing the Hawaiian system of order that existed in pre-Christian settler times requires revisiting the rules that governed its social relations and the legitimation of its structure of authority. Here I focus on one example. Kirch and Sahlins have shown that with the death of each king the boundaries and distinctions, or "control mechanisms" as Clifford Geertz calls them, were undone until they were "re-created" by the successor king. As put by Kirch and Sahlins:

> Mass demonstrations of grief turned into orgiastic violations of social and ritual rules. Differences in rank broke down in the excessive indulgence of sexual appetites, even as the tabus of gender – including restrictions on women's consumption of sacrificial foods – were ignored in free and prodigious eating.
>
> (Kirch and Sahlins 1992: 69)

During this affective binding of time, a new space emerged and the system of order and the rules and rhythms of life to which their living was subjected was suspended:

> And just as the social body suffered the death of the ruler, so each person inscribed the collective disaster on his or her own body. Tearing their clothes and going about dishevelled, people effaced their social being. Inflicting painful forms of self-mutilation, they died (symbolically) with their king.
>
> (Ibid.)

As the authors note, during the grieving process, the heir to the sovereignty was kept apart, lest they be subject to the general pollution. The heir's retreat ended when "the bones of the dead king were ritually sanctified as a guardian god" (ibid.). According to an account by Samuel Kamakau, a vocal Christian convert and native Hawaiian historian of the nineteenth century, the mourning period lasted for about 15 days (1991: 35). After the period of mourning and with the deceased king's bones deified, the new ruler, who had been temporarily removed to another district, was permitted to return and reconstitute a new order by proclaiming the new rules of the new reign. Kamakau without doubt was looking at the ritual as more fitting to a version of time that correlated with nineteenth-century time-scales. In this version, what was foregrounded was the measurement of time. The duration of the practices was made meaningful by a measurable, quantifiable, and set timescale (i.e., 15 days) that was taken as neutral, universal, and inherently shared. But this way of apprehending the temporality at work in the phenomenon of mourning places too much weight and value on the neutrality of time-keeping which, I argue, is neither universal nor a central feature of Polynesian temporalities. In fact, I propose that it is the expression of "collective disaster" that warrants attention and may suggest a different spatial and temporal experience and, hence, formation at work – one that is meaningful in relation to native frames of reference rather than the extension (i.e., ordering difference from sameness) of settler time. Another way to put this would be to say the temporality of time-keeping undercuts the actual event and what matters to those participating in the dynamic process of collective grief. The desire to control and confine the suspension of social prohibitions and the public display of collective mourning into a set number of days thus giving the event a sense of predictable order, says more about the pressures of an "interpretive schema" on Kamakau's historical account (Hindess 2007).

## Land and blood

In this section, I illustrate the temporal orientation of a specific symbolic order and governing structure through a discussion of the concept of blood quantum. The daily newspaper *Honolulu Star-Advertiser* published a story on 29 December 2015 by *Associated Press* reporter Jennifer Kelleher, "DNA Tests Urged for Homestead Applicants". Kelleher's story described the plan of the DHHL to enact new rules, allowing the use of DNA as admissible evidence for authenticating Hawaiian ancestry. The news story provides an unexpected perspective on the temporal tensions around the role of blood rules and the making of Hawaiian identity.

The news story carried a response from Native Hawaiian law professor Williamson Chang, who suggested that identifying Hawaiians based on their blood quantum was a very un-Hawaiian idea. Elaborating on this point, Chang explained that Hawaiians "are not people who divide" and "the idea of Hawaiian is much broader than race . . . If it weren't for the federal government, Hawaiians wouldn't have a reason to be concerned about blood quantum" (Kelleher 2015: B3). Chang's remarks allude to the historical and social complexities of colonial relations. They are suggestive of an entangled, messy, conflicted, uneven, and painful set of experiences from which land laws in Hawai'i related to blood quantum was shaped.

In 1921, the US Congress passed and signed into law the Hawaiian Homestead Commission Act (HHCA). The HHCA provides for the rehabilitation of the native Hawaiian people through a government-sponsored homesteading program.

As law professor Rose Cuison Villazor writes in the *California Law Review*, the significance of the act was that "it represented a step towards providing Native Hawaiians lands they were entitled but denied as a result of colonialism" (2008: 819). Before the HHCA became law, Congress conducted a series of hearings in 1920 on the conditions of Native Hawaiians. Villazor notes that "Testimony provided at the hearings emphasized Hawaiians as a 'dying race,' stating, for example, how the 'number of full-blooded Hawaiians' dropped tremendously from 142,500 in 1826 to 22,500 in 1919" (ibid.: 821). The hearings not only brought attention to the persistently high mortality rates suffered by Hawaiians, they also underscored the point that the proportion of lands in Hawai'i held by Native Hawaiians was very small. According to Villazor, Congress concluded from the hearings that "the alienation of Native Hawaiians from their lands caused them economic, social, and psychological damage as well as cultural loss, and it determined that the establishment of a land base was necessary to rehabilitate Native Hawaiians" (ibid.: 821). Thus, the HHCA put aside "203,500 acres of lands to be used for homestead leases for the residences and the farm lots of Native Hawaiians" (ibid.: 819). To determine which Hawaiians would benefit from the HHCA and be eligible for land, the US Congress implemented a blood quantum rule.

The HHCA defines Native Hawaiians as those who are "descendants of not less than one-half part of the blood of the races inhabiting the Hawaiian Islands previous to 1778". Villazor touches on one of the disconcerting consequences of the rule when she states:

> The original proposal employed a 1/32 blood requirement, which would have been a broader and more inclusive bloodline distinction than the current fifty-percent requirement that was adopted, in large part because of the protests of the sugar industry. In adopting the higher requirement, the law consequently fixed Native Hawaiian identity along a fifty-percent blood quantum criterion.
> (Villazor 2008: 821)

The inauguration of the jurisprudential underpinning of Hawaiian identity, which "fixes" their identity/identification to blood criterion, makes prominent the colonial present and the many ways in which so many Hawaiians (including myself) are obliged to think, speak, and act in ways that remain tied to modernist constructions of humanity. The juridical and administrative language based on blood measurement ascribes Hawaiians an identity that makes them identifiable in a very specific way (Descombes 2016). Under the blood quantum rule, as Kauanui put it, "Hawaiians were no longer simply evoked in relation to their status as natives, commoners, and U.S. citizens but were instead constructed as a beneficiary class that entailed 'full-blood' status" (1999: 132). Does this particular form of institutional recognition, based on blood measurement and a function of a specific temporal and epistemological order and not a universally shared one, undermine possibilities for other ways of being recognized and acknowledged as Hawaiian? What is denied, devalued, lost, excluded, or compromised by the construction of Hawaiian as a beneficiary class that entails full-blood status?

Earlier I noted that the US federal government used a blood quantum criterion with American Indians to determine their tribal status. Blood quantum rule is part of the norms and dynamics of settler governance. Kauanui, in an oft-cited critical essay, "'For get' Hawaiian entitlement: Configurations of land, 'blood', and Americanization in the Hawaiian Homes Commission Act of 1921" (1999), elaborates on how blood quantum policy was introduced and established in Hawai'i. Kauanui identifies the key participants, stating that:

> Two prominent Hawaiians, beside [territorial Senator John H.] Wise backed the HHCA: the Reverend Akaiko Akana and Prince Jonah Kuhio Kalaniana'ole – the former a witness who testified before the Committee on the Territories, and the latter a congressional delegate from the Territory of Hawaii – supported the notion of rehabilitating Hawaiians.
>
> (Kauanui 1999: 128)

Kauanui asserts that the supporters and opponents of the HHCA included

> ... direct descendants of the first missionaries in Hawai'i who were territorial representatives and/or represented the business elite in Hawai'i; white American representatives on the US continent and from the territory; and Prince Kuhio Kalaniana'ole, who was Hawaii's sole delegate to Congress.
>
> (Ibid.: 128)

Focusing on the different intentions held by the supporters and opponents, Kauanui wryly adds:

> most of these different motives begged the question as to whether this land might already belong to Hawaiians. In the common sense of U. S. hegemony, "returning Hawaiians to the land" thus effaced the alternative of *returning the land to Hawaiians*.
>
> (Ibid.: 129; emphasis added)

Kauanui argues that in hearings on the second draft of the bill, the interests of business, particularly the sugar industry, became prominent. To appreciate this point, she is worth quoting at length:

> Those based on the continent were not particularly bothered by the one thirty-second blood quantum criterion for "native Hawaiian." But territorial representatives and other citizens, economically invested in the debate, argued strongly against such inclusive definitions and, through their presentations of "local knowledge" about Hawaiians proposed a legal construction of "part-Hawaiians." Disagreeing with the one thirty-second blood quantum rule, they argued that "part-Hawaiians" were a threat because of their supposed aggressive and enterprising nature. According to this argument, the focus on mixed-race often worked to make a class distinction among Hawaiians.
>
> (Ibid.: 132)

What this crucial passage illustrates is how boundaries based on blood worked in conjunction with the creation of social class divisions. Recalling the points raised in the introduction of this chapter, this compels us to ask about the temporal legacies of colonial relations and their material inheritances. Under what symbolic order and logic can part-Hawaiians be a threat to Hawaiians with fifty per cent or more blood quantum? What should be made of this fundamental division to protect some Hawaiians ("full") and not other Hawaiians ("part") based on their blood amount? How does this social and moral economy of the racialized body normalize what it differentiates? What should we make of the use of blood in constructing both capability and recognition? Should it concern us that full-blooded Hawaiians are invoked as vulnerable and in need of care, protection and "rehabilitation", while Hawaiians with less than 50 per cent blood quantum are marked as enterprising, and therefore should be excluded from the provisions of the bill? The settler-sanctioned assumptions about Hawaiians that underwrites the bill correlates with (but is not simply reducible to) notions of racial inferiority/superiority that have been used in other contexts concerning alleged indigenous inability. The former is associated with a complacent, laid-back, easy-going, indolent body (i.e., those bodies with more Hawaiian blood) unable to do for itself, while the latter (with less Hawaiian blood) is associated with an industrious, hard-working and ambitious one.

These distinctions are built around the metaphor of blood purity and its specific temporal inscriptions. They carry certain assumptions about the abilities and future potential of each group. In testimony to the US Senate Committee on Territories in 1920, A. G. M. Robertson, a former judge of the Territory of Hawai'i, offers his view of the distinction between a "part" and "pure", or full-blood, Hawaiians. Robertson asserts:

> The part Hawaiian, the part Caucasian, the part Chinese, the part Portuguese are a virile, prolific, and enterprising lot of people. These part Hawaiians have had the advantage, since annexation especially, of the American viewpoint and the advantage of a pretty good public school system, and they are an educated people. They are not in the same class with the pure bloods.
>
> (Cited in Kauanui 1999: 133)

Apart from the many and complicated ways in which "blood" can signify, Robertson's remark rests on the idea that a Hawaiian's lack or abundance of industry and economic ambition is *carried* and *passed* down in the blood. In other words, their fundamental alterability resides inside blood. In this way, blood is understood as an "active agent" responsible for catalysing a disposition (Robertson 2012).

It is important to make note here that Robertson's remarks about mixed blood go against a popular idea of the time, which saw mixed unions or "miscegenation" as perpetuating populations incapable of progressive improvement – a nativistic fear related to the degradation of American stock. Robertson's viewpoint implies that blood portion is what makes or breaks an individual's life chances. The assumptions about whiteness figures deeply in Robertson's remarks yet is not made explicit. Interdisciplinary artist Coco Fusco, in her essay "Racial time, racial marks, racial metaphors", writes convincingly about whiteness as exceeding corporeality and having a presence without ever having to name that presence:

> Whereas systems of racial classification from the eighteenth century onward reduced people of color to the corporeal, whiteness was understood as a spirit that manifests itself in a dynamic relation to the physical world. Whiteness, then, does not need to be made visible to be present in an image; it can be expressed as the spirit of enterprise, as the power to organize the material world, and as an expansive relation to the environment.
>
> (Fusco 2003: 37)

We saw this in the modes of perception discussed earlier that gave rise to the figure of the indolent Hawaiian. At this point, it is useful to look at the gendered connotations in the phrase the "spirit of enterprise". Sara Mills, in an essay called "Gender and colonial space", analyses the gendered nature of colonial spaces. Mills is not the first to explore that relationship; it has been the subject of inquiry by many feminist theorists. But what is significant for our purpose is foregrounding the complexity of gendered spatial relations within colonial contexts (Mills 2003: 692). It follows from this that Robertson's remarks are made intelligible and meaningful within a conventional spatial-temporal settler perspective. The bifurcation between public and private/domestic spheres of association is an unstated assumption that operates in Robertson's remarks. For example, full-blooded Hawaiians are associated with vulnerability and in need of protection, and are presented as being unable or ill-equipped to navigate public spaces of enterprise and venture. Many feminist theorists have critically analysed the public/private sphere divide, since the private/domestic is positioned as primarily a women's space (Mills 2003: 698). This mode of perception, which locates full and part Hawaiians within the bifurcated public/private spheres, reinforces a stereotypically masculinist framework and its settler spatial-temporal formation of social institutions and relations.

Although Kauanui's emphasis on the motivations behind the blood quantum debate is important, I want to propose that questions of temporality and knowledge systems might also bear on our thinking of the making and remaking of identity. Blood quantum criterion is a specific, transplanted, and *not* universal construct for establishing identity/identification or group membership. In the US context, the use of blood measurement has a long history with regards to American citizenship (Snipp 2003; Wolfe 2004). The historical development of the two concepts "race" and "citizenship" were closely linked (Wolfe 2004: 67). In the case of Hawai'i, the use of blood quanta was an institutional and pragmatic intervention if you will – of "government" for a "problem" – which the settler state encountered with a declining Hawaiian population. Addressing the contemporary effects of this historical entanglement on Hawaiian processes of identity constitution, Rona Halualani in *In the name of Hawaiians: Native identities and cultural politics* writes, "Genealogical practices and their cultural political force throughout Hawaiian history have been reduced to a unidimensional, state-surveilled requirement for the completion of an already predetermined legislative identity" (2002: 131). Her observation not only confirms what Ermarth has said about the convention of historical time, but also references another practice of collective belonging and identity constitution that is not based on blood quanta.

## Time-identity-citizenship

From the late eighteenth century onward, the notion of *indolence* was crucial in categorizing Native Hawaiians in spatial and temporal terms. The construct of the indolent Hawaiian surfaced in different representations and arguments. The construct was generated in and by a perceptual orientation and symbolic system that took the specificity of their temporal frames as given and neutral. Consequently, the frames enact what Kevin Bruyneel (1997) has referred to as "colonial time", in which temporal boundaries are constructed between an advancing, industrious and enterprising set of people and a static and fixed set of people. The effects have had significant material consequences for Hawaiian people. Colonial time worked to partition European and American settlers from Native Hawaiians and divide Native Hawaiians from each other in hierarchies of social and moral value based on blood measurement: partitions and divisions that are entangled with the present.

In *Beyond settler time: Temporal sovereignty and indigenous self-determination*, Mark Rifkin argues that "Native peoples occupy a double bind within dominant settler reckonings of time. Either they are consigned to the past, or they are inserted into a present defined on non-native terms" (2017: vii). Rifkin questions the scholarship that attempts to show or that insists upon Native peoples' coevalness moving along with and toward the future like all other people (ibid.: viii). An emphasis on coevalness he says, "tends to bracket the way that the idea of a shared present is not a neutral designation but is, instead, defined by settler institutions, interests, and imperatives" (ibid.) that undermine their temporal sovereignty. Rifkin's remarks echo what Mignolo, Wynter, and Ermarth contend about time and temporality. While attuned to the politics of how a historically specific experience of time – as unity, singularity, and neutral – became generalized and naturalized, they are also well aware of discrepant temporalities.

For many scholars with a critical orientation, race, class, and gender are the central objects of inquiry and analysis. From a sociological disciplinary perspective, these constructs form the axes that define inequality in modern society, particularly in the US. Time or temporalities do not figure prominently in the analysis of these social constructs. Yet, as this chapter has attempted to illustrate, scholarship in that area might delve deeper into how temporal orientations are entwined with processes of identity and citizenship. Admission to citizenship indicates, at least theoretically, equality within the polity and in the case of Hawaiian people equality with non-natives and to use Rifkin's phrase the "non-native infrastructure". In pursuing a line of inquiry that takes into account time and temporality, we might pause to consider what temporal tensions exist or emerge when maintaining

Native Hawaiians (or Native peoples more generally) inhabit a shared modernity. While this question may seem like an abstraction, important links to schooling can be drawn. I have argued (see Tavares 2017) that schooling and higher education are sites in the political struggle for self-determination, for decolonizing educational practices, and for indigenizing curricula, research methods, and institutions, not just in Hawai'i but around the world. Rarely do we see these reform efforts confront what Hindess calls the "temporal ordering of humanity" (2007: 333). What forms of affinity are practicable without shared temporal references and discursive frames? How would conceptualizations of identity or citizenship change in light of their temporal making and remaking? These questions underline some starting points that are worthy of notice. They speak to the "spatialization of time" (Mignolo 1995) and the "temporalization of difference" (Hindess 2007), an angle explored by few education scholars writing on education and citizenship or Indigenous self-determination.

## Acknowledgements

I want to thank Julie McLeod and Grace Livingston for their valuable feedback on earlier drafts of this chapter.

## References

Bruyneel, K. (1997). *The third space of sovereignty: The postcolonial politics of U.S.-Indigenous relations*. Minneapolis: University of Minnesota Press.

Descombes, Vincent. (2016). *Puzzling identities* (S. A. Schwartz, Trans.). Cambridge, MA: Harvard University Press.

Ermarth, E. D. (1995). Ph(r)ase time chaos theory and postmodern reports on Knowledge. *Time & Society*, *4*(1), 91–110.

Ermarth, E. D. (1998). Time and neutrality: Media of modernity in a postmodern world. *Cultural Values*, *2*(2&3), 355–367.

Fusco, C. (2003). Racial time, racial marks, racial metaphors. In C. Fusco and B. Wallis (Eds.), *Only skin deep: Changing visions of the American self* (pp. 13–48). New York: International Center of Photography/Harry N. Abrams.

Halualani, R. T. (2002). *In the name of Hawaiians: Native identities and cultural politics*. Minneapolis: University of Minnesota Press.

Hawaiian Homes Commission Act (c 42, 42 Stat 108). July 9, 1921. Retrieved January 20, 2017 from http:dhhl.hawaii.gove/wp-content/uploads/2011/06/HHCA_1921.pdf.

Hindess, B. (2007). The past is another culture. *International Political Sociology*, *1*, 325–338.

Jarvis, B. (2017, January 22). The disenrolled. *New York Times Magazine*, 52–60.

Kamakau, S. (1991). *Ka Po'e Kahiko The People of Old*. Translated from the newspaper *Ke Au'Oko'a* by Mary Kawena Pukui. Honolulu, HI: Bishop Museum Press.

Kauanui, J. K. (1999). "For get" Hawaiian entitlement: Configurations of land, "blood" and Americanization in the Hawaiian Homes Commission Act of 1921. *Social Text*, *59*, 123–144.

Kelleher, J. S. (2015, December 29). DNA tests urged for homestead applicants. *Honolulu Star-Advertiser*, B1, B3. Retrieved January 20, 2017 from www.staradvertiser.com/2015/12/29/hawaai-news/dna-tests-urged-for-homestead-applicants/.

Kirch, P. V. and Sahlins, M. (1992). *Anahulu: The anthropology of history in the Kingdom of Hawaii* (Vol. I). Chicago, IL and London: University of Chicago Press.

Lyotard, J.-F. (1988). *The differend: Phrases in dispute* (G. Van Den Abbeele, Trans). Minneapolis: University of Minnesota Press.

Mignolo, W. (1995). *The darker side of the Renaissance: Literacy, territoriality, and colonization.* Ann Arbor: University of Michigan Press.

Mills, S. (2003). Gender and colonial space. In R. Lewis and S. Mills (Eds.), *Feminist postcolonial theory: A reader* (pp. 692–719). New York: Routledge.

Rifkin, M. (2017). *Beyond settler time: Temporal sovereignty and indigenous self-determination.* Durham, NC and London: Duke University Press.

Robertson, J. (2012). Hemato-nationalism: The past, present, and future of "Japanese blood". *Medical Anthropology, 31*(2), 93–112.

Snipp, M. C. (2003). Racial measurement in the American census: Past practices and implications for the future. *Annual Review of Sociology, 29,* 563–588.

Tavares, H. M. (2017). Postcolonial studies and education. In B. Warnick and L. Stone (Eds.). *Philosophy: education. Macmillan interdisciplinary handbooks: Philosophy series* (pp. 141–152). Farmington Hills, MI: Macmillan Reference.

Toulmin, S. (1990). *Cosmopolis: The hidden agenda of modernity.* New York: Free Press.

US Senate, Committee on Territories. (1921). *Hawaiian Homes Commission Act, 1920: Hearings before the Committee on Territories, United States Senate, Sixty-Sixth Congress, Third Session, on H. R. 13500.* Washington, DC: Government Printing Office. Retrieved January 20, 2017 from www.doi.gov/sites/doi.gov/files/migrated/ohr/upload/HHCA-House-Hearing-Dec-14-1920-for-HR-13500.pdf.

Villazor, R. C. (2008). Blood quantum land laws and the race versus political identity dilemma. *California Law Review, 96*(3), 801–837.

Wolfe, P. (2004). Race and citizenship. *Organization of American Historians Magazine of History,* 66–71.

Wynter, S. (1984). The ceremony must be found: After humanism. *Boundary 2 12*(3), 19–70.

Wynter, S. (1995). 1492: A new world view. In V. L. Hyatt and R. Nettleford (Eds.). *Race, discourse, and the origin of the Americas: A new world view* (pp. 5–57). Washington, DC and London: Smithsonian Institution Press.

# Section III

# Mobility and contexts

# 12 Context, entanglement and assemblage as matters of concern in comparative education research

*Noah W. Sobe and Jamie Kowalczyk*

Decontextualized education research has the rather obvious blindspot of ignoring how it is that the specificities of local environments, relationships and phenomena shape and construe what occurs in and around educational settings as well as how particular knowledges, actors and institutions are drawn together in various arrangements. For this reason, the idea that education research needs to be *contextualized* is generally taken as widespread commonsense. Yet, what it means to contextualize and how researchers in the field of comparative and international education should take up questions of "context" in their work remain both unresolved and neglected. This chapter proposes approaching context as more a "matter of concern" than a "matter of fact" (Latour, 2004b). In the spirit of advancing the practice of "criss-crossing comparison" (Seddon, McLeod and Sobe, this volume), we map out an approach to context as a process of interweaving. As such, the social embeddedness of education is understood as interwoven through the relationality of objects, actors and environments, with the researcher her or himself playing an important "entangling" role in the construction of educational research contexts.

Though the importance of "contextualization" is widely recognized in education research, there is no agreement on how to do this, nor what it means for comparative research methods. As education researchers who are at once located in North American academic homes and enmeshed in a number of globe-spanning academic circuits, we observe that context is often dichotomously framed either as something to be eclipsed or as all-important and inescapable (Sobe and Kowalczyk, 2012). Analogous to the somewhat sterile debates about "qualitative" and "quantitative" research, one can schematically identify currents in comparative and international education that maintain that schools, teaching and learning have universal qualities that facilitate the portability of best practices and lesson learning. From this perspective, comparison becomes a science of *ceteris paribus*, a science of learning how to control for contextual factors to properly construct knowledge. Alternately, our field also contains research currents which hold that educational interactions have a situational specificity that forecloses the easy possibility of "transfer". From this angle, comparison itself can sometimes appear as a modernist artefact and governing tool linked to neo-colonialism. In this chapter, our goal is less to collapse these dualisms than it is to frame out a mode for thinking about context that will facilitate the enactment of criss-crossing comparative education studies that allow us "to look both at and behind the landscape of tangible things to surface patterns and processes of knowing and doing that configure globalising education" (Seddon, McLeod and Sobe, this volume).

## Taking big "C" Contexts and little "c" contexts as matters of concern

One of the key issues that weaves across this 2018 *World Year Book* is the question of how to approach embeddedness and situatedness. As we have discussed in a previous publication titled "Exploding the cube" (Sobe and Kowalczyk, 2013), much comparative education research treats context as pre-existing, "there whether you like it or not" surroundings to be identified and taken into consideration at the outset of a project. The most common expression of this is Mark Bray and R. Murray Thomas's (1995: 475) proposal that educational comparisons can be framed by situating a study where a particular geographic/locational level (e.g. classroom, country, world region) intersects both with the particular "aspect of education and of society" (e.g. curriculum, educational finance, political change) and the "nonlocational" demographic group under consideration (e.g. ethnic groups, age groups, the entire populations). Our chief critique of this approach is that it treats contexts as what Latour (2004a) would characterize as *matters of fact*,[1] whereas matters of fact possess "clear boundaries", have predictive value and are "risk free objects", a *matter of concern* is a risky "tangled" business (ibid.: 22–23) that engages the unexpected and the emerging. Too often context has been treated as a matter of fact and invoked as a unity that is always already-there, waiting to be observed and described via stable categories. In pace with Latour, we do not propose to move away from matters of fact as any step away from a realist attitude. Instead, we hold that a realist understanding of the facts of the matter means that the researcher's attention must be directed to how contexts are made.

One strategy for taking up context as a matter of concern is to distinguish between what we have referred to as big "C" Contexts and little "c" contexts (Sobe and Kowalczyk, 2013). This move is indebted to the distinction Gee (1990, 1999, 2015) proposed between big "D" Discourse and little "d" discourse. Big "D" Discourse refers to historically and socially constructed constellations that permit one to perform or identify particular "kinds of people" or kinds of activities. Discourse includes little "d" discourse, or "language-in-use" (1999, 2015), where language coupled with other particular "actions, interactions, objects, tools, technologies, beliefs, and values," (2015) come together in practices that authorize or challenge particular ways of being and doing. We suggest that it can be useful to distinguish between big "C" Context as the set of historically and socially significant Discourses within education research that interweave actors and objects and govern what it is possible to think and to do, and little "c" contexts as the set of named elements that are seen as comprising a given setting.

In this schema, locational descriptors are one part of big "C" Context. It is by now well-trodden ground to question methodological nationalism in educational research (Dale and Robertson 2009; Shahjahan and Kezar 2012), yet the answer is not simply for researchers to disabuse themselves of thinking about nations. It is instead to ask *and make a part of the research* how nation forms and "national imaginaries" – through the ways that they themselves are assembled – shape and are shaped by the educational phenomena or processes under examination (see, e.g. Popkewitz 2008). Similarly, it is incumbent on the comparative education researcher to probe concepts like "civilization" and "urban" when they are encountered, to understand what is being gathered together in these notions and to what effects. Additionally, to grapple with transnationalism in globalizing time-spaces of education calls for an interrogation of the politics of scale – again, not to force a pre-arrayed schema onto a particular situation but rather to delve into the Context that includes the specific forms and frames that social embeddedness takes (c.f. Wastell 2001).

The categories "political", "economic" and "cultural" also merit examination as forms of big "C" Context. To use these categories in the making of context underscores the ways that the categories of big "C" Contexts create knowledge about characteristics over which rule can be exercised (Rose 1999). This phenomenon is clearly illustrated by the "newly discovered island" heuristic employed by neo-institutional sociologists of education (Meyer et al. 1997) to explain the ways that institutionalized world models define and de/legitimate local agendas. They predict that if a previously uncontacted island were discovered, its inhabitants would be pressured to begin organizing themselves according to world models that have their origin in North America and Europe but have since been spread widely around the globe. The island would be conceptualized as "a society" with "an economy" and "a government" and it would enter into a surprisingly standardizing machine of academic knowledge production. As Meyer and colleagues are well aware, to splice out Context into different dimensions in this manner is to construct domains of action and surfaces of intervention.

The features of big "C" Contexts are the black-boxed units of reference that often appear in research studies in a short-hand manner, as if possessing unquestionable and stable analytic power. For most of its history, the field of comparative and international education has been entirely incorrect when analysing the relation between schools and nations: the critical error being to treat the nation-state as an explanatory independent variable from which most of the salient aspects of schools and school systems flow, when instead the nation needs to be taken as something that needs to be explained (Sobe 2014). Big "C" Contexts, too – as we will discuss in greater detail in the next section in reference to the traditional separation of "objects" and "contexts" – need their share of explaining. We maintain that this is a matter of concern of significant political and ethical import because individual instances of little "c" context are only intelligible through Contexts with a "big C".

## Entanglement and relationality

The comparative education researcher who takes Context as a "matter of concern" is not interested in the traditional object of study contained within a context, but rather examines the relationality between objects and contexts: how they come to be intelligible and conjoined, and to what effect(s). This approach raises to the surface the question of what makes it possible for us to see objects as objects – particularly as problems to be studied. As indicated in the introduction to this volume, "entangled approaches" can be particularly useful for studying and understanding these relationships.

In a foundational piece on *Histoire Croisée* (commonly translated into English as "entangled history") Michael Werner and Bénédicte Zimmermann (2006) have outlined a research approach that aims to overcome some of the limitations of comparative history as it is traditionally undertaken, as well as some of the limitations of transfer research. Much comparison embeds a thinking about time-spaces that requires the deployment of a series of mechanisms to fix and pause the flow of time so that a cross-sectional object can be stabilized and discerned. This kind of thinking is tied to the making of context as a matter of fact where the researcher pulls out one particular moment from a flowing heterotemporal and heterospatial assemblage, what Žižek calls a process of "decoherence", when from "the coherent multiplicity of superposed states" one option "is cut off from the continuum of others and posited as a single reality" (Žižek 2016: 50). Transfer approaches focus on temporally unfolding processes (as is evidenced by the educational borrowing and learning research literatures mentioned above) but are frequently marked by invariability in the categories of analysis and an inability to adequately deal with complex situations where movements are reciprocal and in multiple directions at once (cf. Stoler 2001). Werner and Zimmermann's *Histoire Croisée* is an attempt to move research beyond transfer and beyond comparison by putting interaction, intersections and inter-crossing at the centre of the analysis and by giving renewed attention to reflexivity. Entangled history can usefully refer to "analysis of the tangling together of disparate actors, devices, discourses and practices – with the recognition that this tangling is partly accomplished by said actors, devices, discourses and practices and partly accomplished by the historian her/himself" (Sobe 2013: 100).

An entangled approach accesses the concept of the "assemblage" (see also Larsen, this volume), which is an as if anti-structural structural concept that permits the researcher to speak of emergence, heterogeneity, the decentred and the ephemeral in social life and social interactions that are nonetheless ordered and coordinated. George Marcus and Erkan Saka (2006: 102) describe the assemblage as maintaining the idea of a structure while at the same time evoking movement and change. In this way, it is both spatial and temporal. The ideas of Deleuze form an important basis of much work around assemblages, which he saw as:

> a multiplicity which is made up of many heterogeneous terms and which establishes liaisons, relations between them, across ages, sexes, and reigns – different natures. Thus, the assemblage's only unity is that of co-functioning . . . It is never filiations which are important, but alliances, alloys; these are not successions, lines of descent, but contagions, epidemics, the wind.
>
> (Deleuze and Parnet 1987: 69–70)

The contingency and constant shape-shifting of an assemblage do not, however, de-emphasize the work that is involved in bringing and fusing together disparate elements to create something that informs, shapes and is itself re-shaped by human actions and forms of social organization.

The notions of entanglement and assemblage invite us to spend less time trying to crisply demarcate the boundaries between an object of interest and its "context", and instead to direct our energies towards understanding social embeddedness by studying education phenomena and practices as assemblages. If the traditional approach to contextualization is to situate a research object within a particular, prescribed hierarchically arranged space at a given moment, rather than a "placing", Werner and Zimmerman emphasize movement and intercrossings, so that attention shifts what emerges over time. The object of analysis becomes two things at once: one, the assemblage that is often mistaken for "context" and two, the effect (policy, practice, phenomena) that it constitutes (what we might think of as the traditional "object" of study): "Intercrossing is thus obviously an aspect of both the realm of the object of study and the realm of the procedures of research related to the researcher's choices" (2006: 44).

Entangled analysis engages in empirical and reflexive practice through "pragmatic induction" (ibid.: 46) where research begins with "the object of study and the situations in which it is embedded, according to one or more points of view . . . subject to continual readjustments in the course of empirical investigation" (ibid.: 47). If we conceptualize criss-crossing comparative education as similarly marked by continual readjustments and intercrossing over the course of a study, then it also becomes possible to see contexts and objects in relational terms – and in terms of their historicity as forming an unstable, changing and heterogenous assemblage, which is partly made visible by the processes and entities under investigation and partly by the researcher.

## The messiness of interweaving and researcher entanglement

In our effort to rethink "contextualization" as a necessary component of academic research we have found it useful, albeit with a sense of irony, to return to the etymology of the word (Sobe and Kowalczyk 2013). This allows us to put aside the sediments of "background" and "placement" and "location" that have accrued over time and rearticulate the relationship between Context and object. From the Latin verb *texere*, meaning "'to weave," and with the prefix *con*, or "with," *contexere* has the meaning "to weave together" or "to interweave". Embracing the *contexere* notion of interweaving usefully reminds us to pay attention to the way, as feminist scholars have long pointed out, that researchers themselves are entangled in that which they study. It also invites us to consider the researcher as one who – in the Levi-Straussian model of the *bricoleur* – actively weaves historical artefacts and elements together to fabricate social embeddedness. In this vein Latour (2004b: 246) usefully reminds us that "the critic is not one who debunks but one who assembles."

Thinking of contextualization as *contexere* invites us to think about contexts as being made over and over again as the researcher tracks and accounts for needed adjustments categories and knowledges over the course of the study. These constant adjustments trace both the messy ways in which people, objects and ideas interconnect/intercross, and the multiple perspectives embedded within the making of contexts, inclusive of the researcher's perspective(s) and intervention(s). Werner and Zimmermann propose that an entangled, criss-crossing approach,

> ...integrates into the operation of contextualization carried out by the researcher the referential dimension of the objects and practices analyzed, taking into account both the variety of situations in which the relationships to the context are structured and the effect that the study of such situations exerts on the analytical procedures.
>
> (Werner and Zimmermann 2006: 47)

Taking this approach to researcher entanglement necessitates a high degree of comfort with ambiguity and "messiness", as well as with the likelihood that a focus on relationality will illuminate many things at once. In the effort to engage a criss-crossing comparative education, educational practices, phenomena and policies can usefully be approached as "messy objects", a term used by Fenwick and Edwards, who propose that

> Any changes we might describe as policy – new ideas, innovations, changes in behavior, transformations – emerge through the effects of relational interactions and assemblages, in various kinds of more-than-human networks entangled with one another, that may be messy and incoherent, spread across time and space.
>
> (Fenwick and Edwards 2011: 712)

In tracing out interactions and assemblages, the role of the researcher is both to entangle and detangle.

Though in this chapter we have proposed several strategies for reworking how context is articulated in comparative and international education; we still consider the challenge of social embeddedness an ongoing problem. As an issue at the core of changing space-times of education, contexts – both big "C" and little "c", interwoven and entangled assemblages – remain an important matter of concern for our field.

## Note

1 In recent work, Bray, Adamson and Mason (2007) have usefully reflected on limitations to the cube, particularly, for example, on the ways that the various filters could be reframed. The geographic filter could be expanded to allow a focus on countries affected by a particular colonial experience (Manzon, 2007) or on countries/regions with religious commonalities. Bray and his colleagues have even proposed that multiple cubes could be arrayed along a temporal axis to afford comparisons across time. While they do recognize significant limitations, including the definitional "slipperiness" (2007: 370) that emerges when the units of comparison delineated in the cube are actually deployed

by researchers, they nonetheless note, "good comparative education researchers will necessarily consider factors along each of the axes [of the cube] before they isolate the variables pertinent to their hypotheses" (Bray, Adamson and Mason 2007: 371).

# References

Bray, M. & Thomas, R. M. (1995). Levels of comparison in educational studies: Different insights from different literatures and the value of multilevel analyses. *Harvard Education Review, 65*(3), 472–490.

Bray, M., Adamson, B., & Mason, M. (2007). *Comparative Education Research Approaches and Methods.* Hong Kong, China: Comparative Education Research Centre, University of Hong Kong.

Dale, R. & Robertson, S. (2009). Beyond methodological "isms" in comparative education in an era of globalization. In R. Cowen & A. M. Kazamias (Eds.), *International handbook of comparative education* (pp. 1113–1127). Dordrecht: Springer.

Deleuze, G. & Parnet, C. (1987). *Dialogues.* New York, NY: Columbia University Press.

Fenwick, T. & Edwards, R. (2011). Considering materiality in educational policy: Messy objects and multiple reals. *Educational Theory, 61*(6), 709–726.

Gee, J. (1990). *Social linguistics and literacies: Ideology in discourses. Critical perspectives on literacy and education.* London, UK: Falmer Press.

Gee, J. P. (1999). *An Introduction to Discourse Analysis: Theory and method.* New York: Routledge Press.

Gee, J. P. (2015). Discourse, Small d, Big D. In K. Tracy, C. Ilie & T. L. Sandel (Eds.), *The international encyclopedia of language and social interaction* (pp. 418–422). Boston, MA: Wiley-Blackwell.

Latour, B. (2004a). *The politics of nature: How to bring the sciences into democracy* (C. Porter, Trans.). Cambridge, MA: Harvard University Press.

Latour, B. (2004b) Why has critique run out of steam? From matters of fact to matters of concern. *Critical Inquiry,* 225–248.

Manzon, M. (2007) Comparing places. In Bray, M., Adamson, B., & Mason, M. (Eds.), *Comparative Education Research Approaches and Methods.* Hong Kong: CERC, 85–121.

Marcus, G. E. & Saka, E. (2006). Assemblage. *Theory, Culture & Society, 23*(2–3), 101–106.

Meyer, J., Boli, J., Thomas G., & Ramirez, F. (1997). World society and the nation state. *American Journal of Sociology, 103*(1), 144–181.

Popkewitz, T. (2008) *Cosmopolitanism and the age of school reform: Science, education, and making society by making the child.* New York: Routledge.

Rose, N. (1999). *Powers of freedom: Reframing political thought.* Cambridge: Cambridge University Press.

Shahjahan, R. J. & Kezar, A. J. (2012). Beyond the "national container": Addressing methodological nationalism in higher education research. *Educational Researcher, 42*(1), 20–29.

Sobe, N. W. (2013). Entanglement and transnationalism in the history of American education. In T. S. Popkewitz (Ed.), *Rethinking the history of education: Transnational perspectives on its questions, methods and knowledge* (pp. 93–107). New York: Palgrave.

Sobe, N. W. (2014). Textbooks, schools, memory and the technologies of national imaginaries. In J. H. Williams (Ed.), *(Re)constructing memory: School textbooks and the imagination of the nation* (pp. 313–318). Rotterdam: Sense.

Sobe, N. W. & Kowalczyk, J. A. (2012). The problem of context in comparative education research. *ECPS Journal, 6,* 55–74. www.ledonline.it/ECPs-Journal/allegati/ECPS-2012-6_Sobe.pdf.

Sobe, N. W. & Kowalczyk, J. A. (2013). Exploding the cube: Revisioning "context" in the field of comparative education. *Current Issues in Comparative Education, 16*(1), 6–12.

Stoler, A. L. (2001). Tense and tender ties: The politics of comparison in North American history and (post) colonial studies. *Journal of American History, 88*(3), 829–865.

Wastell, S. (2001). Presuming scale, making diversity – on the mischiefs of measurement and the global: Local metonym in theories of law and culture. *Critique of Anthropology, 21*(2), 185–210.

Werner, M. & Zimmermann, B. (2006). Beyond comparison: Histoire croisée and the challenge of reflexivity. *History and Theory, 45*(1), 30–50.

Žižek, S. (2016) *Disparities*. London: Bloomsbury.

# 13 Governing (im)mobile academics in global times

## An analysis through spatial/mobilities historical sociology

*Marianne A. Larsen*

## Introduction

Academic scholars today are compelled to be mobile, as transnational scholarly exchanges and research collaboration have come to be considered necessary components of a successful academic career. Indeed, over the past two decades there has been a dramatic increase in the numbers of mobile scholars engaging in research collaboration and partnerships with scholars in other countries. In the context of new academic knowledge decoupled from specific national and local cultures, "knowledge and curricula that will 'travel' – ones that will be bought and consumed in as many places in the world as possible" is now privileged (Robins and Webster 2002: 11).

To this end, higher education institutions (HEIs), governments, and regional associations across diverse global settings have enacted policies and practices to encourage and facilitate this transformation of knowledge through academic mobility. However, these shifts are occurring alongside contradictory pressures that work in ways to either force academics to be mobile (who do not want to be) or immobilize them against their will. Together, these related but contradictory processes of mobility/immobility reflect broader geopolitical, knowledge-economy discourses that privilege the production of transnational knowledge that is multi-authored, multi-disciplinary, and multi-institutional, motivated by global ranking schemes and innovations in information and digital communications technologies (Fahey and Kenway 2010; Urry 2002).

In this chapter I problematize the ways in which higher education scholars are expected and compelled to be mobile or, conversely, are unable to move across borders. Utilizing a framework I call Spatial/Mobilities Historical Sociology, I explore the ways that mobility infuses the lives of higher education scholars. I review contemporary and historical manifestations of scholarly mobility and immobility to demonstrate how academic spatialities and (im)mobilities are entangled with temporalities that are uneven and unequal. I argue that the glo-balized academic profession is governed through mobility in uneven ways, as some academics enact their choice to travel, while others are forced to be mobile, and others are simply unable to move across borders. In this way, mobility is viewed not solely as a set of flows, but as a political technology enabled through connections. Thus, mobility and immobility are viewed not as distinct processes, but as being embedded within and paradoxically presupposing each other. Together the pulling and pushing, openings and blockages across time and space that (de)limit academic mobility constitute the global academic assemblage.

## Spatial/mobilities historical sociology

I bring together key ideas from contemporary mobilities and spatial theories to construct a sociological framework suitable for the analysis of scholarly mobility. The spatial and mobilities "turn" illustrates growing interest in the complex, intertwined relations and inseparability between time, movement and space, the social, and the historical. Spatial and mobility theorists consider the social world as being fundamentally spatial, networked, and mobile. Indeed, it is at the juncture where mobilities allow us to question taken-for-granted assumptions about space as a "closed container, backcloth or constraint" (Fenwick, Edwards, and Sawchuk 2011: 133) that both mobilities and spatial analyses emerge.

Spatial and mobilities theorists deploy a relational approach, focusing on the complex relationality of objects, knowledge, people, and places connected through movement, flows, and networks. Mobility is viewed both as a "relationship through which the world is lived and understood" (Adey 2006: 270), as well as a lens through which to research the complex relational dynamics between the movement of information, objects, and people (Sheller 2011). Likewise, a relational notion of space implies understanding that space not only exists in concrete and separate forms, but also as sets of relations between individuals, groups, and objects. As Murdoch explains, relational space is "an undulating landscape in which the linkages established in networks draw some locations together while at the same time pushing others further apart" (quoted in Warf 2009: 75). Thus, attending to idea of relationality allows us to see the connections, multiplicity, and simultaneity of space, place, movement, and time.

There are a number of spatial/mobility metaphors or analogies that illustrate this relational, network, and fluid concept. One is the metaphor of "assemblage" derived from the French *agancement*, which means the coming together of different and heterogeneous elements or objects that enter into relationship with one another to form a whole. Most contemporary social theorists using the term to study the complexity of the social world have been inspired by the work of Gilles Deleuze. Bryant explains how Deleuze conceptualizes assemblage:

> Assemblages are composed of heterogeneous elements or objects that enter into relations with one another. These objects are not all of the same type. Thus you have physical objects, happenings, events, and so on, but you also have signs, utterances, and so on. While there are assemblages that are composed entirely of bodies, there are no assemblages composed entirely of signs and utterances.
>
> (Bryant 2009: n.p.)

Within an assemblage, the relationships of component parts are neither stable nor fixed. Rather, assemblages are relational, in which the heterogeneous and individual parts have agency and are implicated within one another. Assemblages are also fluid and in flux; they can both come together to form territorial organizations and they can mutate, transform, be displaced or replaced (Müller 2015). There is also a temporal aspect to assemblages. As Marcus and Saka note, "The time-space in which assemblage is imagined is inherently unstable and infused with movement and change" (2006: 101).

Another related spatial/mobility metaphor is the network derived from Manuel Castells's (1996, 2006) work on the network society, which is based on an interpretation of space as a set of relations that transcend the territorial location of the nodes that constitute a given network. Castells (2006) conceptualizes the network society as an assemblage based on networks, resulting from the interaction between the new technological paradigm and social organizations at large. Power is exercised not through the government or other institutions, but via networks, through sets of exclusions and inclusions.

Both network and assemblage metaphors facilitate our understanding of the social world as a set of relations between heterogeneous elements of individuals, groups, objects, organizations, and institutions. Moreover, assemblages and networks are both structures and structuring agents. In other words, there is no particular privileging of the macro over the micro, or vice versa. Through networks and assemblage, "new territorial organizations, new behaviours, new expressions, new actors and new realities" are produced (Müller 2015: 29). These are useful tools for studying the structural, process, agency, and the aesthetic. As Marcus and Saka explain:

> Assemblage thus seems structural, an object with the materiality and stability of the classic metaphors of structure, but the intent in its aesthetic uses is precisely to undermine such ideas of structure . . . It generates enduring puzzles about "process" and "relationship" rather than leading to systematic understandings of these tropes of classic social theory and the common discourse that it has shaped. It offers an odd, irregular, time-limited object for contemplation.
>
> (Marcus and Saka 2006: 101)

Likewise, networks also allow us to see how both structures and agency constantly combine and connect to change the very structures and dynamic of the network (Beech 2015).

Spatial and mobilities theorists also emphasize the productive capacity of space and mobility (and the relationship between the two). Soja (1996), for example, emphasizes the performative aspect of places that are produced by (and at the same time produce) social activity. Places are performed into being as individuals inhabit them, and conversely individual and group identities are performed into being by the places they occupy and traverse.

Finally, spatial and mobilities theorists pay attention not only to the movement and connections between elements of the network/assemblage and the space they occupy, but also to what (or who) is not mobile and able to connect. Mobilities scholars, for instance, focus not only on mobility, but on potential and blocked movement, as well as "who and what is demobilized and remobilized across many different scales, and in what situations mobility or immobility might be desired options, coerced, or paradoxically interconnected" (Sheller 2011: 2). Indeed, we cannot understand mobility without the concomitant process of immobility or fixity. While mobility and immobility may be understood as fundamentally different, there are no distinctions between these processes. They each are embedded within and presuppose the other.

This is a historical sociology of the becoming of the global academic that attends to structure and agency, space and time, mobility and immobility. I attempt to understand the relationship of personal activity and experience, on the one hand, and social organizations and institutions on the other, as being constructed across time and place. This, as Abrams in his seminal book on *Historical Sociology* asserts, "makes the continuous process of construction the focal concern of social analysis" (1982: 16). Mobilities and immobilities are at the core of this analysis, which attempts to illustrate how together they operate in ways not only to construct, but also to govern, the global academic.

## Scholarly mobility: an overview

According to mobilities scholars, there are five types of mobilities. The first consists of the physical travel of people for work, leisure, family life, pleasure, migration, and escape. The second concerns the physical movement of objects to producers, consumers, and retailers. Imaginative travel occurs through memories, texts, images, television, and films. Virtual travel happens both in real time and on the Internet transcending geographical and social distance. And finally communicative travel is enacted through person-to-person messages via letters, cards, SMS, text messages, face-time, Skype, and other forms of social media (Urry 2007; Larsen, Urry, and Axhausen, 2006).

We can examine each of these types of mobilities within the context of academic work. Academic mobility plays a crucial role in facilitating the discovery and dissemination of new knowledge. Short-term academic mobility consists of travelling for research meetings and workshops, symposia and conferences, student co-supervision and/or examination, and teaching at overseas branch campuses. Long(er)-term academic mobility involves academic exchange, taking up academic positions abroad and engaging in cross-border research collaborations, transnational research networks or international clusters of excellence (Fahey and Kenway 2010; Hallet and Eryaman 2014, Teichler 2010).

In *Globalizing the Academy*, Urry (2002) examines how knowledge production is deterritorialized through mobility. Scholars no longer work alone within their separate departments and disciplines located within individual universities and nation-states. Rather, they are compelled to work within and across new multi-author, multi-disciplinary, and multi-institutional transnational spaces utilizing physical, virtual, and communicative travel.

Indeed, according to results of the Fourth Global Survey on Internationalization, respondents in Africa, Asia and Pacific, and the Middle East cited international research collaboration (IRC) as the most important internationalization activity. Given this focus on IRC, it is unsurprising that outgoing faculty or staff mobility was the second highest ranked activity amongst respondents from Africa, Asia and Pacific, and the Middle East; in Latin America and the Caribbean it was ranked third (International Association of Universities 2014).

Academic mobility is made possible through various push and pull factors, barriers, and incentives. Push factors or barriers include a lack of job opportunities in the home country or threats stemming from repressive regimes where human rights violations put scholars' lives at risk. Pull factors include the availability of academic positions abroad, and the existence of familial and friendship networks. At the higher education institutional level, we can consider incentives such as policies to recruit foreign faculty, funding to support transnational knowledge collaboration, and tenure and promotion expectations to engage in international research. Pull factors (or incentives) at the destination government level include positive visas and study permits, immigration, and trade policies, as well as subsidies for fellowship and transnational research programs, as well as regional policy initiatives such as the Bologna Process in Europe. Transnational organizations also play a role in facilitating scholarly mobility. Furthermore, pull factors include a personal desire to broaden one's knowledge, to experience and learn about other cultures (Hallett and Eryaman 2014; Kim 2010; Rumbley, Altbach, and Reisberg 2012; Vassar and Barrett 2014).

## Historicizing scholarly mobility

Academic mobility is not new; thus I insert here some brief notes to historicize the educational present. The history of peripatetic scholars dates back to the ancient world, with renowned philosophers such as Aristotle, Confucius, and Plato travelling to teach and study with other scholars. There were several centres of higher learning throughout the ancient world, including Alexandria, Athens, Cairo, Nalanda, Nanjing, and Takshashila (near modern-day Islamabad). Scholars travelled to and from these noted centres of learning to enhance their learning and generate new knowledge. For example, Nalanda University, in ancient India, attracted scholars from places as distant as China, Korea, Indonesia, Japan, Mongolia, Persia, Sri Lanka, Tibet, and Turkey (History and Revival 2016).

Throughout the Golden Age of the Islamic Empire (from the mid-eighth to mid-thirteenth centuries), there was considerable mobility amongst Muslim and non-Muslim scholars between the East and the West. During this era, intellectual culture was based on integrating and fusing knowledge through cooperation amongst a range of scholars from diverse cultural, linguistic, religious, professional, and geographical backgrounds. New knowledge was produced and preserved through the work of mobile scholars during the Global Age. As Al-Haque has argued, "Islamic scholars helped to unite the intellectual cultures of Arabia, Persia, India, North Africa, and Mediterranean Europe, by blending both non-Islamic and non-Arab intellectual works from various cultural background" (2015: n.p.).

Early Islamic madrasas developed into degree-granting institutions by the tenth century, and became the means for social mobility, attracting scholars who acted as mediators between rulers and their subjects. Throughout the Golden Age, the Islamic empire produced around sixty centres of learning, including the Great Library of Alexandria, the House of Wisdom in Baghdad, Al-Azhar in Cairo, and centres of learning in the Iberian cities of Seville, Granada, Valencia, and Cordoba. Scholars from across the ancient world travelled to these centres of higher learning to preserve and generate knowledge, participate in academic debates, and engage in research projects (Al-Haque 2015; Lyons 2009; Welch 2012). As Welch explains, between the eighth and fifteenth century, "scholarly centres of the Islamic world popularized Arabic as the language of science . . . attracted scholars from far and wide, and produced teachers whose fame spread with their peripatetic profession" (2012: 72).

Throughout the medieval period, other centres for higher learning were established, further enhancing scholarly mobility. In the continent of Africa, the "university" of Timbuktu, a centre of higher learning located in present-day Mali, attracted scholars from around the ancient world (Jeppie and Bachir Diagne 2008). Medieval universities developed in Europe as well, and from the twelfth through to the sixteenth century, academic mobility reached its height in Europe, with scholars participating in pilgrimages (*perigrinationes*) to university cities to engage in learning. These travelling academics brought manuscripts and books back to their country of origin and contributed to the global spread of knowledge throughout the medieval world (de Wit 2002). Indeed, within the context of European history of higher education, the sixteenth century was called "the golden age of the wandering scholars" (de Ridder-Symoens 1996: 418).

## Mobility exclusions

This history of scholarly mobility would not be complete without noting the expulsion of Islamic scholars from Islamic centres of higher learning on the Iberian peninsula by the middle of the thirteenth century, when the army of Castile destroyed Islamic centres of learning in Cordoba, Seville, and Valencia, forcing many scholars to leave Spain. Fear, intimidation, and religious intolerance continued throughout the thirteenth to seventeenth centuries, with the progressive expulsion of hundreds of thousands of Muslims scholars from southern Europe (Welch 2012).

Fast forward 750 years and, today, Muslim scholars continue to confront barriers to their mobility. National policies based on anti-Islamic sentiment make obtaining visas to travel difficult, if not impossible, for Muslim scholars. The most recent and blatant example of this was the executive order "Protecting the Nation from Foreign Terrorist Entry into the United States", issued by US President Donald Trump in early 2017, which suspended the entry of nationals from a number of Muslim-majority countries (Iran, Iraq, Libya, Somalia, Sudan, Syria, and Yemen) for 90 days. Academics from those countries were among those affected by the order and unable to enter the US to study, teach, participate in research collaborations with US scholars, and attend conferences there. Reflecting upon the role of entry visas in facilitating or hindering mobility, Bauman argues that access to global mobility has "been raised to the topmost rank among the stratifying factors ... Some of us enjoy the new freedom of movement *sans papiers*. Some others are not allowed to stay put for the same reason" (1998: 87).

This points to the way in which mobility always needs to be theorized in light of immobility practices. Opportunities to be mobile are dispersed unevenly contributing to widening forms of social inequity, pointing to the disjunctive geopolitical power dimensions of academic mobility. Here, I turn to the topic of inequalities in academic mobility in considering both the limits to transnational mobility and knowledge production, as well as negative consequences of forced mobility. I argue that rather than conceptualizing mobility and immobility as two separate processes, they are directly linked and presuppose one another, constituting what I call the global academic assemblage.

Mobilities scholars examine the conditions that enable and coerce different people to be more mobile. Network capital is the capacity to move and is constituted by elements such as the possession of appropriate documents (e.g., visas and study permits), money, qualifications; relationships with distant others; access to information and contact points, as well as transportation vehicles such as cars, trains, and airplanes; the availability of communication devices and appropriate, safe, and secure meeting places, and the time and other resources to manage and coordinate mobility (Urry 2007). I would add to this list competency in the English language, which has largely become the lingua franca of higher education worldwide (Jenkins 2013).

Through network capital, opportunities to engender and sustain social relations with those who are not necessarily physically close by are made possible:

> This form of capital makes the world spatially and temporally smaller by affording long bridges and fast connections between geographically dispersed people, partly because imaginative, virtual and communicative travel allows people to be in a sense in two or more places at once.
>
> (Larsen et al. 2006: 4)

The notion of network capital emphasizes networking capacities, which are dependent on co-presence. In other words, network capital makes possible opportunities for those geographically distant from one another to meet up face-to-face.

Depending on the degree of network capital and motility (mobility potential), some people are hypermobile by choice, some are mobile but not by choice, and others are less mobile or not mobile at all. A scholar involved in an international research network that demands regular face-to-face meetings with other scholars in the network has a high degree of motility and is very mobile. However, a scholar who works from home using the Internet to conduct most of his or her collaborative research also has a high degree of motility without actually moving. This is in comparison to a scholar at risk of political persecution in their home country with very low network capital and motility in terms of choice and who is unable to move (Larsen 2016). Thus, we can see how access to network capital determines who is socially excluded and who is not, and in which situations mobility may be desired and in which situations it may not.

Beiter outlines different types of restrictions imposed on the mobility of scholars:

- denying an entry visa to a foreign scholar, who has been invited to deliver a lecture at a local university, because the authorities disapprove of the content of the lecture;
- confiscating the passport of a scholar on their return from another country where they have given a lecture at a university, in retaliation for the content of the lecture;
- denying a scholar access to an area in their own country to collect data there, as a form of punishment for academic content previously circulated; or
- expelling a foreign scholar lawfully from the country, because they have published content disapproved of by the local authorities. (2016: 246).

Academic mobility exclusions have a long history of being based on racial and religious discrimination, as we have seen above, as well as gender. Referring to international survey data from 1996, Welch writes that

> Although gender disparities were marked among the whole population in each nation surveyed, what this suggests is that the opportunity to travel and study abroad actively discriminates against women academics. Men take more opportunities to travel and study than women, or are more able to do so.
>
> (Welch 2008: 297)

The reasons for this are complex, but are generally associated with the challenges women academics face in trying to balance academic and family responsibilities. Moreover, some faculty might be reluctant to leave "home" to teach abroad in a branch campus or engage in long-term research collaboration due to difficulties associated with leaving and/or bringing their families. We also need to consider the challenges of juggling transnational family ties and dual career paths, which place particular demands on women who are less able to be mobile (Geddie 2013; Vohlídalová 2014).

Mobility exclusions also include academics who are forced to be mobile. Forced academic mobility includes early career, postdoctoral and junior scholars who, given the precarious nature of academic work, are forced to move from one short-term contract position to another across national borders in the hopes of securing a more permanent position (Ackers 2008; Kim 2010). In many other cases, scholars from Global South countries are forced to leave their own countries to secure stable employment in Global North HEIs. The regions most affected by brain drain are the Caribbean, the Pacific, sub-Saharan Africa, Central America, and South East Asia (Amazan 2014; Teferra 2008; World Bank 2011).

Brain drain, a form of mobility exclusion, deprives countries of important human capital, and restricts the ability of Global South countries to sustain themselves and compete in the global knowledge economy, further exacerbating global inequalities. Within the context of African higher education, brain drain has led not only to substantial outflows of African graduate and scholars, but comes at a considerable financial cost, given the billions of dollars spent on salaries for Western expatriates to compensate for the loss of professionals in sub-Saharan Africa (Chien and Kot 2011). Furthermore, Ishengoma (2016) argues that North-South research partnerships are counterproductive for capacity building in Tanzanian universities because they contribute to brain drain, as Tanzanian faculty members go abroad to take up academic positions, depleting their own higher education institution (HEI) of important human resources.

Most problematically, scholars whose academic freedom is restricted through the repression of their research, publication, teaching, and learning are often forced to leave their home countries and become mobile scholars. Civil strife in countries such as Ethiopia, Turkey, and Syria has forced many academics to leave their own countries against their will. Forced mobility can also be the result of political persecution targeting scholars who have published content disapproved of by the local authorities, and who are either forced to leave or forced to return home (Beiter 2016). The latter occurred in Turkey following the crackdown in 2016, when authorities demanded that all Turkish scholars working abroad return home immediately. Various organizations have emerged to assist scholars who are compelled to become mobile or immobile due to political persecution and civil strife within their own countries. These include the Scholar Rescue Fund and Scholars at Risk, based in New York, and the Council for At-Risk Academics, based in the United Kingdom (Amazan 2014; Armstrong 2016; O'Keeffe and Pásztor 2016).

And finally, global academic (im)mobility also includes scholars who are prevented by their own national governments from travelling abroad. In some cases, upon return from teaching abroad, a faculty member's passport is confiscated when the content of their lectures have been deemed unacceptable by local (home) authorities (Beiter 2016). For instance, following the 2016 government crackdown in Turkey, Turkish authorities imposed a wide-ranging ban on all work-related, international travel by scholars (Banks 2016; Scholars at Risk 2016).

## Discussion: constituting the global academic assemblage

In mapping a history of scholarly (im)mobility, we can see continuities across time and space. However, there are some fundamental differences between pre-modern manifestations of scholarly mobility and the intensification of current processes associated with movement across borders. Some have argued that scholarly mobility in the pre-modern age was motivated by desires to preserve and spread humanistic and scientific knowledge, and to discover new forms of learning, leisure, and friends (de Ridder-Symoens 1992). Today's academics are much more likely to feel the pressure of being compelled to be mobile in relation to knowledge economy policy discourses that urge them to engage in transnational research collaborations, teach abroad, and attend international conferences. Mobility is now viewed in instrumental terms as the rational means for the production of knowledge that is multi-sited, interdisciplinary, and multi-authored, and tightly linked to national economic goals.

Global rankings of universities are central to these processes. Rankings shape contemporary universities as internationalized institutions in multiple ways such that to be world-class is now associated with performance indicators associated with "international outlook". The Times Higher Education (THE) Ranking System takes into account the international mix of the student population and the faculty. Similarly, the QS World University Rankings privilege HEIs with significant numbers of international students and international faculty numbers. Mobility processes associated with transnational knowledge production are deeply embedded within these ranking schemes (Larsen 2016). Thus, institutional, governmental and intergovernmental policies privileging academic mobility and transnational knowledge generation need to be considered within light of the growing pressure for HEIs to compete with one another in the socio-spatial regime of the global knowledge economy in order to enhance their international reputation measured through global rankings.

Furthermore, scholarly mobility is also considered an instrumental means to enhancing national economic development goals. Beginning with the Erasmus program in 1987, there have been many European Union initiatives that aim to drive and strengthen economic growth through intra-European scholarly mobility. These include the "Bologna Declaration" of 1999, the European Commission's "Europe 2020 Strategy", and its 2013 communiqué on "European higher education in the world" (de Wit, Hunter, Howard, and Egron-Polak 2015). Canada's "International Education Strategy: Harnessing our knowledge advantage to drive innovation and prosperity" (Government of Canada 2014) is yet another example of government policies that privilege academic mobility, primarily amongst students, as a vehicle to foster national economic growth.

Power relations are at the core of both mobility and immobility processes. Who is able to be mobile and who is not? Who chooses to be mobile and who is forced? Which spaces are characterized by inclusion and which spaces, by exclusion? These are the kinds of questions that mobility and spatial scholars ask, recognizing how certain mobility processes engender and reinforce social inequalities, and others do not. Feminist scholar Skeggs alerts us to the power relations embedded in mobility and space. She explains how "Mobility and control over mobility both reflect and reinforce power. Mobility is a resource to which not everyone has an equal relationship" (2004: 49). This focus on mobility exclusions necessitates tracking the power of discourses and practices of mobility in creating mobility and immobility. Structures and systems make mobility possible for some and impossible for others. As Bauman explains,

"Mobility climbs to the rank of the uppermost among the coveted values – and the freedom to move, perpetually a scarce and unequally distributed commodity, fast becomes the main stratifying factor of our last-modern or postmodern times" (1998: 2).

Moreover, spatial and mobilities theorists have been influenced by Foucault's work on governmentality to problematize the effects of (im)mobility across space and time. Bærendoldt has coined the term "governmobility" – ruling through connections – to illustrate the ways in which mobilities become self-governing principles. He argues that governmentality "works through bodily, technological and institutional forms of self government, which are enacted relationally and embedded in systems" (2013: 29). Clearly, Bærendoldt borrows from Foucault's idea of governmentality, the governance of populations through moral self-conduct, alerting us to the ways in which modern states are embedded in relations of people. In other words, mobility or circulation becomes the main issue in modernity with power relations tightly embedded within and between the circulation of people, ideas, and things.

Interestingly, urban planners in the nineteenth century (e.g., Haussmann's renovations of Paris between 1853 and 1870) were deeply concerned with the mobility of citizens. Organizing and regulating mobility became the main vehicle to addressing urban problems in order to secure the safety of the population. The enabling processes of urban planning can be understood as assemblages:

> For the city, biopolitics [of urban planning] meant certain societal *dispotifs* in assembling the social and spatial life of people . . . The examples of these ways of assembling the city is a central illustration of how societies became, or have become, governmentalised.
>
> (Bærendoldt 2013: 24)

Similarly, scholars today have been governmentalized through the assembling of their spatial and mobile lives. Within the global academic assemblage, the relationships of the various component parts (i.e., students, scholars, texts, policies) are not stable or fixed. Rather, the assemblage is constructed through fluid and heterogeneous relations that are made manifest through mobility. Moreover, the global academic assemblage is not simply constituted by the mobility between scholars, but also the forced mobility of some and lack of mobility of others. In this respect, it is crucial to understand that "While mobility and fixity may easily be classified as two distinct types of dynamic from the perspective of mainstream categories, they in fact enjoy no such distinction. Each presupposes the other" (Sassen 2001: 261).

Thus we can see how power is exercised through mobility, relations and networks, and related sets of exclusions and inclusions. Networks connect and draw people and institutions together, while pushing others further apart. As Massey explains in her account of the impact of one individual's seemingly independent decision to travel by a particular route and transport mode on those who are less powerful:

This concerns not merely the issue of who moves and who doesn't, although that is an important element of it; it is also about power in relation to the flows and the movement. Different social groups have distinct relationships to this anyway-differentiated mobility; some are more in charge of it than others; some initiate flows and movement, others don't; some are more on the receiving end of it than others; some are effectively imprisoned by it.

(Massey 1994: 149)

Ask the Syrian academic in exile what she thinks of academic mobility and you will get a very different response from a Canadian scholar like myself who elects to engage in transnational research collaborations to better position myself for academic promotion. Yet, we are together assembled in a regime infused with power relations characterized by both mobility and immobility processes, inclusions and exclusions.

## Conclusion

Historicizing the present has allowed us to see the temporal nature of the global assemblages of academics. However, while there are continuities with the past, it is also important to recognize that today's world is

... moving differently and in more dynamic, complex and trackable ways than ever before, while facing new challenges of forced mobility and uneven mobility ... there is a new convergence between physical movement of people, vehicles and things; information production, storage and retrieval; wireless distributed computing and tracking technologies.

(Sheller 2011: 1)

Mobility for scholars today is inevitable and has become a constant quest of limitless possibilities never fully achievable. One can never engage in enough international travel, transnational knowledge production, and mobilization to be deemed a successful academic. Drawing upon historical sociology in my attempt to interpret and interrogate mobile academic processes, I have illustrated how both mobilities and immobilities are central to our understanding of what it means to be a self-governing academic in today's world. The spatial-mobilities sociology framing this analysis has provided a new set of questions and lenses for analysing academic mobility historically and in the contemporary era. I have explored the unevenness of academic mobility and limits to academic mobility that (re)produce inequalities in higher education in terms of location and the valuing of particular types of knowledge over others. Societies are made through mobility, as are institutions (e.g., universities) and those who work within them. In this respect, contemporary forms of scholar mobility and immobility need to be understood as a power-laden, self-governing global academic assemblage.

# References

Abrams, P. (1982). *Historical sociology*. Somerset, UK: Open Books.

Ackers, L. (2008). Internationalisation, mobility and metrics: A new form of indirect discrimination. *Minerva*, 46, 411–435.

Adey, P. (2006). If mobility is everything then it is nothing: Towards a relational politics of (im)mobilities. *Mobilities*, 1, 75–94.

Al-Haque, R. (2015). History of internationalization in higher education: A medieval, non-European Islamic perspective. Paper presented at the Comparative and International Education Society (CIES) Annual Conference. Washington, DC, 9 March 2015.

Amazan, R. C. (2014). When the Diaspora returns: Analysis of Ethiopian returnees and the need for highly skilled labour in Ethiopia. In B. Streitwieser (Ed.). *Internationalisation of higher education and global mobility* (pp. 169–185). Oxford: Symposium.

Armstrong, W. (2016). Turkey's brain drain: Purges and fear are driving Turkish scholars out of the country. *War on the Rocks*. Retrieved 1 March 2017 from: https://warontherocks.com/2016/09/turkeys-brain-drain-purges-and-fear-are-driving-turkish-scholars-out-of-the-country/.

Bærendoldt, J. O. (2013). Governmobility: The powers of mobility. *Mobilities*, 8(1), 20–34.

Banks, M. (2016). Turkish science reels from travel ban. *Physics World*, 26(9), 16.

Bauman, Z. (1998). *Globalization: Human consequences*. New York: Columbia University Press.

Beech, S.E. (2015). International student mobility: The role of social networks. *Social and Cultural Geography*, 16(3), 332–350.

Beiter, K. (2016). The protection of the right to academic mobility under international human rights law. *Academic Mobility*, 11, 243–265. doi: http://dx.doi.org/10.1108/S1479-36282014000011019.

Bryant, L. R. (2009, 8 October). Deleuze on assemblages [Blog post]. Retrieved from: https://larvalsubjects.wordpress.com/2009/10/08/deleuze-on-assemblages/.

Castells, M. (1996). *The rise of the network society*. Oxford: Blackwell.

Castells, M. (2006). The network society: From knowledge to policy. In M. Castells and G. Cardoso (Eds.). *The network society: From knowledge to policy* (pp. 3–21). Washington, DC: John Hopkins Center for Transatlantic Relations.

Chien, C-L. and Kot, F. C. (2011). New patterns in student mobility in the Southern African Development Community. In Southern African Regional Universities Association (Ed.). *Building regional higher education capacity through academic mobility*. Paris: UNESCO Institute for Statistics.

de Ridder-Symoens, H. (1992). *A history of the university in Europe. Vol. I: Universities in the Middle Ages*. Cambridge: Cambridge University Press.

de Ridder-Symoens, H. (1996). *A history of the university in Europe. Vol. II: Universities in Early Modern Europe (1500–1800)*. Cambridge: Cambridge University Press.

de Wit, H. (2002). *Internationalization of higher education in the United States of America and Europe: A historical, comparative, and conceptual analysis*. Westport, CT and London: Greenwood Press.

de Wit, H., Hunter, F., Howard, L. and Egron-Polak, E. (2015). *Internationalisation of higher education study*. Brussels: European Union.

Fahey, J. and Kenway, J. (2010). Moving ideas and mobile researchers: Australia in the global context. *The Australian Educational Researcher*, 37(4), 103–114.

Fenwick, T, Edwards, R. and Sawchuk, P. (2011). *Emerging approaches to educational research: Tracing the socio-material*. London and New York: Routledge.

Geddie, K. (2013). The transnational ties that bind: Relationship considerations for graduating international science and engineering research students. *Population, Space and Place, 19*(2), 196–208.

Government of Canada (2014). *International Education Strategy: Harnessing our knowledge advantage to drive innovation and prosperity.* Ottawa: Queen's Printer.

Hallett, F. and Eryaman, M.Y. (2014). Beyond Diaspora: The lived experiences of academic mobility for educational researchers in the European higher education area. In Maadad, L. and Tight, M. (Eds.). *International perspectives on higher education research: Academic mobility* (pp 61–78). Bingley, UK: Emerald.

History and Revival. (2016). Retrieved 25 October 2016 from: www.nalandauniv.edu.in/about-nalanda/history-and-revival/.

International Association of Universities (2014). *IAU 4th global survey: Internationalization of higher education: Growing expectations, fundamental values.* Retrieved 1 August 2016 from: www.iau-aiu.net/content/iau-global-surveys.

Ishengoma, J. M. (2016). Strengthening higher education space in Tanzania through North-South partnerships and links: Experiences from the University of Dar es Salaam. *Comparative and International Education, 45*(1), 2–18.

Jenkins, J. (2013). *English as a lingua franca in the international university: The politics of academic English language policy.* Abingdon: Routledge.

Jeppie, S. and Bachir Diagne, S. (Eds.). (2008). *The meanings of Timbuktu.* Cape Town: HSRC Press.

Kim, T. (2010). Transnational academic mobility, knowledge and identity capital. *Discourse: Studies in the Cultural Politics of Education, 31*(5), 577–591.

Larsen, J., Urry, J. and Axhausen, K. (2006). *Mobilities, networks, geographies.* Aldershot: Ashgate.

Larsen, M. A. (2016). *Internationalization of higher education: An analysis through spatial, network and mobilities theories.* New York: Palgrave.

Lyons, J. (2009). *The house of wisdom: How the Arabs transformed Western civilization.* New York: Bloomsbury Press.

Marcus, G. E. & Saka, E. (2006). Assemblage. *Theory, Culture & Society, 23*(2), 101–109.

Massey, D. (1994). *Space, place and gender.* Oxford: Blackwell.

Müller, M. (2015). Assemblages and actor-networks: Rethinking socio-material power, politics and space. *Geography Compass, 9*(1), 27–41.

O'Keeffe, P. and Pásztor, Z. (Eds.) (2016). Syrian academics in exile. *New Research Voices: International Journal of Research from the Front-Line, 1*(2), 1–162.

Rumbley, L. E., Altbach, P. E. and Reisberg, L. (2012). Internationalization within the higher education context. In D. Deardorff, H. de Wit, J. D. Heyl and T. Adams (Eds.). *SAGE handbook of international education* (pp. 3–26). Thousand Oaks, CA: Sage.

Sassen, S. (2001). Spatialities and temporalities of the global: Elements for a theorization. In A. Appadurai (Ed.). *Globalization* (pp. 260–278). Durham, NC and London: Duke University Press.

Scholars at Risk (2016, July 21). Turkish authorities impose travel ban on higher education professionals. Retrieved 18 September 2016 from: www.scholarsatrisk.org/2016/07/turkish-authorities-impose-travel-ban-higher-ed-professionals/.

Sheller, M. (2011). Mobility. *Sociopedia.isa.* doi: 10.1177/205684601163.

Skeggs, B. (2004). *Class, self and culture.* London: Routledge.

Soja, E. W. (1996). *Thirdspace: Journeys to Los Angeles and other real-and-imagined places.* Malden, MA: Blackwell.

Teferra, D. (2008). The international dimension of higher education in Africa: Status, challenges, and prospects. In D. Teferra and J. Knight (Eds.). *Higher education in Africa: Status, challenges and prospects* (pp. 44–79). Accra, Ghana & Boston, MA: AAU/CIHE.

Teichler, U. (2010). Academic staff mobility. In U. Teichler, I. Ferencz, and B. Wächter (Eds.). *Mapping mobility in European higher education, Vol. 1: Overview and trends* (pp. 1–10). Brussels: European Commission.

Urry, J. (2002) Globalizing the academy. In K. Robins and E. F. Webster (Eds.). *The virtual university? Knowledge, markets, and management.* Oxford: Oxford University Press.

Urry, J. (2007). *Mobilities.* Cambridge: Polity Press.

Vassar, D. and Barrett, B. (2014). *US-Mexico academic mobility: Trends, challenges, and opportunities.* Houston, TX: Institute for Public Policy of RICE University.

Vohlídalová, M. (2014). Academic mobility in the context of linked lives. *Human Affairs,* 24(1), 89–102. doi:10.2478/s13374-014-0208-y.

Warf, B. (2009). From surfaces to networks. In B. Warf and S. Arias (Eds.). *The spatial turn: Interdisciplinary perspective* (pp. 59–76). London: Routledge.

Welch, A. (2008). Myths and modes of mobility: The changing face of academic mobility in the global age. In M. Bryam and F. Derwin (Eds.). *Students, staff and academic mobility in higher education* (pp. 292–311). Newcastle: Cambridge Scholars Publishing.

Welch, A. (2012). Seek knowledge throughout the world? Mobility in Islamic higher education. *Research in Comparative and International Education,* 7(1), 70–80.

World Bank. (2011). *Malaysia economic monitor: Brain drain.* Washington, DC: World Bank.

# 14 History education, identity formation and international relations

*Eleftherios Klerides*

## Introduction

The 2006 Stocktaking Report of UNESCO on the state of school history in Southeast Europe notes that:

> History teaching plays an important role in the development of identity. In Southeast Europe, as elsewhere, history education has commonly been used as a tool for promoting nationalistic ideologies. However, it has also gained recognition as having a key role in the process of reconciliation, democratization and long-term stability.
>
> (UNESCO 2006: 7)

This statement captures a certain truth in the ontology of modernity – the use of history teaching as a social technology for the production of specific subjectivities, e.g., the use of traditional history for the making of *homo nationalis* or of new history of the making of *homo interculturalis*. But it does not capture other important truths about the perceived relationship between the teaching of history and identity formation. It tells us very little about political principles and social structures that permit and, at the same time, constrain how identities and the subjects, as well as the role of history teaching in their construction, can be imagined in particular contexts. Also, it tells us almost nothing about the complex ways in which the different forms of imagining this relationship may interact and be connected to each other.

To articulate these obscured truths and bring to the fore the temporal and spatial contingency of imagining the form of the relationship between history teaching and identity formation, the current chapter employs concepts from international political theory, especially those of realism, liberalism and constructionism (e.g., Karns and Mingst 2010). With noticeable exceptions (Cowen 2002; Jones 2007), such conceptual frameworks have not been adopted to understand and explain the historical and political and ideological underpinnings of UNESCO's or other similar modernist thinking. Rather, social and psychological theories tend to prevail and resulting interpretations (e.g., Nakou and Barca 2010; Psaltis et al. 2017; Schissler and Soysal 2005), like the statement itself, offer a limited view of a complex reality. Focusing on social groups and institutions "below" and "above" states, existing studies do not reveal the principles and structural possibilities of the international system that have created – and sustain – these "supranational" and "subnational" actors and have shaped their aspirations and behaviour. As a result, the beginnings of a shift in the relationship between history teaching and identity, as well as the contexts within which it occurs, tend to be incorrectly located in the aftermath of World War II, obscuring continuities with the interwar period. Also, this shift is often projected as "progress" and the "latest" stage in the history of education, while the resulting rivalry in imagining the link of history education and identity tends to be treated in Manichaean terms. International relations theories, I argue in this chapter, hold the promise of helping us construe both this shift and the rivalry in new, more complex ways.

The chapter is divided into three sections. In the first section, an attempt is made to locate the emergence and dominance of the imaginary of traditional history teaching and the making of *homo nationalis* within the interstate system. The second section discusses major historical and structural changes in international relations that resulted in the creation of new networks and technologies of knowledge building within which the imaginary of new history and *homo interculturalis* has gradually developed – and through which it has been diffusing across the world. In the third section, (some of) the possibilities of interaction between the two antagonistic imaginaries are examined.

## National states, *homo nationalis* and traditional history

International relations theorists locate the origins of the international system in mid-seventeenth-century Europe. Bringing an end to the Thirty Years War, the Treaty of Westphalia marked the emergence of states that have been – at least in theory – equal and free of external interference to determine their own internal affairs within a certain territory. Realism in the tradition of Thucydides, Machiavelli and Hobbes is useful in explaining how the system of sovereign territorial states has worked since that time.

The point of departure of realism (Goldstein and Pevehouse 2014: 43–81; Karns and Mingst 2010: 45–50) is the assumption that states, like individuals, are self-interested entities, act rationally to promote or protect their interests and are acquisitive, aggressive, or defensive. Given the absence of an overarching authority, the international system is, for realists, a vertically organized system of fluid power politics in which certain rules prevail: competition and the pursuit of advantage are the basis of relations, insecurity and conflict are the norm, and deterrence-of-aggression and balance-of-power are the sources of peace and stability.

In realist thought, the historical rivalries amongst the European states were driven not just by the expansionist ambitions of governments and domestic considerations. More importantly, they were made possible by the very *structure* of the interstate system itself. In pursuing their own self-interests, defined as maximizing security, individual states had to be prepared for war, a process which itself generated insecurity in other states that sought to respond in kind. The result of the so-called "security dilemma" (Glaser 2010) – itself a negative consequence of the international system's anarchy or lack of a central authority – was the emergence of a self-help environment that pushed state rulers to seek to maximize *power capabilities*. The ability of states to maximize their power and ensure their security was dependent on "a successful process of *extraction*" (Held 1992: 95; emphasis original); that is, on a state's capacity to extract resources – including human resources – in support of its endeavours. It was within this context that governments sought to build administrative, bureaucratic and coercive structures – including mass schooling – in order to aid both the legitimacy of state authority and the control, coordination and mobilization of their populations, when this was judged as necessary.

With the rise of nationalism in the eighteenth and nineteenth centuries, the requirements of extraction in the system of states led to the deployment of *national identity* as a means of ensuring legitimacy, regulation and mobilization (Anderson 1991). National identities were promoted to cultivate amongst disparate populations a sense of belongingness to national communities on the basis of allegedly shared characteristics, and by means of "imagined" solidarities, to grant states the natural right and moral monopoly to speak and act for nations. The loyalty of populations was something that had to be *won* and this involved a claim by states to be legitimate because they secure and defend the needs and safety of their populations in a dangerous world. In the emerging system of states, populations were not dutiful subjects, but they were, as members of nations, active citizens in representative democracies, possessing both rights and obligations (McGrew 1992).

This triad of territorial sovereignty, national membership, and democratic citizenship has spread across the world, becoming eventually a universal norm and giving rise to today's system of states. While European expansion in times of exploration and colonialism helped to diffuse these ideas, the collapse of Spanish and Portuguese rule in Latin America in the early nineteenth century, the process of mass decolonization in Africa and Asia after 1945, and the break-up of the Soviet bloc in the late twentieth century have increased the number of sovereign territorial states, consolidating this system.

Although realists recognize that at least since the interwar period, states have shared the global stage with intergovernmental and non-governmental organizations, they believe that these actors have minimal influence on state behaviour and the international system, not least because they lack enforcement powers. To influential realists such as Hans Morgenthau (1948) and Kenneth Waltz (1979), their creation is contingent on and reflects the distribution of power amongst states in the international system and, thus, they are deployed by powerful states as instruments of foreign policy to further their national goals. Less powerful states, say these realists, join the bandwagon by means of fear of being left behind (or outside). In light of this, they maintain that state power capabilities (military, economic, technological, cultural) and the formation of alliances and balances-of-power are still the basis of order and stability in the international system, while the security dilemma remains a perpetually unresolved puzzle.

Seen from a realist point of view, the institutionalization of history as a school subject in the nineteenth and twentieth centuries is related to the rise and consolidation of the system of nation-states. Abetted by the "nationalization" of historical scholarship (e.g., the work of Jules Michelet in France or Constantine Paparrigopoulos in Greece) and the break-up of humanistic letters into distinctive knowledge areas (Repousi 2012), the teaching of history entered school curricula for a specific purpose: to contribute to the making of *homo nationalis*, the type of subjectivity dictated by the needs of national antagonisms for survival and supremacy in the international system. British educator Simon Laurie perceived history teaching in the mid-nineteenth century as "an abuse of time" if not used to bring to children "knowledge of wonderful deeds done in the discharge of patriotism and duty" (cited in Marsden 1989: 513–514); or, in the words of a German handbook for history teachers published at the beginning of the twentieth century: "history education should strive for a real, decidedly German spirit. If this is not achieved, it has failed its most splendid goal" (cited in Wilschut 2010: 695).

As the international system expanded with the addition of new states, the usage of history teaching to constitute the national subject followed the same pattern. In dismissing history education reform recommended by UNESCO after 1945, Indian delegates stressed that "in India . . . the need for history to contribute to the development of national consciousness [is] particularly important" (cited in Luntinen 1988: 344). Similarly, the Ukrainian Ministry of Education asserted following the collapse of Soviet rule that one of the aims of the new mid-1990s history curricula was to "educate pupils in a patriotic spirit so that they cultivate a love for their nation" (cited in Janmaat 2005: 24).

In the relevant literature (e.g., Anderson 1991), the national subject is defined by beliefs in the unity and purity of the nation and its longevity and superiority over other nations. It is also held to be typified by a sense of pride in being member of the "imagined community", by a respect of national values and tradition, by an emotional devotion to the homeland, as well as by patriotic ideals of public duty, including the subordination of self-interest to the good of the community and the spirit of sacrifice for country. As Jones maintains, "people were even prepared to die in order to defend their sense of nationhood, placing the preservation of national government above world peace and security" (2007: 328).

As a result of the inclusion of history teaching in the "grammar of schooling", history classrooms and lessons, history curricula and textbooks, commemorative rituals, maps, history teachers and history training programs, all emerged as key institutions for materializing the production of *homo nationalis*. In all these locations of "identity-work", the aim of teaching history has been to tell pupils "the biography of the nation" and to tell it from a "drum-and-trumpet" perspective that glorifies "us" and disparages "them" (Grosvenor 1999; Marsden 1989; Wilschut 2010). School history has strived to explain to pupils the primordial origins of the nation and its unbroken continuity in time, to extol its triumphs and to mourn its tragedies, and to recount the noble deeds of its great statesmen and heroic generals. School historiographies have also sought to trivialize, even omit the nation's wrongs, focusing instead on, even inventing, crimes and injustices of other nations.

Moreover, the national story has been narrated in ways that perform several other interrelated functions (Klerides 2010). It naturalizes the nation in the eyes of pupils (and teachers) as the privileged category of historical representation. It also promotes the homogeneity of the nation irrespective of social class, gender, religious, or ethnic divisions. And finally, it summons pupils to identify with the nation by cultivating a sense of pride amongst them.

In this context, political and military history, being narrated "from above" and organized on the basis of chronology, have dominated history education. Within the spirit of the "grand narrative" conception of the nature of the discipline of history (Burke 1991), the content of school history was accepted as "heritage" (Lowenthal 1998) and thus its transmission and acquisition became an end to itself. That is, traditional pedagogy viewed history as a body of factual information about the past for teachers to faithfully transmit, as carriers of truth, and, pupils to passively obtain, as assimilators of value-free knowledge. In Slater's formulation, traditional history sees the teaching of "history *primarily* as a socialising instrument, emphasising the knowledge and *acceptance* of society rather than a critical understanding of it" (1989: 7; original emphasis). The origins and political underpinnings of this other history teaching paradigm, which "is *primarily* mind-opening, *not* socialising" (ibid.: 16; emphasis original), are best explained, I argue below, by liberal approaches to international relations.

## Governance, *homo interculturalis* and new history

Unlike realists who see the laws of power politics as relatively timeless and unchanging in the international system, liberal theorists view international relations as slowly, incrementally evolving in time and becoming more and more peaceful. In their view, along with the spread of democracy and the expansion of trade, the waning of war results primarily from international cooperation and the gradual build-up of pieces of global governance.

The point of departure of liberal theories (Goldstein and Pevehouse 2014: 85–96; Karns and Mingst 2010: 35–45) is a set of assumptions about human nature, world order, and the potential for peace which differ from realism. Liberalism holds that human nature is basically good and rational, social progress is possible, and human behaviour is perfective through institutions. Even if anarchy pushes states to pursue their own interests, states, like human beings, are capable of forgoing immediate interests in order to further the long-term well-being of the community to which they belong – and hence ensure their own safety and prosperity. Seen as a "universal human community" in the eighteenth century and a "global village" in the twentieth, the world is, for liberals, a system of state, interstate and non-state actors, who not only learn from each other, but also have the potential to work together to overcome common problems and promote the *collective good*.

From the perspective of this belief system, insecurity and rivalries are not inevitable in the international system. Emanating from inadequate institutions, lack of information about other nations and misunderstanding, these core problems of international relations can be eliminated via *bilateral* and *multilateral* action and reform, liberals believe. As Iriye (1997) puts it, "cultural internationalism", that is, the promotion of cross-national understanding is or must be the keystone of security. Or, in the words of Glaser, "although competition is a security seeker's best choice under some conditions, cooperation is preferable under other conditions. The international system does *not* consistently favour competitive policies" (2010: 7; original emphasis).

In the literature (Goldstein and Pevehouse 2014: 86–87; Karns and Mingst 2010: 36), the writings of Immanuel Kant are often seen as laying the rationale of bilateralism and multilateralism. More than 200 years ago, the German philosopher urged state leaders to develop international institutions to facilitate cooperation as a necessary condition for "perpetual peace". He believed that in the absence of an overarching authority in the international system, stability and order would evolve from the ability of states to develop and follow mutually advantageous rules. Through *reciprocity*, not a central authority and the exercise of power, rules are forced, he argued.

The principle of reciprocity is at the core of liberal thinking in international relations. As the foundation stone of cooperation, it accounts for the proliferation of intergovernmental and nongovernmental organizations since the interwar period, characterizing much of their work. In this view, interstate and non-state actors are not instruments of the foreign policy of powerful states, as realists claim. Rather, they serve as arenas of cultivating in state leaders habits of reciprocal contributions and concessions in the process of mutually beneficial decision making and, therefore, of creating "international regimes" (Krasner 1982) – formal and informal, governance-related principles and procedures – that improve a state's behaviour in relation to other states.

To liberals, this tendency to enmesh states in transnational activity results not only in the betterment of their behaviour in the international system by partially transferring territorial sovereignty to supra-territorial forms of authority. More importantly, it heightens, and further reinforces, their sense of *mutual dependency*, leading to patterns of *integration*. Integration, liberals believe, often starts from the spheres of intellectual and economic cooperation, with the conviction that this will "spill over" into other domains including politics. In light of this, liberals believe that international cooperation arises out of the basic, or functional, needs of the global society of states and peoples as a realization of their interdependency and common destiny in the world.

From the liberal perspective, *homo nationalis* is incompatible with the principles of cooperation and integration. This basis for enacting international relations is seen as dictating a different type of subjectivity, *homo interculturalis*, the image of which harks back to the universalism of Enlightenment. In the available literature (e.g., Beck and Grande 2007), *homo interculturalis* is depicted as a peace-loving subject with mentalities and attitudes about "us" and "them" that differ from *homo nationalis*. Rather than seeing the world as a vertically organized society of discrete nations, this subjectivity understands the world as a single, universal community of common fate, organized horizontally into multiple equal, overlapping, and permeable cultures. Instead of convictions in the purity and superiority of the nation (and the inferiority of other nations), the intercultural or cosmopolitan subject is characterized by beliefs such as "different but equal" and "united in diversity", and attitudes such as tolerance to, and respect for, cultural pluralism.

History education, albeit in a new form, is held to have an important role to play in the making of the intercultural subject. This sort of imagining the perceived relationship between history teaching and identity emerged as a reaction to its global*ized* form of traditional history and *homo nationalis*. Like governance itself, the global*izing* imaginary of new school history and *homo interculturalis* grew gradually and incrementally due to, and primarily in the contexts of, international cooperation.

### From textbook revision to new history

The earliest calls for reforming traditional history are traced as back as the late nineteenth century in the politics of intergovernmental and non-governmental organizations associated with the international peace movement, such as the Interparliamentary Union, and the European socialist labour movement (Schüddekopf 1967). These bodies maintained that history textbooks were sources of misunderstanding among nations and advocated their revision in a spirit of international understanding.

In the aftermath of World War I, the question of textbook revision reappeared in the politics of national actors whose profession was education (UNESCO 1949, 1953). Guided by certain individuals such as German radical school reformer Siegfried Kawerau and French teacher trade unionist George Lapierre, teachers' unions and educational societies criticized the militaristic and chauvinistic tenor of their countries' textbooks. In light of this critique, national surveys and comparative enquiries made their appearance in Europe, Japan and the Americas as methods of substantiating these claims. This early textbook research was carried out independently from each other and aspired for *unilateral* action by governments and teachers. It did not touch upon issues of didactics, albeit there are cases where teachers practiced progressive pedagogies (Aldrich 1984). Rather, the main focus of this research was the *contents* of textbooks. The main concern of researchers and collective bodies was how to devise critical textbook analyses for the purpose of improving textbook contents with a view to a better understanding among nations. In this context, certain criteria about the examination and improvement of textbooks were put forward through meetings and reports, such as the elimination of factual errors and the avoidance of defamatory generalizations.

The League of Nations, responding to pressures from professional groups to include textbook revision within the scope of its activities, became eventually the international centre of the interwar textbook revision networks (Fuchs 2007). Through *L'UNESCO oubliée*, that is, the League's "forgotten" organization of Intellectual Cooperation (Renoliet 1999), it played a key role in coordinating and encouraging international efforts to examine and improve textbooks. This organization, comprising the International Committee on Intellectual Cooperation (ICIC), the International Institute of Intellectual Cooperation (IIIC), National Committees of Intellectual Cooperation and numerous commissions of experts and advisors, aimed at fostering, in the words of Alfred Zimmern, the first deputy director of the IIIC, "the international mind". This mind was defined as "a general mentality among the peoples of the world more appropriate to cooperation than the nationalistic mentality of the past" (cited in Laqua 2011: 223–224).

After abandoning the controversial idea of an international history textbook, the organization of Intellectual Cooperation focused on changing only parts of "'dangerous' textbooks" (UNESCO 1949: 14). From the mid-1920s onwards, it pursued a textbook revision program, which had limited success, since adherence to it was voluntary. The organization's first priority was the elimination of incorrect and incendiary passages about other nations. Suggested in 1925 by the Spanish representative, Julio Casares, and adopted by the League's Assembly in 1926, the Casares Resolution inaugurated a standard procedure for bilateral revision. This method provided that a country's National Committee, finding an objectionable statement in a foreign textbook, may notify the corresponding National Committee of the offending country, recommending changes. Parallel to the search for harmful statements, the ICIC and the IIIC encouraged National Committees to examine their country's textbooks and look for passages of objectively written history, especially in relation to controversial topics. It was believed that the circulation of such model passages, for example, through reports such as IIIC's *School Text-Book Revision and International Understanding* (1933), would encourage the writing of less biased textbooks. The third line of action was multilateralism, for example, in the form of *The Declaration on the Teaching of History* (1937). In addition to the eradication of tendentious passages and the promotion of model ones, multilateralism aimed at acknowledging the importance of giving a large place in a nation's textbooks to the history of other nations.

The League of Nations took up an issue that already had a tradition in the Americas, especially in Latin America. Pernet (2015) notes that American efforts to reform history teaching including the proposal of a uniform textbook of the history of the Americas, emerged from the ideological contexts of US-sponsored Pan-Americanism and Latin American *arielismo* (a concept used to articulate a contrast between spiritually elevated intellectual activity and more pragmatic commercial and material culture). Both the advocates of asserting the common aspects of the "American" experience, as well as those who insisted on cultural difference between "Anglo-Saxon" and "Latins", agreed that it was of necessity to teach the history of the Americas in a non-nationalistic way. This idea was being put forward both prior to and immediately after World War I in various forums such as the International Conferences of the American States, and resulted in the signing of a series of bilateral and multilateral conventions for textbook revision in the 1930s (UNESCO 1953).

This tradition explains in part why Latin American scholars were at the forefront of the League's initiatives to revise textbooks, which further reinforced this aim in the Inter- and Latin American contexts. The Argentine ICIC member Leopoldo Lugones, speaking from within "the spirit of harmony typical of the Latin American Republics", proposed at a 1924 meeting of the ICIC that the organization of Intellectual Cooperation should focus its attention on history teaching as the political conscience of the public was based on historical knowledge. Instead of narratives of conflict between nations and military exploits, he stressed that there should be an emphasis on the interdependency of peoples to foster the conscience of the "genus humanum" (cited in Pernet 2015: 135).

The most elaborate and successful multilateral effort to revise textbooks in the interwar period came from *Föreningarna Norden* (Elmersjö 2015). The Norden Associations were founded in 1919 by Denmark, Norway and Sweden – and their number increased with the inclusion of Iceland (1922) and Finland (1924) – with the mandate of promoting cooperation between these countries. Their mandate, according to Elmersjö, derived from a shared belief that nationalisms had eradicated the historical cultural bonds amongst the Nordic peoples and their common Nordic identity ought to have been "resurrected". In this context, the method of mutual textbook revision emerged as an instrument of promoting "a 'regional' nationalism called 'Nordism'" (Elmersjö 2015: 728).

From the angle of these Associations (Vigander 1967), the enactment of this method was a gradual process. During the first stage (1919–22), experts from each country carried out surveys on the textbooks of their own country, searching for and eliminating tendentious treatment of the other Nordic peoples. The second stage (1928–31) was characterized by efforts to include in textbooks more knowledge about the history of the other countries. The third stage began in 1932. At this stage, the Norden Associations' Joint Committee for History Teaching and permanent Commissions of Experts in each country were formed to carry out "a thorough *mutual* examination" of textbooks (Vigander 1967: 47; emphasis original).

While adopting ideas about textbook revision that were also available internationally, the Norden Associations devised new methods too. These methods, dealing with divisive issues in Scandinavian history, are the beginnings of today's suggestions for common textbook projects and multiperspectivity in history writing, especially in conflict and post-conflict settings (Pingel 2008). They include the articulation of: (a) parallel narratives of a disputed historical event that reflect different national accounts, (b) a negotiated, bridging narrative of the disputed event, and (c) a broad description of the grounds for dispute between historians from different nationalities (Elmersjö 2015).

After World War II, Nordic textbook initiatives were taken up by UNESCO and the Council of Europe. They appeared in key publications of these agencies, such as *A Handbook for the Improvement of Textbooks and Teaching Materials as Aids to International Understanding* (UNESCO 1949: 33–34), and *History Teaching and History Textbook Revision* (Vigander 1967: 20–21, 43–64). They were also circulated in various international meetings that the two agencies organized after 1945. In 1950, for example, UNESCO held an international seminar in Brussels on textbook improvement and representatives of the Norden Associations were invited to share their experience. At the seminar, a booklet written by Haakon Vikander, the Secretary of the Norwegian Commission of Experts, and entitled *Mutual Revision of Textbooks in the Nordic Countries*, was handed in and discussed by participants. In the booklet's foreword, the Associations were depicted as "the forerunner" in textbook revision and "an example to learn from" (Elmersjö 2015: 738–739).

Instead of a Nordic identity, however, the Norden Associations' ideas were circulated by the two international agencies in support of different, but interlinked imaginings of the subject. While UNESCO has been founded in 1946 with a mandate of promoting a world citizen framework of identity, the Council of Europe's focus has been, since its founding in 1949, on the cultivation of a European identity (Klerides and Zembylas 2017). The underlying assumption of these imaginings is that in addition to their distinct national identities, the peoples of Europe (the Council) and the world (UNESCO) share a common dimension in their identity as a result of mutual dependency and influences.

Both the Council and UNESCO have regarded history teaching as a key tool in promoting the vision of European and world subjectivities, respectively. The point of departure of their effort to improve textbooks was the interwar criticism of textbooks as sites of militarism and ultra-nationalism that needed to be purged. Building on the work of professional societies and the organization of Intellectual Cooperation, the two agencies dealt with the textbook problem in two ways (Luntinen 1988, 1989; Stobart 1999). In their early work, they sought to improve textbook contents by removing errors, omissions, distortions, one-sided presentation of events and stereotypes, which, it was asserted, served the purpose of glorifying one's own country at the expense of other nations. To this end, they borrowed and elaborated textbook revision criteria invented during the interwar period and, at the same time, created new ones. Under their auspices, this work was expanded and became the focus of the undertakings of other international institutions, such as the Georg Eckert Institute for International Textbook Research, with "the bilateral consultation method" (UNESCO 1953: 40) being adopted as the most effective model for ethnocentrism eradication.

The bilateral method originates in the Franco-German effort of history textbook reform that started in the interwar period (Siegel and Harjes 2012). Historians from both sides of the Rhine responded to French and German teachers' criticism of the nationalistic tenor of textbooks, meeting together for the first time in Paris in 1935 to discuss some of the most contested issues in the two nations' past, including the causes of World War I. History teachers and textbook authors, Jules Isaak from France and Arnold Reimann from Germany, were the driving force behind this meeting. Isaak and Reimann met at the 1932 International Conference for the Teaching of History, one of the forums jointly founded by

French and German teachers and historians in the interwar period, with the aim of "blowing a current of international air into the teaching of history" (Siegel and Harjes 2012: 380). But nationalism made the 1935 meeting's goal of reconciliation impossible and the joint recommendations were marred by interpretative discord and buried in the ashes of World War II.

In the late 1940s, German and French teachers' unions called for renewing textbook reform. Meeting in Paris in 1951, French and German historians reopened discussions and this time managed to come to complete consensus. Siegel and Harjes (2012) point out that the successful conclusion of Franco-German textbook reform rested to a large extent on the efforts of two unlikely partners – both ardent patriots and veterans of World War I – French historian Pierre Renouvin and his German counterpart Gerhard Ritter. As the chief authors of the 1951 Franco-German Historians Agreement, Renouvin and Ritter engaged not just in a truth-seeking process. More importantly, their interaction was one of arduous negotiation and compromise that forced them to push aside their scholarly principles and national prejudices in order to find a new role for history teaching in shaping identity. This process resulted in an agreement remarkable not only because it became the ideological basis and symbol of Franco-German rapprochement, but by shifting textbook focus from military and diplomatic history to social history, it also became the foundation of the idea of a Western European community, as well as of commonalities between Euro-American cultures (Siegel and Harjes 2012).

Thus, parallel to the eradication of ethnocentrism, both UNESCO and the Council of Europe revived the interwar practice of bringing together historians and other scholars of different nationalities to build up consensus (through mutual concessions) on the topics and glossary of a global perspective on history (UNESCO), and a European point of view of history (the Council). As products of both scholarly research and multilateral negotiation, these novel perspectives were to be subsequently incorporated in revised textbooks. Perhaps the most characteristic example of the post-war effort to "denationalize" historical scholarship is UNESCO's project of the *Scientific and Cultural History of Mankind* (1952–69) (Luntinen 1988, 1989). This project, alluding to the proposal of Argentine historian Roberto Levillier and the League of Nation's subsequent initiative of writing a multi-volume history of the Americas (1934) under the tutelage of the IIIC and by American and European historians, focused less on political history and more on transcultural exchanges among the peoples of the world (Pernet 2015).

The revision of history textbooks broadened its scope after the end of the Cold War. From the early 1990s onwards, the emphasis was no longer only on the contents of textbooks. It has also been laid on pedagogy and didactics, on the general aims and objectives of history curricula, on history teachers and their training, and, on young people and their perceptions of history (Pingel 2008). The invention of a "novel" pedagogical paradigm of history teaching in the 1970s and early 1980s in the professional practices of history educators and teachers in Western Europe, especially in England and France, played a decisive role in widening the scope of textbook revision.

In England, a new approach called "new history" emerged out of concerns about the place of history in schools (Phillips 1998). In the late 1960s, there was a widespread feeling among history teachers that history was losing out as a curriculum subject with the growth of social studies and this was attributed to the traditional method of memorizing the facts. Anxiety about history's future triggered its reconceptualization. The Schools' Council History 13–16 Project, *A New Look at History* (1976), was the most articulated attempt to rethink history teaching. In this work, the purpose of history teaching was no longer considered to be the transmission of the facts. Rather, its aim was declared to be the promotion of historical thinking through inquiry methods and the use of historical sources. Apprenticeship in the historian's craft meant helping pupils to develop historical skills – for example, to study events from different and competing perspectives. It also required them to be taught history's defining concepts, such as fact and interpretation.

In France, and at about the same period, journals such as *Les Cahiers Pédagogiques*, institutions such as the *Institut National de Recherche et de Documentation Pédagogiques*, and educators such as Suzanne Citron, Joseph Leif, and Louis François put forward similar ideas about history teaching. For example, Leif maintained that pupils should learn about "the historian's method", while François declared that teachers should promote historical investigations that would give pupils "the immense happiness of discovery" (Waldman 2009: 206). The "*nouvelle histoire*" emerged out of the Annales School's rejection of *histoire événementielle*. This led history teachers to call into question not only traditional history's emphasis on the facts, but also its thematic coverage. Like new history, *nouvelle histoire* focuses less on political history and more on social history.

The broadening of academic history's thematic base, as well as the shift in the philosophy of history in universities from the ideal of "history as truth" to that of "history as interpretation" (Burke 1991), were amongst the conditions that made the invention of these new approaches possible. On both sides of the Channel, new approaches to history teaching were also shaped by the pedagogic ideologies of the time – namely, *pédagogie de l'éveil* in France (Best 1973) and child-centred pedagogy in England (Plowden Report 1967). Based on the psychological theories of Jean Piaget, Benjamin Bloom, and Jerome Bruner, these pedagogic ideologies of progressive education depicted knowledge as a medium for educational ends, teachers as facilitators of learning, and students as active learners creating their own understanding of the world.

In the 1990s, institutions of global governance, such as the Council of Europe, UNESCO and the Georg Eckert Institute, have adopted this paradigm. In its teacher handbook, *History Teaching and the Promotion of Democratic Values and Tolerance* (Gallagher 1996), the Council deterritorializes and redefines new history as a universal norm that all must adopt:

> In the 1990s, the fundamental nature and purpose of history teaching has been re-assessed and the earlier view of school history as a "body of knowledge", simply to be learned and regurgitated, has been challenged . . . The teaching of

> history . . . should be an "explanation-seeking" pursuit . . . achieved through an enquiry-based, problem-solving pedagogy . . . Instead of being asked to accept one interpretation, as offered in the old school textbooks, pupils should be challenged to derive their own views from the study of a variety of evidence and perspectives.
>
> (Gallagher 1996: 18)

New history appears in UNESCO's publications, too. Citing the above-mentioned handbook, UNESCO's *Guidebook on Textbook Research and Textbook Revision* promotes "[t]his shift from treating history as a body of knowledge to be remembered, to a perception of history as a process of rational investigation of the past, based on reference to a variety of evidence from different viewpoints," as a key principle for revising history textbooks (Pingel 1999: 24). This guidebook was written by Falk Pingel, the Deputy Director of the Georg Eckert Institute between 1993 and 2009, highlighting the emergence of an "eduscape" (Carney 2010), based on the recommendations of new history.

Although traces of new history can be found in the work of international institutions at earlier times, these actors fully adopted this paradigm in the context of their renewed interest in school history due to the resurgence of nationalism and ethnic conflicts in the post-socialist bloc. This gave impetus to the eastward expansion of the western expert networks of textbook revision, as well as their proliferation (Klerides 2014). In these networks, where "exchange of information and expertise" and "cross-fertilisation of ideas and experience" take place (UNESCO 2006: 58–59), new history has emerged as the latest stage in educational development. "While some educational systems still adhere to curricula which offer a broad sweep of history, sometimes referred to as Plato to NATO", notes the Council, "others have recognized that quality rather than quantity may be the more appropriate route. That is to say, they concentrate on developing historical understanding and awareness and the skills essential for historical interpretation" (Council for Cultural Cooperation 1995: 60). More importantly, new history has been projected, in these networks, as "best practice", through which cosmopolitan narratives of identity and tolerant subjectivities are to be enacted, instead of nationalistic, intolerant ones. The Council urges its member-states to reform their history textbooks in order to "provide opportunities for pupils to acquire and develop the key historical skills of investigating, evaluating, critical thinking and problem-solving. These are the tools by which we can eliminate nationalistic bias and prejudice in history" (ibid.: 1995: 69).

## History teaching and identity formation as a field of possibilities

While the emergence of a new global*izing* imaginary of the perceived relationship between history teaching and identity is seen from liberal perspectives as progress, its making is explained differently from the realist position. Since power politics is an unchanging feature of the world system, realists would argue that both the articulation and the diffusion of the imaginary of new history and *home* *interculturalis* have been contingent upon certain (and shifting) geometries of international power relations.

Thus, from the realist point of view, Latin American interwar initiatives of history textbook revision were promoted in and through the League's organization of Intellectual Cooperation for realpolitik reasons. Pernet (2015) notes that some Latin American scholars and diplomats saw these initiatives as an opportunity for internationally marginalized Latin American states to sit at the same table with European powers, while others hoped that these initiatives would have provided a counterweight to US power in the Western Hemisphere.

Likewise, rather than being a product of mutual contributions and concessions, realists would argue that history textbook revision in occupied Germany (and Japan) emerged out of the policy of "re-education" that the military governments of the Allied Powers pursued (and imposed) after 1945 (Dierkes 2010). In particular, they would highlight the role of the French military government in helping bring Franco-German history agreement to a successful conclusion. For example, Raymond Schmittlein, the French Director of Public Education in occupied Germany, sponsored many of the meetings between German and French historians and teachers. He also established a new institute for the study of history in Mainz, designed "to pave the way for Franco-German rapprochement" and "promote the study of the History of Europe and its unity" (cited in Siegel and Harjes 2012: 390).

More broadly, realists would point to the threat of Soviet expansion and the US policy of containment in post-war Europe as the *raison d'être* of the Franco-German rapprochement, the promotion of a shared Western European identity and the projection of commonalities between American and European cultures. Bilateral and multilateral textbook revisions were expected to play a key role in helping to bring about patterns of Franco-German, European and transatlantic integration.

Realists would also quickly stress that the work of the Council of Europe in encouraging the rewriting of history textbooks along the suggestions of new history, in the Balkans, the Black Sea and the Caucasus, is part of the European Union's security strategy in its "eastern neighbourhood" (Klerides 2014). History textbook revision, they would conclude, has been dependent on the most powerful state(s) in the world system (often alluding to the US). Instead of competition as the basis of international relations, the most powerful state(s) has been promoting a new world order based on the principle of cooperation (McGrew 1992).

This rivalry of interpretation between realism and liberalism about the motivations of the emergence and expansion of a new imaginary of history teaching and identity making does not just reflect hermeneutic disputes over the past. It is also underpinned by normative conflicts over the future and the sort of history and identity that ought to be promoted in schools: traditional variations of history teaching as a tool for the making of nationally minded subjectivities or new forms and patterns of history teaching as a technology for the production of more cosmopolitan subjects? I suggest that these normative antagonisms are best explained by social constructionist approaches to international political theory.

Social constructionism is a newer approach to international relations (Goldstein and Pevehouse 2014: 96–103; Karns and Mingst 2010: 50–52). While there are many variants, all constructionists locate the study of the formation of international relations within the realm of broad social relations and the social construction of reality. In contrast with the assumption of fixed, timeless preferences in theories of realism (states fight for power) and liberalism (states, organizations, interest groups, and individuals want more peace), they rely on social interaction among the various actors of the international system to explain their interests and behaviour. To leading social constructionist theorists such as Martha Finnemore (2004), neither power nor peace exist independently of interactions between states, interstate and nonstate actors and individuals. Rather, their behaviour and interests, she stresses, are shaped by socially constituted rules and norms which change over time. In this view, national sites and tools (created as a result of realism) and spaces and networks of international cooperation (emerged out of liberalism) are interlinked arenas where state bureaucracies, interest groups, and "norm entrepreneurs" (Goldstein and Pevehouse 2014: 101) interact with each other in complex ways to articulate, reconstruct, or perpetuate certain understandings of the social world. As Wendt puts it, "the social construction of international politics is to analyze how processes of interaction produce and reproduce the social structures – cooperative or conflictual – that shape actors' identities and interests and the significance of their material contexts" (1995: 81).

Seen from this perspective, the relationship between history and identity is construed as a socially constituted field where various actors, operating within the logic of either competition or cooperation and being located at different scales in the international system, have been struggling not only to associate history teaching with the production of certain subjectivities. More importantly, they have been attempting to do so along the lines of either the global*ized* or the globaliz*ing* imaginary. Specific possibilities emerge as a result of social interaction between conflictual and cooperative logics. One possibility is change due to the penetration of elements of the global*izing* imaginary in the entrenched institutions of the global*ized* imaginary. Perhaps the most obvious *change* is the production of bilateral histories – for example, the Franco-German textbook of *Historie/Geschichte* – and multilateral ones – such as the Southeast European countries' Joint History Project. The eradication of overt ethnocentrisms, for example, the disappearance of overtly stated derogatory generalizations against the character of other peoples from the surface of national history textbooks, is another obvious change (Koulouri 2001). A less obvious one is what was mourned as "the loss of the first person plural in school history textbooks" (Phillips 1998: 128); that is, the detachment of textbook writers from the textbook discourse of the nation and the mitigation of the way in which pupils are summoned to identify with this discourse.

A second possibility is the *blending* of elements from the two imaginaries. Many scholars (e.g., Nichol and Dean 2003) show that history textbook writers and history teachers prefer to marry traditional and new history elements rather than change their established practices solely on the merits of either paradigm. For writers and teachers, the major concern is the balance between old and new perspectives:

a genuine desire to be able to develop critical thinking skills and an understanding of historical methodology in pupils without abandoning some
cherished characteristics of their former rationale and practice such as chronological perspective . . . an appropriate depth of content and the opportunity
to use the dramatic storyline.

(Cited in Truman 1990: 17)

Klerides (2010) points out that this mixing of traditional and new history leads
to hybridization and the emergence of a fused imaginary of history teaching and
identity formation. The two imaginaries, he writes, are not always combined
effectively, and heterogeneity is a source of ambivalence, ambiguities and contradictions in history and identity, which tend to oscillate, for example, between
historical objectivity and subjectivity, or between nationalist and internationalist
motifs of identity. Klerides further asserts that such indeterminacies have their
logic not only in difficulties, of how to combine elements from the two imaginaries. They also derive from dilemmas – not only of how to inculcate historical
thinking in pupils without abandoning their socialization with basic facts, but also
of how much of the national story needs to be reconstructed to accommodate
international perspectives.

A third possibility coming out of interaction between competing and cooperative principles and structures is the emergence of *"restoration" projects*
and *"cultural wars"* over school history and identity, often with unpredictable
ends. While for some actors of the global politics the imaginary of new history
and *homo interculturalis* is considered as pedagogical and historiographical
progressivism, others perceive it as an attack on education, collective memory and the nation. For example, conservative politicians including Margaret
Thatcher, right-wing historians (e.g., Geoffrey Elton) and philosophers (e.g.,
Roger Scruton), and new right pressure groups, such as the Hillgate Group,
the Centre for Policy Studies and the Campaign for Real Education, were all
crusading against new history in England throughout the 1980s and 1990s
(Phillips 1998). These critics of new history expressed their concerns that
schools were failing to instil a sense of national identity in pupils, declared that
the loss of chronology and knowledge of basic facts was anti-educational, and
believed that the study of historical sources was the activity of historians, not
schoolchildren. It was within this context that Thatcherite governments set in
motion reform aimed at "restoring" traditional history and national values in
schools. Just as new right groups and individuals saw new school history as
"historical amnesia" and "anti-education", teachers' unions, local education
authorities, departments of education in universities, and the Labour Party
responded to reform arguing that the right was attempting to "hijack" history
for political indoctrination.

One of the possible outcomes of these symbolic wars is "the Defeat of New
History" (Kokkinos 2008: 44). Nowhere is this truer than in France, where the
*Ministère de l'Education Nationale*, under successive Socialist governments led
by François Mitterrand, managed to "restore" in the 1980s the traditional study

of the great periods and personages of French history (Waldman 2009). Yet, the revision of history textbooks according to the suggestions of "cultural internationalism" may materialize at a later time when circumstances are different. In the context of interwar Nordic cooperation, the Norwegian Association rejected a 1919 Danish proposal for mutual textbook review on the grounds of national sovereignty. This idea was unanimously accepted in 1932, after it was officially adopted by the League of Nations (Vigander 1967).

The revision of history textbooks along multiperspectival lines is also disputed in borrowing contexts where multiperspectival textbook revision practices "move in" from elsewhere. Rejecting claims that Cyprus's history textbooks are monocultural and opposing the idea of their rewriting by both Greek Cypriots and Turkish Cypriots, Orthodox Church leaders and philologists urged in the 2000s that "our Greek consciousness must build walls and must not allow malicious plans to harm . . . our Greek identity which is none other than . . . our historical consciousness" (cited in Klerides and Zembylas 2017: 424). It is also possible for textbook revision to be reversed. A few years after the Republican Turkish Party of Cyprus produced and put into use new textbooks (2004) that included elements of new history, the National Unity Party withdrew these textbooks in 2009, reverting to more traditional ones (Beyidoğlu et al. 2010).

## Conclusion

In searching for new and perhaps more complex ways of understanding modernist rationales for using the teaching of history as a technology for the making of certain subjectivities, this chapter employs concepts from international political theory. It argues that realist, liberalist and constructionist approaches to international relations are useful in helping us to identify the political principles and social structures that made different modalities of imagining the relationship between history and identity possible. They also assist us to bring to the fore and articulate the temporal and spatial contexts within which the different imaginaries of history and identity are produced and sustained, rearticulated and contested.

Not only is this line of thinking incomplete in terms of identified principles, structures, contexts, or forms of relationships but, I suggest, it also begs for further elaboration on the basis of an *aggregative* potential. Aggregation is a process through which an attempt is made to combine insights and analytical tools from these three different approaches. In light of this, future scholarship must be focused on, for example, whether the notions of expert networks (liberalism), interaction possibilities (constructionism) and power politics (realism) can be brought together to address more adequately the issue of how the relationship between history teaching and identity formation is materialized under certain circumstances. Such aggregative exercises are very ambitious in nature, even elusive. They are scholarly exercises, however, which evolve from more realistic understandings of the world and exercises that we have not fully explored yet in many fields and sub-fields of education.

# References

Aldrich, R. (1984). New History: an historical perspective. In A. Dickinson, P. Lee and P. Rogers (Eds.). *Learning history* (pp. 210–224). London: Heinemann Educational Books.

Anderson, B. (1991). *Imagined communities*. London: Verso.

Beck, U. and Grande, E. (2007). *Cosmopolitan Europe*. Cambridge: Polity Press.

Best, F. (1973). *Pour une pédagogie de l éveil* [Toward an Awakening Pedagogy]. Paris: Librairie Armand Colin.

Beyidoğlu, M., Jetha-Dağseven, S. Karahasan, H. and Latif, D. (2010). *Re-writing history textbooks*. Nicosia: POST Research Institute.

Burke, P. (1991). Overture: The new history, its past and its future. In P. Burke (Ed.). *New perspectives on historical writing* (pp. 1–24). Cambridge: Polity Press.

Carney, S. (2010). Reading the global: Comparative education at the end of an era. In M. Larsen (eds), *New thinking in comparative education* (pp. 125–142). Rotterdam: Sense.

Council for Cultural Co-operation. (1995). *Against bias and prejudice*. Strasbourg: Council of Europe.

Cowen, R. (2002). In the minds of men: The shifting contexts of interculturality. In *Interculturael: Balance y perspectivas* (pp. 171–180). UNESCO.

Dierkes, J. (2010). *Postwar history education in Japan and the Germanys: Guilty lessons*. London: Routledge.

Elmersjö, A. (2015). The Norden Associations and international efforts to change history education, 1919–1970: International organisations, education, and hegemonic nationalism. *Paedagogica Historica*, 51(6), 727–743.

Finnemore, M. (2004). *The purpose of intervention: Changing beliefs about the use of force*. Ithaca, NY: Cornell University Press.

Fuchs, E. (2007). The creation of new international networks in education: The League of Nations and educational organizations in the 1920s. *Paedagogica Historica*, 43(2), 199–209.

Gallagher, C. (1996). *History teaching and the promotion of democratic values and tolerance: A handbook for teachers*. Strasbourg: Council of Europe.

Glaser, C. (2010). *Rational theory of international politics: The logic of competition and cooperation*. Princeton, NJ: Princeton University Press.

Goldstein, J. and Pevehouse, J. (2014). *International relations*. New York: Pearson.

Grosvenor, I. (1999). "There's no place like home": Education and the making of national identity, *History of Education*, 28(3), 235–250.

Held, D. (1992). The development of the modern state. In S. Hall and B. Gieben (Eds.). *Formations of Modernity* (pp. 71–126). Cambridge: Polity Press.

Iriye, A. (1997). *Cultural internationalism and world order*. Baltimore, MD: Johns Hopkins Press.

Janmaat, G. (2005). Ethnic and civic conceptions of the nation in Ukraine's history textbooks. *European Education*, 37(3), 20–37.

Jones, P. (2007). Education and world order. *Comparative Education*, 43(3), 325–337.

Karns, M. and Mingst, K. (2010). *International organizations: The politics and processes of global governance*. London: Lynne Rienner.

Klerides, E. (2010). Imagining the textbook: Textbooks as discourse and genre. *Journal of Educational Media, Memory, and Society*, 2(1), 31–54.

Klerides, E. (2014). Educational transfer as a strategy for remaking subjectivities: Transnational and national articulations of 'New History' in Europe. *European Education*, 46(1), 12–33.

Klerides, E. and Zembylas, M. (2017). Identity as immunology: History teaching in two ethnic borders of Europe. *Compare: A Journal of Comparative and International Education*, *47*(3), 416–433.

Kokkinos, G. (2008). Metaksy Melacholias kai Eksegersis ["Between Melancholy and Revolution"]. In A. Andreou (Eds.). *H didaktiki tis istorias kai h erevna sta sxolika echgiridia* [History education and research on history textbooks] (pp. 21–67). Athens: Metechmio.

Koulouri, C. (2001) (Ed.). *Teaching the history of Southeastern Europe*. Thessaloniki: Centre for Democracy and Reconciliation in Southeast Europe.

Krasner, S. (1982). Structural causes and regime consequences: Regimes as intervening variables. *International Organization*, *36*(2), 185–205.

Laqua, D. (2011). Transnational intellectual cooperation, the League of Nations, and the problem of order. *Journal of Global History*, *6*, 223–247.

Lowenthal, D. (1998). *The heritage crusade and the spoils of history*. Cambridge: Cambridge University Press.

Luntinen, P. (1988). School history textbook revision by and under the auspices of UNESCO Part I. *Internationale Schulbuchforschung*, *10*, 337–348.

Luntinen, P. (1989). School history textbook revision by and under the auspices of UNESCO Part II. *Internationale Schulbuchforschung*, *11*, 39–48.

Marsden, W. (1989). "All in a good cause": Geography, history and the politicization of the curriculum in nineteenth and twentieth century England. *Journal of Curriculum Studies*, *21*(6), 509–526.

McGrew, T. (1992). A global society? In S. Hall, D. Held and T. McGrew (Eds.). *Modernity and its futures* (pp. 61–116). Cambridge: Polity Press.

Morgenthau, H. (1948). *Politics among nations: The struggle for power and peace*. New York: Knopf.

Nakou, I. and Barca, I. (2010) (Eds.). *Contemporary public debates over history education*. Charlotte, NC: Information Age Publishing.

Nichol, J. and Dean, J. (2003). Writing for children: history textbooks and teaching texts. *International Journal of Historical Learning, Teaching and Research*, *3*(2), 1–29.

Pernet, C. (2015). In the spirit of harmony? The politics of (Latin American) history at the League of Nations. In A. McPherson and Y. Wehrli (Eds.). *Beyond geopolitics: New histories of Latin America at the League of Nations* (pp. 135–153). Albuquerque, NM: University of New Mexico Press.

Phillips, R. (1998). *History teaching, nationhood and the state: a study in educational politics*. London: Cassell.

Pingel, F. (1999). *UNESCO guidebook on textbook research and textbook revision*. Paris: UNESCO.

Pingel, F. (2008). Can truth be negotiated? History textbook revision as a means to reconciliation. *Annals of the American Academy of Political and Social Sciences*, *617*, 181–198.

Plowden Report (1967). *Children and their primary schools*. London: Her Majesty's Stationery Office.

Psaltis, Ch., Carretero, M. and Cehajic-Clancy, S. (2017) (Eds.). *History education and conflict transformation*. Basingstoke: Palgrave Macmillan.

Renoliet, J. (1999). *L'UNESCO oubliée: la Société des Nations et la coopération intellectuelle, 1919–1946*. Paris: Publications de la Sorbonne.

Repousi, M. (2012). Oi protes ekdoches tis Ellinikis istorikis ekpaideusis telos 18ou-telos 19ou aiona [The beginnings of Greek history education, end of 18th-end of 19th century].

In S. Bouzakis (Ed.). *Panorama istorias tis ekpaidevsis* [Overview of history of education], Vol. A (pp. 481–498). Athens: Gutenberg.

Schissler, H. and Soysal, Y. (eds.) (2005). *The nation, Europe and the world: Textbooks and curricula in transition*. New York and Oxford: Berghahn Books.

Schüddekopf, O-E., (1967). History of textbook revision 1945–1965. In Council for Cultural Cooperation (Ed.), *History teaching and history textbook revision* (pp. 11–41). Strasbourg.

Siegel, M. and Harjes, K. (2012). Disarming hatred: History education, national memories, and Franco-German reconciliation from World War I to the Cold War. *History of Education Quarterly*, *52*(3), 370–402.

Slater, J. (1989). *The politics of history teaching: A humanity dehumanised?* London: Institute of Education.

Stobart, M. (1999). Fifty years of European cooperation on history textbooks: the role and contribution of the Council of Europe. *Internationale Schulbuchforschung*, *21*, 147–161.

Truman, P. (1990). Teachers' concerns over the current vogue in teaching history. *Teaching History*, *58*, 10–17.

UNESCO (1949). *A handbook for the improvement of textbooks and teaching materials as aids to international understanding*. Paris: UNESCO.

UNESCO (1953). *Bilateral consultations for the improvement of history textbooks*. Paris: UNESCO.

UNESCO (2006). *Fostering peaceful co-existence through analysis and revision of history curricula and textbooks in Southeast Europe*. Paris: UNESCO.

Vigander, H. (1967). History textbook revision in the Nordic countries. In Council for Cultural Cooperation (ed.), *History teaching and history textbook revision* (pp. 43–64). Strasbourg.

Waldman, A. (2009). The politics of history teaching in England and France during the 1980s. *History Workshop Journal*, *68*, 199–221.

Waltz, K. (1979). *Theory of international politics*. New York: McGraw.

Wendt, A. (1995). Constructing international politics. *International Security*, *20*(1), 71–81.

Wilschut, A. (2010). History at the mercy of politicians and ideologies: Germany, England, and the Netherlands in the 19th and 20th centuries. *Journal of Curriculum Studies*, *42*(5), 693–723.

# 15 Towards a mobile sociology of education

*Paolo Landri*

## Introduction

Space-times of education in Europe and all over the world are being transformed in complex and unexpected ways. The changes concern, in particular, the institutional boundaries – that is, the material, cognitive, and social infrastructures sheltering education spaces from and filtering the risks of dealing with the contingencies of the social and economic worlds (Masschelein and Simons 2015). By relating these transformations only to the current trends of the neoliberal agenda could be, to some extent, simplistic and underestimates the complex dynamics of change. To improve our understanding of these transformations, and keep a critical edge, I will argue that we need to develop forms of investigation able to display the unintended consequences of the dominant dispositifs, the multiple enactments of the modifications of the space-times of education, and the related effects. A promising area of reflection and empirical research in that sense is being developed in the interference among socio-material approaches and education studies (Actor Network Theory [ANT], Science and Technology Studies [STS], Feminist Studies) (Fenwick and Edwards 2010; Fenwick, Edwards and Sawchuk 2011; Fenwick and Landri 2012). This chapter is interested in comprehending how this interference may expand the sociology of education. The socio-material turn represents an invitation for the sociology of education to *move beyond itself*. By considering some examples from a Special Issue I co-edited (Landri and Neumann 2014), I will discuss three implications of the "moving beyond": a) from the human-centred approach in the conceptualization of social interaction to the co-implication of humans and non-humans in social ties; b) from the dominant methodological nationalism in most of the investigations in education policy to consider the increasing post-national scenarios in education, and c) from the attention to policy to a more complex accounts of practice in education fields. The chapter unfolds as follows: firstly, I will briefly describe the dynamics of transformation of the space-times of education and the limits of the current explanations of these changes; secondly, I will reflect on the effects of moving sociology of education beyond itself.

## Changing space-times of education

In the latest decades, educational systems are being interested in the multiple changes that are modifying the spaces and the times of education. Loci and the timeframes of education practice are under the pressure of an epidemic of global, regional, and national reforms aimed at transforming the traditional configuration of the space-times of education, made of topologies of education partially independent from the socio- and economic dynamics. It is then increasingly difficult to describe the space-times of education as enclosed, embedded, or bounded by such state-nations, societies, regions, schools, classrooms, etc., and to defend these boundaries as "proper ontological regions" (Massa 1991). We are witnessing, in particular, repeated attempts at reshaping the material and the social arrangement of the configuration of schooling as a particular invention, and a form of gathering characterized by suspension, profanation, and forms of attention. At the moment, it is not sufficiently clear if the projects of change are intended to tame, or neutralize this "form of gathering", or to transform the space-times of education to resume the possibilities of the morphology of the school as a mode of organizing (Masschelein and Simons 2015). A functionalistic logic of the space-times of education that related them to socioeconomic needs appears to take the lead, and the institutional boundaries defending the configuration of the schooling as space-times of suspension of the natural and unequal order are slowly eroded by the epidemic of reforms. Here, the "good intentions" of changing the space-times of education to upgrade this institution to the changing conditions of contemporary societies are mixed with the logic of advanced capitalism that tends to neutralize the scholastic form and to domesticate it into its philosophy of governmentality.

The problematization of the institutional boundaries is mainly made visible by the *construction of the new dispositifs of accountability*, by the widespread use of the *new digital technologies for the governance and the education practice*, and by the *increase of the mobilities of people*.

The development of new systems of evaluation is translating education systems all over the world in spaces of commensurations. A complex infrastructure of data fabricated by the OECD, the World Bank, and UNESCO is supporting, via educational indicators, a massive project of representation and visualization of education systems and practice that is oriented to make them transparent, to improve the steering capacity of governments in the shaping of education policies and reducing their costs. The fabrication of these spaces of commensuration are enacting new space-times of education (such as the European space of education, or the global space of commensurability of the PISA project) with the effect of displacing the governing of education from the here-and-now of teaching and learning to complex assemblages of local, regional, and global expectations (Grek 2010; Lawn and Normand 2015).

The diffusion of digital technologies is, as well, a condition of possibility for border crossing, and a challenge for the education practice. The promise of educational events and interactions occurring potentially everywhere and anywhere is a significant challenge to the classical topologies of education. Virtual worlds, e-learning platforms, games for learning, MOOCs, e-books, interactive white-boards are changing the circulation of knowledge and modifying the materiality of learning, by creating unexpected opportunities of interconnection between time and space zones. Digital technologies are increasingly important in the governance of education, since they are deeply imbricated in the way education policies are enacted (Williamson 2015) and, at the same time, they are playing a constitutive role in the enactment of the contemporary space-times of education (Sørensen 2009). It is even quite difficult to conceive of current education practices without making reference to how they accompany, augment, and help teaching and learning. The culture of double-click learning and the rhetorics of immediacy in learning are powerful discourses supporting the unfolding of digital space-time-material associations across the borders of states, classrooms, societies, schools – that is, overlapping, or partially disrupting the classical "envelopes" of education in modern industrial societies. This digitalization is sustaining the emergence of new identities of learners (Bennett, Maton, and Kervin 2008), and are influencing, as well as making, new teacher identities (Perrotta, Czerniewicz, and Beetham 2015). As a matter of fact, the increasing co-implication of humans in the fabrication of new socio-technical dispositifs of education is the condition for the emergence of novel identities able to inhabit the new digital topologies of education. Of course, digital technologies are opportunities to enhance the circulation of knowledge, to make it more mobile, and potentially more open, albeit they are not a panacea for social and educational inequalities. While they contribute to new forms of democracy to reducing inequalities, they also introduce new forms of inequality and concentrations of power.

New questions for the space-times of education are finally related to the increasing mobilities of people. The emergence of new regional spaces of education, such as the European space of education, the policies of harmonization at the level of higher education following the effects of the Bologna Process, the flows of "forced" migration from developing countries and countries in war zones, are reshaping the movements of students, learners, workers, and migrants, and transforming educational needs. Institutional boundaries are criss-crossed, and new associations are developing to networking space-times of education. The increasing mobilities of people raise the issues of making comparable educational experiences, of understanding what is transferable, and of what is recognizable regarding knowledge and competencies across the space-time of education. Here, the search for new educational standards (like ECTS for example, or the EQF in the case of the Europeanization of education) opens new possibilities of interconnections, and comparability (Gibb and Hamdon 2010).

What are the recurrent explanations of this dynamics of change? Are there principal reasons triggering this complex restructuring that is affecting the classical topologies of education? And what is the role of educational knowledge regarding the changing modification of space-times? In other words, is there a "context of context" that could ultimately provide key ingredients to read the current transformations? Before furnishing some responses to these questions, it is important to recognize the performative character of any production of educational knowledge (and indeed of any knowledge endeavour) (Law 2012). As a matter of fact, educational knowledge is influenced by and is affecting the modification of space-times of education. Further, there is some knowledge that is more complicit with the dominant rhetoric, while other forms of knowledge prefer to assume a critical perspective, whereas the meaning of "critical perspective" could also be open to multiple possibilities (Biesta 2015). Recently, it has been possible to register the shift of sociological and comparative education studies towards forms of *cosmopolitan policy analysis* (Simons, Olssen, and Peters 2009; Ball and Shilling 2017). This change of perspective mirrors the cosmopolitan turn in social sciences (Beck and Sznaider 2006). Education policy is realized in new sites, new locations often outside the scale of the single nation-state. In dealing with the risks of methodological nationalism, education policy analysis can no longer be limited to the boundaries of the nation-state and should be able to describe those complex assemblages of states, actors, circuits of expertise, enterprises, international organizations, etc. concurring to the formation of contemporary education policy. To be relevant, in other words, it should rethink the historicity of its categories, and accept the challenge of the transformations of space-times of education. It is expected to reveal the complexities of the changes, their paradoxes, dilemmas, and possibilities: it should contribute to developing a critical edge. Usually, the current shifts in the space-times are related to the mutually reinforcing processes of globalization, widespread neoliberalism, and the restructuring of the influence and power of the nation-state (Ball and Shilling 2017). Overall, these three broad "contexts of contexts" dominate the plot of the explanations of contemporary dynamics of systems of education. Globalization, and neoliberalism, however, are the key aspects. Whereas globalization describes the disruption of the singularities of the experiences of education policies and practices, and the increase of the interdependence and interconnection of the space-time of education, neoliberalism provides the direction of globalization by driving the universalization of market-based relations, and supporting the creation of entrepreneurial selves. States are attributed a diverse role: they are expected to play as market makers or are substituted by other actors in education policies in complex heterarchies and network forms of governance. While this explanation is supported by empirical data, and represents a notable enrichment in the understanding of the contemporary developments, it focuses mostly on the effects of the convergence of space-times of education. By giving the sense of "putting things into a frame", it depicts a complex, and somewhat coherent *panorama* of the emerging topologies of education, and provides a novel context in which the space-times of education can be located. Like any panorama in a meta-narrative, it provides a "big picture" that makes order and coherence between the micro, the meso, and the macro. It works as the notions of "risk society", or "liquid society", that illustrates main features, and provides the directions of the transformations developing on the scene. These meet the desire of readers and listeners of having an overall description of a field, while they are always the product of local sites and of particular points of view (Latour 2005). There is no need to assume it as being at the start, or to consider it the end of the investigation.[1] An interesting move to enhance our understanding of the complexities of the changes, could be to consider the panorama as a sensitizing framework and, more radically, to put the very setting of space-times of education under scrutiny. This epistemological shift could help in taking further steps forward in the investigation of the current *cosmopolitics of education* without having a pre-formatted overall context. The notion of "cosmopolitics" problematizes the humanistic assumptions of the cosmopolitan turn (Latour 2004). The question is to comprehend the disruption, the emergence, and the consolidation of the space-time of education, by making little assumptions about the "Big Pictures". Promising directions of research and reflection in this respect could be found in the interference between socio-material approaches and education studies. I will illustrate in the next section how this interference has the effect of displacing the sociological investigation of education beyond its usual territories.

## Mobile sociology of education

Socio-material studies of education have not a long history. While they have some antecedents in the classics of education studies, they slowly emerged in the last two decades through the interaction between science and technology studies (STS) and studies of education. STS is a broad area of scholarship with diverse orientations, and theoretical approaches focused on technoscience; i.e., on knowledge production, and circulation in scientific and technological circuits, and on the interplays between science, technologies, and society. It is an interdisciplinary area (anthropology, sociology, informatics, etc.) that contributed to the detailed description of knowledge-in-the-making, and brought to the forefront the materiality of human and nonhuman associations. STS shifted investigation from the epistemology of the scientific disciplines, and from the classic sociology of science to the inquiry of science as a practice, ending in rethinking the "social", and focusing attention on the sites of production of science and knowledge.

The "planetspeak" discourse of knowledge society accelerated the interests of many researchers towards STS: large investments in knowledge and innovation were emerging, yet it was becoming ever clearer the singularity of knowledge as an economic resource and the difficulties of making it a lever for wealth production. Actor Network Theory (ANT) and After ANT were key perspectives here, since they provided basic vocabularies that spread quickly in many fields of investigation. Later, other theoretical orientations were imported, from feminist ANT; in addition, other sensibilities were considered and imported, by supporting a renovation of social science vocabularies. The interaction between STS and education studies is reflected in a notable set of research projects and publications in authored and edited books, special issues in international and national journals (a provisional list should include, for example, Nespor 2002; Fenwick and Edwards 2010; Fenwick et al. 2011; Fenwick and Landri 2012; Sørensen 2009; Gorur 2012; Landri and Neumann 2014; Williamson 2016; Gorur 2016). It attracted the interest of many scholars coming from many professional and scientific backgrounds and contributed to the enrichment of their vocabularies. The interaction is a challenge to consolidate conceptualizations. In the case of the sociology of education, it is an invitation to rethink the sociological perspective. I will highlight, in particular, how the socio-material turn expands the sociological understanding, by considering: a) the co-implication of humans and nonhumans; b) the making of

Table 15.1 Characteristics of the case-studies

| Case studies | Gorur (C1) | Grimaldi & Barzanò (C2) | Celeuman et al. (C3) | Decuypere & Simons (C4) |
|---|---|---|---|---|
| Object | Australia "quick recovery" from initial shock in PISA (2000–03) | The "merit turn" in Italian education system | Inspection and auditing process of all teacher-training programmes in Flanders | Digitalization of academic practice |
| Aims | How comparability in education is constructed | How the global idea of "merit as lever for modernization" and its related technologies have flowed into a regional education space | Bring to the forefront the work of standard | The constitution of academic practice in digital times |
| Theory | ANT and Sociology of Measurement | Governmentality studies and ANT | ANT and Post-ANT | ANT and Post-ANT |
| Research methodologies | Documents analysis, interviews with policy advisors and experts of international large-scale assessment (2008–12) | Documents from official and public web resources | Experimental mode of description | Textual and visual accounts of academic practice |

Table 15.2 Summary of effects of moving sociology of education beyond itself across case studies

| Effects/case studies | Gorur (C1) | Grimaldi & Barzanò (C2) | Celeuman et al. (C3) | Decuypere & Simons (C4) |
|---|---|---|---|---|
| Co-implications H/NH | Imbrication of ESCS, ISEI, ISCED and other indicators in many networks | Assemblage of standardized tests, rewards, prizes, Ministry of Education, meritocracy advocates, constructive critics | Inspection meeting inscripted in textual and digital forms | Humandigitality: the digital "swarm" as infrastructure of contemporary academic work |
| The making of the global and/or the local | The global space of education as space of commensurability | Space of education as an arena of competition between more able and less able in Italy | Equivalence of professional teacher profile and teacher training across Flanders | Redistribution of one-day academic work in regions of activities |
| From policy to practice | Depuration work: writing reports for policy makers and technical reports for experts | Policy assemblage of "merit turn" enact and enrol a set of disparate practices Practices of resistance | Practices of inspection | Interlocking practices in academic work |

the global and the local, and c) the movements between policy and practice. I will offer some illustrations of these points, by drawing on some examples from a collection of research included in a Special Issue I co-edited (Landri and Neumann 2014). Methodologically, I have selected four articles from the collection where this interaction was explored (see Table 15.1). These essays concerned: teacher education (Ceulemans, Simons, and Struyf 2014); the merit turn in an evaluation of teaching and head teaching performance (Grimaldi and Barzanò 2014); the making of the space of commensurability in PISA (Gorur 2014), and academic practice in digital times (Decuypere and Simons 2014). I have re-read and compared them, and drawn some possible implications regarding how the sociomaterial turn mobilizes sociology of education (see Table 15.2).

### The co-implication of humans and nonhumans

One of the effects of the interaction between STS and education studies is the infusion of a *posthuman view*. The sociological view tends to depict interactions with the assumption that the "social" is defined regarding human-to-human relationships. While it is admitted that the "social" includes objects and technologies, in most sociological descriptions, etc. they are marginal, or peripheral: at most, they are tools or a fixed part of the context. The stage of agency is dominated by the humans that are at the centre, and humans are "above the things". A basic sociological vocabulary separates persons and things (Esposito 2014, 2016). In a posthuman view, the capacity to act is redistributed, and the attention shifts in considering how objects, technologies, matter participate in the agency. It becomes a research question to understand to what extent they are active participants in the scene of action under investigation. The sociological research is then invited to focus: a) on the assemblages of humans and nonhumans, and b) to understand the "networky" character of the human; i.e., its being as an assemblage as well. In following this principle, the investigation is directed to reveal the "missing masses" of education policy and practice, and how materialities shape educational agencies. In analysing educational policy, the whole machinery of the policy assemblages and, in particular, the co-implication of humans and nonhumans, is brought to the forefront. In her research project on how comparability is constructed in large international-scale assessment (PISA), Gorur describes how OECD experts and consultants are involved in negotiations and discussions about the measurement of equity in education that are usually hidden in the public debate (Case 1 in Table 15.1). Since equity in education could be interpreted in multiple ways, the issue for experts of measurement and for making measurement comparable across different countries is to give a stable and precise definition to calculate it and make it calculable in replicable ways. For measuring equity in PISA, three sets of data are collected: a) performance data from standardized tests, b) student questionnaires, and c) school questionnaires filled by principals. PISA then provides information about how students of different socio-economic groups perform regarding learning outcomes. Equity, then, is a measure of the degree of independence of the outcomes from socio-economic status. The more students' outcomes are accounted for by factors of gender, family, economic status, race, etc., the more iniquitous the education system. To calculate socio-economic status, PISA relies on the ESCS index elaborated with the data gathered through student question-naires. The measure of ESCS in PISA 2000 combines five indicators and depends particularly on ISCED (International Standard Classification of Education) and the ISEI (International Socio-Economic Index of Occupational Status), with new indicators developed specifically for PISA to calculate ESCS. However, ISCED and ISEI have been far from stable and accurate. Similarly, the indicators devised for PISA are also unstable. While these indicators are always at the centre of end-less discussions, they are nonetheless the basic ingredients for the appraisal of the equity of education across countries and are so imbricated in multiple networks of calculation and policies that they are difficult to change. Even a slight alteration in this infrastructure of data and protocols is revealed to be very costly. Moreover, not only policy knowledge but also the translation of education policies requires the enactment of complex socio-materialities (Cases 2 and 3 in Table 15.1). Case 2 focused on the heterogeneous network that has emerged around the goal of evaluating teachers and schools, and rewarding the "merit" that coheres through the amalgamation of standardized tests, rewards, and prizes. The Ministry of Education, meritocracy advocates (intellectuals, journals, foundations, etc.), as well as constructive critics (trade unions, professional associations, journals, etc.) aimed to put into practice a policy of meritocracy in Italy. They hoped to defeat, or at the least, limit, the open critics who contested the very possibility of teacher evaluation and its appropriateness for the education field. The nonhumans, in this case, did not play a peripheral role; they are oriented to create a different world of education populated by "deserving" and "nondeserving" teachers. Case 3, instead, illustrates the inspection practice, by following the traces of teachers' professional profiles. The study describes how the inspection practice enacts an inspection meeting, how the professional profile is instantiated in a concrete training course and self-evaluation reports, folders, books, study guides, etc. The research high-lights how what happened in the inspection meeting becomes inscripted in textual and digital forms and the work needed to maintain an equivalence between the profile, the curriculum, the course, the assessment, and the mutual orientation of the colleagues. In looking at the socio-materialities, the interface between humans and nonhumans comes to the fore, and it is clearer how the materialities contrib-ute to shaping education policy and practice; i.e., what is inscripted, delegated, and the effects regarding agency. Finally, the focus on socio-materiality reveals the "networky" character of the human, as a being in constant experimentation in connection with technologies, spaces, and objects. Case 4 addresses the recom-position of academic practice; in particular, it refers to a detailed analysis of the working day of six professors from different countries, universities, and research fields. Putting aside a contextual approach that relates the current transformation of the academic work to grand narratives (globalization, neoliberalism, etc.), the research project is interested in understanding the everyday practices of academ-ics, and how digital technologies reshape the academic activities. This view allows visualizing the different regions and the relative operation of the academic work.

The analysis of the recomposition reveals how digital objects and technologies constitute the infrastructure of academic work, a digital "swarm" that connects the disparate regions of the academic practice. Indeed, the pervasiveness of the digital leads to a problematization of the distinction between human, nonhuman, digital, material, etc., and a recognition that each actor in the network is human and digital at the same time, so that it is possible to talk of *humandigital* academic practice. The attention to the co-implication of humans and nonhumans suggests moving from abstract to detailed descriptions of the many embodiments of the sociologies of education.

### The making of the global and the local

A second effect of the interaction between STS and education studies is the enrichment of the sociological imagination of space and the solution it offers to the challenge of *methodological territorialism*. A socio-material gaze escapes from the pitfall of *methodological nationalism* (Dale and Robertson 2012); i.e., a release from the tendency to enclose societies existing in nation-states and to assume that comparing societies implies comparing nation-states. In following the concept of methodological nationalism, the global space appears as a space made of regions with clear boundaries where all the citizens living within these borders have a unique identity (e.g., the Italian, the French, etc.). In other words, the space-times of education could be explicitly assigned to a fixed Westphalian geopolitical arrangement. The equivalence between societies and nation-states is deeply rooted in the history of sociology, that has developed its vocabularies by looking at the emergent successful modern societies compared with alleged "backward" societal states of affairs (Urry 2000). Sociology of education frequently oriented its research agenda on topics and research questions shaped by education reforms and issues arising at the national level. A recent collection of the histories of the sociology of education in different countries all over the world confirms the persistence of the national interests besides the widespread reform epidemic and global discourses (knowledge society, lifelong learning) (Osipov, Ivanova and Dobrenkov. 2013). On the other hand, the growing interests towards the investigation of the globalization of education raise the risk to accept and "leave untouched" some of the rhetoric of "globalloney". A more sophisticated understanding of the space-times of education, then, is needed to develop the sociological imagination. The interaction between STS and education studies offers a possibility to put under scrutiny: a) the *making of the global*, and b) *construction of the local*. The re-reading of the four cases cited above gives some illustrations of the directions of this problematization. Case 1 describes the making of the global, by analysing the subtleties of the machinery of OECD-PISA, one of the most influential enactments of a global space of commensurability. Globalization is not taken for granted, it is, rather, problematized, and the knowledge processes supporting and partly performing globalization are opened as a matter of public concern. Case 1 informed us about the infrastructure of data shaping a global space-time of education, as well as the struggles, and the negotiations accompanying the calculation of equity in education. In this way, the global is not understood as a "container" but as a construction of a knowledge infrastructure, and it is possible to have information about the re-design of post-national scenarios in education. Cases 2, 3, and 4, on the contrary, offer examples of the *making of the local*. While the logistics of globalization can "touch down on earth", the local is not less fabricated than the global. Case 2 focuses on how the emphasis on "merit" in Italy arises when a global idea – merit as a measure of calculation for the modernization of education – is considered as the possible solution for improving the "low" quality of the Italian education system, at least as indicated in international assessment datasets. The case also shows how the translation of this idea into tentative technologies of measurement (policy trajectories: PT1, 2, 3, and 4) aimed at distinguishing the enhanced "ableness" of teachers and head teachers, by reshaping the space of education as an arena of competition. This investigation shows how the local is reshaped through dispersed, yet related, policy trajectories. Case 3 explains how a standard, a professional profile of teacher competencies, reshapes teachers' education in Flanders. It does so, by describing in accurate and detailed case-studies the workings of standardization in teacher-inspection practices. We are invited to recognize that the standard is localized, and contributes to shaping teacher education. Finally, Case 4 helps us understand how analysis of day-to-day local academic practices could be redistributed in many areas of activities, whose complexity lies in the interconnection of many technological and social activities; what is revealed is that the "micro is more complex than the macro". In all these cases, sociological investigation of education is invited to move from the usual territories of the nation-states to problematize the actual configurations of space-times of education (the global and the local), by revealing their present histories, how they connect multiple sites and reconstitute new sites.

### Between policy and practice

A third effect of the interaction between STS and education studies is the suggestion to move from policy to practice. To some extent, and in some cases, this hints at putting aside policy to focus only on practice. "Policy" is a key topic of interest for the sociology of education. In most cases, the national sociologies of education consolidated as epistemic communities are helpful for producing knowledge about education policies, and it is well known how the "turn to policy" has been a key feature in the recent history of the sociological investigation in education (Ball 2008). There has been, however, and still is, an unfinished debate on "what is a policy?" (Vidovich 2007; Ball 2015). The interaction with the STS approach, here, consists in re-introducing and giving more space to "practice". There is not enough space here to demonstrate how "practice" is a concept with a long tradition of interest, even in the social sciences. In any case, to make a long story short, the socio-material turn is a vehicle fostering a return to practice, and to consider policy from the angle of practice (Landri 2012; Gorur 2011). The four cases we discuss here offer interesting examples of what it means regarding sociological view. In Gorur's study (Case 1), the response to the issue – how comparability is achieved in international large-scale assessment – is provided by looking at the "mundane and tacit practice and the range of selections and decisions that are folded into international comparisons" (Gorur 2014: 69). In this way, we are invited to consider the knowledge coming from these big globalizing projects not as a matter of fact, and to pay attention to the knowledge practices. Here, comparability is not a given; it is, rather, a tentative accomplishment. It is possible to understand as well all the "depuration work" consisting, for example, in separating reports for policy-makers and technical reports intended to account for the community of the researchers as well as for the experts. A double version of the same investigation is then provided for different audiences: a) an objective version for the needs of the policy-makers; and b) a version for the interested in the subtleties "behind the scenes". Case 2 illustrates, in particular, the policy assemblage of the "turn to meritocracy", and the set of disparate practices it was able to enact and enrol. Similarly, it brings to the fore the practices of resistance and recalcitrance that were activated to contrast and combat sometimes openly the strategy of meritocracy. The meritocracy policy assemblage was intended to connect the Ministry of Education, the tests, the candidates, the schools, and the unions. In instances of recalcitrance, some of these same entities were involved. Trade unions defended the winners and the losers in the competition to select the most "able" teachers and head teachers. Lawyers entered in support of those who "lost" to file the appeals to the regional administrative juries. The "turn to meritocracy" enacted practices of resistance too: in one of the selected provinces for the experiment, no school accepted the proposed changes. The interest for practice is even more striking in Cases 3 and 4 (the Flanders study and the study on academic practice). Here, policies remain deliberately in the background, and the focus is on the work of standardizing done by the professional teacher profile on the one hand, and on the other hand the recomposition of academic practice in the digital age. In Case 3, there is the description of the inspection practice and the analysis of some of the policy effects of the adoption of the teacher profile. Here, the attention is on the auditing processes of the teacher-profiling programs in Flanders. The focus is on the commissioners' work, the inscription devices and the results of the inscription to display the standard protocol followed to understand to what extent the training program aligned with the teacher profile. The move is helpful in displaying the power of teacher profiling but, also, that standardization work is never-ending work. Case 4, finally, is oriented to offer a technique for describing academic practice in the making. The epistemological position, here, tends to distance itself from a pre-formatted reading of this practice in dominant discourses, and represents the practical orientation in the various directions of the academic work to understand the role of digital objects. These four examples display how education practice is not completely controlled, and governed by the policies. Whereas the policy is interested in framing, the practice tends to overflow. The space-times of education appear, then, to balance between the forces of framing and overflowing, between ordering and disordering.

## Conclusions

The current transformations of the space-times of education are a challenge to education studies. The classic configuration of space-time was associated with a particular ordering of epistemic communities and related vocabularies. However, the emergent features of education systems relate to border-crossing, transnational mobilities, and technological changes with new forms of movements and novel forms of immobility and marginalization, and require a rethinking of the educational investigations. This chapter has explored a promising area of research: the interaction between education studies and STS, paving the way to the socio-material turn in education, and reflected on what effects this interference could have in the case of the sociology of education. I have done an experimentation of re-reading, by drawing on a collection of case studies done within this frame, edited in a special issue with a colleague in an international journal. I have argued that the interaction moves sociology of education beyond itself. I have discussed three implications, and also given some empirical illustrations, of this "moving beyond": 1) from a human-centred view to one that includes the co-implication of humans and nonhumans in education policy and practice; 2) from a limited spatial imagination towards a more complex description of the space-times of education, and 3) from a dominant attention to policy to a more complex analysis of practice. Overall, these movements are an invitation to a mobile sociology of education; i.e., for multi-sited sociological investigations intended to give visibility at the materialities of education, the complex reshaping of post-national scenarios, and the complexities of education practice. They are oriented to give a critical edge to the sociology of education, by expanding the sociological understanding and imagination. First, it invites us to pay attention to how

> . . . educational interplays are not constituted by individual minds moving in a disembodied space of persons and things, but rather by *networks*, that is by assemblages and intertwinements of persons, persons, and things, things with things assuming, through notable investments in forms, occasional and contingent sociomaterial configurations.
>
> (Landri and Viteritti, 2016)

Secondly, it expands the spatial imagery of sociology of education often enclosed in the regional topology of nation-states, failing to recognize the same fabrication of nation states, the multiple intersections between globalizing and localizing practices, and the development of multiple topologies of education. Thirdly, it invites us to consider the overflow of practice: education is not completely determined by the framing of policy. Empirically, it is possible to highlight many possible enactments of policy in practice, to describe practices of resistance, as well as education practices developing outside the dominant circuits of knowledge and policy. It means that at least in principle the "planetspeak-discourses", the grand narratives of the changing space-times of education do not account for, and rule, education practice entirely. In order to describe the current transformations, and to perform them differently, there is the need to rethink the sociological gaze. This view suggests to reinforce the investigation in the *cosmopolitics of education*. The "cosmopolitics of education" reads the current transformations as complex, often contested and unfinished socio-material assemblages, where the classic "human-centred" and modernistic world of education is being transformed in unexpected ways, with both potentials and risks. Whereas the cosmopolitan view leaves unproblematized the humanistic assumptions of the common world of education, the research on the cosmopolitics of education considers the making of a "common world of education" an open-ended and debated question that involves, rather, the reassemblage of human and nonhuman configurations, where the priorities of the humanistic assumptions of education are "put on the table". The socio-material turn displaces therefore sociology of education beyond some of its usual territories (the human, the nation-state, the policy) to enrich its understanding and imagination. In sum, it invites the sociological investigation of education to follow a *nomadic thinking and practice* that underline the openness of everyday life, its being ontologically in becoming (Braidotti 2011), and the effects of translations (Latour 2005). This call for movement, and for being sensible to mobilities, should not be assimilated with a refusal of the traditional places, or to an emphasis on the contemporary tendency to (fast) movement. Moreover, it is not a denial of the inequalities and the sufferings that are perpetuated by the emergent cosmopolitics of education. It is rather a plea for inhabiting, and moving across, sites to describe, problematize, and explore the contemporary emerging landscapes of education practice: an epistemological and political experiment to test whether or not they are heading to liveable space-times of education.

## Note

1 A parallel critical appraisal of the issue of the "context" in education is in Sobe and Kowalczyk (2013).

## References

Ball, S. J. (2008). Some sociologies of education: A history of problems and places, and segments and gazes. *The Sociological Review*, 56(4), 650–669. doi: http://doi.wiley.com/10.1111/j.1467-954X.2008.00809.x.

Ball, S. J. (2015). What is policy? 21 years later: Reflections on the possibilities of policy research. *Discourse: Studies in the Cultural Politics of Education*, 6306, 1–8. doi: www.tandfonline.com/doi/abs/10.1080/01596306.2015.1015279.

Ball, S. J. and Shilling, C. (2017). General introduction. In S. J. Ball and C. Shilling (Eds.). *Education policy studies* (pp. 1–20). London: Routledge.

Beck, U. and Sznaider, N. (2006). Unpacking cosmopolitanism for the social sciences: A research agenda. *British Journal of Sociology*, 57(1), 1–23.

Bennett, S., Maton, K. and Kervin, L., 2008. The "digital natives" debate: A critical review of the evidence. *British Journal of Educational Technology*, 39(5), 775–786.

Biesta, G. (2015). On the two cultures of educational research, and how we might move ahead: Reconsidering the ontology, axiology and praxeology of education. *European Educational Research Journal, 14*(1), 11–22. doi: http://eer.sagepub.com/lookup/doi/10.1177/1474904114565162.

Braidotti, R. (2011). *Nomadic theory. The portable Rosi Braidotti.* New York: Columbia University Press.

Ceulemans, C., Simons, M. and Struyf, E. (2014). What – if anything – do standards do in education? Topological registrations of standardising. *European Educational Research Journal, 13*(1), 73–88.

Dale, R. and Robertson, S. (Eds.). (2012). *Globalisation and Europeanisation in education.* London: Symposium Books.

Decuypere, M. and Simons, M. (2014). On the composition of academic work in digital times. *European Educational Research Journal, 13*(1), 89–106.

Esposito, R. (2014). *Le persone e le cose*, Torino: Giulio Einaudi editore.

Esposito, R. (2016). Persons and things. *Paragraph, 39*(1), 26–35.

Fenwick, T. and Edwards, R. (2010). *Actor-Network Theory and education.* London: Routledge.

Fenwick, T. and Landri, P. (2012). Introduction: Materialities, textures and pedagogies: socio-material assemblages in education. *Pedagogy, Culture & Society, 20*(1), 1–8.

Fenwick, T., Edwards, R. and Sawchuk, P. (2011). *Emerging approaches to educational research: Tracing the socio-material.* London: Routledge.

Gibb, T. and Hamdon, E. (2010). Moving across borders: Immigrant women's encounters with globalization, the knowledge economy and lifelong learning. *International Journal of Lifelong Education, 29*(2), 185–200. doi: http://dx.doi.org/10.1080/02601371003616616.

Gorur, R. (2011). Policy as assemblage. *European Educational Research Journal, 10*(4), 611–622.

Gorur, R. (2012). The invisible infrastructure of standards. *Critical Studies in Education, 54*(2), 132–142.

Gorur, R. (2014). Towards a sociology of measurement in education policy. *European Educational Research Journal, 13*(1), 58–72.

Gorur, R. (2016). Seeing like PISA: A cautionary tale about the performativity of international assessments. *European Educational Research Journal.* doi: http://eer.sagepub.com/lookup/doi/10.1177/1474904116658299.

Grek, S. (2010). International organisations and the shared construction of policy "problems": Problematisation and change in education governance in Europe. *Educational Research, 9*(3), 396–406.

Grimaldi, E. and Barzanò, G. (2014). Making sense of the educational present: Problematising the "merit turn" in the Italian eduscape. *European Educational Research Journal, 13*(1), 26–46.

Landri, P. (2012). A return to practice: Practice-based studies of education. In P. Hager, L. Alison, and A. Reich (Eds.). *Learning practice and change: Practice-theory perspectives on professional learning* (pp. 85–102). London: Springer.

Landri, P. and Neumann, E. (2014). Mobile sociologies of education. *EERJ, 13*(1), 1–8.

Landri, P. and Viteritti, A. (2016). Introduzione. Le masse mancanti in educazione. *Scuola democratica, 1*, 7–21.

Latour, B. (2004). Whose cosmos, which cosmopolitics? *Common Knowledge, 10*(3), 450–462. Retrieved from: http://search.ebscohost.com/login.aspx?direct=true&db=hlh&AN=13808804&lang=es&site=ehost-live.

Latour, B. (2005). *Reassembling the social. An introduction to Actor-Network Theory.* Oxford: Oxford University Press.

Law, J. (2012). Collateral realities. In F. D. Rubio and P. Baert (Eds.). *The politics of knowledge* (pp. 156–178). London: Routledge.

Lawn, M. and Normand, R. (Eds.). 2015. *Shaping of European education: Interdisciplinary approaches*, London: Routledge.

Massa, R. (1991). *La clinica della formazione*. In R. Massa (Ed.). *Saperi, scuola, formazione. Materiali per la formazione del pedagogista* (pp. 89–120). Milano: Unicopli.

Masschelein, J. and Simons, M. (2015). Education in times of fast learning: The future of the school. *Ethics and Education, 10*(1), 84–95.

Nespor, J. (2002). Networks and contexts of reform. *Journal of Educational Change, 3*(3–4), 365–382. Retrieved October 30, 2013 from: http://link.springer.com/article/10.1023/A%3A1021281913741.

Osipov, A., Ivanova, V. and Dobrenkov, V. (Eds.). (2013). *Global sociology of education.* Veliky Novgorod: Novgorod State University.

Perrotta, C., Czerniewicz, L. and Beetham, H. (2015). The rise of the video-recorder teacher: The sociomaterial construction of an educational actor. *British Journal of Sociology of Education, July*, 1–17. doi: www.tandfonline.com/doi/full/10.1080/01425692.2015.1044068.

Simons, M., Olssen, M. and Peters, M. (2009). Re-reading education policies: Part 1 The Critical Education Policy Orientation. In M. Simons, M. Olssen and M. Peters (Eds.). *Re-reading education policies* (pp.1–35). Rotterdam: Sense Publishers.

Sobe, N. W. and Kowalczyk, J. A. (2013). Exploding the cube: Revisioning "context" in the field of comparative education. *Current Issues in Comparative Education, 16*(1), 6–12. Retrieved from: http://search.ebscohost.com/login.aspx?direct=true&db=eue&AN=95007997&site=ehost-live.

Sørensen, E. (2009). *The materiality of learning: Technology and knowledge educational practice.* New York: Cambridge University Press. Retrieved October 20, 2014 from: www.cambridge.org/us/academic/subjects/psychology/educational-psychology/materiality-learning-technology-and-knowledge-educational-practice#.UnDY2EOgCKw.mendeley.

Urry, J. (2000). *Sociology beyond societies.* London: Routledge.

Vidovich, L. (2007). Removing policy from its pedestal: some theoretical framings and practical possibilities. *Educational Review, 59*(3), 285–298. Retrieved from: www.informaworld.com/openurl?genre=article&doi=10.1080/00131910701427231&magic=crossref.

Williamson, B. (2015). Digital education governance: Data visualization, predictive analytics, and "real-time" policy instruments. *Journal of Education Policy, 31*(2), 123–41.

Williamson, B. (2016). Digital education governance: An introduction. *European Educational Research Journal, 15*(1), 3–13. doi: http://eer.sagepub.com/lookup/doi/10.1177/1474904115616630.

# Index